SCHOOL OF ORIENTAL AND AFRICAN STUDIES
University of London

Please return this book on or before the last date shown

Long loans and One Week loans may be renewed up to 10 times
Short loans & CDs cannot be renewed
Fines are charged on all overdue items

Online: http://lib.soas.ac.uk/patroninfo
Phone: 020-7898 4197 (answerphone)

3 1 JAN 2006

- 3 DEC 2007

1 4 JAN 2008

2 1 JAN 2008

1

Modern
Thai Literature

Modern Thai Literature

With an Ethnographic Interpretation

HERBERT P. PHILLIPS

In association with
Vinita Atmiyanandana Lawler
Amnuaycaj Patipat
Likhit Dhiravegin

University of Hawaii Press • Honolulu

Library of Congress Cataloging-in-Publication Data

Phillips, Herbert P.
    Modern Thai literature.

    Bibliography: p.
    Includes index.
    1.   Thai literature—20th century—History and
criticism.   2.   Thai literature—20th century.
3.   Literature and society—Thailand.   4.   Thailand—
Civilization—20th century.   I.   Title.
PL4200.P44   1987   895.9'1'09003   86–30816
ISBN 0–8248–1065–1

*To Lauriston Sharp and the memories of
Clyde Kluckhohn and John F. Desmond,
who introduced me respectively to
Thailand, ethnography, and literature*

Contents

Preface

This book is simultaneously about Thai literature and about the writing, reading, and cultural purposes of that literature. The materials that represent these two interests are presented separately, but in their exposition they constantly refer to one another. While there is no perfect way to deal with this kind of cross-reference problem, we think that some people might find it more comfortable to read the book backwards—by which we mean that individual selections be read first, their associated introductions second, and the material on ethnographic context and the selection process third. The principal reason the book was not actually arranged in this sequence is that it would have violated customary narrative expectations that "context" ought to come first, introductions second, and literary substance last.

The origins of the book lie in part in the friendships that over the years I have developed (initially quite serendipitously, later more systematically) with a variety of Thai writers. It was these friendships and the writers' own preoccupations with the staggering changes that were occurring in their lives that made me so aware of literature as a source of ethnographic understanding. Years earlier, I had worked with Thai villagers (Phillips 1958, 1963, 1965, and Hanks and Phillips 1961) who were also keenly aware of the rapidly changing nature of their culture, but as a group they were hardly as outspoken, as literarily accomplished, or as diverse in their perspectives as are the people whose views are presented here. It was my workaday contact with Thai writers that also made me aware that they represent a social structural type—a group of people who are functioning as the codifiers of their society's collective experience—and that writers everywhere in the world have become increasingly important, if only because of the almost universal explosion in literacy rates during the latter part of the twentieth century. In this cross-cultural sense, I came to realize that the book was really a case study in what one such group of people think, how they came to be what they are, and how they organize themselves and relate to their larger society.

By having been witness to many of the events they describe, fictionally or otherwise, I was also keenly aware of the time-boundedness of this material, and for the necessity for a study like this to be conducted at least once every decade or two. I suspect that a period of less than a decade may not really provide sufficient time perspective to identify either major historical movements or individual writers who are likely to have a lasting impact upon their culture's intellectual history. I also suspect that having known several of these writers personally and having spent numerous hours talking with them about their work, motives, and self-perceptions, I have a somewhat different perspective on their literary activities than would be derived solely from an analysis of their texts.

This project could never have been pursued without the involvement of the three persons identified as having an "association" with the enterprise. My friend and colleague of more than two decades, Professor Likhit Dhiravegin of Thammasat University, served as my sponsor with Thailand's National Research Council. More important, he spent hours regaling me with his insights into the political dimensions of Thailand's intellectual life and his predictions and analysis of Thai political events. Amnuaycaj Patipat played a critical role in locating, screening, discussing with me, and helping me to understand the hundreds of selections that were examined in the process of making our final choices. His understanding of both his society and the nature of the research process is profound, and I shall always be indebted to him for tolerating my American sense of intellectual pugnaciousness and suspiciousness. Dr. Vinita Atmiyanandana Lawler was my alter ego in the translation and frequent retranslation of almost all the materials contained in this book. We worked together as a team for hundreds of hours, alternating translation responsibilities and constantly monitoring each other to make our English as faithful as possible to both the meaning and intent of our authors' texts.

As a reading of the texts might suggest, our translating style was extremely conservative or "tight," sometimes sacrificing fluency for awkwardness in order to convey what we perceived to be the complexity or richness of the original Thai. In many places we were forced to talk *about* Thai meanings rather than provide renditions of them, and our numerous translation notes often ask the reader to shift attention from the text itself to its exegesis or commentary. This device is not unusual in "ethnographic translation," but it does require a degree of forbearance on the part of the reader. An equally problematic issue was the question of our own English style, and the possibility that the work of these many different writers might come to be covered by a kind of literary patina, as if they were all the product of a single author. It is our sense that we have permitted our writers' individual voices and messages to remain distinctive, but the possibility that we have overedited cannot be totally precluded.

In the course of preparing our materials, I asked students in a series of seminars and several of my colleagues—most of whom knew very little about Thailand—for their views on both the selections and my commentaries. They provided the feedback for the kind of information that ethnographically uninformed, but otherwise highly perceptive, readers wanted for interpreting the material. I am especially indebted to Sadeka Arebi, Jerry Bass, Jeanne Bergman, William A. Collins, Jennifer DeBouzek, Alan Dundes, James Faubion, Jamilla Feldman, Stephen Foster, Regina Garrick, Nelson Graburn, Deborah Knaff, Nancy Lutz, Victoria Mukherjee, Kirin Narayan, Laurel Rose, Wendy Rose, John Stough, and Amin Sweeney. I am of course also indebted to those colleagues and students who know a great deal about Thailand and who critically reviewed portions of the manuscript, particularly Benedict Anderson, Thomas Blair, Christopher Court, Jonathan Habarad, Charnvit Kasetsiri, Pamela Myers-Moro, Thamsook Numnonda, Yos Santasombat, Vicharat and Juree Vichit-Vadakan, and Pansak Vinyaratn. Funds for portions of the research were provided by the Ford Foundation through the American Council of Learned Societies, by the Institute of East Asian Studies, the Humanities Research Committee, and by the Faculty Research Committee of the University of California, Berkeley, for which I am also most grateful.

Finally, my debt is greatest to my wife, Barbara Haxo Phillips, not only for tolerating for so long all those little narcissistic acts that many book writers indulge in (being there but not being there because I was absorbed in the phrasing of some inchoate idea) but, more importantly, for reading almost as many versions of this text as I have, and for being my most honest critic.

HERBERT P. PHILLIPS

Note on the Romanization of Thai

Except for titles, personal names, and familiar place names, Thai terms have been transcribed according to a modification of the Haas phonetic system (Mary Haas, *Thai Vocabulary*, 1955, and *The Thai System of Writing*, 1956. Washington, D.C.: American Council of Learned Societies). The modification involves the omission of the five tonal markers, the voiceless unaspirated stop ?, and a different representation of certain vowels.

Briefly, the system is as follows: voiced unaspirated stops are written *b*, *d*, and (only in final position) *g*; voiceless unaspirated stops are *p*, *t*, *c*, and *k*; voiceless aspirated stops are *ph*, *th*, *ch*, and *kh*; voiceless unaspirated spirants are *f*, *s*, and *h*; voiced semivowel sonorants are *w* and *j*; voiced nasal sonorants are *m*, *n*, and *ng*; the voiced lateral sonorant is *l*; and the voiced trill sonorant is *r*. The vowels are written thus: front unrounded, *i, ii, ia, e, ee, ae, aeae*; central unrounded, *y, yy, ya, oe, oeoe, a, aa*; and back rounded, *u, uu, ua, o, oo, au, auau*.

PART I

An Ethnographic Interpretation

The Ethnographic Context
of Thai Literature

This book is intended to be two things: a presentation of some of the major writings published in Thailand during the 1960s and 1970s, including observations on their cultural and historical significance, and an analysis of the role and function of literary figures and the purposes of literature in Thailand during this same period. Originally, my associates and I had hoped that the book might also provide an intellectual history of Thailand during these decades, but if it does this, it is more by implication than by systematic design.

Although the book contains literature and is about literature, its primary purpose is not literary, but cultural: to show what some of the most sensitive, reflective, articulate—and sometimes theatrical and bumptious—members of Thai society think of their own culture and experience and, to the extent that it can be conveyed in English translation, how they think about such things. The writing of literature is seen here as integral to the social process, as both historical precipitant and product. Our concern is with its meaning to its creators and readers, not with its ultimate aesthetic value—with the exception of those aesthetic considerations that are an aspect of meaning in Thai thought. By the same token, literary issues that are sometimes presumed to cut across different cultural traditions—"imaginativeness" and "originality"—are given relatively little attention in this volume, if only because our interest is in literature as a noetic expression of a social and cultural milieu rather than as a vehicle for artistic inventiveness and ingenuity. The latter qualities may be present, but more as serendipitous than as defining features of the literary enterprise. If in the 1970s there emerged in anthropology a tradition of treating cultural forms as literary and dramatic texts, the thrust of this effort is toward treating literary works as embodiments of culture.[1]

Thus, whatever their other attributes, the writers and thinkers whose work is presented here are viewed as "key informants" on Thai society—their "keyness" being a function both of their intellectual and verbal skills and such contextual factors as their training and recruitment, social and personal identities, networks of colleagues and friends, and the amount of time and energy they give to their craft. The latter considerations make what they do as much a social and cultural activity as a creative activity. They also mark our writers as rather special key informants in that the information they provide is not primarily a result of an ethnographer's eliciting techniques, as it is with most anthropological informants, but rather of the positions they hold in Thai society. They are people who are socially situated to talk about things that in their culture are judged to be "important," sometimes because they already are and other times merely because these writers say they are. Thus, the issues that they address, and that the anthropologist independently chooses to interpret, are essentially self-selected.

Writers also differ from anthropological informants in another important respect. The people for whom they are writing are obviously not foreigners but rather are people much like themselves. The communication taking place is (exempting the complexities of the translation process) totally intracultural in nature. It is this fact that makes literature such a valuable corpus of knowledge for anthropological inquiry. What is being communicated—in content, meaning, assumption, and purpose—is, above all, "the native's point of view."[2]

The Role of Literary Figures

If literary figures are inherently interesting to an anthropologist because of their sensitive renditions of the native's viewpoint, it is their functional attributes—what they do in or for their society—that makes them structurally significant and that commands our analytic attention. Through their writings literary figures do a number of different things. They entertain or amuse; mobilize public opinion for social action; glorify, beautify, sacralize—and often desacralize—cherished beliefs or institutions; create cynosures for public attention and raise social consciousness; and crystallize new ways of looking at things, although typically what is being looked at is already quite familiar. However, underlying all these contributions is a single noetic purpose: to provide their readers with a codification of the world that is cognitively and aesthetically credible and, in so doing, to define what is right and wrong with the universe, what is consequential, and what should be remembered. The remembering function, although from a motivational point of view often only a by-product, is especially significant, if only because literature is a permanent, preservable record of the self-judgments of a society at different points in time. In this respect, it serves as a major data base of a society's intellectual history.

Whether our Thai writers see themselves in such analytically enlarged terms is quite another matter. Many translate what they do into much narrower personal considerations. Some say they write merely to make some extra money; others to gain public esteem and attention; and some because they have a compulsion to write. Some admit to more psychologically complex reasons, such as writing in order to impose a sense of intellectual discipline upon themselves or to fulfill an image of themselves that involves certain *noblesse oblige* requirements, for example, sharing their wisdom or expertise with others (see Phillips 1975:340–342).

However, a significant number explicitly view their writing as a way of coming to terms with the large historical forces that are impinging upon their society. Like men and women of letters in many places, they are particularly sensitive to the adequacy of conventional cultural explanations —whether things are what they seem in terms of the contentions of conventional wisdom but also whether they are not at all what they seem. What makes their task historically important, at least in their own eyes, is their awareness that they are living during a period when their culture is undergoing unprecedented social change and the traditional categories for understanding things no longer work or are no longer persuasive. Much of what they are about has to do with documenting the breakdown in traditional understandings and, to a lesser extent, trying to create newer, more viable alternatives. In a few domains (religion, and perhaps the family) it also involves demonstrating the strength and resilience of some of the traditional postulates of Thai culture.

The background of change and social ferment that dominates our authors' concerns also makes the spirit and emphasis of our work very different from that found in many anthropological studies. Lévi-Strauss has argued that what most clearly characterizes an anthropological sense of inquiry is the anthropologist's concern with the unconscious foundations of social life. He asserts (1963:18) that most of us work among people from whom "it is very difficult to obtain a moral justification or a rational explanation for any custom or institution. When he is questioned, the native merely answers that things have always been this way," and that consequently there is little intellectual utility in asking natives to account for their actions or, if such justifications are available, taking them very seriously. While this kind of assertion is probably an accurate rendition of the experiences of some anthropologists and of the Rousseauesque presumptions of a great many more (and clearly an excellent rationale for Lévi-Strauss's special kinds of analyses), it is wholly inimical to the thrust of our work. However one might view the quality of any individual selection, all the native material presented in this book represents original, self-conscious, and creative efforts on the part of their authors. In both their reflectiveness and assertiveness, they are the quintessence of "moral justification" and "rational explanation." In fact, from an existential point of view, they may even go beyond that because, as many of our authors acknowledge, writing is inherently an act of artifice and contrivance—reducing the flow, open-endedness, and richness of life to words, and to the constraints of the literary genres in which one works. It is wholly an act of intellectual design and construction.

The Social and Political Setting

Our selections were all written during the period from 1960 to 1976 against a background of profound political, social, and psychological change. By 1960, the Gilbert and Sullivan ethos of the Phibun Songkhram regimes of the World War II and post-World War II periods had passed into Thai memory, and the basic changes in the nature of Thai life that Field Marshal Sarit Thanarat had initiated after his coup of 1957 (and which were carried on by the Thanom regime after Sarit's death in 1963) were firmly in place. These included the realities and myths of "national development," massive road building programs that resulted almost immediately in equally massive movements of people, things, and ideas throughout the nation; the arrival of American military and economic aid programs, as well as agents of the CIA; the sending of increasing numbers of Thai students overseas for higher degrees; and administrative efforts aimed at integrating Thailand's northeastern provinces into the mainstream of the Thai polity. This last endeavor included sending the putatively "best" rather than, as was traditional, the putatively "worst" administrators to the Northeast and investing millions of *baht* to develop the town of Khonkaen as a "new northeastern urban center."

A few years later, the level of compulsory education in Thailand was changed from four to six years; construction began on three regional universities in Chiengmai, Khonkaen, and Songkhla; and Thai television (which in 1955 had been the first television system on the Asian mainland) was broadcasting throughout the kingdom. By mid-decade, most of the seven airbases used for bombing Vietnam and Laos had been completed, and the 55,000 American soldiers necessary for manning these bases were joined by another 6,500 troops per week on "rest and recreation" tours from Vietnam. This influx of soldiers transformed the Patpong and New Petchburi Road areas of Bangkok into major red-light districts, the exhibitionistic nature of which had never before been known in Thailand; the small provincial towns in which the American airbases were located underwent similar, if socially more disruptive, transformations. Simultaneously, foreign businessmen began to respond to the investment inducements of the Thai government, with Ford, Bristol-Myers, and Mercedes-Benz among the first of hundreds of multinational corporations that were eventually to open assembly plants in the kingdom. Also, "world-class" hotels were rapidly constructed to serve a burgeoning tourist industry, and the seaside village of Pattaya quickly became one of the major resorts of Asia. Equally important, a few native millionaires were beginning to be identified, and the Bangkok Bank was opening branches in virtually all provincial towns and even in a few foreign countries; within the next two decades it was to grow into the largest bank in Southeast Asia. Furthermore, in the expanding economy, most high school and college students had relatively little difficulty in obtaining positions, and the category "middle-class" began to be used more frequently in Thai public discourse.

If all this economic activity was contributing to an increase in the GDP averaging approximately 7 percent per year, it was also contributing to the emergence of numerous social tensions. Bangkok seemed suddenly to change from one of the safest to one of the most dangerous cities in the world, and national crime statistics soared. Along with the concept of "middle-class," the concepts of "rural–urban gap" and "maldistribution of income" gained increasing consciousness. At the same time, "insurgency" was breaking out in the Northeast among disaffected Thai peasants, most of whom felt shut off from the burgeoning social and economic opportunities; in the North among abused Hmong tribal peoples; and in the South partially under the aegis of the Pattani Independence Movement, most of whose members were Muslims. While these "jungle soldiers" collectively never exceeded 8,000 persons, they triggered the mobilization of immense numbers of police, soldiers, and Ministry of Interior bureaucrats to deal with them. By the end of the decade, the Communist Suppression Operations Command (CSOC) had become the most powerful and financially favored governmental agency in rural Thailand.

The growth of economic activity and the development of powerful bureaucratic empires also raised the level of greed and corruption within officialdom and in the nation as a whole, so that by the close of the decade a moral reaction had begun to take shape. The National Student Center of Thailand (NSCT) was originally created by authorities as a mechanism for co-opting student activists and monitoring their political activities. But almost immediately after the inception of the center in 1969, NSCT members began to campaign against governmental corruption, the overly favorable treatment of Japanese and American interests, and the arbitrary acts of the "three tyrants"—the prime minister, Field Marshal Thanom Kittikachorn, the deputy prime minister, Field Marshal Prapart Charusathien, and Col. Narong Kittikachorn (the last being the son of Thanom and son-in-law of Prapart.) It was the issue of governmental corruption—specifically, the misuse of a military helicopter for a hunting holiday and the transparent nature of the lie denying that use—that triggered the Student Revolution of 1973.

The Student Revolution of October 14, 1973, which overthrew the Thanom military government, ushered in the most exciting, chaotic, and ultimately painful period of Thai history in this century. The months immediately following the revolution were marked by a spirit of giddiness and pride as well as by the somewhat unrealistic expectation that the moral passion of students (an inherently transient population) would provide sufficient authority to transform the structure of Thai society. This interval was followed by a period of intense, but chaotic, mobilization when all kinds of groups—new and old farmers' organizations, student groups, labor unions, political parties, public interest groups—vied with one another through demonstrations, strikes, rallies, and a variety of happenings to gain public support and somehow to begin that process of transformation. But the sheer cacophony of demands and the disagreements of competing groups made such a transformation impossible. Even groups that had previously been linked, such as university and vocational students, came to compete with one another in an essentially class-based manner. The internal bickerings of the popularly elected civilian governments established after the revolution and their inability to meet the impossible demands made upon them reinforced the sense of anomie that came to permeate all aspects of public life. A series of unsolved political murders, all of leftist activists, also added to the anxiety of the time. While there was in fact untrammeled political freedom throughout the period, it was the inability of the various elements of society—except the rejected political far right—to join together into a coherent historical movement that pointed to the demise of the democratic period. Nor was the tension of the time assuaged by the small group of university students who insisted on acting as a kind of Greek chorus for the moral inadequacies of Thai society as they continued to demonstrate on one issue or another.

It was one such demonstration—involving a perhaps unintentional act of lèse majesté—that lead to the events of October 6, 1976, when Thammasat University was stormed by right-wing mobs and Border Patrol Police. At least forty-six students were killed, hundreds of others were wounded, and hundreds more were arrested and stoned as they were driven away from the scene of violence. It was the burning alive, lynching, and beating of so many Thai by other Thai that became so clearly etched in the public memory, an act of carnage that had no precedent in Thai history. A military coup was implemented immediately "to restore stability," followed by the installation of the regime of Thanin Kraivichien, which ruled the nation incorruptibly, but also with extraordinary repression and inefficiency, for the next year.

The events at Thammasat and the activities of the Thanin regime brought down a pall upon Thailand. Books were burned (including those from which many of our selections were taken), publishing firms were closed, a highly restrictive curfew was instituted, thousands of people were arrested, and thousands fled, some to other countries but most to northeastern Thailand and Laos, where they joined the jungle soldiers and where their added numbers suggested the possibility of genuine civil war. However, to mount a war takes time, and before that possibility could develop the Thanin regime gave way in October 1977 to a much more liberal and self-confident regime headed by General Kriangsak Chomanan. Equally important, internal ideological differences, the devastating mass murders in Cambodia, and the real hostilities between their mentors, China and Vietnam, began to eat away at the moral and political authority of the Marxists; returning defectors frequently spoke of "our hardcore CPT [Communist Party of Thailand] members being crazier than those in Cambodia." When an honorable amnesty program was instituted by the government and promises were made of a freer and more secure society, most of those who had fled to the jungle (including some of our contributors) returned and reintegrated themselves into the mainstream of Thai life.

The Kriangsak regime gave way in 1980 to the even more broadly based and open regime of General Prem Tinsulanonda, who brought university intellectuals into his government, expanded self-governing rural development programs, and continued apace Thailand's movement toward industrialization, the last fueled by recently developed natural gas resources in the Gulf of Thailand. Since 1980, the principal thrust of Thai society has been the even more rapid expansion of the middle class, in provincial as well as urban areas; the explosive growth of consumerism (including the construction of massive, air-conditioned shopping malls); and the perception of the United States as a competitor with, rather than as a model for, Thai economic interests, particularly in agriculture.

Culture and Literary Priorities

In any society, the ordering of literary priorities has its own cultural logic. Thus, to claim, as was done earlier, that the work of Thai writers is inherently original and creative is not to claim that the writers themselves necessarily assign their highest priority to such values. They clearly do not lack an appreciation of creativity nor deny the personal pleasure that it affords.[3] But given all the purposes that writing can serve, there are attributes of the literary act that are valued higher. Thus, the daring of a work—its boldness, spirit of outrage, sometimes its simple macho quality—is considered to be more significant. In fact, boldness is so important that even when it is a form of windmill tilting, as in "What Kind of Boat?" and "Chewing Out a Special Class," it is deeply appreciated and approved. Similarly, the entertaining qualities of a literary effort—how well it diverts, amuses, provides relief from one's natural state of boredom—are also more highly valued than the originality of its conception

or message, although originality is often the essential ingredient of entertainment.

The reasons for these kinds of priorities are complex and multiple.
The appreciation of boldness, for example, has to do historically with
the emergence of the Thai middle class and with writers changing from
being primarily a literati associated with the court (those who reflect
upon and glorify values that maintain the status quo) into an intelligent-
sia (heretics and dissenters who are attempting to bring forth new intellectual orientations). Indeed, the very passion of one's language (see
"Fishiness in the Night" and "Big Shot as Toad") is a way of highlighting
one's contrast with the delicate, euphemistic gentility of the literati. In
this sense, it serves as an expressive marker of the author's social or ideological position. Another, more contemporaneous source of the boldness
is the stylish rhetoric (or, more precisely, what is believed to be the stylish
rhetoric) of the modern, international world—whether it be the language
of protesting students in Berkeley or Paris or the tumbling prose of a
Norman Mailer. Thus, to express oneself with passion and fury or bitterness and irony is to be *au courant* and a thoroughly modern thinker. Still
another source is the journalistic background of many Thai authors (in
this collection, nine of the twenty-five contributors) and their identification of themselves variously as members of an influential "fourth estate,"
as muckrakers, and as people who have a flippant, impatient, or cynical
view of the world. The latter (not uncommon to journalists in many
places) are intensified versions of characteristics that are already widespread in Thai culture and undoubtedly account for some of the appeal
of these authors.

The priority given to literature as entertainment is perhaps even more
deeply rooted in Thai culture, although as a genre "comedy" obviously
has universal human appeal. In Thailand, however, the entertaining elements of writing (or speech, dance, painting, fantasy, folklore, or, for
that matter, anything that is conceived and communicated) go far beyond
the limits of any conventional genre. As the anthropological literature
demonstrates (see Phillips 1965:54–66), *sanug,* or fun, is such a central
feature of Thai life—pursued, encountered, and interwoven with virtually everything that Thai do—that it is felt to be inherent to the expressive process. It appears not only in the content of messages, but in its
forms, as in "Concerning *Farang*" and the names of the characters in
"Getting Drunk Abroad." It is something that people are constantly alert
to, and it makes its way even into tragedy (in "Grandma," the purgative
qualities of papaya or the market value of watercress) and solemn political criticism (the mother's character in the play *Naaj Aphajmanii.* It is
also a favorite way of communicating about weighty social issues: crime
("I Lost My Teeth"); ecological destruction (the end of "The Chao
Phrayaa River is on the Verge of Dying"); peasant revolution ("Social

Work"); technological modernization ("Headman Thuj"); the profligacy of university students ("I Am a University Student"); corruption ("A Telephone Conversation the Night the Dogs Howled"); or bureaucratic pretension and waste ("What Kind of Boat?"). In fact, some Thai authors argue that these kinds of issues are intrinsically so tedious—as much for their familiarity as their immorality—that readers will rise and attend to only those interpretations that are entertaining. While this observation might in itself be considered a bitter commentary on the views that Thai writers have of their own society, it is also a superbly human and realistic response in a culture whose ultimate explanations are prescribed by Buddhist doctrine.

These observations have been made principally to emphasize the necessity to think in terms of the cultural values that actually animate literary activity and to caution against facile intercultural assumptions about the meaning of literature to those who produce and enjoy it. There are a few additional considerations, as much social structural as thematic, which impinge upon the role of literature in a place like Thailand. These considerations also challenge some standard anthropological premises about the nature of literature and literary figures in the non-Western world. Again, the real issue here may simply be the extraordinarily rapid rate of change in Thailand and other Third World nations and the seeming inability of Western analytic categories to keep abreast of the impact of such change on ongoing social processes.

The Cultural Status of Contemporary Literature

The first of these considerations, although perhaps the most inchoate, is historically the most significant. It has to do with defining and assigning a status to contemporary writing as an independent intellectual and aesthetic phenomenon. From an intercultural point of view, a great deal of contemporary non-Western writing (like much of contemporary non-Western art) lacks a clear and recognizable status, if only because it emerges out of a historical situation still dominated by two earlier, more established literary traditions—folk or oral literature on the one hand and a classical literature on the other. (While oral literature is found in all societies, classical literature is typically limited to societies with "Great Traditions." See Redfield 1955 for the authoritative formulation of the concepts "Great" and "Little" traditions.)

The "domination" has to do with the greater historical depth of the two prior traditions, the assumption that such depth makes them more culturally "natural" or legitimate, and the literary values that are attributed to them. Thus, in comparison with modern writing, oral literature is viewed as more direct, earthy, and sagacious but also freer and more fanciful. Because it typically has no identifiable authors and is often linked to religion and other forms of social solidarity, it is also considered more expressive of agreed-upon cultural values. By the same token, it is viewed as more obvious or blatant in its revelation of the group's unconscious psychological preoccupations.[4] There is, in addition, an element of intercultural snobbery or effeteness operating here, at least for those who perceive ethnic differences in Rousseauesque terms: that is, in looking at literary material from an alien culture, most of us are more willing to be persuaded—or at least charmed—by the aphoristic wisdom of a folktale than by the more complex inventions of a college-educated urbanite. The former is presumed to be more "authentic" and simpler (even in cases where it may be symbolically more complex), while the latter, if more sophisticated, is considered more adulterated and contrived. That the modern material uses familiar expository forms—the novel, short story, critical essay—is seen as further evidence of its parvenu quality, even when, as in the case of the novel, it may not actually be warranted.[5] Inherent in all of this is the view that oral literature is the product of an innocent, irrecoverable past and that modern writing is the product of a vibrant, but jaded, present. The snobbery breeds upon contempt for the familiar—or in this case what seems more familiar. (A similar kind of logic often characterizes the evaluation of non-Western art. For a brief, but brilliant, analysis of how perplexing designs are defined as something familiar so that they can then be more easily denigrated, see Graburn's 1978 essay: " 'I Like Things To Look More Different Than That Stuff Did': An Experiment in Cross-Cultural Art Appreciation." In both cases, the denigration is a result of not understanding the meaning of the material in native terms.)

On the other side of the literary equation, "classical literature," in contrast to modern writing, is viewed as more elegant, elaborate, mythical, and more concerned with ultimate or prototypic issues such as the nature of the socal order, heroism, beauty, loyalty, and other modes of human perfection. As in folk literature, there is in classical literature little hesitation in blurring the human, natural, and supernatural worlds. (This blurring is not eschewed in contemporary writing; see "Grandma," for example. When it occurs it is accepted as a natural extension of the traditional belief rather than as an invention of the modern imagination.)

In Thailand classical literature was usually written and recited as poetry rather than prose, with the result that there was comparatively greater concern with the aesthetics of language per se—its lyrical qualities and how it could be fashioned to conform with prosodic rules (see Mosel 1961 and Simmonds 1963). In matters of literary evaluation, the beauty of language and imagery, both aural and conceptual, was rated more highly than the originality or profoundity of the message being communicated. These criteria continue to operate into the present generation and, among other things, make any translation of Thai poetry inherently deficient. The difficulty of translating Thai poetry, particularly its sonorous qualities, may well be the reason for the relative paucity of classical Thai literary texts in other languages. The *Ramakian,* the Thai version of the *Ramayana,* has been translated (see Dhaninivat 1961 and Cadet 1971), as have a few important selections of drama and poetry (see Chappell 1972, Drans 1947, Ingersoll 1973, Pramoj 1958 and 1965, and Simmonds 1963 and 1971). But most foreign language materials are mainly summations of or commentaries on original texts (see Dhaninivat 1947 and 1954, Ginsburg 1972, Purachatra [Prince Prem Chaya] 1949, 1955 and 1959, Rajadhon 1956 and 1961, Rutnin 1975, Schweisguth 1951, and Yupho 1963). Another reason so few texts have been translated is undoubtedly related to the fact that the stories have always been more accessible in visual form—as temple paintings, murals, engravings, designs on lacquerware cabinets, and the like. And for whatever reason, foreigners have seemed more responsive to the aesthetics of the visual than to the aesthetics of the poetic.

Finally, as is true almost by definition, much of the classical literature was written or staged for the pleasure of the elite, and significant portions were written by the elite themselves.[6] The support of literary activity was viewed by virtually all Thai monarchs as a critical attribute of the royal role (see Gedney 1982). Certain monarchs of the past two centuries —particularly Rama I, II, and VI—are remembered for the virtuosity and dedication with which they pursued their own writing. To this day, many Thai speak of literary talent as an implicit, but essential, attribute of the power of kings. Indeed, literary talent (perhaps as an extension of rhetorical virtuosity) was assumed to be part of the charisma, karmic status, and superior civility not only of kings themselves but of the whole ambience of the court. Although the tradition has perhaps attenuated over time, it has been exemplified in the twentieth century in Prince Damrong Rajanubhab and Prince Narisara Nuwatiwongse during the reign of Rama V, in the courtiers of Rama VI, and in the writings of Prince Dhaninivat (regent during the 1950s), Prince Wan Waithayakorn (Thailand's late, great word modernizer and also president of the United Nations General Assembly), and Prince Prem Purachatra (the most dedicated editor-translator of Thai classical literature).

Among the contributors to this book, at least three self-consciously model their own literary roles, at least in part, upon their royal ancestors or heroes (M. R. Khukrit Pramoj on Rama II; Sulak Sivaraksa on Prince Damrong and Prince Narisara; and M. L. Boonlue Kunjara Debyasuvan partially on her older sister, who was reared at court, but mostly on a more generalized notion of royal responsibility.) A fourth contributor, Vasit Dejkunjorn, is perhaps even more critically involved in this tradition. Some suggest that notwithstanding his brilliance as a satirist and the likelihood that his material will be published only posthumously, one of his principal functions as commanding general of the Royal Guard was to serve as unofficial palace chronicler and historian of the reign of the present king, Rama IX.

Classical Thai literature continues to have a significant impact on contemporary Thai culture. As a cynosure of verbal eloquence and of the accomplishments of the past, it is taught in public schools and in the universities and is performed at the National Theatre and on radio and television. Some educated Thai also speak of participating in family poetry recitations, particularly when they were children; although these were sometimes readings from the classical literature, they were more frequently demonstrations or training sessions in committing poetry to memory and in proper modes of elocution. All of this was part of a more generalized complex—class-linked, although not exclusively so—associated with a life of gentility and civility.[7] At another level, classical Thai literature is one of the major symbols of the nation's identity and is used as an insignia for presenting Thailand to the international world. It is especially favored by the tourist industry, which urges visitors to see and to photograph classical dance dramas and to purchase tapes of classical poetry readings—presumably more for their exotic sound than their meaning.[8]

Of more direct relevance to our interests is the role that classical literature plays in the system of literary metaphors and allusions used by informed men and women. As the selections in this book demonstrate, contemporary writers simply assume that knowledge of classical sources is part of the normal intellectual apparatus of their readers, and they cite that literature to convey a more precise and complete understanding of experience. For most educated Thai, there is no more apt image of rage than *Phra* Wesandorn's toward Chuuchok in the Jataka tale (see "Lord Buddha, Help Me?"), or of fear than the image of flowing blood in *Phra Lauau* (see "Fulfilling One's Duty"), or of the nature of the traditional Thai hero than that embodied in *Phra Aphajmanii* (see *Naaj Aphajmanii*). Literary "classics" everywhere have this kind of aesthetic and rhetorical function; the point here is simply the pleasure and pride that Thai have in using their tradition in this manner.

Yet for all its elegance and emphasis upon the prototypic, Thai classical literature is clearly not of this world in its subject matter, sense of reality, or timeliness. As one modern writer expressed it, "our *wanakhadii* [classical literature] belongs to the world of museums," as heirlooms to be appreciated for their eloquence and aesthetic integrity but also as things that are essentially tangential to modern experience. From this point of view, the cultural status of classical literature is parallel to that of oral literature: as the latter is symbolic of the innocence and simplicity of the past, classical literature is symbolic of the beauty and grace of the past. But the historical depth of these traditions—that which seemingly makes them more culturally "natural" or legitimate to ingenuous outsiders—is also the basis of their marginality or liminality in contemporary Thai consciousness.[9]

The cultural status of contemporary literature must be defined in terms very different from those that apply to these earlier genres. For one thing, the aesthetic thrust of modern writing is based upon an entirely different set of literary interests. If oral literature is animated by a spirit of peasant sagacity and unpretentiousness and classical literature by a courtly panache and a concern with the sonority of language, modern literature is animated by a spirit of realism, immediacy, and narrative honesty.[10] It is a literature of ideas, events, and actions relating to the on-going social world rather then one of sound patterns and prosodic rules, recondite symbols, or complex internal states and motivations. The fact that it is written in narrative, rather than poetic, form, with the built-in requirements that narrative has (and that poetry often eschews) regarding the sequencing of images and ideas, their intellectual coherence, and their general necessity "to make sense" in terms of workaday verbal patterns, reinforces its realism. To both authors and readers, the strength of modern writing derives much more from its noetics than from its aesthetics—its capacity to conceptualize what is experientially familiar. To what extent this conceptualization might also be lasting or profound only time can tell.

Contemporary writing does have in common with its literary precursors a diffuse concern with ethical problems and issues, or at least with phrasing human experiences in these terms. There is a premise here, widespread throughout Thai culture and thought, that virtually all problems have moral solutions (or moral dimensions with which people must come to terms), which each person, through his or her own act of will, is capable of implementing or, conversely, of neglecting or violating. The frequency with which moral issues emerge from our material—sometimes as central points but more often in the references and allusions used to cast an argument—testifies to the tenacity of this tradition.

It is in its social dimensions, however, that contemporary literature differs most markedly from the earlier genres. Paralleling so many of the other changes that have occurred in Thai society as a whole, the Thai literary enterprise has been transformed into an extraordinarily open-ended intellectual process, with contemporary authors writing about as many things as people speak about. This open-endedness is not total: political censorship in Thailand is real, even if it is capricious; also, the uncertain economic state of many writers, particularly the less-established ones, and the fickleness of public preferences, always constrains what is actually written and published. But in contrast to both oral and classical literature, contemporary literature is self-consciously felt to be a mode or vehicle for intellectual exploration, discovery, and experimentation. This is not a borrowing of the Western notion that if literature is to be valuable it must be original, or that it somehow represent or embody what is avant-garde. Thai do not subscribe to a belief in the inherent goodness of the innovative or creative. Rather, what is important from a Thai point of view is that literature clarify or reveal that which is obviously real but unrecognized; that it make people think about what previously was improper (or dangerous or irrelevant) to think about; that it give shape, meaning, and identities to things. However they might strike a Western observer, these are the kinds of literary values that have explicitly informed or inspired writers such as Khamsing Srinawk (in his account of a middle-class teacher on the make), M. L. Boonlue Kunjara Debyasuvan (in her description of the tension between a modern husband and a traditional wife), Suchart Sawadsii (in his merging of sex and aggression), Witayakorn Chiengkul (in his drama of generational conflict), Suchit Wongthed (in his observations on Thai students, both at home and abroad), and most of the contributors to this volume.

The real social issue here is the fact that Thai literature has changed from being, on the one hand, an elite activity dominated by a small number of literati producing work that was socially approved and aesthetically appealing to the elite themselves and, on the other, a peasant literature that was inherently legitimate because of its universality into a literature of the intellectual marketplace. While this marketplace has been extremely sensitive to the prevailing freedoms and repressions of domestic politics, its fundamental historical character has been the constant expansion of the wares it has offered, the number of people who have patronized it, and its own internal competitiveness. Over the past century written literature has moved from the palaces of princes into the raucous ambience of a Thai bazaar. The rivalry among ideas, styles, themes—and ultimately between alternative visions of the nature of experience—is intense. As a consequence, contemporary writing has a much greater degree of variability, individuality, and substantive richness than is found in either of the earlier genres.

The competitive spirit of the literary marketplace stimulates considerable intellectual richness and the formation and fission of literary *phuak,* the various colleagues, friends, teachers, and disciples with whom most writers surround themselves and who serve variously as critics, guides, and general sources of intellectual, emotional, and sometimes financial support. Thai literary *phuak* are not planned, self-consciously organized groups. While membership in *phuak* is not permanent, their composition at any one time is reasonably clear, and readers and other authors sometimes know a particular writer's *phuak,* his past *phuak,* and the broad outlines of various *phuak* loyalties and rivalries. As a group, Thai writers are no less vain than men and women of letters in most places, and *phuak* solidarity is constantly being tested by those who are particularly daring, self-sufficient, or contentious. Among the contributors to this book, whose work spans a sixteen-year period, there are at least five identifiable *phuak,* most of which, because of internal divisions and normal changes of career, have had numerous overlapping members.

Many successful writers acknowledge that the competition also stimulates the publication of a substantial amount of literary pap. Younger writers in particular seem motivated by a constant but usually vain search for literary formulas that somehow will ignite their reading public and bring them instant fame. Because publication costs are relatively inexpensive and the ethos of the bazaar assumes that every new product may be a winner, it is easy for most material to get some exposure, even if it is only by vanity publication. The result is a market that in quantitative terms contains a large percentage of material that is difficult to take seriously. This may simply be a statistical by-product of the highly experimental nature of the present Thai literary situation. In a low-risk, high-yield market, the prevailing spirit is that anything goes.

This "anything goes" spirit is in fact one of the most pervasive themes of the entire Thai literary scene, animating the publication of both the best and the worst writing. It is more an attribute of the attitude and perception of writers than it is a substantive theme of the literature itself, although its qualities resonate through several of our selections (see particularly "Concerning *Farang,*" "Madame Lamhab," "Paradise Preserved," "A Telephone Conversation the Night the Dogs Howled," and "What Kind of Boat?"). Essentially it is an attitude in which daring, a readiness to bet or gamble, flippancy, the pose of self-confidence, wide variations in social class and social manners, and a sense of the transiency of almost everything are felt to permeate all of social life. Above all, it embraces the belief that virtually nothing is to be taken seriously, least of all oneself or one's work. Since success or failure is usually the result of forces beyond one's control, almost anything is worth trying. One can never anticipate what will impress or appeal to others (even if it impresses oneself), and thus one must always be prepared to be simultaneously cynical and sanguine about the outcome of things—although the cynicism is probably the more apparent, if only because it is more self-protective.

Literacy and Its Institutions

The transformation of Thai literature into an intellectual marketplace has been accompanied by, and ultimately is based upon, an even more significant cultural event—a dramatic increase in the nation's literacy rate. Thailand obviously is not unique in this regard. Everywhere in the world, more and more people are learning to read, and the emergence of universal literacy may prove to be one of the monumental achievements of the twentieth century. Whatever increasing literacy actually does to a society, it certainly gives its members broader access to the total store of human knowledge and contributes, at least indirectly, to the meritocratization and perhaps the democratization of social processes.[11] By making more ideas more readily available to more people, it also increases the competition between ideas—as much in a social sense as in an intellectual sense.

Literacy rates by themselves say nothing about what is actually read, by whom, and for what purposes. Rather, they are measures of a society's commitment to the reading process and of the complex institutional apparatus that develops around reading. This apparatus includes the teaching of reading and writing; the recruitment and training of writers; the creation of printing and publishing houses and of mechanisms for disseminating publications, such as bookstores, networks of magazine stands, and the like; and the development of libraries and other facilities for the preservation of books. Other, more subtle, symbolic factors are the presence or absence of a craft tradition associated with printing; the extent to which books are, like art or jewelry, objects to be collected, appreciated, and sometimes used as markers for their owners' social positions; and the extent to which public libraries are lending or noncirculating, or, in the home, whether books are kept in unlocked cabinets as family possessions available to all or under lock and key as the personal property of a specific family member. (In years past, children in Thai homes had to ask permission and obtain a key to read a book, thus creating a complicated social transaction out of simple intellectual curiosity.)[12] In various ways all these are indices of the status and value that a society as a whole accords to its literary pursuits.

The changes that have occurred in Thailand during recent decades have been impressive. Although the nation has had a written language for more than seven hundred years, and the beginnings of universal public education since 1892, the official literacy rate was only 54 percent at the end of World War II (National Statistical Office 1965:131). By 1970, it had increased to 82 percent, and in the Bangkok area to 90 percent. Unfortunately, in all areas of the nation, the female literacy rate was invariably lower than that of males by 10 to 15 percent.

As is true in many places, these official literacy rates are based upon census-takers simply asking respondents if they (and other household members over the age of ten about whom they presumably know) are "able to read and write," without any attempt to distinguish between functional and fantasized literacy. Some Thai informants indicated that they have always assumed that "literacy" meant "reading and writing one's name," while others spoke of "reading and writing personal letters," and still others referred to "reading a newspaper." More reliable indices of functional literacy are the statistics on schooling. By 1970, 45 percent of the nation's population over the age of six had either completed or was in the process of completing four years of education, which, under normal circumstances, provides sufficient training to read a newspaper. However, these figures are undergoing dramatic change as more and more Thai children are attending school for longer periods. Thus, by 1980, 97 percent (7.4 million people) of the kingdom's elementary school-aged children, and 25 percent (almost 2 million people) of the nation's secondary school-aged children were enrolled in school, the vast majority of the latter on a tuition-paying basis. By 1981, 4.2 percent (a quarter of a million people) of those Thai between the ages of eighteen and twenty-three were attending college or technical and business school equivalents (National Statistical Office 1981:42–43).

It is impossible to determine, at least at this level of statistical generality, what proportion of the functionally literate population actually reads the work produced by contemporary Thai writers, although in numerous instances selected writing (for example, some of the novellas and literary criticism of M. L. Boonlue Kunjara Debyasuvan; M. R. Khukrit Pramoj's novel *Sii Phaeaendin* [Four reigns]; and the poetry of Angkarn Kalayaanaphong and Suchit Wongthed) are required reading in schools and universities, and thus are read by millions. More important, certain publishing practices in Thailand give writers greater access to potentially more readers (in a comparative, per capita sense) than is perhaps the case in Western societies. Most Thai authors first publish their material in newspapers or in weekly and monthly magazines. Novels, novellas, and short stories are also serialized for publication in daily newspapers and in weekly magazines ("The Enchanting Cooking Spoon" was originally serialized in three installments). In this format, they are read by scores of thousands of readers.[13] Only the most popular or valuable of these writings are later made available in the more integrated, durable, and prestigious form of a book. One result of this system of duplicate (or, more precisely, sequential) publication is to provide writers with multiple royalties, although this too has its own cultural phrasing. Each edition of a book is considered to be independent of any prior publication, and rather than receiving a percentage on copies sold, authors receive a single sum for the total number of copies of that edition being printed, usually in print runs of 2,000 to 6,000 copies, although renowned writers often merit a single printing of 10,000 to 20,000 copies. If there is evidence that sales will exceed a particular printing, the author either negotiates an additional printing at a higher price or, more frequently, takes his rights to another, higher-paying publisher. Some best sellers have been issued by as many as a dozen different publishers. Although there is considerable variation in the retail prices of Thai language books, hardcover books typically sell in the 30–100 *baht* range (US$1.50–$5.00) and paperbacks in the 8–60 *baht* range (US$.40–$3.00).

This system of multiple formats and royalties is in part a modern response to a situation in which writers traditionally received a mere pittance for their labors.[14] Thus, even the original 1960 magazine version of "The Enchanting Cooking Spoon" brought its author only 150 *baht* (US$7.50) for each of the three installments. In recent years, payments have become somewhat more respectable: by the mid-1970s a serialized novel could, depending upon the credentials and status of the author, bring 500–4,000 *baht* per installment. It was not until very recently that the economics of the literary enterprise permitted a few Thai (Suchit Wongthed, Sulak Sivaraksa, Suchart Sawadsii) to devote themselves full time to professional writing, mainly because they derived part of their income from their work as editors or journalists. To date, no Thai known to us has yet been able (or willing) to pursue a career devoted exclusively to creative writing.

It should be noted that from the point of view of the cultural values and symbols embodied in their careers, the success of Suchit, Sulak, Suchart, and a few others is no mean accomplishment. Excepting the independently wealthy and some special elite women, the pursuit of serious writing had for decades been seen by most Thai as a kind of juvenile indulgence—something that one did as an idealistic and unfettered youth but relinquished as the exigencies of life turned to marriage, family responsibilities, and the necessities of "making a decent living." In fact, among the established minor tragedies of Thai life were those numerous talented young men and women who were forced to give up their "serious writing" and turn instead to careers in advertising or public relations or work as speech writers and hacks for politicians. (Aspects of this pattern are hinted at in "Paradise Preserved" and *Naaj Aphajmanii*.) Whether as major intellectual innovators or simply as indicators of the natural evolution of Thai society, people like Suchit, Sulak, and Suchart have clearly overcome the traditional system of expectations. Through their own talent, energy, and a certain capacity "to arrange things" (financial supporters, good staffs) they have moved into full-fledged adulthood, maintaining their roles as intellectually creative men who could also support themselves, their families, and even their (sometimes substantial) *phuak* of disciples. From a historical and social point of view, the symbolism of their accomplishments is perhaps just as important as the content of their writings.

There is one other mode of literary distribution that merits special mention. Although it is still only an incipient practice, more and more of the writings of contemporary authors are being reprinted in cremation volumes (see the Introduction to "Big Shots and *Likee*"). This custom of distributing books to guests attending funeral ceremonies originated with King Chulalongkorn during the latter part of the nineteenth century and thus is unique to Thailand rather than a practice of the wider Theravada

Buddhist world. Including a biography and photographs of the deceased, cremation books were traditionally made up of selections from the Buddhist canon, classical poetry, patriotic songs, and the like. While most such texts were stock items (like gravestones in the West) family members nevertheless exercised great care in selecting material that would honor the deceased. That some contemporary writing should begin to be used for this purpose attests to the aesthetic and emotional esteem that this literature has come to be accorded in Thai society. Since cremation books represent approximately 30 percent of the books published in Thailand, their potential readership numbers in the scores of thousands of people.[15]

Finally, as a result of borrowing patterns and group readings (particularly those in village Thailand, which may involve illiterate listeners), the number of copies printed or sold always represents a gross underestimation of the number of people who actually read or hear a work. The actual number of readers of any given work is a function of its significance, cost, durability, and availability from other sources. (Because of the high import duties on copying machines, xerography is extremely costly and is used only when there are no alternatives.) The rule of thumb used by most publishers is that for every book, magazine, or newspaper sold there are at least five people who read or hear the text; a few estimates increase the ratio (8 to 1 and 10 to 1) but none goes under it.[16] Thailand's first and most influential "intellectual magazine," *Sangkhom-saat Parithat* [Social science review], rarely had press runs of more than 8,000 copies, but because of its attempts to examine cultural fundamentals, it, or selections from it, came to be read by five to ten times that many people.[17] Similarly, one of our selections, "Relations with Colleagues," from the novel *Naaj Amphur Patiwad* [The revolutionary district officer], even after being serialized in a daily paper became the first fictional effort in Thai history to have sold more than 100,000 copies and to have been read by more than a half million people within a year of its publication. Given the basic facts about literacy and educational attainment in Thailand, these figures, and the cultural commitments they imply, are not unimpressive.

Although such patterns are not unique to Thailand, their magnitude represents a critical element in the nation's total institutional structure of publishing and reading. It is our view that these patterns are both cause and consequence of reading being somewhat more of a social act and, correlatively, somewhat less of a private, psychological act than we customarily think of it in the West. People not only read, but they debate, confabulate, and banter about what they read. The quality of writing styles, the descriptions of fictional heroes and villains, the elegance or foolishness of intellectual arguments, the latest rhetorical outrages are all grist for the mills of discussion, social exchange, and the individual's desire to be in touch with the world beyond his or her private experience.

People lend and borrow books, magazines, and articles so that they can participate in the pleasures of gossiping and deliberating about the world of ideas, affairs, and the imagination and because such lending and borrowing is in itself an expression of their sociality. For some there is undoubtedly an element of class affectation operating here, in the sense that being able to carry on an informed and animated discussion of an important literary work is a marker (to oneself as well as to others) of being civilized, *au courant,* and a member of the educated elite. However, Thai seem to be less pretentious and more mutually supportive, playful, and relaxed about their literary exchanges than people in many countries.[18] They also appear to be more trusting about lending books to friends and more attentive to caring for and returning them on time than is true elsewhere.

Perhaps the clearest demonstration of the maturing status of the literary enterprise in Thai society was the appearance in 1979 of the monthly *Loog Nangsyy* [The world of books], the first Thai-language magazine to be devoted exclusively to literary criticism and book reviews. Its press runs of 6,000 to 8,000 copies indicate a readership of 30,000 to 40,000 people, if the pattern holds true. The implications of such an effort—that there are now a sufficient number of new books published and a sufficient number of potential readers who want to know about them to make a magazine devoted to examining them economically viable—is no small accomplishment in a society that did not even use the book review genre until after World War II.

In the end, however, the cultural value and status of contemporary Thai literature does not reside primarily in the numbers of people who read it. Unlike movies, television, and radio, this literature is not meant to indulge the tastes of mass audiences or to maximize the economic interests of its creators, although Thai writers clearly appreciate the additional income their writing provides and sometimes their works are adapted for television or movies. Rather, like serious authors everywhere, Thai write because they (and their readers) believe they have something true, important, or aesthetically compelling to say and that, whatever the size of their audience, they must first be judged in these terms.

Censorship

Irrespective of literary merit, audience size, or a publisher's business sense, publication has in recent years been constrained by the reality or threat of censorship—not only the external censorship exercised by police but, perhaps even more effectively, the self-censorship of publishers, editors, and authors. The latter is a function of the former in that police have had the authority not only to seize allegedly offensive mate-

rial but to close down the total operation of a publisher, even confiscating his printing presses. Thus, everyone involved in the editorial process is made to feel responsible not only for particular texts but for the entire organization, including the jobs and incomes of associates or subordinates. This is not to deny the development of certain stratagems aimed at circumventing the constraints of censorship: underground publication; the use of a multiplicity of pseudonyms by certain authors (since frequently authors as well as texts are considered dangerous by censors); and the creative use of humor, hyperbole, and little symbolic conceits that, while brilliantly integrated into the text, make unmistakable political points. However, for all the imaginativeness of the literary response, censorship casts a constant, if low grade, pall of anxiety over the entire enterprise. It is always there as something to worry about.

For certain authors censorship is as much reality as it is anxiety. Poet, philologist, historian, and Marxist thinker Chitr Phoumisak (see "Fishiness in the Night") was one of the most prolific but least published writers of the 1950s and 1960s—both circumstances due largely to the fact that for most of this period he was in jail for political reasons. Although three different regimes (Phibun, Sarit, and Thanom) prohibited his work from being published or sold, dog-eared, mimeographed versions of many of his writings circulated privately among friends and the intellectually curious. Among the latter were numerous people who considered Chitr's political conceptions bizarre but who were nevertheless awed by his literary talents. He was killed by the police in the mid-1960s, and after the Student Revolution of 1973, he was fashioned into a Marxist martyr, and his works were among the best selling and most broadly critiqued writings of the 1973–1976 period. After the coup of 1976, his publications, along with those of many others, were again suppressed, this time by the Thanin regime. Lately they have taken on some of the qualities of "historical documents" and are once again being widely and openly circulated.

Few writers have suffered the outright suppression of Chitr Phoumisak (let alone incarceration or murder), although numerous writers, fearing for their own safety, have spent extended periods in exile. Perhaps the most famous of these was Kularb Saipradit, Thailand's most articulate creator of social protest fiction of the 1940s and 1950s, who, like Chitr, was jailed for "treason" during the Phibun era, and who, after his release, fled to China where he spent the final years of his life. Among the contributors to this book, Khamsing Srinawk, Sulak Sivaraksa, Puey Ungphakorn, Seksan Prasertkul, Anud Aaphaaphirom, and the author of "The Telephone Conversation the Night the Dogs Howled" went into exile after the coup of 1976. (Of these, one spent several unforgettable weeks in jail being questioned by the police; another was almost lynched as he was trying to leave the country; still another had the total inventory of one of his bookstores confiscated by the police; and three spent several months in the jungle trying to decide what to do with their lives.) As is the case with virtually all Thai writers, it is difficult to disentangle the literary activities of these individuals from the other activities they have pursued or the roles they have played (or have had thrust upon them) in Thai public life. By the same token, it is difficult to disentangle the reality or threat of censorship from all the other tactics that are normally used by those competing for political power or primacy in Thailand. In fact, the persons just cited were forced to leave Thailand (at the time, with good reason to fear for their lives) not because of anything specific they had written but rather because of the roles they had come to play in the larger theatre of Thai public life. Most of them have since returned to Thailand and are pursuing productive, relatively unharassed lives. The point here is that, like most people (Americans in their judgments of the political aspirations of Norman Mailer or Gore Vidal; French in their perceptions of André Gide or Jean Paul Sartre), Thai do not afford any special political privileges to those with literary talent. The majority Thai view is that for all his brilliance as a poet, Chitr Phoumisak was also a genuine revolutionary, and he played out a role that if not inevitable was certainly explicable in terms of the historical realities of Thai culture.

While the legal authority for censorship has varied over the years, its fundamental character was crystallized in Proclamation 17 of the 1957 "Proclamations of the Revolutionary Group," the basic charter of the military regimes that governed Thailand during the late 1950s, most of the 1960s, the early 1970s, and, with some important modifications, the late 1970s. Phrased in terms of newspapers, this document unabashedly describes the nature of the restrictions on all publications:

> . . . the authorities shall attach and destroy such papers and attach the machine on which such papers were printed for such period as they may think appropriate but not longer than six months . . . if any paper publishes matter of the following nature:
>
> 1) any matter infringing upon His Majesty the King, or defamatory, libellous, or contemptuous of the Queen, royal heir, or regent;
>
> 2) any matter defamatory or contemptuous of the nation or Thai people as a whole, or any matter capable of causing the respect and confidence of foreign countries in regard to Thailand, the Thai government, or Thai people in general, to diminish [This clause prohibits criticism of the conduct of Thai foreign relations and, more specifically during the 1960s, criticism of the United States military presence in Thailand];
>
> 3) any matter ambiguously defamatory or contemptuous of the Thai government, or any ministry, public body, or department of the government without stating clearly the fault and matter [This and the following clause are perhaps the most vexing to the creative writer, if only because the essence of effective public criticism in Thailand is teasing ambiguity];
>
> 4) any matter ambiguously showing that the government or ministry, pub-

lic body, or department of the government has deteriorated, is bad, or has committed a damaging offense without showing in what matter and particular;

5) any matter promoting approval of Communism, or apparently [*sic*] a Communist plot to disturb or undermine national security;

6) any false matter of a nature tending to panic, worry, or frighten the people or matter tending to incite, or arouse disorder, or conflict with public order or morality, or prophecies concerning the fate of the nation which might upset the people [Although this last phrase is directed toward seers and shamans, it is also used against the authors of such statements as "if the government continues policy X, it will have the following adverse results"];

7) any matter using coarse language tending to lower national morals or culture;

8) any official secrets. . . .

Notwithstanding their imperious tone, few of these dicta have actually been enforced in an open or public manner, and when they have it has usually been for lesser offenses such as slander or defamation of character. Rather, they seem to function in a backstop manner, as ultimate sanctions to other, more frequent, equivocal, but personally more disquieting censorial acts—"visits of inquiry" from the police (sometimes at home, sometimes at the office; sometimes a lone officer, sometimes a commissioned officer and a squad of armed men); "words of warning" from an unknown official that are passed through a series of intermediaries; or anonymous letters or phone calls, phrased so they are taken seriously. (That such communications might be the work of eccentrics or the mentally disturbed is inconceivable to most Thai, if only because "politics" is too serious a matter to be admitted into the mental life of the neurotic or psychotic. That they might be "dirty tricks" or even "friendly jokes" is within the realm of Thai possibility, but just barely.) It is difficult to judge the effects of these more ambiguous forms of censorship upon those who experience them. People who report them usually do so with a sense of pride about their own stalwartness and, even more, with a sense of delight about their ability to spar with and outwit a police official.[19]

On the other hand, there are others who report the understandable fear and hatred they felt when their homes were invaded late at night by armed, uniformed men who ransacked their shelves in search of potentially illegal documents and who, after creating a mess or taking a few volumes, simply left. To our knowledge, none of these actions has ever resulted in any arrests or trials, of either victims or perpetrators. More important, victims seem to respond not as though they were the specific targets of an act of political intimidation (although at some level of consciousness they certainly know this) but rather in terms of being the unlucky victims of the kind of uncontrolled police hooliganism that can touch anybody at anytime. Nor do the few people we know who have undergone this kind of intimidation admit to the possibility that it has in any way muted their readiness to voice their social and political views.

Clearly, censorship is as much an "institution" of literacy as are publishing houses, libraries, and literary salons. At one level, the very existence of censorship laws, and of a police mechanism for "implementing" them, betrays the sense of power that the Thai political establishment assigns to the publication process and the dissemination of ideas. Whatever the literacy rates, the quantity of pap that might be produced, or the homely purposes to which it is sometimes put, writing is nevertheless perceived as having major consequences for the nature and direction of Thai society and to that extent is defined as something that must be controlled or monitored. On the other hand, it is also true that in Thailand, censorship is as haphazard and counterproductive as it is intellectually harassing. It not only has been unable to prevent underground publication and distribution but in fact has stimulated it. It has to some extent made better writers of some by inspiring them to finesse censorial strictures with literary wile and flourish, and it has kept some lazy writers out of the marketplace (by justifying their rationalizations that their work would never get by the censors or would create difficulties for their publishers). In this sense, censorship has helped raise the general level of sophistication of the cat-and-mouse, fun-and-games ambience that most Thai treasure in their public life, the central purpose of which is to mock official pretense and absurdity. Too, although censorship in no sense created it, it has helped sustain and legitimize a more or less permanent anti-establishment tradition among certain elements of the Thai literary community. (For an excellent discussion of the history and genealogy of this tradition, see Chitakasem 1982.) Yet, for all its inefficiencies and self-defeating qualities, censorship has had the ultimate sanction of Thai law and thus the capacity to come down at any time against real or fanciful offenders. In reality, of course, it has not come down at "any time" upon possible violators. Censorship has always ebbed and flowed with the currents of Thai politics and with the anxieties and calculations of its political leaders. Writers can read these currents as well as, or perhaps better, than anyone else, and they know when censorship is likely to be irrelevant or critical to what they are about. However, it is the legitimacy of censorship in legal terms that has made it a constant focus of literary attention.

Fashioning a Literary Sample

One of the basic premises of this study is that literary works are refractions or distillations, rather than reflections or replicas, of the life and thought of the societies in which they are written. In our view, their content is as contingent upon the situation of the author—his or her personal prejudices, social positions, and rhetorical purposes—as they are upon the cultural realities to which the writing ultimately refers. They are also contingent upon the communicative expectations of writers and readers —emergent and creative as well as traditional. It is for all these reasons that we have found it necessary to give as much attention to the social and personal context of the literary enterprise as to the texts themselves.

If the metaphors of "refraction" and "distillation" describe the relationship between literature and real life, they are also relevant to the relationship between the materials contained in this book and the total corpus of contemporary Thai writing. In their very nature our materials are neither a random nor representative sample of this literature (although admittedly the very idea that a body of literature might somehow be "statistically represented" is to us a bit peculiar). Nor are our selections the product of some abstract theoretical model for assembling such a volume. Rather, they are essentially the result of a series of on-the-ground compromises among a number of specific, sometimes mutually contending, ethnographic aims.

We first sought materials that would convey the scope of Thai literary activity in terms of its substantive themes, the genres used, and the variety of persons who define themselves as writers. This emphasis upon scope, rather than quality or depth, is an expression of the anthropological preoccupation with the richness and multifarious nature of cultural traditions and of our concern with establishing the parameters of these traditions. It is probably also a reflection of the nonelitist bias of anthropology and our view that all human expressions, both within and between cultural traditions, are of equal value. One consequence of this bias was the attempt to eschew making comparative judgments about aesthetic merit, imaginativeness, or originality or, more significantly, using such attributes as criteria for selection. Thus, we make no claim, even implicitly, that our materials necessarily represent the "best of Thai writing."

To be sure, one of the three substantive standards we used in choosing a selection was its "intellectual persuasiveness to a native Thai audience." And indeed in numerous instances—the imagery (but not necessarily the conceptualization) of "Grandma"; the confessional nature of M. R. Khukrit's "I Lost My Dog"; the euphony of "Oh! Temple, Temple of Bot!" and "Fishiness in the Night" (which in both cases is lost in translation, but which may be suggested by explanation)—Thai associates have insisted that we have identified some of the most memorable examples of contemporary writing. But these are Thai, not Western, standards, and as these and other selections repeatedly demonstrate, it is both too easy and dangerous to make false surmises about the congruence, or even the overlap, between these standards. Even if false surmises are reduced and cultural differences explained, there may still be a significant aesthetic hiatus, if only because so many of our selections were originally written to be appreciated, savored, and responded to emotionally rather than to be used as an object or source of intellectual exegesis—which of course is very much our own purpose. But this is the kind of risk that every writer takes in offering his work to the public and subjecting it to the private readings of others. Variation in interpretation and use is simply inherent to the literary process.

Our concern with scope automatically created other problems, the most serious of which was the necessity to omit from this collection novels or other lengthy works, the critical factor being the likelihood that any single novel might in volume equal or exceed our entire space allowance. Some supportive Thai colleagues have suggested that the omission might not be as significant as it would seem because—again, from their native point of view—the novel is not as "culturally natural" as is, for example, poetry. By this they mean that the novel is not as familiar and widely appreciated a genre as poetry and is not characterized by as much verbal ingenuity and euphony. Certainly the "beauty" of Thai poetry derives from its capacity to synthesize, often epiphanally for Thai readers, semantic and aural aesthetic elements. But the narrative possibilities of the novel afford far greater scope for the representation of human character and for the development of a sense of social complexity and of the sheer unpredictability of human experience. (It is probably not fortuitous that the richest and most ramified text in this collection—the abridged novella, "The Enchanting Cooking Spoon"—is also the longest.) At one point, we considered resolving the conflict between scope and depth by fashioning a collection comprised of six to eight abridged novellas but rejected this idea on the grounds that it would result in an overly restrictive representation of Thai writing. We eventually concluded that a mix of genres—essays, poems, short stories, a drama, a novella, songs, social commentary, a chain letter, and even a chapter from a novel—would best serve our purposes, although in no case was a work selected because it represented a particular genre. Precedence was always given to the literary substance, not to the form, of a selection.

Perhaps the most intractable problem we faced was how much emphasis should be placed upon particular authors rather than upon particular selections, and correlatively, the extent to which an effort should be made to find selections that would somehow represent an author's distinctive literary outlook. We found some excellent pieces by relative unknowns—typically individuals who wrote early in their careers but moved on to other things—while we often had difficulty locating appropriate works by writers who had achieved considerable literary stature. For example, "Senii Sawaaphong" (a pseudonym), is renowned for his sensitive portrayals of how the 1932 revolution completely altered the interpersonal relationships between social classes, demonstrating the fallacy of the widely held Western perception that the revolution had little impact upon Thai social structure. But it is virtually impossible to abstract out of Senii's writings the subtlety of this interpersonal revolution without either violating the integrity of the original texts by over-abridgement or translating an excessive amount of contextually necessary, but analytically tangential, material. Similarly, in several places we have made reference to the work of 'Rong Wongsawaan, who is widely recognized as one of the first Thai authors to write about the emotional and interpersonal, as well as biologically pleasurable, aspects of sexual relations. But if 'Rong's work is original and provocative in Thai, its English translation is not in our judgment particularly edifying, beyond perhaps some of its symbolism, (certain plants and other natural substances used to seduce lovers or the symbols appearing in the incantations used by prostitutes to attract or retain customers and the like).

In the end, we decided to give precedence to the value of an individual selection rather than to the literary or social stature of its author. However, there were several writers whose historical significance demanded that they be included (M. R. Khukrit Pramoj, Chitr Phoumisak, M. L. Boonlue Kunjara Debyasuvan, Khamsing Srinawk, Dr. Puey Ungphakorn, Sulak Sivaraksa), and in these cases we selected materials that expressed at least some aspect of their intellectual vision. Over the years these individuals have written so much that any selection would in its nature be a misrepresentation of the catholicity of their interests and outlook, but this kind of problem is unavoidable in any anthology. What is more important is that in every instance we tried to select material that addressed a significant social, historical, or psychological issue and that also contributed to the variation and balance of our entire effort. Obviously, M. R. Khukrit Pramoj will not go down in Thai history for his concern with the existential loneliness of man or Chitr Phoumisak for his views on the pornography of Bangkok. But these issues were of sufficient interest to the authors themselves and of sufficient centrality to the culture of their time to merit a place in this collection. We also decided that since it was the substance of the selections rather than the stature of the authors that must be given precedence, inevitably some authors would be represented by more than one selection. Thus, the multiple appearance of certain authors is simply a result of their own broad-ranging interests rather than of any favoritism on our part.

Criteria for Selection

Three substantive criteria were used in selecting our material: (1) the historical importance of a particular selection; (2) the extent to which it expressed or revealed aspects of Thai culture or thought; and (3) its intellectual persuasiveness to a native Thai audience. These criteria were not considered to be mutually exclusive.

The historically important materials were perhaps the easiest to identify. Some, like "My Beloved Brother, Thāmnu" or "Oh! Temple, Temple of Bot!," are almost as famous as the historical situations they commemorate. Others, like "Getting Drunk Abroad" (the internationalization of Thailand), "I Lost My Teeth" (the dramatic increase in threats to the physical security of ordinary citizens), "Headman Thuj" (the emergence of the "development" ethos), or "Lord Buddha, Help Me?" (the decline of sacred values), mark some of the most significant, and probably irreversible, changes that have occurred in Thailand during the second half of the twentieth century. Our selections in no sense represent a calendrically precise historical record, if only because the issues they address are part of a still unfolding temporal process.

Most of our selections fall into the second category, works that inform us, at various levels of consciousness, how Thai apprehend the universe. Although we had no preconceptions about what kinds of expressive materials would be included, it quickly became obvious that certain themes would be prominent, if only because Thai literary concerns are as patterned as any other domain of culture. Particularly apparent were the use of humor; the need to convey an abstract and compulsive sense of morality; the defining of human beings in terms of their capacity to play-act and posture; an overweening concern with the comparative status of people and the markers of their status (speech patterns, clothes, kinesthetic styles); the stoical, non-Faustian, and thoroughly realistic acceptance of personal failure and death as inherent and omnipresent features of the human experience; the psychological chaos of the modern world (although as many writers seem to be stimulated by this chaos as are frightened by it); and the presentation of the writer himself as a cynical, ironic, and tough-minded commentator on contemporary experience.

The third consideration—a work's persuasiveness to its native audience—may ultimately be the most important criterion we used in selecting material, but in our hands it was probably the least rigorously implemented. It is "important" in the sense that it focuses specifically on determining what is arresting or meaningful to Thai and thus on drawing English readers into their cognitive world. But it was "least rigorously" implemented because of our willingness to compromise this "emic" (native-centered) concern for the "etic" (cross-cultural or observer-centered) concern of providing material that would attract or engage the sensibilities of Western readers. We determined "native persuasiveness" simply by asking Thai friends and associates why they preferred various selections, although admittedly we were most attentive to those items that stimulated our own perplexity, disappointment, or sense of uncertainty. The various dimensions of this issue are discussed more fully below. But whatever their impact on English-language readers, "The Wholesome Intention of *Khunnaaj* Saajbua," "My Dog Is Missing," "Big Shots and *Likee*," A Telephone Conversation the Night the Dogs Howled," "Fishiness in the Night," and "Chewing Out a Special Class" were chosen in large part for their rhetorical effectiveness in Thai.

The Selection Process

The process of selecting material was not too different from that followed in most bibliographic searches, except that it involved asking authors, colleagues, and friends to suggest, judge, and in some cases even lend us items for photocopying. Friends led to other friends, and certain works led to others. At one point, one of us casually remarked to a friend that our materials seemed excessively somber and self-critical and that we were a bit concerned about the anti-humor tilt of the data we had so far gathered. During the next few weeks we were inundated by Thai light-headedness in all its forms—from this friend, his friends, and their friends. Libraries were of limited use in locating material, but the availability of large numbers of anthologies and several helpful bibliographies greatly expedited selection.

Two of us examined and evaluated more than two hundred and fifty items, both serious and humorous, and many of them were also discussed with associates and writers with whom we were particularly close. Some of our evaluations were intense, long-winded, and contentious, and occasionally required checking our own views against those of several other people (see, for example, the Introduction to "The Paradise of the President's Wife"); in other instances, it was almost immediately apparent that a prospective item was inappropriate to our purposes, and it was quickly set aside. However, it was through this evaluative process that our initial pool was eventually reduced to a "candidate list" of sixty-seven pieces which, in turn, was reduced to the thirty-four presented here. The nature of these final selections is not dramatically different from that of the thirty-three items that were not used. The two lists differ mainly in the historical significance of particular works and, more generally, in their editorial subtlety, polish, or panache. Some items were dropped simply because they overlapped topically or stylistically with others that were retained.

The tone and configuration of the thirty-four final choices do differ in some significant respects from the two hundred-odd items that were originally eliminated, however, and these differences are relevant to judging the nature of both our materials and the larger domain that makes up the Thai literary enterprise.

First, our selections use a style of exposition that in general is more muted and softly turned than that of many of the items that were rejected. Although the differences here are of degree rather than kind, we repeatedly encountered works that were almost embarrassing in their literalness, narrative single-mindedness, and blatancy, and we rejected such items primarily on these grounds. It was as if their authors did not trust the critical capacities of their readers. We are not sure whether such narrative literalness is a consequence of the didactic tradition in Thailand ("everything must be explained") and its inherently patronizing attitudes or of writers' uncertainties about their readers' sophistication in a rapidly changing marketplace. Too, we are not sure whether the authors of our final selections are more "modern" or "international" in their outlook (which presumably would make them more appealing to us) or are simply better writers than their rejected compatriots. But whatever the case, they use a mode of discourse that, at least in an internal comparative sense, is more supple and shaded than that used in most of the writings we encountered.

Second, all writings appearing in our final list had to be reasonably coherent in their English rendition, and many of the rejected items simply did not meet this standard. "Coherence" is an elusive attribute, and what is "incoherent" in one language or to one reader can make (or be reworked to make) thorough sense to another. Our standerd of coherence was whether a selection made sense to Thai readers and, when it did, whether it merited the kind of intellectual scaffolding that, although often distracting, would make it meaningful in English. Our final selections include several examples of writings that at first glance suggest coherence difficulties ("Concerning *Farang*," "What Kind of Boat?," "Fishiness in the Night") but which, when accompanied by a gloss, are thoroughly explicable in English.

The coherence problems of the rejected items were not of this order. Rather, they emerged from a mode of discourse sometimes punctuated by, sometimes flowing with, non sequiturs, circular arguments, and ritual abstractions. Some readers saw this as "ordinary" Thai writing, which, they asserted, "should never be taken too seriously, anyway." Others—more charitably and, we think, considerably more accurately— saw this as a device used by authors either to communicate their own inner states (disdain, irresponsibility, haughtiness, and sometimes honest confusion) or to bring some attention to themselves (in the manner in which any outrageous verbal act can make its source the center of attention). Thus, if this more kindly interpretation is correct, these instances of "incoherence" are (consciously or otherwise) more modes of emotional display than they are modes of textual exposition (ingenuous or otherwise). This is not to suggest that such displays are unimportant or that they do not resonate in compelling ways with the emotional and cognitive needs of their readers; on the contrary, the impulse toward letting one's primary process "go" is in many places, including Thailand, exceedingly powerful.[20] However, these displays cannot be assigned a coherence they do not have. One of our selections, "Chewing Out a Special Class," does suggest some of the incoherence we have been alluding to, but its essential arguments are more intellectually pointed and tightly organized, and its other qualities significantly more engaging, than those found in the many items we rejected.

In addition to these stylistic issues, there are several substantive areas which loom large in Thai intellectual culture but which for a variety of reasons we decided to de-emphasize or to handle in special ways. First, our materials say little about the ferment of contemporary Buddhism— its politicization, the concern of many Thai about the role of monks in the modern world, and the anxiety that some have about the continuing viability of Buddhist belief and practice. While there are references to some of these issues (see "The Wholesome Intention of *Khunnaaj* Saaj-bua," "A Telephone Conversation the Night the Dogs Howled," and "Lord Buddha, Help Me?"), we have eschewed any focused discussion of them, in part because they have already been addressed in some detail in the literature (see Tambiah 1976, Keyes 1977, and Suksamran 1977 and 1980) and in part because the discourse on them has occurred more at the level of debate and hardened intellectual position than at the expressive, connotative level that represents the thrust of our materials. Furthermore, a large part of this debate is less about Buddhism than it is about bringing into the religious domain some of the standard ideological bifurcations of Thai political life, the nature of which is amply represented in several of our selections.

Similarly, our materials say very little about the Thai intellectual preoccupation with parapsychology—shamanism, fortune-telling, the meaning and value of amulets, ritual cloths, incantations, and, more generally, understanding and controlling the supernatural. While this is not a broad-ranging literature, it is of historical depth and cultural elaboration, involving the steady production of books, articles, and a wide variety of tracts. Most of these take the form of catalogues, pharmacopoeias, didactic essays, and histories (of amulets, spirits, and the lives—often the several lives—of famous monks). While all of this may represent superb source material for symbolic analyses, very little of it looms large in creative writing. When it is used at all, the supernatural usually comes into play for unexceptional purposes, such as to describe aspects of a character's personality or as a device for indicating an atmosphere of anxiety or crisis (see "A Telephone Conversation the Night the Dogs Howled"). In fact, the supernatural is so thoroughly integrated into the belief system of most Thai readers that it essentially obviates the use of such themes in the development of a Siamese equivalent of Western science fiction or horror writings; that is, they are simply too real to serve as the basis of fictionalized fantasies.

Of an entirely different order is the relative underrepresentation we have accorded to materials concerned with the nature of Thai economic life. Here the principal significance of "economics" is that it has served as the engine of so many of the other social and psychological changes that have occurred in Thailand during the period represented by our writings. Several selections do address or allude to the impact of economic interests and values on the workaday lives of people. Thus, "Lord Buddha, Help Me?" is in large part about the psychological consequences of poverty in a situation of rising expectations, and it is economic considerations that most clearly move or complicate the lives of the characters in "Madame Lamhab," "Paradise Preserved," "Fulfilling One's Duty," and "Relations with Colleagues." Even in "The Enchanting Cooking Spoon," it is the economic position of the hero and heroine that makes the entire story possible.

Yet, none of these works really conveys the overriding motivational power that the pursuit of money has come to have in Thai society. In terms of its generality, moral acceptability, and the amount of psychological energy it is able to mobilize, the pursuit of money ranks along with the search for karmic redemption, social status, power, and "fun" *(sanug)* as one of the dominating forces of Thai culture. Indeed, lately its significance may have exceeded or subsumed all these other cultural concerns, as more and more Thai use such aphorisms as "the business of Thailand is business" or say that their country is no longer being run by soldiers and bureaucrats but by bankers and businessmen.

For all its social importance, however, this emergence of a Thai equivalent of the Protestant ethic (although in historical actuality, it is much more the infusion into Thai culture of a *nanyang,* or overseas Chinese, ethic) does not easily translate into literary terms. Most Thai write about economic pursuits as bureaucratic issues—as five-year plans, investment opportunities, trade balances, problems in income distribution, the value of which is presumed to be self-evident—or they incorporate these findings into ideological commentaries on such things as "the rural-urban gap," the rigidities and inequities of the Thai class system, and the like. A considerable body of literature is produced in both genres, typically as reports from government agencies and banks, news articles, pamphlets, seminar reports, and published lectures.

What is intriguing about all these modes of discourse, however, is their lack of any explicit concern with what drives people to make money, the joy that they might derive from it, and what they do with it once they have it. (An exception here is perhaps "The Enchanting Cooking Spoon," in which wealth received as a gift, rather than through the hero's own effort, is redistributed to the deserving, thus underscoring the hero's sense of decency.) There is not even much concern with the array of implicit pleasures that in real life constantly attend economic activities, such as the pleasure of negotiating or bargaining with others, the satisfactions of gambling or taking chances (and the sense of freedom and daring that they imply), or the sense of control over others that money so frequently provides.

The economic issues addressed or alluded to in our selections are essentially off-shoots of this kind of institutionalized thinking, although, in accord with Thai literary tradition, the works carry the additional moral message of reminding readers what an excess of avarice can do to human beings; too, in accord with that morality, they present greed as a characteristic of the individual rather than of the sociocultural system. (The message of "Relations with Colleagues" may be an exception.) In the end, economic pursuits are for the vast majority of the writers and readers of Thai literature fundamentally practical matters having to do with feeding, clothing, housing, and caring for oneself and one's family rather than matters to be memorialized, condemned, or even evaluated. Among our selections, this spirit of practicality is conveyed perhaps most authentically, if thoroughly prosaically, in the speeches of the partygoers in Suchit Wongthed's "Getting Drunk Abroad." Theirs is the way that most Thai, irrespective of class, educational background, or social pretension, think about their economic interests.

The Literary Boundaries of the Selections

A few words must be said about some of the tactical decisions that were made in assembling this collection. These decisions had to do mainly with setting limits on its intellectual and historical scope.

First, it was decided that the anthology would not include any book

reviews. Given the culturally reflexive functions that book reviews frequently serve, the decision to exclude them was not taken lightly. However, in reality Thai book reviews parallel the writings they review, and
any single review or small number of reviews would both misrepresent
the scope of the genre and not add much to our understanding of the literature to which they refer. In general, Thai reviews are like reviews
everywhere; some are informative and even profound, while others are
nothing more than extended abstracts of the original works. In tone and
thrust, they sometimes do differ stylistically from reviews published in
the Western world. Thai reviewers tend to be kinder and more mutually
approving of one another in their evaluations than are their Western
counterparts, which may be a function of the fact that they and the
authors are fewer in number and often know each other personally. At
the same time, Thai criticism can be far more persnickety than its Western counterpart, focusing on minor or tangential flaws in a text. Often
these peripheral criticisms serve as displacements for more devastating,
but unstated, criticisms—all of which is in accord with more general patterns of Thai public discourse.

A second, and more significant, decision had to do with whether or
not to merge social and political commentary and analysis with poetry,
short stories, and other more purely expressive genres. After a great deal
of deliberation, we decided to follow Thai, rather than Western, literary
practice and to combine the two modes, although continuing to give the
preponderance of our attention to the more expressive genres. The issue
here is that although Thai distinguish between analytic and creative writings in the same sense that Westerners do, they do not award the distinction any overriding literary or cognitive significance. Virtually all of the
contributors to this collection write in both modes, and some will even
meld the two within a single selection. Thus, Khamsing Srinawk's "Paradise Preserved" begins as a fictional creation but concludes as an ideological commentary. Even more typically, many writers use poetic or allegor-
ical forms explicitly to analyze or comment upon political and historical
events. (See the two selections by Dr. Puey Ungphakorn, Vasit Dejkunjorn's "Concerning *Farang*," Chitr Phoumisak's "Fishiness in the Night,"
Suchit Wongthed's "Oh! Temple, Temple of Bot!," and Sulak Sivaraksa's
"What Kind of Boat?" among others.) From a Thai point of view, such
efforts are to be responded to in terms of both their aesthetic and political
perspicacity.

The decision to include both kinds of writings was also prompted by
the desire that our collection reflect accurately Thai intellectual preoccupations. In these terms, there is no doubt that "politics" represents the
critical cynosure of Thai intellectual life. Individual Thai may be more
interested in making money or merit, in achieving fame, or having "fun,"
but politics is the life-blood of Thai intellectual discourse. It is what

members of the educated public most frequently gossip about, try to predict, plan for, are entertained by, and about which they most actively seek information. *Ngaanmyang*, literally "the work of the nation," represents that outer world of affairs. It is the world of interpersonal presentation, negotiation, and machination. To assemble a book of Thai literary works without giving *ngaanmyang* its appropriate weight would be to miss the fundamental point of such an enterprise.

The 1960–1976 Time Frame

A third, and obviously critical, decision had to do with the time frame of our selections, 1960–1976. Clearly any collection like ours requires some kind of temporal perimeter, and this particular period was chosen because in our view it had a certain historical unity. Too, we wanted a span of time that was sufficiently lengthy to permit the identification of themes and issues of perduring historical substance.[21] Some Thai colleagues, inspired by a cyclic conception of their history, suggested 1955 as an aesthetically more suitable starting point. This was the year of the "Hyde Park" free speech movement, and they and others cited this movement as the historical precedent for the intellectual ferment of the 1973–1976 period. But, in fact, the "Hyde Park" period had its own precedents (even some of the same political actors) in the liberal Pridi Phanomyong-dominated regimes of the mid-1930s. More importantly, it is clear that government-endorsed or -sanctioned intellectual freedom is only one of several factors contributing to a society's total intellectual ambience, although its relative rarity in Thailand may account for why some Thai view its periodic reemergence as the kind of event that should be memorialized in a book like this.

We selected the 1960 date because it marks a clear and convenient historical dividing line. The 1976 cutoff date was selected because it marks one of the major traumas of Thai history, the consequences of which were impossible to predict at the time and have not yet really been worked through or resolved. Many thoughtful Thai are still profoundly confused by the state of mind that produced the hatred and brutality that accompanied the storming of Thammasat University; by the ideological attractiveness and organizational talent of the extreme right as contrasted to the seeming inadequacies of the left and the middle, especially with regard to the emphasis that each gave to overt and covert modes of mobilization; by the adaptability—particularly the co-optive powers—of such seemingly conservative institutions as the palace, the military, and the business community; by the return of a semblance of self-control to elements of society (on both the right and left) that previously had seemed untrammeled in their expressiveness. Above all, people are still confounded by the destruction of their own innocence by the events of the 1973–1976 period, and by the loss of their belief in the power of morality to play a controlling role in human affairs. The other side of this is their perception that after all of the turmoil of the period there have been few significant changes in the structure of Thai society, excepting perhaps some increased responsiveness on the part of the Thai establishment and a contraction in the influence of those on the political extremes. For those who perceive history in more aesthetically meaningful terms, the turmoil of the 1973–1976 period may be seen simply as the inevitable result of a decade and a half of uncontrolled change and excess and the trauma of the Thammasat massacre–Thanin repression–retreat to the jungle as a historically necessary, if inherently painful, part of the process of cultural retrenchment.

The passage of time heals a great deal (or aids the processes of forgetfulness), and there are powerful drives in all Thai to get on with the present and the future, rather than to dwell on what was or might have been. But such drives notwithstanding, the events of the 1973–1976 period still comprise an undigested portion of Thai history, an era that remains to be evaluated, understood, and somehow fitted into the concerns and ethos of the present. It is the absence of such an evaluation and our own inability to understand yet the nature of that fit, that has induced us to end our account at 1976.

The Community of Writers

Although a work of contemporary literature is clearly the product of the motivation and imagination of an individual author, it is profoundly social in at least two respects.[22] First, being a mode of communication, its language, subject matter, and symbolism are inherently social; it is precisely for this reason that it is appropriate to consider writers as "key informants" on their society. It is also social in another respect: writers participate in and sometimes contribute to literary traditions; they serve literary apprenticeships and model themselves on or depart from the interests and skills of earlier writers; they have literary friends, enemies, admirers, and detractors. Thus, writers represent something of a community or subculture within their larger society.

Social Organization and *Phuak*

To what extent this "community" occurs naturally, with a corporate identity, function, or locality (in the sense that a village, factory, or Buddhist temple has such attributes), is problematic. Most Thai writers are, and see themselves as, inordinately busy people who in addition to being writers are also variously teachers, farmers, bureaucrats, journalists, artists, shop owners, celebrities, housewives, university rectors, generals, prime ministers, revolutionaries, and the like. The crucial point is that most authors are simultaneously members of a number of different "communities," all of which compete for their time, energy, and commitment. Thus their writing inevitably represents only a small part of their total professional performance and identity, although, for many, a very precious part. Most also are, and see themselves as, proud people who, although in no sense denying the debts they owe others, consider their work to be mainly an outcome of their own talent and interest rather than an expression of an unfolding literary or intellectual tradition. There may be a few arguable exceptions (perhaps Seksan Prasertkul or

Chitr Phoumisak), but on balance, their pride of authorship is far greater than their sense of solidarity with, or obligation to, any specific social or political movement.[23]

Yet, at another level, most authors have a keen sense of "a literary community"—its fashions, internal divisions, coalitions, recruitments, and changing *phuak*. Since the community is sufficiently small and centered in Bangkok (although not exclusive to the capital), virtually everyone knows the thrust of everyone else's work, and many know each other personally.[24] They have seen each other perform in public—at university seminars and lectures or on television panel discussions. Thus, they have a sense not only of their colleagues' ongoing ideas and interests but, equally important, of their rhetorical talent and panache—a not insignificant matter in a culture in which any public presentation is evaluated as much for its theatrical impact as for its intellectual substance. More important, a large number of them have worked together closely, either as peers or in employer-employee and teacher-disciple relationships. It is in the context of these relationships that so many of the loyalties and jealousies that characterize Thai literary and intellectual life are initially fashioned.

It is the intellectual consequences of such relationships that make them historically significant, however. The point is that not only do writers work together and develop likes and dislikes for one another, but that these likes and dislikes directly affect the nature and shape of the ideas they present in public, or at least this is what they and other Thai believe to be the case. Thus, several observers close to the Thai leftist movement have seriously argued that one of the main reasons for the sorry intellectual state of Thai Marxism—particularly the absence of a vision or conception of a "Thai Marxist society" (as contrasted to Chinese or Vietnamese versions)—is the personal animosity felt by several leftist writers (including some represented in this volume) that derives from their years as young coworkers at one of Thailand's largest publishing houses. They so grated upon one another, as much on personal grounds as on matters of ideological style and emphasis, that they simply would not talk with each other about larger issues of mutual interest. It is as if they were overcome by a sense of either Thai or bourgeois self-absorption, and rather than risk public confrontation or open conflict or, more importantly, the loss of face that would accompany a reconciliation, they opted for ideological silence—all of which express interpersonal patterns (and also explanatory ones) that are deeply rooted in Thai culture.

But the opposite outcome is also possible. Thus, there is no doubt that much of the success of the journal *Sangkhomsaat Parithat* (see n. 17) in providing intellectual leadership and legitimacy to the aim of ending Thailand's participation in the Vietnam War was a direct result of the mutual trust and respect felt by three or four people who pooled their intellectual resources to mount a long-term campaign of public education and persuasion. The social structure of this little group was critical to their activity, both in terms of their division of labor and in terms of the way they were seen by the public. Even the age-grading of the group eased the ways in which they dealt with one another in that it defined patterns of relative experience, deference, and respect. The editor, Suchart Sawadsii, was the youngest member, but the most energetic, and a superb organizer of informational sources and of contributing authors. A few years his senior was the author of "A Day in the Life of Pat," the scion of a prestigious Thai banking family, with close ties to the American peace movement, the Thai foreign ministry, and the large community of foreign correspondents stationed in Bangkok—factors that contributed to his work on the foreign policy implications of the war. Still older by a few years was Khamsing Srinawk, symbolically the representative of the interests of Thai villagers (both on the basis of what he wrote about and where he lived). As one of the nation's most famous creative writers, he enjoyed ties to the international intellectual and scholarly community. His attention was focused on the impact of the war on Thai culture and society. In the background, silently endorsing the enterprise (but such a symbolic role was quite enough), was Dr. Puey Ungphakorn, at the time one of Thailand's most influential bureaucrats and in the international world, a cynosure of Thailand's success as a developing nation. These social considerations were a crucial part of the group's public image, testifying both to the respectability of their views and to the spectrum of Thai interests they represented. Thus, in a very real sense, the success of their enterprise depended not only upon the pooling of their skills and their ability to get on with each other but also on the fact that they represented mutually reinforcing positions in Thai society. It was the interlocking of these various considerations that made their effort both intellectually and historically consequential.

In these two cases, the political content of the authors' views made them particularly amenable to group pressures and the expectation that they would somehow represent or be the product of a consensually fashioned "position." (It was the violation of this expectation by equally valid personal considerations that makes the case of the discordant Marxists so historically revealing.) However, group pressures—and the *phuak* with which they are associated—can be based upon a variety of considerations. Thus, M. L. Boonlue Kunjara Debyasuvan, until her death, was the leader of a literary *phuak* (and simultaneously of at least two other *phuak* concerned with the teaching of English and with national educational policies) whose internal unity was based upon her own charismatic personality, her symbolic links to traditional court culture, and above all, to an intellectual message that focused on sexual equality, the professional competence of women, and their special commitments to a sense of excellence[25] The vertically oriented nature of this *phuak*—focused on a single dominant personality—is perhaps more characteristic of Thai *phuak* than are the peer-oriented *phuak* noted earlier, and here "group pressures" have as much to do with maintaining the solidarity (and ultimately the moral power) of the teacher-disciple relationship as they do with promoting a particular literary vision. (For an interesting description in English of a disciple's perception of her teacher, see Mattani Rutnin's 1978 observations on Boonlue, particularly pp. 2 and 101–109.) The strength of Boonlue's leadership was undoubtedly abetted by the fact that she had actually been the teacher to several generations of students, many of whom became teachers to others, and among whom were several writers. A significant part of her intellectual influence also derived from her role as presumed literary heir of Daukmaajsod, her older half-sister and Thailand's greatest literary apologist for the *phuu dii* —the genteel, obedient, ladies of grace of an idealized Thai elite (see "The Enchanting Cooking Spoon" and "Madame Lamhab"). While as a good younger sibling and subtle-thinking Thai, Boonlue never directly challenged the legitimacy of her sister's vision, she nevertheless completely redefined the desiderata of the modern Thai heroine. In her formulation, the new protagonist became a person of energy, intellectual talent, and forthrightness who contributed as much to the world of affairs as to the world of her family (for example, Chaarinii and to a lesser extent Adcharaa in "The Enchanting Cooking Spoon"). Boonlue's message not only represented an idea whose time had come, but it had come in part because she was its spokesperson, carrying out a role that her sister had previously played—albeit with a very different message. To most reflective Thai, the contrasting visions of the two sisters are not so much a matter of historical irony as they are an expression of the normal unfolding of a historical process, each sibling accurately portraying the changing ideals of her own milieu. Similarly, although most will not declare whether the idea or its author has priority, they perceive the power and legitimacy of Boonlue's views as reinforced both by the precedents of her sister's work and by the elite positions they each successively held in Thai society.

Parallel to Boonlue's situation in some respects is the *phuak* that has been maintained over the years by M. R. Khukrit Pramoj. In terms of the numbers of people involved, it is probably the most important literary *phuak* of the past half century. However, its basis has not been ideological consensus or a literary vision or even the charisma of its leader but rather the characteristic loyalties that develop between employer and employee. Since 1950 the constituents of the *phuak* have been the numerous people who have worked on or contributed to Khukrit's various publications: *Siam Rath* daily newspaper; *Siam Rath Sabadaa Wicaan,* a weekly review; and *Chaawkrung,* a monthly feature magazine. (Khukrit has simultaneously been the leader of at least four other *phuak:* the Social Action Party on whose platform he successfully stood as prime minister; a group of bankers, investors, and hotel owners; a group of directors and performers concerned with classical Thai dance drama; and the inhabitants of several villages that have been linked with his family since the reign of Rama II and for whom he considers himself principal patron.) Because Khukrit is not easily identified with a clearly delimited literary message (see the Introduction to "My Dog Is Missing") and also because of their own variability, the members of this *phuak* have little intellectual unity. What they do have in common is a clear sense of obligation to Khukrit for having given them the opportunity to pursue their writing at a reasonably good salary and with a ready-made reading public. Since many were recruited right out of college, he afforded them an excellent situation in which to learn, experiment with, and refine their craft. While many went on to other interests and activities, they almost all feel the abiding sense of gratitude that most Thai feel toward someone who backed them during the early, fragile stages of their careers. This is true even for those who also resent what they view as Khukrit's over-directive ways—a sentiment that is perhaps intrinsic to the nexus of talent and clientage, particularly when the clients' patron is, like Khukrit, as fully talented as any of them.

Khukrit has such an excellent record in identifying high-quality people who actually fulfill their promise that simply being a member of his *phuak* carries the mark of professional merit, as if one had been invited to join an honor society of verbally or rhetorically talented people. Like any patron, however, he has also made some mistakes. Perhaps his most famous mischoice—in terms of the ironies of patron-client relationships —was his hiring and training of Samak Sundaravej who, under the byline of Mauau Dii ("Dr. Good"), became one of Khukrit's most popular *Siam Rath* columnists and in time parlayed this popularity, based upon a superb sense of rhetorical bombast, into a political career. A decade after hiring Samak, Khukrit lost his seat in parliament to Samak in an election that simultaneously forced Khukrit to relinquish his prime ministership. Whatever the personal meaning of this turn of events, most analysts of the Thai political scene recall the situation in terms of the replacement of one of Thailand's most socially responsible political leaders by one of its most outrageous.[26] Some also see it in terms of the risks of patronage: although most clients feel indebted to their patrons and would never consider directly challenging the latter's superior status, all clients also perceive their patrons as means to or devices for their own advancement and, if faced with a conflict between these two desired ends, it is to be expected that they will opt for their own interests.

While historically real and instructive, this kind of confrontation is rare. We have outlined it here mainly to illustrate some of the permuta-

tions of the Thai patronage system. In most instances, the system operates the way it is supposed to. When either patrons or clients are
unhappy with one another or feel that they have outgrown each other or
simply feel the tug of other opportunities, they typically separate with a
sense that their time together, at least until near the end, has been mutually
advantageous.

One of the most troublesome problems in trying to understand what
actually goes on in Thai patronage is the fact that almost all our data are
provided by clients, not by patrons. It is the client who acts out, who
reports his pleasure or displeasure, and who, from the public's point of
view, decides to stay with or to leave the patron. Obviously, clients are
constantly being discharged by their patrons, but it would be beneath a
patron's dignity to feel obliged to explain his actions to the outside world
or, for that matter, to anybody. In fact, "good patrons" are those who
create the circumstances for their clients' voluntary resignations rather
than the justifications for having to fire them. By the same token, sensitive clients see the writing on the wall and depart well before their patron
is forced to act.

We have dwelled on these specific *phuak* because of their visibility, historical importance, and relevance to the works in this volume. Space limitations prevent us from examining several other, equally significant
mainstream *phuak*. However, we would emphasize that for all the
impact that any particular *phuak* has upon the Thai literary scene and
upon the formulations and fortunes of its constituent members, it is only
one of several sources of the literary identity of any writer.

Beyond *Phuak* Affiliation

There are numerous writers who for various personal reasons or at certain points in their career simply resist affiliation with any *phuak*. The
author of "Relations with Colleagues," who uses the pseudonym "Bunchookh," is such a person. Despite his fame and success, he is virtually
unknown to most members of the Thai literary community. There is no
doubt that his preference for isolation and anonymity is motivated at
least in part by his desire to protect himself from vengeful or paranoid
bureaucrats in the Ministry of Interior who, correctly or incorrectly,
might believe themselves to be portrayed as characters in his fiction.
Even a person like Khamsing Srinawk has at times avoided *phuak* affiliation, as he did during the early years of his career when he was experimenting with his style and talent and later, on a more episodic basis,
when he felt he had to get away from everybody simply to have time to
write. (One of Khamsing's most frequently used literary allusions is the
jungle as a source of protection against the intrusion of others; see "I Lost
My Teeth.") Khamsing, like many Thai writers, has, at bottom, an

ambivalent attitude about *phuak* membership: on the one hand, he appreciates the camaraderie and intellectual give-and-take and perhaps even the increased sense of power and protection that is intrinsic to the *phuak's* "social unity"; on the other hand, he fears the possibility of having his own individuality and identity submerged by the group and also the tendency of many Thai to find other people guilty, liable, or otherwise indictable simply by virtue of their associations.

A second consideration constraining the significance of any particular *phuak* is that most writers—irrespective of their primary affiliation—are constantly subject to the influences and pressures from other, cross-cutting *phuak*. Thus, all the time Vasit Dejkunjorn was a member of Khukrit's *Siam Rath* group, he was simultaneously a member of a less clearly defined group of *saajlom saeaengdaeaed* ("taking the breeze and the sunshine") writers. He and others might even deny that this was a *phuak* in the usual meaning of the term, but in the early 1960s theirs was a popular, widely practiced, and frequently copied literary style which emphasized the wit, delight, and foolishness of upper- and upper-middle-class life. The symbol of this *phuak*-cum-genre was the weekend frolic at the beach, from which the group's title is derived. As time passed, the "breeziness" of their heroes and heroines changed from a behavioral ideal into an object of social ridicule. Vasit, inspired by a satirist's vision of the universe (see "Social Work"), was one of the people most responsible for this changing perception. However, most of the things he ridiculed (the playboy life; the idleness of the wealthy, particularly their wives and adult children; the unending Thai search for higher social status) continue to represent some of the pivotal values, or at least fantasies, of numerous upwardly mobile young Thai.

In addition to their links to alternative, and sometimes competing, *phuak,* virtually all Thai writers have worked out special dyadic relationships with peers, patrons, and occasionally even "enemies." These ties are as varied in form, function, and motivation as are most relationships in Thai culture. Two of our contributors, for example, so enjoyed each other's company and their wives got on so well together that one man built a small weekend–vacation house on the other's rural property (and primary residence), and they have spent hundreds of hours together discussing life, Thailand, their professional plans, and their writing. In another case, the overseas education of one of our contributors was paid for in part by another contributor, the latter motivated by his admiration for his friend's intellectual talents, the friend's dire financial need, and the likelihood that the friend would make a major intellectual or literary contribution upon his return to Thailand.

Similar, if more subtle, considerations seemed to have attended the arrangement between Angkarn Kalayaanaphong and Sulak Sivaraksa, which has come to be recognized as one of the most successful "collaborations" of recent times. This recognition is undoubtedly abetted by their public image as an odd couple: the reclusive and bemused Angkarn, who admits to being more comfortable with the trees and the stars than with people (see "Grandma"), and the aggressive and tough-minded Sulak, whose brazenness as a social critic seems to many readers to know no bounds (see "What Kind of Boat?"). Initially, it appeared that Sulak was simply Angkarn's patron; although the latter's drawing, painting, and poetry had been seen by a small group of university people, it was not until Sulak began to use the artwork on the covers of *Sangkhomsaat Parithat* and to publish the literary material in the journal that Angkarn's fame began to spread. Angkarn was soon receiving commissions from hotels and other corporations for his murals, and Sulak was introducing his poetry to the international world, mainly by arranging translations into English. One of Angkarn's poems ("Scoop Up the Sea") was supposedly translated by the American poet, Allen Ginsburg, but since Ginsburg could neither read nor understand Thai, it was obviously Sulak, as go-between, who did most of the work. Thus, over time, the relationship changed from Sulak being primarily Angkarn's patron into being his agent, and, to a certain extent, even his client, as Angkarn's work brought increasing attention, stature, and even subscriptions to *Sangkhomsaat Parithat.*

Not all of Sulak's relationships have had this quality. Irrespective of his contributions to Thai intellectual life, Sulak is perhaps best known to the Thai public for his continuing, *ad hominem* attacks on M. R. Khukrit Pramoj. Sulak originally depicted Khukrit as a fallen literary idol—a person whose pretensions to intellectual and aesthetic greatness had been totally eclipsed by his unacceptable interpersonal style (*Sangkhomsaat Parithat* 3, 2 [1965], reprinted in English in Sivaraksa 1973 and 1980). However, as time passed and Khukrit became increasingly public and political in his activities, Sulak's criticisms became more hostile and broad-ranging, and even more personal, in their thrust. For more than two decades Khukrit's response to all this has been silence.

Whatever the validity of the allegations or the appropriateness of the response, the dynamics of the situation may be seen in terms of at least three different (but culturally familiar) kinds of factors. First, to most it is clearly a case of Sulak, the younger and lesser known, using Khukrit to bring some attention and importance unto himself. While the interpersonal exploitation here is unabashed, it is also simply the other side of what occurs (admittedly more willingly and openly) in most patron-client relationships. Also, it is seen as a frequently used tactic in intergenerational adaptation and conflict, if only because of the inherent unevenness in the power and prestige of the parties involved. Second, irrespective of Sulak's motives, some see this as a case of abstract justice, of Khukrit finally being treated in a manner similar to the way he himself has treated others. To what extent those who voice this judgment would dare to be like Sulak, and express this view in public, is quite another matter. Third (but in the kind of baroque speculation that appeals to many Thai) a few see the case as a genuine, but ultimately doomed, attempt on the part of Sulak to bring some of the British spirit of literary rivalry and one-upsmanship into the Thai situation. Their view is that Sulak, who likes to see himself as a "British old boy," had hoped to get Khukrit, another "old boy," to rise to the occasion and engage in what to both would be a familiar pattern of mock conflict. What was not envisaged, they suggest, was either the profundity of class consciousness involved or that it would become an instrument of interpersonal combat; they argue that Khukrit, a Thai aristocrat and Oxford graduate, would never deign to engage a plebeian like Sulak in such an enterprise. In Khukrit's Trollopean view of Thai social structure, Sulak was simply putting on red-brick college British airs that would not be dignified with a response.

We have provided this detail not to document the underside of Thai literary life, but rather to underscore the reality of such issues and the attention that Thai writers and readers give to them. Of course, any attempt to show an emperor without his clothes will almost anywhere draw an audience. What makes this case significant in terms of Thai culture are the symbolic aspects of Sulak's claims, particularly those that "make sense" to a Thai audience and almost automatically lend credibility to his views. Thus, whatever his real motives, the mere fact that Sulak is younger than Khukrit makes him a figure of enlarged vulnerability and gumption. He is the perennial youth who has dared to criticize someone older and more important—something that in an ideal Thai world is not supposed to happen but when it does (as it must) is felt to be refreshing and emancipating, as are all releases from Oedipal constraints. The other side of this is the assumption that, unless he has gone mad, the younger and inherently vulnerable Sulak would have never dared to say such things unless they were in some way tenable.

Sulak's grievance against Khukrit also rides on another symbolic device that is ultimately more telling. It is the grievance of the bright, imaginative, hard-working, up-by-the-bootstraps member of the middle class who feels that his social and personal value is denied or insulted by an entrenched and supercilious member of the old elite who does not fulfill even his own standards of civility, such as giving others time, attention, and their psychological due. While Sulak clearly does not feel this way about all representatives of the old elite, he is nevertheless appealing to a middle-class sense of affront that has been experienced and elaborated continuously since the 1932 revolution. In this sense, Sulak's honoring of middle-class sentiments is the antithesis of the hauteur attributed to Khukrit. Sulak's message is one with which most of his readers can identify; Khukrit's (or that assigned to him) is one to which most aspire.

Whichever is more sucessful, they both plumb sentiments that lie deep in the Thai experience.

Intellectual Genealogies

The preceding material on the organization of writers essentially concerns the reciprocal ways in which members of the literary community impinge upon one another and define each other's status. There is one other source of literary identity that must be mentioned, and that is the sense that almost all Thai writers have of their own intellectual genealogies—their relationships to specific literary figures who they feel have stimulated, taught, or inspired them or in whose footsteps they feel they are following. In our judgment, these links have the most lasting impact on the writing of most authors and on their views of their own literary positions. Inevitably some of them are more the result of an author's own construction or projection than they are real bilateral relationships, as for example, when Khukrit sees his own career as writer, literary administrator, and patron of the arts as a modern replication of the activities of his ancestor, Rama II. This is not a crass attempt on Khukrit's part to magnify his own status or even an attempt to point out an amusing historical parallel. Rather, as in almost all such cases, it is an effort to root one's own activity, and definitions of its value, in the precedents and continuities of Thai history. Its primary purpose is to affirm that what one is doing has been done and honored in Thailand for a long time. One gains inspiration and strength from one's literary models, not social status.

Other kinds of genealogical ties may involve a senior writer who has actively responded to a younger writer's request for guidance or training. In fact, the ties may even take on the formal attributes of a teacher-disciple relationship, as, for example, when Sulak Sivaraksa approached *Phya* Anuman Rajadhon, the late doyen of Thai philological and folklore studies, asking for training in literary criticism and social analysis. The formality of their relationship was solemnized in a ritual in which Sulak literally prostrated himself before his teacher, swearing fealty and dutifulness. From that time on *Phya* Anuman considered Sulak (both privately and publicly) his principal intellectual heir. That Sulak turned out to be far more serious, strident, and broad-ranging in his criticism of Thai society than his guru was to both of them secondary to their ritual tie to one another. Equally important, the "genealogical factor" did not stop with *Phya* Anuman. Sulak's link to *Phya* Anuman projected him further back into Thai history through *Phya* Anuman's own links to Prince Damrong (who had been *Phya* Anuman's supervisor and predecessor at the National Library) and Prince Narisara (who considered *Phya* Anuman his "scholarly friend"). It was this series of direct, personal con-

result of the sales that the prizes stimulate than of the prize money itself. A few writers have even pointed to these prizes as evidence that one can now make a respectable living in Thailand through one's writing.

Different from the above are the voluntary organizations concerned with the dissemination of literature or the welfare of writers. Although its membership is small, the Thai Writers Association has had some success as a pressure group in getting publishers to pay higher royalties and in getting newspapers to devote more attention to literature and authors in their feature sections. Somewhat different in thrust is the Thai branch of PEN International (for "Poets, Playwrights, Editors, Essayists, and Novelists") which has served as a conduit for the translation and placement of Thai writings in foreign literary magazines or in anthologies of Asian and world literature; too, its members often serve as hosts for visiting literary dignitaries. With links to departments of literature in Thai universities, and through them to colleagues in other nations, as well as to other PEN branches, the Thai PEN has perhaps been the major force in promoting Thai literature to the world as a whole. In addition, there are scholarly societies like the Social Science Association of Thailand or the Siam Society that either publish intellectual magazines or hold public lectures that occasionally focus on literary issues. Also, although university literary associations and their magazines serve more specialized interests, they have played a major role in training Thai writers and in helping them to establish their literary credentials. Both Chitr Phoumisak and Vasit Dejkunjorn originally sparked the public's attention through the work they presented in student publications while enrolled as undergraduates at Chulalongkorn University.

The overriding quality of all this activity is its spontaneity, viability, and expanding institutional influence. There is a sense that "things are happening" in the Thai literary world. During the past few years, for example, some of Bangkok's newspapers, particularly those catering to the upper middle class and the elite, have begun to include a "literary page" as part of their Sunday supplements. However unremarkable this innovation may seem, it is precisely the kind of practice that is bringing the work of Thai writers to increasingly larger, and socially more influential, audiences. Familiarity with and perhaps even the reading of contemporary literature may in time become as much a part of the cultural universe of these audiences as is their knowledge of Thai politics, fashion, Buddhism, entertainment, and all the other things that absorb the mental life of modern, aspiring Siamese.

Finally, some of the large international foundations have begun to express serious interest in Thai writers and writing. The Toyota Foundation has established a "Know Our Neighbors" publication program designed to translate into Japanese some of the best of contemporary Southeast Asian writing and has already issued several works, including

nections to a golden age of Thai scholar-bureaucrats that provided the emotional support and justification for the intellectual position the Sulak tried to establish for himself, with considerable success, during the 1960s and 1970s. In the symbolic terms of Thai culture, the ritual link was just as good as—perhaps even better than—a genetic tie to these half-brothers of Rama V who, for many modern Thai and certainly for Sulak, personify some of the most creative minds in Thai history. Of course, like any genealogical link, this one was inherently bi-valent: on the one hand, it rationalized Sulak's serving as a modern advocate for these persons and, in so doing, honoring them and their values; on the other hand, it permitted Sulak to become involved in their original honor and prestige and, in so doing, feeling (or at least hoping) that some of their qualities would rub off on him.

The dynamics of this situation are not without paradox. A ritual relationship is more binding than a "flesh and blood" tie in that it is voluntary and its ritual features make it more difficult to abrogate than a genetic tie. But if a ritual relationship is personally more binding, it is also socially more vulnerable, if only because it raises suspicions about the motives of the persons who create such a relationship. It is simply assumed that although the ostensible purpose of the link is to honor and show respect to another person, it simultaneously serves to advance the interests of both parties. Most such relationships are essentially private, however. They are known to others only when one or both of the participants choose, for their own reasons, to make the matter public. In this instance, it was *Phya* Anuman—who delighted both in the respect shown to him by Sulak and in the latter's intellectual talent—who talked most openly about their relationship.

Most literary genealogies lack the ceremonial qualities that linked Sulak to *Phya* Anuman and the Princes Damrong and Narisara. In fact, Sulak would be the first to admit that his ritualizing of the relationship was meant, at least in part, as a metaphor for some of the social values that over the years have come to be associated with these historical figures. A more typical expression of the genealogical tie between writers is perhaps found in the relationship between Khamsing Srinawk and Kularb Saipradit, although both the etiology and emotional contours of their relationship, whatever its cultural supports, were felt by them as something unique. Khamsing was village born and bred, and one of his childhood fantasies was someday to establish the first newpaper in Thailand devoted to the interests of its northeastern peasants. It was in these terms that Kularb, who was one of Thailand's most famous journalists during the 1930s, became one of Khamsing's childhood heroes. Kularb was widely read in several European languages, particularly in socialist and depression-era literature. By the mid-1930s, however, he had begun to move away from journalism into creative writing, focusing on themes of social justice, class conflict, and "socialist realism." These issues were more popular in the heady years after the 1932 revolution than perhaps at any other time in Thai history, including the 1973–1976 period. It was both the trajectory of Kularb's career and the legitimacy of his literary themes that so stimulated the young Khamsing.[27] In the early 1950s, having served his own apprenticeship as a journalist, he sought out Kularb's friendship and guidance, carrying with him manuscripts of some of his own short stories.

Their relationship was not quite what the childhood fantasy had conjured, mainly because of the numerous pressures upon Kularb. Twenty-seven years older than Khamsing, Kularb was increasingly being viewed by disciples and younger friends as a font of political, rather than literary, wisdom; at the same time, he was beginning to suffer political threats from agents of the Phibun government. There were also suspicions about Khamsing because of his associations with an expatriate American. However, despite these strains, Kularb and Khamsing did read, criticize, and edit each other's work, and it was Kularb's wife, *Khun* Chanid—herself a professional translator of Thai, Chinese, and English—who found publishers for Khamsing's earliest writings.

Looking back at his career, Khamsing sees himself as having been influenced significantly by Kularb, who represented a real-life model of what a writer might do in Thai society and who validated the literary and social value of the themes that Khamsing wanted to address. Also, Kularb gave Khamsing a sense of continuity with a rich literary past—one that might not have the temporal depth (or the elaborate mythology) that people like Khukrit or Sulak might claim for their own literary genealogies but one that extended into an international tradition that, under such labels as socialist realism, has during this century found its way into the literary corpus of almost all nations. Whatever its origins, this genre has under the pressure of historical circumstances become thoroughly integrated into the expectations of Thai literary audiences.

Inevitably, Khamsing's literary interests have also departed from those of his predecessor. Like many of his generation, Kularb saw virtually all his literary characters as pawns swept up and moved by social forces that they were incapable of modifying or shaping. (This kind of totalitarian paradigm was perhaps inevitable for writers of the 1930s and 1940s.) Khamsing is also interested in such forces, but, unlike Kularb, he portrays his characters as constantly calculating, negotiating, and using their limited resources to maximum advantage. Whereas Kularb described peasants as passive victims of an unjust or stultifying Thai past, Khamsing describes them as men and women of substance, some stupid, some bold, but all of complex dimensions. Khamsing has gone beyond Kularb not only in providing a more realistic and humane portrait of villagers but, equally important, in relocating them in the literary consciousness of

Thai readers. Prior to Khamsing's work, virtually all Thai writer[s] [fic]tion treated villagers either as part of an undifferentiated human [back]ground or as simple foils for the interests of upper-class heroes a[nd vil]lains. (In Kularb's view, upper-class adults were usually villains, alth[ough] he held out considerable hope for their sons and daughters.) Pea[sants] could become heroes but usually only after they had relinquished [their] peasant status (through education or some special talent or windf[all].) Khamsing changed all this by bringing villagers to the forefront of li[ter]ary attention, by presenting them as people whose rich inner and ou[ter] lives were worth knowing. He was aided in this effort by an emergi[ng] Thai awareness of the power of peasants to alter history (such as in t[he] recent peasant-based revolutions in China and Vietnam) and by the the[n] nascent bureaucratic interest in trying to "develop" villagers.

Formal Organizations and Institutions

The foregoing has focused on the culturally familiar and personally meaningful ways that writers deal with one another to advance their own careers and their profession as a whole. There is another organizational consideration that must be cited. We are referring to the host of voluntary associations and semipublic institutions that promote the literary enterprise. Some of these are international and national organizations that have taken on the role of literary patrons. For years, the Southeast Asian Treaty Organization (SEATO) awarded an annual prize in literature, and during the 1970s the Association of Southeast Asian Nations (ASEAN) has awarded a similar prize—with Thai writers being consistent winners. Within the kingdom, the royal family sponsors a National Books Committee which has awarded annual prizes in various literary categories, and large private institutions such as the Bangkok Bank and Oriental Hotel have established parallel awards. Like Pulitzer prizes in the United States, these patronage-type competitions involve both honor and money. Notwithstanding the cynical expectations of some writers, the judges of these competitions (many of whom are drawn from university faculties) have to date apparently been professionally impeccable in their deliberations; their selections have included several unknown and unsponsored authors, as well as others who have focused on socially discomforting themes of Thai life, such as corruptibility in Buddhist practice and belief. While some of this prize-giving involves the kind of social fluff that almost always accompanies philanthropy, it also testifies to the value that some elements of the Thai establishment assign to the literary effort. Certainly those authors who have been involved in the competitions as winners or runners-up take them seriously as verification of their own creative merit and potential influence. They also can be sources of considerable additional income; as with most such awards, this is more a

an early romantic novel (set in both Thailand and Japan during the pre-war years) by Kularb Saipradit entitled *Khanglang Phaab* [Behind the image]; two of M. R. Khukrit Pramoj's fictional efforts; and an essay by Sulak Sivaraksa on Dr. Puey Ungphakorn. There is some indication that the Ford Foundation may be interested in sponsoring writers from several Southeast Asian nations in some form of sabbatical leave or seminar program. In addition, agencies of the Peoples Republic of China have expressed interest in translating contemporary Thai writings into Chinese. While these kinds of programs are at various stages of formulation, the very real international attention they signify provides additional stimulus to the entire Thai literary enterprise—both by expanding authors' horizons of what their intellectual impact might be and by inducing at least a few of them to consider their own work in terms of comparative critical standards.

Writers and Class Origin

It should be apparent from the foregoing that, from the point of view of those who read it, the work of Thai writers is very much an urban middle-class and upper-class phenomenon. This does not deny that there are significant numbers of village schoolteachers and monks, petty provincial officials, philosophical pedicab drivers, and a wide variety of closet intellectuals who also enjoy contemporary writing; nor does it mean that these two urban classes are not in themselves open-ended, constantly changing, and extraordinarily varied in the intellectual concerns of their members. But it is clear that at any one time the bulk of the readership of contemporary literature is drawn from these two social classes rather than distributed proportionately throughout Thai society. The reasons for this have to do with such things as lifestyle and self-image, as well as with the time, money, and energy people are able to give to being better informed, intellectually stimulated, culturally stylish, and the like.

Another side of the equation is the social position of the writers themselves; their own class backgrounds; the nature of their links to the people about whom they write, particularly the extent to which they represent (self-consciously or otherwise) the interests of such people; and the question of the sociological verisimilitude of their work, that is, how accurately and completely their writings reflect the complexity of the Thai social order in terms of its constituent groupings (not only classes but ethnic groups, age groups, sexes, regions, urban-rural divisions, and the like).

There are a number of related issues involved here. At the most basic analytic level, it must be recognized that writers are not sociologists, and in the terms attributed to the Shakespearean scholar, Harry T. Levin, their literary efforts are always refractions rather than reflections of their society. What they lack in sociological literalness, representativeness, or scope of coverage is hopefully compensated for by the angle, depth, subtlety, and imaginativeness of their literary perspectives. The perspectives with which they are most comfortable derive from their own personal backgrounds and prejudices. In these terms, it comes as no surprise that the writing of someone like M. L. Boonlue Kunjara Debyasuvan should be infused with an upper-class preoccupation with boredom, frivolity, and intellectual gamesmanship, while the work of someone like Khamsing Srinawk should convey the insecurity of village life and the peasant's sense of irony about his own condition. These emotional elements represent familiar and tacit features of each author's experience, although paradoxically, the act of writing about such conditions raises them to the level of literary consciousness and transforms them into issues for examination, debate, and judgment.

Some writers, of course, utilize perspectives that derive not from what is personally familiar and actually experienced but from what they aspire to and fantasize for themselves. This is clearly the case with Sulak Sivaraksa who, while serving as the most articulate spokesperson for the traditional elite values of civility, social service, and commitment to excellence, approaches them mainly from the perspective of an ambitious and well-educated member of the middle class. With the passion of a convert, Sulak has taken the position that these ideals have significance not only for the elite themselves but for all Siamese who are concerned about integrating into their current historical situation what is putatively most unique and desirable from their own national tradition. He has also been successful in using his advocacy of these values to elevate his own position in the Thai class system—which is testimony to the essential openness of that system and to the role that ideology and talent (as contrasted to birth and wealth) can play in determining a person's status.

Sulak's teacher, *Phya* Anuman Rajadhon, earlier followed a parallel route in moving from his own middle-class origins into the higher reaches of the Thai elite (an accomplishment explicitly acknowledged in his official title, *Phya*). Among our other contributors, Vasit Dejkunjorn followed a similar, if more complex, path to his position as confidant and protector of the royal household. One can also move in the opposite direction: while Anud Aaphaaphirom comes from an elite urban family, his Marxist ideological commitments took him into the jungles of northern Thailand and to China, where he led and promulgated a very different kind of life than his class origins would have presaged.

As these cases suggest, class background is a relevant, but analytically indeterminate, factor in shaping a writer's intellectual outlook. This indeterminacy is simply a result of the fact that people change. They move in and out of social classes; they grow up, and it is impossible to judge what stage or part of their lives will have the greatest or least influence in guiding their literary preoccupations. Thus, there is no inherently valid way to determine the relative weight to assign to an author's early childhood situation, later formal education, serendipitous adolescent encounter, or any other particular set of circumstances that may have contributed to his intellectual development.

While it is true that few modern novels, short stories, or dramas are written in Thai villages or Bangkok slums, it is also true that more than one-third of the contributors to this volume come from precisely such origins.[28] To the extent that they have become figures of social, historical, or aesthetic significance (which is clearly the case with Angkarn, Dr. Puey, Khamsing, or Suchit), these individuals have in the course of their lives effectively traversed the Thai class system, although like intellectuals in most places, their modest financial condition serves to define them more as adjuncts to, rather than as full-fledged members of, the elite or as persons peripheral to the system.

Perhaps the most important consideration to note about the influence of class membership is the highly selective way in which individual authors respond to it in their own work. The point is simply that the tyranny of our abstractions notwithstanding, a category like "class background" never describes a unitary mode of experience. Thus, although Chitr, Khamsing, Angkarn, and Suchit were all born and brought up in villages, they each emerged from that experience with very different visions, not only because of who they are but because of the complexity of village life. Chitr idealized the endogenous purity of villagers while simultaneously seeing them as victims of an exogenous institutionalized oppression. While Khamsing does not deny the presence of oppression—both endogenous and exogenous—he defines villagers mainly in terms of their realism and resourcefulness in coping with their circumstances. Villages are for him places where people get on with their lives rather than wasting time beating their breasts over their plight or pining for a "golden age," whether in the past or future.

In contrast to both, Angkarn pays little attention to social conditions and human arrangements (except to say that human beings are not very nice under the best of circumstances) and instead uses some of the elementary ideas of village Buddhism to locate people in nature and the cosmos. The Buddhism here is a product of the village in terms of its rhetorical qualities—its directness and lack of self-consciousness, as well as the fact that it is animated by the vitality and wonder ("anything is possible") of village supernaturalism. This idiom provides Angkarn's work with both its aesthetic power and sense of reality, the latter mainly because millions of villagers assume Buddhist and supernatural explanations to be absolutely true. Angkarn's work also emphasizes the heightened involvement that villagers have with plants, animals, and the processes of the natural world. In contrast to his three colleagues, Suchit uses his village background more as a frame of reference for informing and working out his viewpoint than as a substantive body of material for description and analysis. There is in his work constant allusion to the rural origins of things, as if the village were the font of so much that is both wonderful and painful in contemporary Thai experience. Thus, while "Lord Buddha, Help Me?" is obviously about the poverty and desperation of urban life, it is also about the aspirations of young village men who are driven to leave their natal soil and get ahead in the world of urban challenge and excitement. Similarly, the model for the student revolutionaries of 1973 in "Oh! Temple, Temple of Bot!" are the village martyrs of 1767, and the continuing symbol of the martyr, "*Chaw Khun* Thauaung," relates to the same milieu. But if the village is the source of Thai idealism and bravery, it is also the place that corrupt officials can most easily ravage, as Suchit so clearly reminds his readers in "Madame Lamhab." One has the sense that for Suchit, the village is not so much a place that can be typified in literary terms as it is a symbol of what is generative, continuous, and consensual in Thai life. It is in his treatment almost a collective representation of Thai culture.

That a group of writers should perceive their common origins in such diverse terms is by no means surprising. Our aim here is to point out that a common class background tells us little in a predictive sense about the meaning and impact of that background on subsequent literary activity. There is also little in these common origins that would have suggested any of the other features of the career patterns of these writers, for instance, that Chitr became a social historian and Marxist martyr; Khamsing, a candidate for parliament, world traveller, and modern dairyman;[29] Angkarn, the nation's most accomplished artist and poet; and Suchit, one of the most productive authors of his generation. The major factor may simply be the remarkable talent of these individuals and their being part of a society—or a historical period—in which at least some of their ambitions were reinforced, challenged, or given free rein.

Writers and Their Constituencies

An inevitable question is the extent to which these and other Thai writers can be considered to promote the interests of the people about whom they are writing. The issue here has to do with the instrumentality and ultimately the politics of literature, in the sense that authors may see themselves as spokespersons for those in or out of power, for those seeking social recognition or esteem, or for ideological positions that to their minds serve these constituencies. There is no simple answer to this question, if only because the literary motivations of writers are so inherently variable. In their most elemental guise, all writers are advocates for their heroes and critics of their villains, most of whom bear some relationship to real human beings. Thus, it is clear whose interests Suchit is representing in "Oh! Temple, Temple of Bot!" and Anud is condemning in "Big Shot as Toad." But having said this, it must also be noted that many Thai writings are less transparent and the purposes of their authors are considerably more complex. In "Lord Buddha, Help Me?" Suchit lays out a much more fundamental, if less ennobling, human problem than the one memorialized in "Oh! Temple, Temple of Bot!"; when he uses cultural shibboleths, it is to suggest the intransigence of the problem he is addressing rather than its resolution by political formula. Here, the very idea of "hero" or "villain" seems irrelevant. Similarly, whatever "The Enchanting Cooking Spoon" might say about the excrescences of upper-class Thai life, it is fundamentally a statement about the conflict between old and new cultural standards and the mutual miscommunication of spouses rather than an ideological position on the status of women. If the heroine is painfully naive, she is also culturally attractive and morally decent; if the hero (or in some lights, villain) is unaware of his passion for interpersonal manipulation, he is at least well-intentioned and morally upstanding in his public manners and his sense of self; even "the other woman" is no wanton hussy but a lively intellectual whose search for erudition somehow justifies her narcissism and her ability to disrupt the lives of others. Here, as in real life, the heroic and villainous qualities of people become blurred, and the author would have gained little from allying herself with or against the interests of any of her characters.

While it is easy to identify works that assert ideological positions and authors who serve as agents for those positions, it is equally necessary to recognize writers who are committed to illuminating the human condition rather than to prescribing for it. The basic problem is that, like so many things in modern Thailand, there really is no institutionalized consensus among writers and readers as to what the purposes and priorities of contemporary writing ought to be. On the one hand, there is a powerful didactic strain in Thai literary tradition which assumes that the raison d'être of virtually all writing is the promulgation of morality by preaching, exhorting, coaxing, ridiculing, being ironic, or enacting some other kind of rhetorical performance. In these terms, writing is defined as inherently political or ideological, and it is simply assumed that writers will promote or condemn the interests of the various groups to which their works refer. (See Rutnin 1978, Poolthupya 1981, Chantornvong 1981, and Chitakasem 1982 for documentations of this tradition.) In recent times, there have been attempts by young, leftist intellectuals to take the tradition even further by making the articulation of political positions ("literature for the sake of life, literature for the people") the highest of all literary values. This movement ended abruptly with the coup of October 1976, but there were already signs of its inherent weaknesses, not the least of which was the fact that there were simply far fewer writers than political activists among those who supported this view.[30] Also, as might be expected, many of the latter had a thoroughly tedious and formulaic conception of the nature of literature and the basis of its appeal.

On the other hand, there is another strain in Thai literary tradition which assumes that the purpose of modern or contemporary literature is to analyze and clarify human problems or conditions and that readers will make up their own minds about how such problems are to be resolved—if they are to be resolved at all. This stream is much less patronizing in its rhetoric, and inevitably the problems it addresses are far more resistant to conventional solutions. In fact, the problems are sometimes so intractable that they are either without solution or only admit to denouements that are aesthetically rather than morally satisfactory. Thus, in "Fulfilling One's Duty," the author creates a series of irresolvable conflicts between competing ethics: the decency of the engineers versus the moral character of the hero; the greater, long-term good of the nation versus the lesser, but more immediate, good of the displaced villagers. In the end, the writer offers what is essentially a rationalization of the hero's conduct—one that gives meaning and virtue to the hero's acts and, in so doing, buffers the pain of the tragedy but never reconciles the moral dilemmas that comprise the basic terms of the story. A similar frame of reference animates "Madame Lamhab," "Relations with Colleagues" (and the novel, *Naaj Amphur Patiwad,* from which the selection is drawn), and even the gentle "Headman Thuj," although the aesthetic devices used in each of the stories differ strikingly from one another.

What all these and related efforts (see "Social Work," "Big Shots and *Likee*," "I Lost My Teeth," and "The Enchanting Cooking Spoon") seem to have in common is that they depict situations in which a hero or heroine presents a persona or rhetorical performance that does not quite succeed but, in not succeeding, somehow heightens his or her essential humanity. In most (but not all) of these stories, the rhetorical performance fails despite the hero's considerable verbal talents. But the corollary of this is that these stories also document the failure of social definitions and connections, in that the characters find themselves in situations where things are very much out of joint, almost the precise opposite of the way they are supposed to be. In "Fulfilling One's Duty," the construction of a dam is not supposed to make people suffer, but it does; in "Madame Lamhab" and "Relations with Colleagues," government officials are supposed to be dutiful and incorruptible, but only the aberrant or naive actually are; in "Headman Thuj," modern conveniences are not supposed to be inconvenient or cause their users anxiety, but they do; in "Social Work," charity is not supposed to be tainted by vanity and alms are not supposed to be stolen, but they are; and so it goes. In fact, the heroism of the characters, or at least their complexity and attractiveness, is very much a function of the anomie that surrounds them. While in the end some muddle through, are left in a state of ambiguity, or even die, they all have a personal integrity that is at least aesthetically arresting.

It is this concern with portraying a world that is considerably less than perfect—but that is nonetheless real—that most clearly distinguishes this second stream of the Thai literary tradition. The authors who move in this stream are not animated by a spirit of moral or ideological certainty and do not serve as spokespersons for any clearly identifiable social groups. Rather, they are singularly involved with gaining some kind of rational understanding and intellectual control over the chaos of contemporary experience. If they have a constituency, it is those readers whose lives and strategies are remarkably similar to those of their fictional creations.

Finally, a few words should be said about how felicitous the work of Thai writers is to the full magnitude of social types and groups that exist in Thailand. This issue can best be understood in terms of two related historical movements, one long-term and the other more recent. First, as was suggested earlier, over the past century there has been a slow, but clearly marked, expansion in the kinds and numbers of people writing and reading literature and in the nature of their literary interests. This enlargement has involved a movement outward from a small circle of royalty and nobility writing for themselves about things that projected their own interesting but parochial experiences; to a somewhat larger group that began to include educated, middle-class bureaucrats whose numbers mushroomed dramatically after the Revolution of 1932; to a yet larger group that began to include writers and readers from peasant and urban proletarian backgrounds; to a still larger group whose literary activities began to manifest a consciousness of significant and perhaps conflicting differences between the various elements comprising Thai society as a whole. The emergence of each successive group of writers and readers was accompanied by an expanding sense of social consciousness and literary legitimacy. Thus, while it would have been inconceivable earlier in the century to write about the life and thought of peasants, such themes became almost a literary rage during the 1960s and 1970s.

The second movement dovetails with this more long-term process. Whether inspired by indigenous or international considerations, it is essentially a Thai version of the sociological hyperesthesia that has swept the world during the second half of the twentieth century, which has resulted in according literary recognition to virtually every group claiming some kind of independent ethnic, religious, regional, economic, occupational, or sexual identity. Thus, the corpus of Thai writing has come to be characterized by a remarkable array of sociological concerns. As our selections demonstrate, there are writings on or about villagers, college students, various elite types, bureaucrats, mothers, monks, headmen, *nagleeng* (hoodlum-protectors), leftists, rightists, society ladies, and characters whose lives have telescoped a variety of social identities (schoolteacher-cum-brothel owner-cum-cabdriver-cum-political flunky). There are many other social types memorialized in the literature for which we have simply had no space: tribal peoples, prostitutes, pedicab drivers, Muslim victims of Thai Buddhist prejudice, tin miners, policemen (both as villains and as figures of sympathy), gigolos, dandies, and factory workers. Inevitably, some of this literature deals with such types in a passing manner, while in other cases it focuses on them to edify a literary or social issue. With the possible exception of the royal household (which is shielded by some very skittish *lèse majesté* laws) and the higher reaches of the military (which while less sheltered are more volatile), there really is no social domain that is exempt from literary treatment.

None of this is to suggest that this outburst of sociological consciousness has necessarily resulted in a more profound or ennobling vision of Thai society. However, it has served to document the complex nature of social life and, most importantly, to inform readers about social worlds that exist beyond their own parochical experiences. There is no doubt that while this cosmopolitan explosion is a reminder of the excitement and richness of modern life, for many readers it also documents the breakdown in the organic solidarity of Thai society. Certainly many Thai, particularly Marxists, have argued that such solidarity was always only a myth, serving to legitimize the prevailing system of power relationships and the specious, self-assigned superiority of the ruling classes. But myth or not, there is no doubt that the earlier solidarity was psychologically authentic and contributed to the stability and order of Thai culture and to the emotional investment that people had in their society.

The cosmopolitan explosion portrays a very different kind of social and psychological world. It is a place inhabited by people who not only do unfamiliar things but things that violate one's morality, expectations, and even cognitive understandings. In this modern world, children moralize to their parents (as in *Naaj Aphajmanii*), spouses talk to one another in order to confound and debate (as in "The Enchanting Cooking Spoon"), people become psychotic by trying to follow the rules (as in "Relations with Colleagues"), or are forced by poverty and frustration even to relinquish their faith (as in "Lord Buddha, Help Me?"). This is not a literature that edifies or elevates the Thai experience, but it is honest, poignant, and realistic. It will continue to be written until there is a paradigmatic rearrangement in the social and intellectual purposes of Thai writers (and their rhetoric) or until the circumstances of Thai culture as a whole undergo significant change.

Some Reflections on Literature and Ethnography

Earlier we indicated that the ethnographic value of literature derives largely from its intracultural nature; that is, since literature is written by natives for other natives, it always communicates an inner view of culture and, to the extent that it is not misshapen by the translation process, is an unimpeachable source of indigenous meanings, assumptions, and purposes.

This essentially unarguable proposition represents the basic premise of our enterprise. But beyond that there is the more complicated issue of how one transforms intracultural meanings into intercultural understandings. It is more complicated because it involves recognizing that a body of literature is never simply a series of texts that speak for themselves but rather is a series of texts designed for readers with certain kinds of expectations. Thus, their transmission to readers of another culture requires not only renditions of the works themselves but exegeses of the meanings they have for native readers in the hope that their foreign readers' normal literary expectations are held in abeyance, expanded, or somehow made responsive to the literature's alien qualities. Another way of saying all this is that the normal reader reflex, "I like this poem," "I do not like that short story," will not do in the intercultural situation, unless one believes that there are cross-culturally valid standards of literary judgment. Rather, the reflex must be tempered by the prior question "What is it about a particular piece of literature that makes it resonate for native readers?" together with an answer that affords some sense of the nature of that resonance. What we are proposing here is that literary interpretation should always be contingent upon ethnographic understanding.

None of this is easy or automatic. For one thing, there are no standards for how much information is necessary to achieve "ethnographic understanding." Furthermore, once such understanding is achieved, there is always the risk that the piece of literature may be overwhelmed or eclipsed by its own ethnographic commentary, a condition enhanced by the presumption that native texts are inexhaustible cornucopias of cultural meaning, waiting to be interpreted. In preparing this book, we were constantly aware of this kind of risk. We also felt pressured by the reports of readers who know little about Thailand but who, having seen some of our texts in manuscript, wanted more and more ethnographic explanations.

Second, there are built-in limits to what any amount of ethnographic explanation can do, if only because ethnography is virtually always about native things rather than renditions of those things. Thus, from the beginning of our project, we were keenly aware that if we were assembling a book of Thai writings for a Thai audience, rather than for an English-reading audience, its entire configuration would have been dramatically different, the point being that whatever our book says about Thai thought and literature, it does not impart a cumulative sense of what kinds of writings most appeal to Thai readers or how Thai literature is presented to Thai audiences. Such a book would contain less interpretive commentary than does ours, be substantively more dense and varied, be either more direct or more convoluted in revealing its political and literary prejudices, and be substantially more didactic in tone. Also, it would probably contain considerably less humor than ours, if only because while Thai have a much more highly ramified sense of the comic than do English readers, they also assume a more serious and ritualized approach to the public presentation of their culture.

A third and even more complicated issue has to do with the nature of the relationship between foreign and domestic literary expectations. While all intercultural interpretations of literature must recognize the realities of cultural differences, they must not assume that such differences are absolute or inherently irreconcilable. One of the most striking qualities of a collection like ours is that while some of the selections jar or are unimpressive or perplexing, there are others that resonate as clearly and pleasurably, or at least as intelligibly, for English readers as they do for Thai, although not necessarily for the same reasons. Much of the literary dissonance present in our material occurs in specific sections or portions of a work that may otherwise be thoroughly readable. Frequently the breakdown in literary expectations occurs at the end of a piece where, after a satisfying literary sojourn, the English reader is simply left dangling with an intercultural message that is somehow off-key or off-the-wall. This situation is particularly obvious in selections such as "Concerning *Farang*," "Paradise Preserved," "Getting Drunk Abroad," "A Day in the Life of Pat," and even "Fulfilling One's Duty." From an intracultural point of view, these endings are, of course, not at all off-key but in fact are densely packed with cultural meaning, some of which we have tried to explicate in notes or in the introductory remarks to the selections. But the act of explication can in itself violate things that in the original text are meant not to be explained but rather to be left unclear, suggestive, pregnant, and essentially open-ended. In this sense, "ethnographic explanation" can sometimes lapse into overinterpretation.

There are certain selections that are difficult to tune to from beginning to end and that are best dealt with by using ethnographic explanation as a kind of cognitive baffle or cushioning. This is particularly so with some of the poetry, such as "What Kind of Boat?," "Fishiness in the Night," "Big Shot as Toad," and "Paradise of the President's Wife," although it also characterizes essays like "A Day in the Life of Pat" or "Chewing Out a Special Class." These selections are not so much exotic as they are filled with in-group allusions and phrasings. An effort on the part of the reader is required to understand not only the meaning of the allusions but also the author's rhetorical intent. In these cases, ethnographic explanation serves to distance the writing, in the hope of providing the foreign reader with a sense of the effect of the work on native readers.

Then there are those selections that seem to be as pellucid in English as they are in Thai. Perhaps the best examples of these in our collection are "Grandma," "The Enchanting Cooking Spoon," "Headman Thuj," and "Lord Buddha, Help Me?" While their Thai origin is in each case unmistakable, they all seem to have the capacity to tap a sentiment or referent that at some level is as emotionally or cognitively meaningful to English readers as it is to Thai, although beyond that level there may be significant divergences in meaning or interpretation. Thus, the underlying appeal of "Grandma" seems to be its pantheistic premise; although it is not salient to Western thought it is nonetheless widely known, appreciated, and most English readers have considerable sensitivity toward it. However, what is intriguing from an intercultural point of view is that a story like "Grandma" is essentially imaginative to English readers, belonging to the realm of the wishful or possible (which perhaps also defines the Western conception of a pantheistic universe), while to Thai readers it is profoundly actual and real, its appeal being based more upon the aesthetics of its presentation than upon the originality of its formulation.

A similar kind of situation obtains with "The Enchanting Cooking Spoon." While the appeal of the story for both Thai and English readers derives from its honest and detailed description of the contours of a husband-wife relationship, most Thai readers attend to the social malaise of the husband, the naiveté of the wife, and their seemingly "natural" (in reality, culturally acceptable) miscommunication. English readers, on the other hand, attend to the double binds into which the husband is constantly tying his wife, his male chauvinism and verbal sadism, none of which can be excused by his pleasing public manners, his own Faustian search for happiness, or his latter-day claims to want to make his spouse happy on her own terms. Both interpretations are as correct as any culturally inspired projection can ever be. However, the point here is not the validity of the competing interpretations but rather the appreciation that both sets of readers have for the reality and poignancy of the literary statement.

Analytically viewed, the common feature of these interculturally engaging stories seems to be the fact that they focus on issues that are ordinarily on the periphery of Western interests or consciousness but that when restated in the terms and assumptions of another culture—where they are anything but peripheral—take on an illuminating or provocative quality. Thus, a story like "Grandma" engages an English reader because it contributes a dynamism and a sense of bilaterality and timelessness to what is otherwise a somewhat inchoate, unilateral Western view of the relationship between human beings and nature.[31] Similarly, a story like "Headman Thuj" charms most Western readers in the gentle, relaxed way it deals with a biological function that, although experienced by all, is almost never touched upon in Western fiction because of its tabooed nature. Here what we would ordinarily avoid or deal with squeamishly is transformed by the bucolic realities of Thai culture into a twinkling commentary on technological change and social pretension.

If there are selections that differ interculturally but can be explained ethnographically and others that are partially different but that nevertheless ring true, there are also selections that seem surprisingly familiar and that in their familiarity can be easily perceived as unexceptional or lesser versions of their Western counterparts, undoubtedly because they violate the basic expectation that products of another culture should be different. Our collection does not have many of these items, if only because we did not wish to disaffect potential readers, and those we did include have other redeeming qualities. Not surprisingly, they are mainly among our politically oriented essays, such as *Naaj Aphajmanii,* "On the Thai Left," and "The Quality of Life of a Southeast Asian."

Notwithstanding the seemingly derived qualities of these kinds of essays in English, the messages that they convey are to Thai readers just as original and meaningful as any of the other works in the book may be to English readers. Things that may seem mundane or self-evident in an English-reading context—a father-son argument over politics (as in *Naaj Aphajmanii*); the necessity for proud and self-righteous youth to be also self-evaluative (as in "On the Thai Left"); the wish for adequate governmental support of basic social services (as in "The Quality of Life of a Southeast Asian")—may in a place like Thailand be exciting, innovative, or threatening to the status quo. One of the functions of a volume like this is to underscore these realities and to remind readers that although Thai and English literary expectations are palpably different, even dramatically different, there are large areas of overlap, so that what is culturally obvious in one place is culturally enlarging in the other.

Finally, a few words should be said about the fidelity of our materials to Thai literary tastes and preferences. First, it is axiomatic that all our materials appeal to some elements of the Thai reading public, if in a few cases it may be primarily to the editors who originally published them. Second, it is inevitable that some Thai literary domains have been bypassed, in part because in our judgment they were not sufficiently edifying or evocative to Western readers and in part because we may have simply missed them. Some of these omissions are culturally interesting but historically trivial, such as the genre of joke and action serials and penny novels written by people like the late P. Intharapaalit and known to virtually every literate Thai adolescent and young adult. Others are more consequential in their consciousness-raising qualities, such as the writings of 'Rong Wongsawaan on the emotional elements of male-female relationships. In some respects, 'Rong's writings are like Thai versions of *Playboy* magazine fiction, on which they are in part modeled; in other respects, they are fine-grained evocations of the complexities of human wishes. But in either case, their publication introduced into Thai culture a sense of the interpersonal subtlety of sexual encounters that previously was literarily inchoate—or such are the claims of 'Rong's admirers.

Perhaps our most serious omission was the large body of literature, primarily by women, which is essentially private musings on the external world. Some of our selections suggest this genre. Thus, Suchit Wongthed's "Lord Buddha, Help Me?" is very much about a man's internal struggle to balance his fantasies about himself with an outside world he neither understands nor can control. But the inner world of this "musing literature" is much less a place for working through personal problems than a place to meander, reflect, and revel in secret and narcissistic understandings. It is a domain where personal thought and feeling contrast sharply with the nonsense going on in the "real world," although the natural features of this external world—the smell of flowers, the feel of falling rain, the sensuality of rubbing one's toes along the muddy bottom of a swimming hole—comprise a large part of one's literary reflections. The most accomplished practitioners of this genre are perhaps the late Suwanee Sukhonta and Wimol Siriphaibul, the latter known more popularly as "Thomyantii."[32] We have omitted their work, and similar efforts, from our collection principally because their characters' thoughts and musings are truly "private," and from a narrative point of view their accounts do not "go anywhere" or "do anything." They are essentially an array of literary still lifes or brief aesthetic vignettes.

Although all our materials appeal to some elements of the Thai reading public, some kinds of writing inevitably have more appeal, and by the same token some obviously have less appeal, than others. We tread very lightly here because, as noted before, the free-market quality of Thai writing has resulted in the absence of any real consensus about literary preferences among those most directly involved in the literary process. Nevertheless, we think that among our selections there are certain literary styles or modes that appeal to virtually all native readers, and that may not be apparent from either our other observations or the general configuration of our material.

Foremost among the works exemplifying these styles are those written in a simple, gentle, straightforward, and unpleading manner. Probably the two best examples of such unadorned prose are "Big Shots and *Likee*" and "The Wholesome Intention of *Khunnaaj* Saajbua." The appeal of these writings is their uncomplicated and unconditional viewpoints, although in both cases the authors are dealing with issues (in *"Likee"* with fantasy, reality, and political tenure, and in *"Khunnaaj* Saajbua" with family relationships) that are of considerable psychocultural import. It may well be that the authors' easy style and uncomplicated viewpoints are a function of the culturally consensual nature of these issues, that is, they can be uncomplicated precisely because most of their readers agree with what they are saying. The clear and simple reinforcement of the culturally familiar is everywhere a primary function of literary activity. Had this volume been more concerned with works that were appealing to Thai readers and less with those that might be informative to English readers, we would have selected more of this type.

Another Thai preference concerns materials written by famous people. Certainly part of the fundamental attraction of the selections by M. R. Khukrit Pramoj, M. L. Boonlue Kunjara Debyasuvan, Sulak Sivaraksa, and Chitr Phoumisak is the social distinction of the authors, although it may be arguable whether their writing is cause or effect of their celebrity. In the cases of Khukrit and Boonlue, their family ties and varied social and occupational pursuits probably preceded any fame attached specifically to their writing; in the case of Sulak, the obverse seems to be true in that he explicitly used his rhetorical talents to achieve a following in the intellectual community; in the case of Chitr, it was the novelty of his ideas and the scope and erudition of his style that led to his becoming an ideological and literary cynosure. But whatever sequence the biographical causalities take, it is clear that readers are attracted to such people because they can partake of the writer's wit, wisdom, charisma, advice, status, insight, or sense of intellectual daring. There is in all of this not only an element of being a literary "fan" or "groupie" but also the traditional Siamese sense that some of the author's celebrity or talent may somehow rub off upon the reader, and that by learning, osmosis, or some kind of halo effect the reader can bask in the intellectual, and ultimately social or political, power to the author.

Lastly, there is that large number of works, perhaps even the majority of our selections, that appeal to readers largely on the basis of their underlying structural features—their moral or ironic endings ("Madame

Lamhab," "Fulfilling One's Duty," "Headman Thuj," "I Lost My Teeth"), their use of a metaphorical chorus perhaps echoing the chanting of Buddhist monks (the ending of "Grandma"), or their being cast as metaphorical eulogies (both the theme and ending of "Oh! Temple, Temple of Bot!"). These features are all rooted in the traditional rhetorical forms of Thai culture—on the one hand, in the rhythms and purposes of Thai folklore, and on the other, in the styles and sonorities of Buddhist canonical practice. Thus, for all their febrile contemporary interests, Thai writers and readers maintain—perhaps despite themselves—some major expressive links to their own cultural past.

Notes

1. Geertz (1972, 1980a, 1980b), Boon (1977), and Becker (1979) are the most eloquent practitioners of the former. This antimetathetic conception of our project was first suggested to me by Jeanne Bergman. I am indebted to her not only for her felicitous formulation but, more importantly, for making me conscious of the historical context, and its associated supports and precedents, for this kind of work. Although our project was planned well before the publication of Geertz's initial statement and was stimulated by several circumstances in my earlier career and life-history, there is no doubt that there was something in the anthropological environment of the 1970s that fostered a more generalized exploration of "literary" interests. Geertz himself has taken the position in his "Blurred Genres" (1980a) essay that lately there has been such a rich mixing of disciplinary interests in all the social sciences and humanities as to constitute the beginning of a paradigmatic rearrangement—what he calls a "refiguration"—of social thought. This is all perhaps an example of what Kroeber (1948:329–342) meant by "the working out" of a basic culture pattern.

2. This phrase, originally used by Malinowski (1922:25), has over the years come to represent the unchallengeable purpose of all ethnographic research. (The complete sentence reads: "This goal is, briefly, to grasp the native's point of view, his relation to life, to realize *his* vision of *his* world.") For some anthropologists, the phrase itself has taken on some of the qualities of an incantation. For others it is an elementary methodological axiom. And for still others, it has become a rallying cry for competing methodological schools (see Goodenough 1956 and 1957; Frake 1962; Sturtevant 1964; Berreman 1966; Geertz 1973 and 1976; Nida 1975; Colby 1975; Colby, Fernandez, and Kornenfeld 1981). The phrase has not, to my knowledge, ever been explicitly applied to literary works.

3. Although there are many measures of a society's concern with creativity and originality, it is not insignificant that the Royal Thai Government did not establish a Patent Office and issue its first patent to a Thai citizen until 1981. The issuance of patents, however, is as much a result of economic and legal pressures as it is an institutionalized recognition of the value of creativity.

4. For discussions of the nature and role of oral literature, see Fischer 1963, Dundes 1965 and 1980, and Toelken 1969. For English-language material on Thai oral literature, see Attagara 1961, Caulfield 1961, Chaudhuri 1976, Feinstein 1969, Krueger 1969, Krull and Melchers 1966, LeMay 1930, Rajadhon 1968, Sibunruang 1954, Toth 1971, and Wells 1964. Except for Attagara's bibliographic effort, virtually all these works represent "oral literature for *farang*"

(Westerners) rather than oral literature as it is actually articulated and used in village Thailand. The materials were selected for publication in English precisely because of their appeal to nonnative sensibilities and in the editing or rewriting were sanitized, idealized, or otherwise refashioned. Also, they have been published in a form that contains little information on their representativeness, native meaning, or context of presentation. This is the manner in which most oral literature from non-Western societies has become available in English over the years. While the literature is neither "wrong" nor useless, particularly in its thematic features, its highly selective nature must be recognized; it is virtually a genre unto itself. With the increasing use of modern folklore collection techniques (for Thailand, see Attagara 1976 and Davis 1974), this skewed situation is slowly being ameliorated.

5. Despite the widely held assumption that it is a European creation, the novel is known to have emerged in at least three different times and places: eleventh-century Japan, fourteenth-century China, and seventeenth-century Spain. To what extent these historical events represented instances of independent invention or of borrowing is unclear, although there is some indication that the Chinese may have been influenced by the Japanese (see Kroeber 1951 and Spearman 1966). However, the early Chinese novel was eventually to have a direct impact upon the development of Thai literary tastes. Thus, after the arrival of the printing press in 1835, the fifth book to be printed in Thailand was a Thai translation of the fourteenth-century Chinese novel *Romance of the Three Kingdoms* (in Thai, *Saam Kok*). The book had been translated during the reign of Rama I (1782–1809) by a group of Thai and Chinese scholars living in Thailand (Senanan 1975:19), and its printing in 1865 stimulated the translation and publication of numerous other Chinese stories. The year 1902 marked the publication of what is considered "the first Thai novel," *Khwaam Phayaabaat*, which was a version of the 1886 Victorian English novel, *Vendetta*, by Marie Corelli.

6. However, it is also true that there was (and continues to be) a "Little Tradition" counterpart to the classical literature of the Thai courts. For all their broad and ad-libbed humor, the performances of *likee* folk drama troupes at village fairs were modeled on the themes and situations presented in classical court drama (see "Big Shots and *Likee*"). The widespread geographical distribution of temple murals portraying themes from the classical literature also demonstrates that there have always been village counterparts to palace artists. This kind of parallelism between the "Great" and "Little" traditions, particularly in terms of the values they embodied, contributed to the fundamental unity of Thai culture.

7. These purposes could also be subverted. See the story, "The Enchanting Cooking Spoon" for a perfect example of how a man uses his knowledge of classical literature, e.g., his allusion to Kritsanaa, the embodiment of spousal perfection, to mark his own sophistication in order to put down his wife.

8. A promotion by Thai Airways International demonstrates its utility even in advertising copy. The advertisement includes a photo of a soaring Thai Airways 747 juxtaposed beneath a section of a mural of the *Ramakian* showing the principals on Rama's chariot. Part of the accompanying text reads; "*For centuries, flight has been part of our everyday life. The practical expressed with gracefulness and beauty. Found again and again in the legendary Ramakian episodes where travel between heaven and earth was a daily necessity. And uniquely Thai.*"

9. In speaking of "the cultural status" of oral and classical literature and their use as symbolic markers of "the past," we are not referring to any inherently objective or perduring qualities of these materials but rather to contemporary modes of classifying and perceiving them. To identify the lasting attributes of "oral literature" would, for example, require us to examine this tradition not only

in terms of its current characteristics but as an ongoing, self-rejuvenating, and constantly changing literary activity. Similarly, a focus on the "objective attributes" of "classical literature" would demand an examination of its history and the various changes it has undergone over the centuries. Our justification for reducing the historical complexity of Thai literature to a few, contrasting structural features is simply a desire to communicate about these traditions in terms of their current meanings and definitions.

The lexical contrasts of contemporary Thai are fully consonant with the above observations, although inevitably they are more subtle. The fundamental contrast is between *wanakhadii* (classical literature) and *wanakam* (modern or contemporary literature). The latter implies, according to one informant, "writing that is of good form, good content, and that is uplifting to the mind." The former has these qualities simply by definition. Both genres can be further qualified: *wanakhadii naa len* is classical literature that is particularly amusing or appealing and *wanakam ruam samaj* is recent literature of high aesthetic excellence. However, because the excellence of *wanakhadii* is inherent (based on its greater age, euphonious language, associations with the court, and the like), it is judged to be always aesthetically superior. No particular date separates classical and modern writing, although there is a diffuse sense that the latter begins in the late nineteenth century. *Nithaanphyynbaan* (legends or myths of original inhabitants) or *nithaanchaawbaan* (legends or myths of villagers) are what we would generally think of as "folklore." *Nijaaj* (as in *nijaajphyynbaan* and *nijaajchaawbaan*) are in most contexts virtually identical to *nithaan,* but because some informants say that they sometimes refer to tales of greater length and narrative complexity and suggest a greater likelihood of truth than do *nithaan,* they are best translated as "oral literature." On the other hand, *nijaajbaraamparaa* are ancient tales which, because of their sheer age, are likely to have less objective truth. Related to both *nithaan* and *nijaaj* are *kati,* which refer to accounts that make moral or ethical points (as in adages and fables). While *nithaan* and *nijaaj* continue inexorably to be both replicated and created in contemporary Thailand, and represent genres that are most widely known and are learned earliest in life, they are nevertheless viewed—by admirers, agents, and unwitting creators—as vestiges of an indeterminate Thai past.

10. In using such terms as "realism" and "narrative honesty" we are referring to cultural phrasings of these qualities rather than to any absolute standards. It should be apparent from the selections in this book that notions of "realism" and "narrative honesty" are constrained by a prior concern that such "realism" and "narrative honesty" have maximum rhetorical impact. In Thailand, words are meant to impress and persuade; however "realistic" or "honest" a text may seem, it is always—like literature everywhere—deliberately fashioned.

11. The social impact of literacy is the subject of an extremely rich, but also intellectually inconclusive, scholarly literature. See particularly Bantock 1966, Cipolla 1969, Cressy 1980, Disch 1973, Eisenstein 1979, Goody 1977, Goody and Watt 1963, Gough 1968, Graff 1976 and 1979, Harman 1970, Havelock 1963 and 1976, and LeVine 1982. The nature of the access that literacy provides, however, is always conditioned by censorship practices, decisions about what is to be translated from other languages, cultural and legal conventions concerning copyrighting and plagiarism, the costs of publication and the efficiencies of distribution, and the like.

12. In general, far more items are kept under lock and key in Thai households than in Occidental homes—not only jewelry, books, and important papers but favorite clothes, cosmetics, hobby materials, and other valuables that might tempt children, siblings, servants, or, for that matter, the master or mistress of the

household. Also, because of mildew and termites and other cellulose-eating insects, books are far more perishable in the tropics than in more temperate climates and in Thailand are usually kept in closed (although not necessarily locked) cabinets. In homes with air-conditioned rooms—inevitably those of the more wealthy or modern—there is a general tendency to display books on open shelves. Although these rooms are almost never locked, they are sometimes off limits to specific members of the household.

13. While the publication figures of virtually all Thai newspapers and magazines are assumed to be inflated (primarily because higher figures are used to justify higher advertising fees), the largest daily in the country, *Thai Rath,* is reputed to print 800,000 copies, at least on the day the national lottery number is published. In contrast, *Siam Rath,* the most reliable and intellectually respectable daily, publishes approximately 25,000 copies, although its weekly review *(Sabadaa Wicaan)* is reputed to have a run of as high as 50,000. The magazine with the largest circulation, *Bangkok,* is reported to print 750,000 copies and the woman's magazine *Satri Sarn* approximately 200,000.

There are approximately fifty daily newspapers in Thailand, half of which are published in Bangkok. There are in addition about sixty weekly newspapers, most of which are published in provincial Thailand. Well-stocked Bangkok newsstands also carry seventy-five to a hundred different general purpose weekly and monthly magazines. These figures must always be approximations, if only because of the "here today, gone tomorrow" nature of the Thai publishing world. Defunct periodicals are often rejuvenated by new owners and editors, sometimes to be published as up-dated versions of their predecessors but at other times as totally different kinds of magazines.

14. The historical reasons for this are obvious. On the one hand, as suggested by the pre-World War II data on literacy, there was not a sufficiently large market of readers to sustain the payment of higher fees. On the other hand, the writing of literature was for many years an avocation of the independently wealthy and justified as a labor of love or as an act of social responsibility.

15. Some private Thai libraries are comprised almost completely of cremation books. In fact, if there are "professional mourners" in certain societies, there are "professional cremation book collectors" in Thailand, people who regularly attend cremations for the purpose of obtaining free books, sometimes for themselves and sometimes for sale or trade. Because the interactions of motivations, actions, and consequences are in the Thai view very complex qualities, doing so does not necessarily diminish the Buddhist merit that is made and shared at a cremation ceremony.

16. In a field study of Thai newspaper-reading habits conducted in the late 1950s, James N. Mosel found village newspaper reading chains involving as many as six different readers and group readings (in which selections from newspapers were read aloud) to as many as twenty people (personal communication).

The contribution that public libraries make to the standard 5 to 1 ratio is unclear, although it cannot be very significant. While there are 326 public libraries in the kingdom, holding more than 2,332,000 volumes (UNESCO 1982), all but a few are noncirculating. (These few include university libraries, tuition-supported secondary school libraries, and libraries which have significant international involvement, such as The Siam Society, British Council, U.S. Information Agency, Neilson-Hays, and the like.) Thai libraries are comfortable, pleasant places in which to work, but in the view of their administrators their budgets simply do not permit the risk of allowing books to leave the premises. As a result, most public libraries serve primarily as book repositories and reference rooms. In a few instances, such as the open-shelf, air-conditioned National Library in Bangkok, they are also major research institutions.

17. Although it is now virtually forgotten, which is perhaps the inevitable result of having ceased publication, *Sangkhomsaat Parithat* is a landmark of Thai intellectual history. Established in 1963 by the then new Social Science Association of Thailand—which was a loose coalition of intellectual representatives of the old, court-centered elite, high-level bureaucrats, and young university professors—the journal was intended to be an outlet for research results and bureaucratic announcements that might have some public relevance. Its printing press was donated by the U.S. Information Agency and the salary for the editor was provided by the Asia Foundation which, unbeknown to Thai (and certainly not to the editor), was at the time funded mainly by the CIA. Instead of becoming the simple kind of newsletter that its founders had anticipated, it self-consciously modeled itself on the British journal *Encounter* (which ironically was also proven later to be funded by the CIA). *Sangkhomsaat Parithat* quickly became the nation's major forum for intellectual debate and controversy, focusing on issues of cultural identity and social change. As a compilation of publicly expressed views, its intellectual honesty and sophistication were unprecedented in Thai history. Toward the latter part of the decade its editorship changed, and like the *New York Review of Books* in the United States, it became the most consistent critic of the nation's participation in the Vietnam War, stressing Thailand's excessive dependency upon the United States. Its editorial leadership eventually went on to other acitivities in the intellectual and literary world.

18. The same might be said about the literary salon, which, like most (but not all) social affairs in Thailand, tend to be less age-graded and more explicitly cooperative than is perhaps the case in other societies. Guests bring their spouses and children; the host will be sure to invite people of several generations; and although there are variations based upon the relative wealth and age of the hosts, the bountiful meals at these gatherings are often the result of careful coordination among participating wives. As in literary salons everywhere, the focus of discussion is books, ideas, politics, and gossip about those not there, but with a spirit of play, laughter, and interpersonal respect, not one-upsmanship. Although some established writers complain about the amount of time they must devote to the salon scene, they also view it as essential to the testing and sharing of ideas and for strengthening and modifying their *phuak* relationships.

19. This is an understatement. On the basis of four different accounts brought to our attention, it would seem that the encounter of a writer or editor with a police officer ostensibly in search of suspicious or indictable evidence represents one of the classical confrontations of Thai life. It is "classical" because the confrontation is between two fundamentally different, but equally valid, sets of cultural values that are meaningful to all Thai. Much of what ensues in the writer-police encounter is a function of whether it involves only two people, one-on-one, and the quality of civility and respect exhibited by the parties toward one another. But dramaturgically—and that is what interests most Thai—the encounter typically has the following elements. The writer sees himself (and assumes the police officer shares this perception) as mentally quicker, more verbally skilled, better educated, and probably of a higher social class (and thus demanding more respect) than the policeman; even if the last is not true, the writer's rhetorical skills would suggest that it is. The police officer, on the other hand, sees himself (and assumes he is seen by the writer) as a man of unlimited power and perhaps even ruthlessness, whose own individual strength is reinforced by a massive bureaucratic organization of underlings and supervisors who would support him in virtually every particular. There are subtleties that complicate the encounter:

the writer must not seem too uppity or flippant and the police officer must not seem too authoritarian or arrogant.

In addition, although the writer might not wish to admit it, his vanity has been inflated by the official attention he is being given. And while the policeman would also not wish to acknowledge it, he has more than likely simply been given an assignment but does not have the slightest idea what he is looking for. Indeed, he may not be looking for anything, but his physical presence alone will serve as a warning to the writer to alter his anti-establishment or socially critical ways. On his part, the writer wants to get through the encounter in a way that will reduce the likelihood of future visits. In a few instances, writers have felt so good about how they have managed the confrontation that, in a Thai reversal of Dostoevski's Raskolnikov–Porfiry Petrovitch relationship, they have tried to educate the police officer in the value of a free press and the unrestrained expression of ideas.

20. Although the motivations and stylistics are obviously very different, there are parallels to this in some of the English-language literature of this century. James Joyce's stream of consciousness comes immediately to mind, as does some of the more recent prose of Thomas Pynchon and John Barth. Although always coherent, Norman Mailer's prose is clearly meant to suggest the speed with which his own mind generates, shifts, and spins around with ideas. While not a "primary process," it is certainly a highly libidinized mode of thought. A similar although perhaps more disciplined, narrative style was used a generation earlier by Thomas Wolfe.

21. As might be expected, most of the published accounts on this period focus on political events and issues rather than on larger social processes. Perhaps the most extensive of these political essays is Girling's 1981 volume. A brief, but excellent, summation of the political history of the period can also be found in Likhit Dhiravegin's 1984 monograph. The best source for the Phibun era is David Wilson's classic 1962 work, although no essay quite captures the spirit of the period as cogently as does Thamsook Numnonda's 1977 paper. The Sarit period is documented most completely in Thak Chaloemtiarana's 1979 study. For contrasting views of the impact of American aid programs see Caldwell 1974 and Lobe 1977; for an insider's view of what Thailand—or at least its elite—gained from such arrangements, see Thanat Khoman's 1973 paper. Establishment views of the insurgency are contained in Tanham 1974, Zimmerman 1978, and Somchai Rakwijit 1974 and 1976; Marxist views are expressed by Turton, Fast, and Caldwell 1978; more analytic views are revealed by Girling 1968 and Thomas 1975. For events during and surrounding the 1973–1976 period, see Morell and Chai-anan's landmark 1981 volume; two excellent papers by Prudhisan Jumbala, 1974 and 1977; and provocative papers by Saneh Chammarik 1976 (on structural factors underlying the 1973 revolution), Anderson 1977 (on the changing structure of society), Somporn Sangchai 1976 and Muecke 1980 (on right-wing organization), and Reynolds and Lysa 1983 (on the development of a Marxist historiography.) For the Thanin period, see Montri Chenvidyakarn 1978 and Girling 1977.

The literature on the post-Thanin period still lacks historical perspective, although papers by Kershaw 1979, Morell and Chai-anan 1979, and Wedel 1982 are interesting summaries, the next-to-last on the intellectuals who went into the hills and the last on those who returned. Areas to which relatively little scholarly attention has been given are the impact of foreign corporate investments on Thai society as a whole and how industrialization, education, and migration—both domestic and foreign—is changing the nature of the Thai class system.

22. The former was not always the case in Southeast Asia. There is considerable evidence that the literary efforts of Southeast Asian courts—original works as

well as adaptations and translations of Indic-derived classics—were very much the product of committee enterprise. Groups of writers met, typically under the direction of kings and princes, and through discussion, modification, and sometimes the syntheses of individual contributions, attempted to create consensually crafted epics, drama, and poetry. Little is known about the politics of such creativity, but given the nature of precolonial Southeast Asian social structure, it must be assumed that these seminars were carefully stratified in terms of status. It was not until the second half of the nineteenth century that the notion of a single, identifiable author of a literary work was widely admitted in Thai society, although there were some exceptions, such as Sunthorn Phuu earlier in the century.

23. The "argument" here has to do with the relative significance that is assigned an author's ideological purity or commitment. Of the two writers just cited (for more complete remarks on their historical positions, see the introductions to their selections), Chitr was by far the more ideologically engaged, perhaps even obsessed. In contrast, Seksan sees ideology as inherently contingent upon historical circumstances and "the actual conditions of society." Also, everything about him indicates a highly eclectic mind that utilizes a bit from Marxism, a bit from Buddhism, a bit from the epistemological framework of modern social science, and a bit from traditional Thai folk wisdom, all in the service of fashioning "a best" explanation. In its freedom from ideological rigidity, the intellectual style is characteristically "modern Thai," although in its eclecticism, it also lacks the spirit of certainty that Thai appreciate in their rhetoric and which, in fact, characterizes most of Chitr's work.

24. It is impossible to determine the number of people actually involved in such a community. Our effort includes samples of the work of twenty-five individuals. With more space and a higher price and a somewhat grander conception, the number of contributors might have been easily doubled. In terms of those whose self-image includes the category "contributing member of Thailand's literary community," we might be referring to perhaps one hundred and fifty people. (For another, but equally unsatisfactory, approach to this issue, see Phillips 1975.)

25. This last relates to the widely shared Thai assumption that there is a "natural" tendency for most things to be done in a half-hearted way and sooner or later to unravel. In contrast to the "natural" (in a genuine Lévi-Straussian sense) is that which is "civilized," well-ordered, tasteful, and characterized by a concern with excellence. Although the property of both sexes (see "What Kind of Boat?" for an expression of masculine concern with excellence), this concern is particularly the province of elite women and those who aspire to their standards, or such was the position of M. L. Boonlue. (See her 1972 novel, *Surat Naari,* for an elaboration of this conception.)

26. By virtue of this April 1976 election, Samak also became Deputy Minister of Interior in the Democrat Party government of M. R. Seni Pramoj, Khukrit's older brother. (However, unlike Daukmaajsod and Boonlue, there was no love lost between these two siblings; if anything, their relationship was an institutionalized, but muted, form of sibling rivalry.) The entire political configuration was to change only six months later with the coup of October 5, 1976, after which Samak became Minister of Interior (a position of inordinate power) in the regime of Thanin Kraivichien. A year later, he lost his post when General Kriangsak Chomanan came to power. Since then, both Khukrit and Samak have continued to be close to center stage in the Thai political drama. With the passage of time, Samak has even tempered some of his rhetorical excesses. Although this book contains no example of Samak's rhetoric, it is very much in the style of (if more extreme than) Anand Seenaakhan's "Chewing Out a Special Class."

27. The concepts of "journalist as culture hero" and "journalist-cum-creative writer" are by no means unique to Thailand. The latter runs both deep and strong in the Western world where there are such varied examples as Daniel Defoe, Charles Dickens, Mark Twain, Sinclair Lewis, George Orwell, Ernest Hemingway, and Albert Camus. The "journalist as culture hero" is perhaps not so clearly defined, but during the nineteenth century such people as William Howard Russell (whose reporting on the Crimean war inspired Tennyson's "Charge of the Light Brigade" and Churchill's correspondence on the Boer war) and Henry Morton Stanley ("Dr. Livingstone, I presume") played such a role. During the twentieth century, Americans such as H. L. Mencken, Walter Lippman, John Reed, Edward R. Murrow, and more recently Walter Cronkite and even Robert Woodward and Carl Bernstein, have taken on such attributes. Khamsing's views of the role of the journalist, and later the writer, were considerably more modest: he saw them as providing the people about whom they wrote with a sense of social identity and importance. He also saw the journalist as providing his readers with practical information—medical, agricultural, educational, economic—for improving their own conditions in the modern world.

28. Because a few of these writers wish to deny or gloss over their own class backgrounds we have intentionally omitted listing them. Those that are mentioned either take pride in or are simply matter-of-fact about their class backgrounds.

29. Thai, like other Asians and most Africans who have passed the age of weaning, have difficulty in digesting the lactose of fresh dairy products. However, when cow's milk or cream is processed into ice cream, yogurt, and similar forms, the lactose content is sufficiently altered to permit the production of adequate lactase for normal digestion. Khamsing's entry into dairy farming was predicated upon the potential market for ice cream and his own access to excellent distribution facilities.

30. To label this as a "movement" may be a gross overestimation. One of the most difficult problems in assessing this kind of activity is to make an accurate judgment about its intellectual and social magnitude. Most discussions of the intellectual ferment of the 1973–1976 period refer or allude to meetings or essays in which "literature for the sake of life" themes were enunciated. Included here was the famous (or infamous) Chiengmai University conference on "Should We Burn Thai Literature?"; the use of labels like *wanakam nam naw* or "polluted literature" to refer to elite literary efforts; and the condemnation of seemingly "friendly" writers who would not join in supporting this politicization. But it is impossible to determine whether there were 2, 20, 200, or 2,000 people involved in this kind of campaigning. One has the sense that the outrageousness and vehemence of the proponents of the "literature for the sake of life" vision gave their position a degree of public attention far in excess of both their numbers and credibility. However, it must also be acknowledged that those involved in "music for life" activity (*dontrii phya chiiwid;* see "Man and Buffalo") had much greater success, undoubtedly because political ideas are more readily packaged in lyrical forms.

31. This is not to deny that there are some specialized Western views of this relationship—evolutionary, ecological, or the kinds of cosmological conceptions articulated by scholars such as Pierre Teilhard de Chardin or Loren Eisley—which are considerably more systematic, comprehensive, and perhaps sophisticated than the view expressed by Angkarn. But it is to say that for a variety of deeply held cultural reasons most ordinary Thai readers are more attentive than ordinary English readers to the links between and ultimate unity of people, flowers, cobras, and dewdrops.

32. "Thomyantii" is also known for her passionate, outspoken right-wing political positions, a factor which played a role in her being appointed to a ministerial post in the 1976–1977 Thanin government. These political views also caused her work to be constantly referred to as "polluted literature" *(wanakam nam naw)* by left-of-center critics, although in reality most of the substance of her writing focuses on the rich inner life of women, not on the outer world of political practice and ideology. Of course, it may well be that describing this inner world is judged by her accusers to be just the kind of useless indulgence that would attract right-wing ladies.

PART II
The Literature

1

The Immutables of Thai Life: Religion, Family, Fun, and the Search for Respectability

Grandma

Introduction

The following short story by Angkarn Kalayaanaphong is perhaps the most beautifully crafted in this collection. Of all our materials, it is the one selection that in concept and emotional power is most "traditionally Thai." The story is about the realities of nature and death, things to which the Thai have always given the most serious attention and about which their religion has provided the clearest, and also the most profoundly satisfying, understanding.

While the story is in part an exercise of the creative imagination, its aesthetic and emotional meaning derives from the premises of Thailand's oral tradition and thus describes events that many Thai accept as genuinely possible, if not real, in the empirical world.

The thoroughly modernized reader should recognize that, although we may have forgotten, the pantheistic premises of this kind of story are not completely alien to the Western mentality. Very much the same view of "the real world" can be found in Tennyson's *Flower in the Crannied Wall* ("Little Flower—but *if* I could understand/ What you are, root and all, and all in all, / I should know what God and man is.") or in Wordsworth's *The Tables Turned* ("One impulse from a vernal wood / May teach you more of a man, / Of moral evil and of good, / Than all the sages can."). What distinguishes this English view from the Thai is that while the former is essentially a lament of man's inability to fully understand nature, the Thai view—which ultimately is both more pantheistic and more moral—demonstrates the integration of nature and man. If human beings can be reborn in future lives as flowers, frogs, or watercress shoots—as Thai Buddhist cosmology fully allows—there is no inherent barrier to their carrying on meaningful conversations in this life, or to a flower even initiating such discussions. It is true that in this story the author tends to juxtapose "man as the doer of evil" and "nature as the source of goodness," but this contrast is more reflective of the author's personal vision or preference than it is something most Thai would assume to be true.[1]

The attitude toward death expressed here—its simple inevitability, its naturalness, even its sensate quality—is perhaps what is most "truly Thai" about the story. It contains no Faustian protest, no convoluted psychological denials, and, other than the attempt to beautify death, no weighty emotional effort "to come to terms with it." In fact, it contains literally only one word of human protest—the adjective "vicious." And the creature to whom this adjective is applied is provided with the most natural justification for its actions: it was mating. Even more "natural" perhaps is the author's attempt to link death to all other processes of the natural world. Unlike most accounts of death, where time is usually stopped, the emphasis here is on the interminable movements of nature: a new day begins to dawn; the dewdrops continue to crackle; a lingering star still glitters. The death of a creature is seen simply as one elemant of or point on these timeless processes.

Angkarn Kalayaanaphong is the most distinctive member of Thailand's aesthetic community. Many Thai consider him to be the nation's only socially recognized "genius"—although this ascription tends to be given grudgingly, in part because of his reclusiveness and his social manners and in part because of the Thai tendency to neutralize others in their public assessments.[2] However, none denies that Angkarn stands alone as the country's most original traditional artist. In a nation of numerous skilled, but highly conservative, craftsmen, he has brought to classical Thai painting and drawing a dynamism and vitality that is almost never seen. His subject matter is drawn from religion, mythology, and nature. Although his work is rarely exhibited, it brings the highest sums awarded to any living Thai artist. An example of his work can be seen on the dust jacket of this book; although it was drawn several years after the writing of "Grandma," the spirit of the two efforts are strikingly similar.

In addition to his distinction as an artist, Angkarn is acknowledged to be one of his nation's greatest poets. Although his poetry is not as singular as his art, it perhaps represents a greater accomplishment, if only because he writes in a country where scores of thousands of people (even the illiterate) are authors and listeners of poetry. Angkarn's poetic fame is based upon the beauty of his language, the juxtaposition of his sounds, and his violation—like e.e. cummings in English, always a meaningful violation—of traditional Thai poetic forms. The subject matter of his poetry is parallel to the subject matter of his art.

Angkarn's narrative work is judged to be his least developed aesthetic talent. "Grandma" is included here not because of its expository depth, but simply because it is a clear, revealing expression of one of the most significant areas of Thai thought. Readers should note that however this story appears to them in this translation, the original statement is considerably more musical, subtle, and precise.

Angkarn was born in Nakornsidhammaraj in southern Thailand in 1926 and was educated at temple, public, and private schools before entering the University of Fine Arts in 1946. He married late in life and is the father of three young children. He speaks only Thai, and other than some brief visits to neighboring countries of Southeast Asia—principally to read his poetry or to be honored—he has spent his entire life in Thailand.

NOTES

1. In a research project that the editor carried out several years ago with Thai villagers on the question of the "inherent nature of man," the majority of villagers viewed human beings as inherently neither good nor evil, as free to move in either direction but with an obvious tendency to prefer evil. If forced to make a choice, Angkarn would probably not disagree with this more flexible judgment.

2. M. R. Khukrit Pramoj often is also judged to be a "genius" but usually in a figurative, rather than literal, sense and as much for his political ability as his intellectual talents.

Grandma

ANGKARN KALAYAANAPHONG

One twilight during rainy season, the downpour has come to an end, leaving a trail of clean white clouds moving in gentle procession. The bushes and the flowering trees turn a brilliant and refreshing green. The setting sun, a ball of red, radiates its beams, bringing forth the rainbows that dine on the droplets left behind. Behind the high mountains, the wind blows gently, shaking the glistening raindrops off the leaves of the mahogany and rubber trees.[1] Down there is a lonely hamlet, a great distance from the center of things.

An old woman, crumbling from her years, lives in an old hut in the middle of a deserted field. Her hair is the color of fog and her face is wrinkled and dried, though the center of her eyes still sparkle. But she is in the dusk of her day, over eighty years of age, her body bent over into a widow's hump.[2]

She belongs to the age of grandmothers, without relatives or friends. For many years she has been picking greens in the field and splitting logs to sell for a living. Now she has grown thin and is constantly ill, missing her meals when there is nothing to eat. One day, after recovering from her most recent illness, she craved some rice and *liang* curry, a curry made of the greenest vegetables.[3] So she left her hut to pick some greens. She noticed the *tamlyng* shoots quivering seductively in the wind. At the

---

From *Sangkhomsaat Parithat* 3, no. 4 (1966).

1. In the Thai text, the sound of the words for these trees—*yung* and *yang*—is more important than their botanical identity.

2. Strictly speaking, the widow's hump is an abnormality of aged females. In this instance, grandma's posture may also be the natural result of the constant stooping that is involved in a lifetime of agricultural labor. Although more pronounced in women, the bowed back is a characteristic of the elderly of both sexes in many peasant societies.

3. This curry is particularly favored by the elderly and those who have been recently ill. While tasty, it is also relatively simple to prepare.

moment she was reaching toward the vine to pluck one of the shoots, another shoot spoke out: "Grandma, please pick me first.[4] That shoot there is my younger sister. Wait until tomorrow, and maybe then she'll have something to talk with you about."

Grandma was at first dumbfounded and then perplexed, but she gathered her courage and answered, "Of course, for most people on this earth, there'll be a tomorrow, but for me, today is always the last day. Nothing is certain. Tomorrow morning when the cock crows close to three o'clock maybe I will have breathed my last. I have already come that close, many times. So today I want to eat some *liang* curry to my heart's content."

The tamarind shrub, entering the conversation, asked her, "Do you have any rice?"

"Well, some. I bought about four or five litres[5] a few days ago. But there's only a little more than a litre left, and it's full of weevils. I'll have to pick them out first. By the time the rice is cooked, the night spirits will be out and it will be time to light the torch."[6]

As soon as the old woman finished her words, the yellow papaya, so ripe that it was ready to fall, said in a loud but trembling voice, "Grandma, take this rich and ripe papaya to eat first." Grandma had not yet recovered from her amazement, but she expressed her deepest gratitude to these plants.

The papaya said repeatedly, "Take me first to eat. I have a laxative that will clean your intestines and will make you feel more relaxed.[7] Then you will make yourself forget your concerns and worries, feel in a pleasant frame of mind, enjoy the rainbow of the seven gleaming rays of the morning sun, and wake up early in the morning breathing in the pure and fresh air, welcoming the deity of the new day who will bestow upon you the divine ray of happiness and will prolong your life span. Grandma, you will have a tomorrow that will go on and on for as long as you wish."[8]

---

4. In the Thai text, the term for "grandma" (*yaa* or "father's mother") is intentionally misspelled, both in the title and throughout the essay. The misspelling seems to have one of two purposes: (a) to suggest a person who no longer has any meaning as a distinctive human being or (b) to suggest a creature whose name, while having no meaning in itself, sounds identical to and combines the different spellings of the words "father's mother" and "grass." The author's ambiguity is left for the readers to resolve.

5. Literally, "coconut shells"—a traditional unit of measurement roughly equivalent to a litre. The measurement has not been used for several decades.

6. A traditional, but commonplace, way of referring to dusk.

7. The papaya does indeed contain a proteolytic enzyme which gives the fruit its purgative qualities.

8. The excess of the papaya's language is muted by phrasing that makes the statement sound like a familiar blessing or a message of consolation.

Grandma asked, "Why can plants talk? In earlier days you were so quiet as to be mute. Or perhaps your compassion lies secreted deeply within you. You are able to bring forth your generosity and your magnanimous mercy so that I can feel the delight of the divine power that has revived my strength and vigor."

At that moment, all the plants of the field declaimed in chorus: "Although we share the same world with human beings we are immune to the influence of mankind's basic character and thought, which is composed of selfishness, small-mindedness, and avarice. By no means do we follow the human example of pretense, deception, and intrigue. Other than Grandma, we communicate with nobody. We see that you are deserted and ignored uncompassionately by the rest of mankind. Because of the deep pathos we feel for you, we can no longer refrain from speaking.

"In fact, the deities have bestowed souls[9] on all living things, but we prefer to be mute. Even though we have our own language, we act as if we did not. We sometimes communicate with each other in our own language, but it is too mystifying to be understood by any human being. At first, we thought that Grandma would breathe her last tonight. But we were fortunate to realize that through the intercession of Divine happiness you have regained your strength, prolonging your life much further."

Grandma listened intently, deeply moved by the chorus.

Immediately, the watercress[10] in the pond behind the hut said, "Grandma, I will put forth new, fresh leaves for you to pick and sell every day in the market. In the future there will be more people in this area, so my price will increase. Grandma, proclaim to everyone that watercress is a superb medicine. After eating me, people's eyesight also improves."

The old woman was so touched that tears streamed down her cheeks. She kneeled down, lowered her body, and raising her hands to her forehead to pay respect, she expressed her gratitude to Mother Earth and all the vegetables and plants, saying, "Grandma really doesn't want to be any trouble at all to you."

"When I pick you don't you feel any pain?"

The watercress quivering in the wind laughed and said, "Only the deities in heaven have such exquisite compassion. Grandma, do you think that the gods that created us would have also bestowed upon us the feeling to know pain? The whole world would then be filled with the cries of our mourning and the screams of our agony as a result of the way we are treated every day and night by human beings. We do speak and we

---

9. *Winjaan,* the psychobiological energy that the individual carries through the cycles of reincarnation. In Thai ontology, all creatures that can vocalize have a *winjaan.*

10. *Phakbung,* a Southeast Asian cress, and one of the most tasty and familiar Thai foods.

do feel many things, but this is because of the wondrous power of our souls.

"Fortunately, we plants have a nervous system that does not know pain. If we were any different, the torment and misery would be too great to bear, and we would just die. Come Grandma, please pick me. I am always happy to produce fresh, new leaves."

After that day, the watercress in the pond grew longer and larger, putting forth beautifully more stems and fresh leaves. The old woman picked them to sell at the market, earning enough to pay for her rice and other food and continuing to live in the old hut. Portions of the palm leaf covering the hut were torn, making a hole through which the twinkling stars glittered. The constellation Orion passed in the sky and the frogs and tadpoles croaked melodiously. It was deep into the night.

This time the old woman has been sick with malaria for several days. Her temperature has risen very high, making her deaf in both ears. She feels dizzy and is talking as if delirious in her sleep. The weather has changed and it is hot and humid everywhere. The dark, sad clouds are hiding the moon. The wind blows stronger, becoming more turbulent and shaking the whole country. The trees are like swings swaying in the rain. Flashes of lightning and thunder strike down with a deafening clap that shakes the whole world. The old woman is panic-stricken and loses consciousness. Her body is soaked with rain. After a few hours, the storm tapers off. The sky begins to fill with the silver and golden rays of morning. The joyous chirping of the Boradok birds and Malaysian parrots can be heard clearly in the distance.

She has regained consciousness, but her fever has not abated. Poor dear, she is delirious. She is confused and goes down to pick some watercress. The watercress cries out in warning, "Grandma, don't come down here. There are dangerous snakes near the edge of the pond. They are mating." However, she does not hear the entreating voice and walks on down, straight ahead.

So it happens, in a moment of fate, she steps on the tip of the tail of a vicious cobra. The cobra is startled. It swings around and bites her fully. The fangs are buried into her. She feels a sudden pain at the back of her foot, so she moves to soothe it with her hand. The cobra strikes again, this time at her hand, and she begins to realize that she has been bitten by a snake. Panic-stricken, she loses consciousness, and falls at the edge of the pond. Before long, the deadly poison of the cobra works its way against the current of her bloodstream. In old age, the woman has little resistance. The poison forces itself through the blood into the depth of her heart, bringing her pulse to an end. The old woman breathes her last. But her eyes are still open wide, as if to express her concern for the vegetables, trees, and flowers who are her companions. Their friendship has no comparison.

A portion of the waning moon still shows faintly and then disappears behind the trees. The day is beginning to dawn. The rain has abated some time ago. The air is calm and chilly, creating an atmosphere of solitude and silence, except for the reverberations of nature. Exploding dewdrops crackle on leaves. Only one lingering star still glitters in the immaculate womb of heaven.

For anyone having the power to hear beyond the range of the human ear the sobbing of the trees and flowers in that field would be very clear. The watercress, the papayas, the tamarinds, and the *tamlyng* shoots are all lamenting and weeping.

A tiny flower with a trembling voice said, "Older brothers and sisters, I am so unhappy because I was hoping this morning to bloom into a bright violet flower. If Grandma could have seen my brilliant color it would have helped to relieve her pain. It is so sad."

The *tamlyng* said, "Look at that! An army of fire ants is eating away at the pupils of Grandma's eyes. They are chewing away at her eyes in swarms. In a few days her corpse will rot and swell. The vultures and crows will peck at her body and feed from her flesh. Her bones will be scattered over the soil and sand. It is so pitiful."

After its lamentations, the *tamlyng* again begins to sob until tears come forth from the center of its pure white blossoms. The tears blend with the dew and overflow the petals, as if they are a stream of remorse mourning the death of this old woman who has said farewell to the world and has disappeared forever.

The Wholesome Intention
of *Khunnaaj* Saajbua

Introduction

While many of the selections touch upon aspects of Thai family life, none really focuses upon the joys or satisfactions of family membership. Several in fact see the family situation mainly as a stage for interpersonal conflict (*Naaj Aphajmanii,* "The Enchanting Cooking Spoon," "Social Work") or as the justification for one's ambition ("Paradise Preserved") or deception ("Madame Lamhab"). It is only in "Headman Thuj" and in "Oh! Temple, Temple of Bot!" that we begin to get a suggestion of the pleasures of family life—in the former a sense of the gentle respect that can exist between husband and wife and in the latter a sense of a mother's pride and concern for her endangered son.

In the following story we get a fairly clear picture of how many Thai would like their family relationships to be. Here life together is animated by a clever and gentle repartee among people who simultaneously are emotionally disciplined, relaxed, and self-accepting. This is the kind of narrative that has to be read carefully because the topics of conversation, while in themselves mundane, are couched in a rhetoric that is very precise. It is the attention that the participants give to this rhetoric that demonstrates the affection and respect they have for one another.

There is one aspect of the story about which Thai readers might feel a little equivocal. This has to do with the role of *Khun* Pin as a henpecked husband and whether the role is admirable, realistic, comic, or the like. Many Thai seem to take the position that although in terms of his own interests a husband should always be more *macho* than he is henpecked, as a member of a well-functioning family he should always defer to his inherently more capable and responsible wife. Husbands are assumed to be both more childish and more worldly (and by the same token, less focused on the needs of the family unit) than their wives. In this sense, the portrait of *Khun* Pin is highly realistic. But if realistic, it also conveys a touch of the husband's inevitable ambivalence. Pin says, "I'm a typical Thai man. I like things to go along uneventfully like this. And it's good to have a strict boss. I like to be ordered around. If I have total freedom I'll forget myself and think I'm greater than I am. So let me be liberated only a little bit, not too much. I'm afraid of myself, to tell you frankly." It is the last sentence that indicates Pin's unavoidable nostalgia for the pleasures of freedom, youthful irresponsibility, and masculine narcissism. Although most Thai men resolve their ambivalence quite admirably—some in the same manner as Pin—all recognize it as the abiding problem of the husband-wife relationship. And there are of course others who resolve their ambivalence in the opposite direction.

The story contains many other touches that are equally realistic: the constant reference to money as the currency of both love and interpersonal control; the narrator's admission of resorting to a little white lie to get his mother to pay his train fare, and his easy dismissal of this minor "extortion"; the Thai preoccupation with foods like cured pork and *lamjaj* as symbols of one's concern for those who extend themselves as well as of one's love.

The author of this story, "Mananya," is one of Thailand's most widely read authors, but little is known about her personal or intellectual background. She is a regular contributor to *Satri Sarn,* the nation's largest circulation women's magazine, and is married to an engineer. It is through her husband's work that she has come to know a great deal about dam construction, all of which has provided the context for her famous short-story series "The Dam People."

Readers who might be perplexed by the meaning of the story's penultimate sentence should see the Introduction to Charnvit Kasetsiri's "Big Shots and *Likee.*"

The Wholesome Intention of *Khunnaaj* Saajbua

"MANANYA"

Khunnaaj[1] Saajbua, my mother, has not been to Russia. In fact, being afraid of cold weather, she will never go there in this life.

"And what about in your next life?" I used to jest.

"You just follow me and see for yourself," was the reply.

Even though she does not know Russia, she is, nevertheless, one of those pro-Russians. I say this because she has a thorough knowledge of Russian laws and charters, especially Article 272 of the Great Queen Catherine, which stipulates: "If citizens are happy in every way, the population will increase of its own accord."

That is the reason why she has never let my father enjoy happiness in every way—as owner of his own body, eating and sleeping to his heart's desire. Father, therefore, has had only one son, which is me, and one wife, Mother.

"Poor Father, you will never know how a minor wife differs from a major wife," I used to tease him.

"Well, they're spelled differently. Ha . . . ha."

"But why do you laugh? Don't you miss an opportunity you ought to be enjoying?"

"You want me to cry or something? I bet, too, you would tell your mother on me if I did. You'd say I regret not having the chance to cheat on my wife, wouldn't you?"

"Oh, my! Father! Oh, Father, how would I dare do that to you? But really we can bet on it: if you did have a mistress, Mother wouldn't do

---

From *Satri Sarn* Magazine 28, no. 37 (December 21, 1975): 23–26, from the short-story series entitled "The Dam People."

1. *Khunnaaj* is an honorific used to address or to refer to a married woman of a well-to-do household. It is used in this story with a touch of hyperbole.

anything. Unless you brought her around in broad daylight, there would be absolutely no fuss."

"What?" *Khun* Pin was taken aback.

"Really," I confirmed, "you don't know anything. *Khunnaaj* Saajbua is really very clever. Mother knows that if and when she openly admits that you have a mistress, you'd take advantage of her acceptance and set up a major camp and a minor camp. You would first be good to one camp and then to the other in various ways. If there were two camps, then there would be fighting, even though at first there might not be any. But if from the very beginning Mother doesn't do anything, you would have to hide and wouldn't dare honor your mistress, and then before you'd know it, you'd get fed up with her—and in the end, Mother wouldn't have to waste her energy fighting.[2] And that's why an intelligent man doesn't bring his mistress around to confront *Khunnaaj* and, for the same reason, why a clever *Khunnaaj* doesn't believe people who say her husband has a mistress."

"Hmm." *Khun* Pin eyed me deliberately. "Very well said. Who taught you to say that, really?"

"It's my innate intelligence."

"So that's your problem," sighed my father.

I am clever like my mother. Among all my friends, I am smarter than everyone else; that is to say, smart enough to know that all of them are foolish. If they were not so foolish they would have recognized a long time ago that I'm smart. Right?

Khunnaaj Saajbua has always ruled her husband and son peacefully, and there has never been any attempt to stage a revolution or coup d'etat. Her government follows the axiom: "Let them eat well and live well but have little money."

"It's good enough to live well and eat well. Why do people want so much? Men and money don't get along, anyway. If you let them have a lot of money, they'd no sooner go astray," she used to say.

"This is what women say, isn't it?" I would challenge her.

"I say it. Now what?" *Khunnaaj* raised her voice sharply.

"Nothing," I hastened to deny. "The reason I asked was because the statement sounded good. A person who says something like that is clever, deep, and respectable. . . ."

"How much?"

---

2. Why a man should get fed up with his mistress is by no means clear in the original Thai, although in general it is expected that he will. Some men get fed up with the hassle of constant deception; others are deprived of the status affirmation that the mistress was originally intended to provide; and others are influenced by mistresses who themselves are fed up with being hidden and unhonored. Because sexual prowess is perceived in terms of number of partners, each sexual attachment is expected to pale rather quickly.

"What?"

"I say how much money do you want from me? You don't have to go around flattering me. If I didn't know you I wouldn't be your mother."

"About 300 will do. Hmm, what's this perfume you're wearing? Smells so good."

"It's my own body odor."

So that naturally tames me. Have you ever read a Chinese story about innate power? It contains this proverb: "Above the sky there's more sky; above man still another person." Thus, above Prakob Plengdee [the author as narrator] there is, of course, *Khunnaaj* Saajbua.

Even *Khun* Pin would tell me, "Kob, you learn to be afraid of your mother now, so that in the future it will be natural for you to be afraid of your wife."

"So that means you're also afraid of your wife?"

"Well, yes. What makes you think I'm not afraid of her, Kob?" The volume of his voice increased so that Mother could hear him clearly. "There's an old saying that it's in the nature of a good man to be afraid of his wife."

"Has your stipend been raised yet?" I whispered.

Don't spread it around, mind you. But my father's daily stipend is 15 *baht* 2 *salyng*.[3] While *Khunnaaj* Saajbua pays for his food and all his personal belongings, this 15 *baht* 2 *salyng* is pocket money. In case he wants to go out and eat noodles, he has to pay for it himself. My father is a retired man, and every day he takes a morning walk with some friends. They walk quite a distance, and later, he returns home by bus. So it's 15 *baht* for snacks, and 2 *salyng* for bus fare. See?

Khun Pin smiled foolishly. "Since the bus fare went up, she's given me one more *salyng*. That makes it 15 *baht* 3 *salyng*. And I have to change my money for a bag of *salyng* coins, so in the morning, when she hands me 16 *baht*. I can give her one *salyng*."

"And what does Mother do with that one *salyng*?"

"Collects them until she has accumulated enough to give to me."

"Huh," I sighed. "Don't you ever feel uncomfortable? This is clearly a dictatorship. Revolt. We must revolt if this is the way things are."

"Oh, no. If it fails, she'll be mad and reduce my stipend to 10 *baht,* and that'll be tough on me. Now go away. Go ask someone else, will you?"

He chased me away. "I'm a typical Thai man. I like things to go along uneventfully like this. And it's good to have a strict boss. I like to be

---

3. At the time the story was written, one *baht* equalled 5 U.S. cents and four *salyng* equalled one *baht*. Thus, 15 *baht* 2 *salyng* equalled 77$^{1}/_{2}$ cents.

ordered around. If I have total freedom I'll forget myself and think I'm greater than I am. So let me be liberated only a little bit, not too much. I'm afraid of myself, to tell you frankly."

"Oh, no! How can you say that? That kind of talk doesn't contribute to the progress of the country."

"Well, I'm not obstructing anyone's progress. I'm just telling you that I like it my own way. I'm not trying to recruit any following."

"Oh, how strange," I say to the breeze. "There are many things for him to like, and yet what he likes is being afraid of his wife."

"Well, now, are you just faking this—so I can pass it on to Mother?"

Khun Pin laughed heartily. "I don't know. Why don't you figure it out. You're so smart, aren't you? Remember there are three types of people you smart guys ought not to challenge or displease. First, the Minister of Finance. Second, the Director of the Budget Bureau.[4] And third, your wife."

I nodded, having thoroughly understood. "But if you're thinking about getting more than 16 *baht.* . . . Sorry, I mean going from 15 *baht* 3 *salyng* to 20 *baht,* then that will be tough, very tough. You know full well *Khunnaaj* Saajbua is stingy."

Khunnaaj Saajbua's stinginess is a well-known fact among our circle of relatives. But let's not talk about it, for you would think I gossip about my mother. And I don't want to have to go to hell for this when it isn't necessary.

When she was younger, *Khunnaaj* liked to go to the movies a lot. She never went to Thai movies, though. She said she couldn't stand those cheap stars. Indian movies? She didn't like them either, because their leading actresses had fat bellies and the actors had syrupy eyes. Chinese movies? No, not them either. She only liked *farang* movies during the period when there were stars like John Wayne, Alan Ladd, Rita Hayworth, Ava Gardner, and Clark Gable. I'm talking about the ones I recall; I am not old enough to remember those of earlier periods. The movies at that time were produced by Fox, Paramount, Rank, and Metro, which used a growling lion as its trademark. *Khunnaaj* Saajbua liked Metro movies so much and paid such attention to them that she was able to detect a special secret—that the lion in the Metro titles did not always growl the same way.

"If the lion growls twice, it's a normal, good movie. If it growls three times, it's a very good one. But if it growls four times, that means it's a four-star movie."

"One growl for one star, so to say," *Khun* Pin used to tease her.

---

4. The Ministry of Finance is the ultimate authority on taxes, the Bureau of the Budget on public expenditures.

"That's right," she answered.

"Your lions are strange, Saajbua. I've only heard about Hanuman yawning stars and moon.[5] But this is a lion. It must be supernatural then."

Khunnaaj gave a look of pretended displeasure. "Well, they're symbols after all. Don't you see, unless they growl a bit differently, they shouldn't be there at all."

Khun Pin nodded. "Shall we say you've succeeded in deciphering the hidden meaning? Perhaps I ought to try to interpret the howls of our dog, Muk. One howl means that it has seen an unmarried ghost, two howls for a ghost couple, and tens of howls for a whole department of ghosts."[6]

"There's no such thing as a 'department of ghosts.' There is only a 'pregnancy ghost,' the ghost which threatens a mother with a child in the womb—two people." *Khunnaaj* Saajbua couldn't help arguing.

"I said '*krom*,' not '*klom*.' I mean people from an entire department who have died, from the director-general down to the janitor."

Khunnaaj Saajbua was cross with her husband for many days, and so it was that *Khun* Pin nearly came to suffer a cut in his stipend. It was good that at that time they hadn't as yet been married too long and *Khunnaaj* wasn't all that strict about money. But nonetheless she was rather thrifty and whenever planning to see any movie she first had to get a word or two from people who had already gone as to how many growls (sorry, I mean how many stars) were ascribed to it. For if the lion did it only once or twice, much as she wanted to, she wouldn't go see that movie. But for three growls, she might reconsider.

Then I moved to Lampang. That's when I was assigned to work on the Geu Lom Dam. Once every month or two, I would return home to visit my parents. On each visit, *Khunnaaj* Saajbua fed me and gave me 20 *baht*. Now, that, I tell you, meant a whole lot of love, particularly when compared to the single *salyng* she gave to Beum, son of Grandma Kheo whom she kind of liked. And so I had no choice but to resort to fooling her in order to extort some money, threatening her with the possibility of being fired should I not be able to buy a return train ticket, and so on and so forth. It was the only way to get 100–200 *baht*. Well, what else could I have done? I had to commit some vice. It was too bad, that's all.

So a great deal of time lapsed between one visit and the next, and I didn't really quite know what to bring home. Nobody liked cured pork,

---

5. In the *Ramakian* (the Thai version of the *Ramayana*) only the genuine monkey god, Hanuman, can produce the stars and moon from his mouth with a yawn. False Hanumans always fail this critical test.

6. The baying of dogs at night is typically interpreted as howling at ghosts or malevolent spirits. The mock argument over "department" and "pregnancy" ghosts that follows is a play on words—*tang krom* and *tang klom,* respectively. In ordinary speech Thai do not distinguish between the pronunciation of *r* and *l.*

and *lamjaj* season was rather unpredictable.[7] In some years *lamjaj* were so abundant that one's mouth twitched when one saw them, and in other years, there were very few of them. Anyway, the better ones were all sent to Bangkok, and the northerners were left with second- and third-rate fruit, if not with those that were downright bad. If you brought them on a visit to anybody, your host would wear a peculiar expression on his face, for he'd inevitably think how cheap you were to be bringing such inferior specimens. I ended up with some copies of *Satri Sarn*, which I always brought along, especially the ones with the "Dam People" series in them.[8] However, on seeing them, my father looked a bit apologetic.

"Pa's eyes aren't so good, so I'd better not read, don't you think?"

Rarely would *Khun* Pin refer to himself as "Pa" as in this instance. He must have felt it very necessary to spare my feelings.

Khunnaaj Saajbua sighed and replied curtly, "You must be crazy."

"Oh, Mother. Do take a look at them. I'm a good writer, you know. Even the editor says that a lot of people like my stories."

"Crazy."

How frustrating. Friends at the dam didn't read them, and neither would Father and Mother. Oh, how this hurt! If I never become great and famous, it will be because of this undermining factor—and nothing else. It's what's called an "environmental hazard."

And while I was deeply hurt and on the verge of tears, I happened to come across Boonrawd, an old friend from high school.

He greeted me uproariously, and after a while said, "Hey, guess what? *Khunnaaj* Saajbua came to see me at the printing house four or five days ago."

"Did she? Did she want to print some *kathin* announcement or what?"[9]

"No. She was asking about the printing fee for a small volume, sort of like a pocketbook, about the length of a series that covers twenty-five to thirty stories. What? You mean you didn't know about it?"

"No." I was gaping. "Whose stories?"

"They're yours, stupid! . . . that 'Dam People' series of yours."

"What?"

"It's true. Hey, are you really *Khunnaaj* Saajbua's son? Where have you been? Hasn't she told you?"

"She really hasn't. I've been home three nights, and she hasn't said a word about it. How strange. I wonder what makes her want to sell pocketbooks."

---

7. The *lamjaj* is a small, lychee nut-like fruit grown mainly in northern Thailand. Together with northern cured pork, it is a popular gift item.

8. The magazine in which this story was originally published.

9. A *kathin* is a ceremony involving the giving of new robes to the monks of a particular temple. Participation is usually by invitation.

"She told me she won the fourth or fifth lottery prize or something like that. So she gave away some of that money to make merit and saved a portion to print your book. Gosh! You should have seen her. She could barely part with the cash."

"If it sells I'll be rich . . . ," I started imagining.

"Hey, it's not for sale," Boonrawd hastened to correct me. "It hasn't been printed yet. She advanced the money and signed a contract for me to carry out the printing when the condition is met. She was afraid paper would get more expensive, so she hurried to sign the contract in advance in order to save some money."

"What kind of condition is it? What are you talking about? I really wonder. I don't think *Khunnaaj* Saajbua has ever read any of my stories, so what on earth could have gotten into her now?"

"Even when they're printed, she won't be reading them," Boonrawd replied with a resigned look on his face. "So you think your mother wanted so much to read you stories? Poor you. No, *Khunnaaj* wasn't thinking about making money. She wanted them printed in her honor, and obviously yours as well, and also she will save some money on the copyright fee. She ordered them printed as cremation books, to be given as gifts at her funeral. That's what they're for!"

Concerning *Farang*

Introduction

The following essay is one of the few selections in this book, perhaps the only one, that in the editor's judgment may become a Thai classic—an essay that Thai will read decades and perhaps centuries from now for what it says about the nature of Thai thought and experience in the mid-twentieth century. Its "classical" nature derives from the fact that for all its simplicity (its relaxed spirit and intentional silliness) it is in actuality an extremely complex document that at one time succeeds at several different levels.

At the most obvious, it is a "shaggy dog" story about the eccentric ways of Westerners. The criticism is gentle and friendly, poking almost as much fun at fellow Thai as it does at Occidentals. The civility of the criticism reflects the general atmosphere of the early 1960s when *farang* were still something of an oddity and well before the full weight of the American military presence had come down upon Thailand. The entire spirit of the essay is quite different from that expressed in "Paradise Preserved," "A Day in the Life of Pat," or "The Paradise of the President's Wife"—all of which were written considerably later.

At a different level, the selection is not so much about *farang* as it is an exercise in the use of suggestion and connotation in verbal discourse. This is a communicative mode which all Thai enjoy and at which many excel. What is extraordinary about Vasit's essay is that from the title to the final paragraph it is an almost uninterrupted, if meandering, stream of intentional polysemantic messages.

The author uses suggestion in at least two ways to create his multiple meanings. First, of course, he uses puns and also triple and even quadruple entendres. The second method is less formal and involves using words and phrases that, although seemingly innocent, suggest a train of thought indicating a violation of what is culturally reasonable or seemly.

It is this violation of the culturally expectable that lies at the basis of all verbal humor. This is also the reason that translations of humor from one cultural setting to another so frequently fall flat; the readers of the translated version do not have a sufficiently clear conception of the culturally expectable to recognize that a violation has occurred.

The author's use of suggestion points to still another feature of the essay, that is, that beneath its gentle satire and its playful use of language there is in fact a serious and specific message. The message is shrouded in allusion and circumlocution, but its meaning and logic are clear to any Thai reader. It is encapsulated in the latent meanings of the paragraph discussing the "reciprocal relationships" between Thai and *farang,* which is the only paragraph in the entire essay actually without any word play.

The message is that, despite all their comic attributes and despite our uncertainty about why, the *farang* are in Thailand only because there is something here they want. In order to obtain that something (whatever it is) they have to give something in return. It is inherent to any process of exchange that the parties risk being cheated, shortchanged, or otherwise made to suffer, thus making things more serious, responsible, and anxiety-laden than we might prefer. Thai and *farang* have to be very careful when dealing with one another. This is the inevitable result of history having brought us together.

This essay was the lead article in a collection of the author's work entitled *Miscellany.* Neither the original essay nor the later collection indicate a date of publication, although contextual considerations suggest that the collection was being sold in 1962. For biographical information on the author, see the short story "Social Work."

Concerning *Farang*

Vasit Dejkunjorn

In using the word *farang*—which will appear here rather frequently—I do not mean the fruit that, like a mummy, is sometimes destined for pickling or that in other cases is dipped into salt, but rather a group of human beings who, not born in Thailand, came here to live and do their thing.[1] And these *farang* came in many different ways. Some came by boat. Some came by flying machine. (Machines that fly?) It is possible that some used their feet[2] to get here from their homelands, but from my several years of studying history, I have never heard of any doing it this way. And since communication and transportation in these modern times are really more convenient than in the time of Father Ramkhamhaeng,[3] I am confident that there is no *farang* who would be so eccentric as to walk to Thailand from America or Europe, even though such an accomplishment would mark him as the most persevering person in the whole world.[4]

From *Saphaehaerakhadii* (Bangkok: Phadungsyksaa Press, ca. 1960).

1. *Farang* has two meanings: guava and Occidentals. Historically, the latter meaning derives from the Thai pronunciation for "franc" or "Frenchmen." Thai distinguish *farang* from Indians, Negroes, Chinese, Japanese, and "others." Ordinarily no distinction is made among types of *farang,* although if context demands, distinctions can be made on national grounds, e.g., Americans, Englishmen, Italians, etc. Since the pickled guava is one of the tastiest of all Thai foods and a mummy is something weird and discomforting, this image, while descriptively possible, is emotionally ludicrous.

2. "To use one's feet" as contrasted with "to walk" is to do something vulgar and coarse. As indicated elsewhere in this essay, *farang* have a tendency to use their feet for purposes other than walking.

3. King Ramkhamhaeng was the greatest king of Thailand's founding dynasty.

4. While perseverance is one of our most desirable human traits, to persevere at something that is not inherently worthwhile or that can be better accomplished by some other means is simply comical. Only Faustian (and funny) *farang* would entertain the thought of there being value in such a walk.

In earlier times, it was difficult to find *farang*. (As I indicated earlier, I am talking about the human *farang,* not the fruit. Therefore, the sentence did not read "it was difficult to find *farang* even as ingredients for medicine," because if it were phrased this way,[5] it would probably cause some misunderstanding. The words might be misinterpreted to mean that we are like a bunch of cannibals who cut up *farang* and use them in our medicine, perhaps creating some panic among those *farang* who are able to read Thai.) The reason that it was difficult to find *farang* in earlier times was because the communications that existed in those times were really not too convenient. Those who wanted to come to Thailand from the European continent had to spend several nights—even months or years—on small ships. And if they came during the wrong season,[6] they might have had to leave their ships and swim all the way from the tip of the Malay Peninsula to Thailand and do this without ever having intended to set records in the freestyle, the breaststroke, or the backstroke.[7] On top of that, after finally arriving in Thailand, they would be most disappointed in finding only a small country, not yet civilized,[8] with no obvious way of producing a profit that was worth the labor that was used in swimming here. And if their purpose in coming here was to propagate religion—well, the Thai people they would meet have such absolute faith and belief in Buddhism that they think the missionaries of other religions are some kind of phenomena from outer space.[9]

Bringing this up to date, we can see that nowadays communication between Thailand and other places around the world is much more convenient and quicker. Even though some *farang* might not recognize why it is important for them to come to Thailand, they keep coming here and just pile up. At first, some of them came only as tourists for fun while others came on commercial and private business. But after they were

5. The phrase "to find something even as ingredients for medicine" is a familiar Thai simile for describing—and exaggerating—the difficulty of finding that thing. It means that the thing is so rare and desirable that it is impossible to find even the infinitesimal amount of it that is necessary for the making of Thai medicine. In this context, the assertion that the simile is not used clearly has the additional purpose (over and above the comic purpose presented in the text) of suggesting a put-down of Occidentals, e.g., that in comparison to pickled guava, human *farang* are not sufficiently desirable to have the simile applied to them.

6. Monsoon season, when shipwrecks are most likely to occur.

7. Once more, this is an attack on the faustian pretensions of *farang,* those strange people who would use swimming as a means of proving themselves. Using one's energy to set swimming records makes as much sense as walking from America to Thailand.

8. This is a Thai transliteration of the English word "civilized," and in this context it is intended as wry nonsense.

9. The original Thai here resists precise translation. This American colloquialism is an approximation of the author's meaning but should not be taken literally.

here, more and more of them said to themselves, "This Thailand is much better than I[10] first thought it was." As for how it is better or where it is better . . . well, you will just have to ask those *farang*. I am a Thai, so how would I know?[11] I only know that right now Thailand is jammed with *farang*. They are all over the place. There are the *Farang U No, I Don't No.*[12] *Farang U Nak, I Baw.*[13] *Farang E CAFE. E GoGo, E Oleang.*[14] *Farang* FAO, *Farang* ECA, *Farang* IOU,[15] and many, many other *farang*—except of course the pickled *farang* and the *farang* that is dipped into chili and salt. (As indicated earlier, I am talking about the *farang* that are human beings.)

On the Thai side of things—well, there are Thai who have made a hobby out of parading through *farang* countries. Counting down from the ministers, there are the ministers' wives, the ministers' children, the ministers' servants, the wives of the ministers' servants, the children of the ministers' servants, the servants of the ministers' children, the wives of the servants of the ministers' children, the children of the servants of the ministers' children, the children of the children of the servants of the

---

10. This is a Thai transliteration of the English word "I." Its Thai spelling means "coughing."

11. This is the characteristic Thai statement of false modesty. However, it is unclear from the context whether the author is satirizing false modesty or is simply being falsely modest.

12. In the original text, these words are written as Thai transliterations of English language sounds. The English sounds, however, have two different, but related, meanings: (1) if written, *"U No, I Don't No,"* the *"U"* and *"No"* are the perfect Thai pronunciation for "UNO," the acronym for "United Nations Organization" (before the word "Organization" was dropped); (2) if written, "You Know, I Don't Know," the words describe the relationship that obtained (facetiously or otherwise) between UN experts and Thai. The author obviously intended both meanings—irrespective of how they are spelled.

13. *"U Nak, I Baw"* has four simultaneous meanings: (1) it is a partial reduplication of the previous play on words, the *"U"* and *"N"* sound of *"U Nak"* here representing "United Nations"; (2) because Thai attend to final consonants as much as they do to initial consonants, the *"U"* and *"K"* sounds of *"U Nak"* refer to the familiar acronym for "United Kingdom"; (3) at its most literal, it means "you are heavy, I am light"; (4) but at a slightly more latent level, it means "you take a crap, I take a piss."

14. The sound "E" is an expletive, *cafe* is the Thai word for "coffee," and ECAFE is the acronym for "Economic Commission for Asia and the Far East," a major UN agency headquartered in Bangkok. *GoGo* is the Thai word for "cocoa" and also the name of the popular cabaret dance of the early 1960s. *Oleang* is Thai-Chinese iced coffee.

15. In this sequence, these acronyms sound exactly like a Thai schoolboy voicing his English alphabet lesson. "FAO" refers to the UN Food and Agricultural Organization; "ECA" refers to the Economic Cooperation Administration, a U.S. government agency; and "IOU" is the familiar symbol for a debt, well known to educated Thai.

ministers' children, and so on and so forth, down to those Thai who have no relationship at all with the ministers—either straight relationships or crooked ones.

It could be said that the Thai and *farang* have worked out a system of reciprocal relationships wherein they each depend upon one another, albeit somewhat chaotically. *Farang* money comes into Thailand and Thai money goes out to *farang* countries. But I don't know whether more goes out than comes in or vice versa. Even if I knew, I would not know how to help either side, other than to feel anxious and worried, but that's the way fate is.

Concerning *farang,* it is widely acknowledged that they are owners of bodies that are taller and larger than those of the Thai. Their bearing, way of walking, and way of talking has a certain elegance and grandeur that makes them seem more awesome than the Thai.[16] For example, they carry their chests higher than we do and when they walk they swing their arms in a shorter arc. But the stride of their legs is longer and when they speak their voices are deeper. If a Thai with an ordinary build were to try to imitate these body movements and were to meet another Thai with the same kind of build, the second person would probably think to himself, "What a swaggering show-off!" But if the second person were larger and more muscular than the first, he might call out loud for all to hear, "What a bloody fool that swaggering show-off is!" and even add a few curses at the end of his exclamation—depending of course on circumstances. This is probably the reason why we rarely find Thai imitating the *farang* way of walking, talking, and gesturing.[17]

Since so many people consider the *farang* style of acting to be attractive, I decided to try to find out what aspects of *farang* behavior are considered unappealing or not so pleasant to look at. I interviewed many people who I thought would have answers to these questions. The answers I received were very similar, but they were almost never to the point. For example, one answer was: "Whatever the *farang* way of appearing and acting is, it is always smart[18] and awesome." Another answer was: "The *farang* cannot rival the Thai—when it comes to beautiful cats and clever thieves." Some people answered by referring to the

---

16. This statement is intended to be both patently true and latently ironic, e.g., while the *farang*'s body is in size and carriage indeed impressive, it is potentially the body of the clumsy klutz.

17. Lest the *farang* reader misunderstand, this illustration of the show-off getting his comeuppance from the bully is not intended as a jab against Thai character. It is rather a simple statement of Thai realism and perhaps even Thai justice.

18. While this is written as a transliteration of the English word "smart," the word has in fact been incorporated into the Thai language where it explicitly means "stylish" or "attractive," as in "smart dresser."

dredge *Manhattan* and to Madsen guns,[19] neither of which has anything to do with the question, but all of which made me wonder whether the people who were answering were crazy.

Finally, I found someone who answered the question most directly. This was Mr. Prachakraa Bunnag.[20] He is not somebody particularly important, and he is not the kind of person whom I thought would have a knowledgable answer to the question. If you are wondering about his importance . . . well, he is about as important as I am. And if you are wondering about how knowledgable he is . . . well, he is not any more knowledgable than I am. The thing is that while we have cooperated in duping other people, the two of us have also cooperated in being duped.

When I asked him, "What is it about *farang* that is not appealing?" he answered, "When they still have not been peeled and are green and bitter."

"Hey . . . I am talking about *farang* that are people."

"Oh. . . ."

That "Oh . . ." went on and on. He had stopped to think as he took a long breath. Fortunately, the thought ended before he suffocated.

I repeated my question: "C'mon. Answer me."

"Oh, *farang* . . . (he finally decided), they are not appealing when they *farang ramthaw*."[21]

---

19. The *Manhattan* was a U.S. naval vessel given to the Thai government after World War II (and which actually played a role in an attempted coup d'etat in 1952) while the Madsen is a make of Scandinavian machine gun well known in Thailand because of its role in some coups d'etat.

20. A well-known friend of the author.

21. The original Thai text here permits three different translations, and thus three different meanings: (1) If translated "when *farang ramthaw*," it means "when Westerners dance," which is meant to suggest that they are unattractive when clumsy; (2) if translated "when like *farang*, they *ramthaw*," it means "when like *farang*, they use their feet in a coarse, vulgar fashion—throwing them onto desks when relaxing, using them to point at things, and the like"; (3) if translated "when they do the *farang ramthaw*," it means "when they do the classical Thai dance 'The Foot Dancing *Farang*'," which is a special double entendre. Unlike most Thai classical dance, which emphasizes hand gestures, this particular song emphasizes (as does all *farang* dancing) the use of the feet; in fact, the song takes its name from that bit of *farang* reality. Thus, for *farang* to do the *farang ramthaw* is to have them imitating us imitating them.

My Dog Is Missing

Introduction

The following soliloquy by M. R. Khukrit Pramoj is the only selection in this book that is included more for what it says about the author and his role in Thai society than for its substantive intellectual content. However, it is a measure of Khukrit's intellectual stature that almost two decades after the essay was first published, it is remembered by many Thai readers almost as much for its moral message as for what it revealed about Khukrit himself.

Thai commentators have often pointed out that the name "Khukrit" is unique in Thailand, having no precedent in Thai history and being shared with no other living person. The same is true about Khukrit's social position and public character. On the one hand, he is, with the exception of the members of the royal family, the single most renowned member of Thai society. On the other hand, he is a man of extraordinary personal complexity. But above all, he is a man of exceptional talent, having taken on a panoply of unrelated activities and having apparently excelled at all.

At various points in his life he has been prime minister, deputy finance minister, and member of parliament; chairman of a constitutional convention and principal author of the resulting Thai Constitution (1974); publisher of Thailand's most influential newspaper and weekly magazine (*Siam Rath* and *Siam Rath Sabdaa Wichaan*); pundit, columnist, radio commentator, TV panel discussant, and adviser on workaday problems; university instructor and lecturer; economist and banker (Bangkok Bank of Commerce); hotel owner (Indra); Hollywood actor (the prime minister in the film *The Ugly American*); professional Thai dancer; photographer; horticulturalist; and the author of more than thirty books. Although the bulk of the latter are compilations of his advice columns (*Panhaa Pracamwan* [Problems of everyday life]), radio commentaries (*Phyan Nauaun* [Your bedtime friend]), and social and political essays

(*Caag Naa Haa Nangsyyphim Siam Rath* [From page five of the *Siam Rath*]), they also include five novels, an essay in religious and philosophical analysis (*Huang Mahanop* [The vast expanse], 1959), two travel accounts (on Japan and Cambodia), as well as historical satire and fiction. Unfortunately, only one of Khukrit's numerous works has to date been successfully translated into English. This is *Phai Daeaeng*, 1955, or Red *Bamboo*, 1961, a novel that describes the relationship between a Buddhist abbot and a local Communist, his lifelong friend.

Some of Khukrit's accomplishments may be as much a function of the structure of Thai society as they are of his own talent, that is, it is obviously easier for a monied, Oxford-educated member of royalty to establish a first-rate newspaper when his competition is concerned almost exclusively with crime, sex, and yellow journalism. However, some of Khukrit's other accomplishments bespeak a man of truly uncommon gifts. Thus, one of his novels, *Sii Phaeaendin* [Four reigns], 1954, is universally regarded as Thailand's greatest literary creation of this century. A two-volume, fictionalized account of life at court from the reign of King Chulalongkorn to the reign of King Ananda, it is at one level a description of the intrigues, loves, food habits, vanities, and sensitivities of the nobility during this final period of "premodern" Thailand. But at another level, the novel lays out the character of a woman, Maeae Phloy, who although completely a fictional creation, may well be the most famous woman in Thai history. She is the prototypic Thai mother: magnanimous, realistic, forgiving, practical, and always loving. Her role in Thai thought is perhaps equivalent to that of Emma Bovary in the French tradition or of Anna Karenina in Russian culture, although the details of her character are completely different from these other heroines. Maeae Phloy is probably also special because she was created in unedited installments approximately one hour before the daily typesetting deadline of Khukrit's newspaper.

Proper historians will eventually judge M. R. Khukrit's place in Thai political and economic history. However, a few words should be said here about his contributions to Thai intellectual life, in which he has been the dominant figure for more than a quarter of a century.

First, although the role is deeply rooted in Thai culture and has been performed by others, few have been as successful as Khukrit in recruiting and supporting those numerous individuals who themselves were to become central figures in Thailand's intellectual and literary leadership. Khukrit gave them their start, employed them, and cultivated them. Among the people included in this book, Vasit Dejkunjorn and Suchit Wongthed are particularly prominent. Prajuun Chanyaawong, Thailand's foremost political cartoonist, and 'Rong Wongsawaan, who wrote extensively about the emotional dimensions of sex (and who later also acted as publisher of some of Khukrit's own writings), were both in his employ for several years. Another such person was Prayad S. Naa Khanaad, the kingdom's most accomplished Thai language newspaper editor.

Some observers have argued that it was also very much in Khukrit's character to have eventually squabbled with all but one of these persons and to have either discharged them or, through their own assertions of independence, to have lost their loyalty.[1] It is the editor's view that this is less a consequence of Khukrit's character than it is an inherent attribute of any Thai situation requiring creative and imaginative people to defer to authority, particularly an authority that is just as imaginative and obdurate as they. There are ample precedents from Thai history of this kind of conflict, such as the relationship between Sunthorn Phuu, Thailand's greatest nineteenth-century poet, and Rama II who, in addition to being king (1809–1824), was a poet of considerable accomplishment. (Khukrit is in fact a direct descendant of Rama II and holds his royal title, *Momraachawong,* by virtue of his ties to this monarch; equally important, he considers his ancestor one of his great literary models.) There are numerous other people who over the years have maintained their loyalty to Khukrit, but they tend to be viewed more as typical Thai sycophants (see Khamsing Srinawk's "Paradise Preserved") than as persons of intellectual or literary distinction.

In contrast to this interpersonal influence, M. R. Khukrit's contributions to Thai literature are much more difficult to assess. As suggested earlier, *Sii Phaeaendin* may well be read for decades, and perhaps centuries, as much for being a source of historical information on the court as for its characterization of Maeae Phloy as the idealized woman and mother. It is also the most unself-consciously "Thai" of all of Khukrit's fictional efforts in that it describes things like malevolent supernatural spirits *(phii)* and baroque family jealousies in totally ingenuous terms, as if the author were simply gossiping with his readers over a backyard fence.

M. R. Khukrit's other fictional efforts seem somewhat more contrived. The best known of these is probably *Phai Daeaeng (Red Bamboo)* —its fame being based upon its politically phrased subject matter and on the fact that it was translated into English. The story is avowedly a Thai version of the Don Camillo situation created by Giovanni Guareschi and made even more famous by the late French actor, Fernandel, who played the role of the Italian Catholic priest in a series of films produced during the 1950s. The story's familiarity to Westerners and its political overtones are probably what made Khukrit's version so eminently translatable.

In the Thai story, the Catholic priest has become Bhikku Krang, the Buddhist abbot of a Central Plain village temple. Born and reared in the community, Krang is a natural leader who wears yellow robes—a relaxed, self-confident person full of wit and sarcasm but with genuine compassion for the stupidity and incompetence of his fellow men. Unlike the Italian situation, the protagonist in the story is not a Communist mayor (since, as Khukrit notes, there has never been a Communist mayor in Thailand, "at least not yet"), but rather his lifelong friend, Kwaen, who is considered by district authorities to be a Communist. Kwaen is a Communist because he calls himself one, but, more importantly, he is a man who mucks up most of the things he touches: he has failed numerous attempts to pass his examinations and advance his career in Bangkok; he all but loses his patrimony; and he is a most ineffective leader of those villagers he had tried to recruit to his Communist ways. Part of the relationship between Krang and Kwaen is based upon the former trying to divert his childhood friend from his wayward and dangerous ideas.

Although most of this is presented by Khukrit in a delightful, non-ideological manner, there is no doubt that one of the morals of the story is that Communists are social failures who blame society for their own inadequacies, while ordinary Thai villagers are men of tolerance, wit, and understanding who have the opportunity of increasing their goodness by becoming monks. While there is both amusement and logic to this argument, it is obviously a bit too contrived to be intellectually persuasive. On the other hand, in 1955 when the book was first published, the category "Communists" typically referred to people about whom almost nothing was known but who were imagined to be monsters, and this account at least helped to redefine the category and give such persons some humanity, reality, and even a bit of foolishness.

M. R. Khukrit's third intellectual contribution has undoubtedly been his most important, at least in terms of his impact on Thai society as a whole. This has been his role as social commentator, critic, advice giver, and general observer of the Thai experience. He has been so successful in this role that over the years he has come to be addressed as *aacaan* ("teacher") by many of his readers, and he has also spawned a few imitators—but none who has ever become a viable rival.

He started responding to readers' questions in his column, "Problems of Everyday Life," almost immediately after *Siam Rath* began publishing in 1950, and since that time he has addressed virtually every major issue confronting Thai society. Known much more for his panache than for his consistency, he has both praised and condemned almost all of the nation's recent political leaders, institutions, allies, and enemies; like Abigail Van Buren ("Dear Abby") in the United States, he has advised people suffering from an extraordinary variety of personal and interpersonal problems; and he has interpreted the most recondite points of Buddhist canon. While at times he writes and thinks off the top of his head ("My mother used to say that I could never stop prattling"), at other times he does precise and thorough research.

Khukrit has addressed so many different issues in so many varying ways that some Thai claim it is impossible to identify in his writing any overarching positions to which he is genuinely committed. While there is some truth to this judgment—if only because his forte is in responding dramatically to a particular situation, not in propounding ideological principles—there are nevertheless certain themes that do appear repeatedly in his work. Thus, his love and respect for the monarchy has over the years been undeviating. However, in contrast to those conservatives who view the monarchy primarily as a sacred symbol and who thus approach it with a fawning sense of awe, he writes like a man who, because he has known monarchs personally, feels trusting and comfortable about them. He gives kings a sense of human proportion that many other Thai are simply too nervous to acknowledge.[2]

Of a totally different order is his concern for nature and its creations: rivers, crickets, flowers, trees, and small animals. Although it was not intentional, it is probably not fortuitous that the two essays by Khukrit appearing in this book should focus on these kinds of matters. The callow Westerner might consider a lost dog a somewhat maudlin issue, but to Khukrit it is the perfect way to talk about the ultimate existential loneliness of man and the alienating qualities (including those that are self-inflicted) of Thai life.

Still different from either of the above is Khukrit's abiding interest in democracy, or in the ultimate sovereignty of the electorate. While the interest has obviously been whetted by his own political ambitions of the past decade, it predates this period by several years. In a very real sense, one of his major aims in founding the *Siam Rath* publications was to educate, explain, propagandize, and cajole the Thai public into undertaking their sovereign responsibilities.[3]

Yet, when all is said and done, the most memorable thing about M. R. Khukrit is not the content of his intellectual positions but rather his unique style or panache. There are many elements to this style: his unpredictability; his rhetorical richness; his willingness to turn against constituents or friends (e.g., overly self-righteous students) on matters of principle; his readiness to express in public certain emotions (anger, depression), which most Thai keep in check; and, above all, his insistence upon hearing only his own very different drummer.

The key to Khukrit's intellectual style is probably the very same factor that made him into a professional actor and dancer—the tendency, shared by many performers, to perceive life itself as a sequence of scenes to which one must always respond effectively and, it is hoped, dramatically and memorably. This in no way is meant to imply that he behaves in a dissembling manner; on the contrary, many of his beliefs are as profoundly held as they are demonstratively conveyed. However, it is meant to suggest that in an interpersonal or public situation, he is constantly "on"—that whatever his sincerity or commitment, he is also trying to be aware of what is happening, how effectively he is communicating, what his impact on his audience might be, and how he can better leave his mark upon them and on the passing situation. As a psychological process, it bespeaks an extraordinary degree of subtlety, quickness, and self-confidence—although never arrogance, since its aim is to affect situations and people not to control them. It is also a position that assumes that others are just as willful, clever, and resistant as oneself.

The following essay is a brief, but famous, example of Khukrit's panache. Needless to say, despite his remonstrations, he later went on to write other essays and to achieve "rank, admiration," and "even the love and understanding" of his countrymen when he was elected prime minister just a few years later. However, these factors are incidental to the essay's real point: to convey to Thai readers that even the most eminent among them suffer the most basic and natural deprivations and, more important, that it is not improper to acknowledge one's emotional distress by sharing it with others. The latter is not so much a case of wearing one's heart upon one's sleeve as it is an attempt to educate the public in the propriety and nonthreatening nature of emotional honesty and directness. Khukrit is essentially saying that to admit one's unhappiness or temporary professional impotence is just as human, and thus ultimately as meaningful, as admitting to all those other emotions—"ambition, . . . rank, admiration, fortune, or even the love and understanding of my fellow men"—that many Thai often drive themselves to experience. While this might seem simple and obvious as an analytic statement, it is much more than that as a cultural and moral proposition—if only because Khukrit is presenting it to readers who have considered the only acceptable public sentiments to be ones like strength, dignity, coolness, eloquence, humor, and the like. In other words, he is arguing in a most stylish way for the legitimacy of emotional expressions that are not at all in style.

The power of his message derives, of course, from the fact that he focuses directly upon himself and his own inner states, about which, in this instance, there is nothing to be gained in falsifying. Too, there is a critical "reality factor" that adds tenability to his statement, that is, most of his readers are aware that at the time he wrote the essay he was living alone, having been separated from his wife and his adult children for several years. While this situation afforded him the freedom and scope to pursue his numerous professional interests, it probably also resulted in personal isolation and real emotional privation. Under the circumstances, it is not at all surprising that he should become so deeply attached to his dog. M. R. Khukrit is in fact confirming his readers' suspicions and acknowledging that even those with eminence, talent, and panache must pay the price.

NOTES

1. The exception is Vasit Dejkunjorn, who very early in his career went into police work and, with no further workaday links to Khukrit, found it both easy and gratifying to maintain a cordial relationship and a sense of idealized obligation toward his former patron. That Vasit was ultimately to have a patron even more powerful than M. R. Khukrit, e.g., the king, is also not irrelevant.

2. This point is developed further in a splendid paper by Roger Kershaw, 1980; see Bibliography.

3. An analyst of the Thai political scene disagrees with the thrust of this judgment and argues that during the late 1960s and early 1970s Khukrit's writings in *Siam Rath* demonstrate a clear anti-parliament bias and a position supportive of the authoritarianism of the military regime. The problem here is the question of the consistency or inconsistency of Khukrit's thinking or even whether the notion of "constancy" is relevant to Khukrit's approach to politics. The comments here on Khukrit's "pro-democratic" sentiments reflect his own self-image as explicitly expressed to the editor during extended interviews in 1965. They are also part of his explanation of why he founded the *Siam Rath*. Most importantly, they are verified a decade later during Khukrit's tenure as prime minister when he headed the most democratically oriented government to rule Thailand since 1946. None of this is to deny that during the interim decade of the late 1960s–early 1970s Khukrit may have also been disenchanted with the democratic process.

Perhaps all of this is related to the rhythm of Khukrit's actual participation in democratic politics. Although it is usually omitted from his list of achievements, Khukrit was in fact the founder of the first political party in the history of Thailand, the Progressive Party *(Phaak Kaawnaa)* that came into being in 1946 and was soon changed into the Democrat Party that was lead by his older brother, M. R. Seni Pramoj, and Nai Khuang Aphaiwongse. It was when this change took place that Khukrit relinquished his participation in democratic politics, not to return for almost three decades until in the mid-1970s he created the Social Action Party, under whose banner he became prime minister.

My Dog Is Missing

M. R. Khukrit Pramoj

My dog is missing.

A black, Thai dog. Male. Thirteen months old. Answers to the name "Sii Mawk."[1]

It is nothing extraordinary and it is probably of no importance to anyone.

But I am more miserable than I can express.

Long ago I rejected ambition.

Long ago I stopped thinking of rank, admiration, fortune, or even the love and understanding of my fellow men.

Long ago I lost interest in the gossip and criticism about me and stopped being afraid of the threats and menacing acts of others. Each day I think of doing things that are useful only to others and not to myself. The loneliness of my heart is beyond measure . . . because I am still only an ordinary human being.

One black dog. He alone made my loneliness bearable.

Every time I went out, he was there to see me off, and whenever I returned home, he was there to welcome me. When I was at home, he would stay close to me. He is the only thing I felt close to. When I was away from home, I would always have the feeling that there was something waiting for me at home that loved me and trusted me without conditions.

Originally published in *Siam Rath,* December 11, 1968; reprinted in *Caag Naa Haa Nangsyyphim Siam Rath* [From page five of the *Siam Rath*] (Bangkok: 'Rong Wongsawaan and His Young Friends Publishing Co., July 1970).

1. "Sii Mawk" literally means "the color of misty fog," but more importantly, it is the name of *Khun* Phaeaen's miraculous horse in the great epic of the eighteenth–nineteenth century, *Khun Chang, Khun Phaeaen.* Most of Khukrit's readers are aware of his special fondness for *Khun* Phaeaen. In fact, Khukrit's famous home in the Sathorn Road area of Bangkok is designed to be a replica of *Khun* Phaeaen's home.

The house was more of a home because of him.

At least there was something reaching my heart, making me feel that I was a human being and not something made of brick and mortar.

On Monday, the ninth of this month, someone, not knowing what he was doing, took my dog into his car for a drive to Bangkapi without letting me know.

The dog got excited and jumped out of the car on Sukhumvit Road between Soi 14 and Soi 22. The search was in vain.

From that morning on, I could neither eat nor sleep. I could do nothing and think of nothing.

I already knew that separation from a loved one meant suffering.

But when that separation happens to oneself, one is incapable of suppressing one's feelings.[2]

I did not want anything or hope for anything that people usually want. I wanted only to keep a dog, a dog that was in no way exceptional or expensive.

And I could not safely keep even this little thing.

What causes me so much anguish is knowing that the dog must be suffering as much as or more than I am. He must be trembling in fright because he has been separated from his beloved owner.

Because he is a dog, he has no way to know or to understand Lord Buddha's teaching: *"Biiyehii Wiibayokhoo Thukkhoo"* or "separation from the loved one is suffering."

If I knew he was already dead, I would have to reconcile myself to the inevitable and accept it.

But I just don't know.

So in one stroke, I have lost my ties to life, because what was already there was just a thin web. One slight yank and it snapped.

I am writing all of this not to ask for anybody's help and not out of the hope that I will be given sympathy or pity.

The matter is too trivial and also no one can do anything for me.

I have written this because I do not know what else to write about.

And I probably will not have the wit to write anything again for a long time.

If I do write, I will have to force myself.

And if I have to force myself to write something, it is the same as writing nothing.

So it is better not to write at all.

---

2. This and the preceding sentence have reference to the Buddhist premise that if one knows the cause and effect of things, one should be able to handle a situation more effectively, including one's own emotional responses. The premise is made more explicit in the Buddhist teaching cited later in the text.

Madame Lamhab

Introduction

In Thailand, as everywhere else on earth, people sometimes use their language in such a stylized way that the message they are communicating seems virtually programmed; a listener can almost predict what a speaker is going to say, how he is going to say it, what the sequence or contrasts of his utterances are likely to be, and, above all, what his intent is.

The following "interview" is an extraordinary example of just such communication. Although fictional in nature (only the place "Phayao District, Chiengrai Province," is real), every Thai has known or encountered a woman like Madame Lamhab. In this situation, Madame Lamhab's purpose is to present herself to others—and equally important, to herself—as a decent, constrained, sometimes witty, but always supportive wife and mother. Her overwhelming concern is to act and to think like a *phuu dii*—literally, a "good person," but more precisely a person of civility, propriety, and dignity. Traditionally, *phuu dii* were members of a rank of land-owning elite, but in this century the term has come to refer to a behavioral style, a manner of carrying and presenting oneself, rather than to a social position.

While men are also *phuu dii* (they are just, gentle, and authoritative), the cultural conception of a *phuu dii* is more fully developed in the case of women. In fact, many of the novels of Daukmaajsod, Thailand's greatest female author of this century, are adumbrations of the many facets of the female *phuu dii*.

Madame Lamhab is a *phuu dii* not only because she strives for goodness and claims her goodness, but because she also reveals small touches of personal honesty, intelligence, and self-effacement. She does not try to conceal her lowly village background but acknowledges it and builds upon it. Because she is, like all *phuu dii,* an excellent conversationalist, her speeches, for all their aphoristic predictability, demand the listener's attention. They even have a certain contrapuntal quality as she moves back and forth between self-praise (her bright son and dedicated husband) and self-criticism (her not-so-bright middle daughter). That her admiration should fall on her men and her regret on a daughter is also very much on target. Throughout her presentation, she asserts self-confidence and self-acceptance, although never to excess; these qualities are always subservient to her concern with morality and integrity.

As acknowledged by the author in the last few lines, the central issue of this story is whether Madame Lamhab is telling the truth. From a Thai point of view, this issue is exceedingly subtle. While it would be easy to say that in her lengthy declarations on all the terrible things that she and her husband do not do she is simply protesting too much and is thus dissembling, it would be just as accurate to say that she carries on in this manner because she is enraptured by the sound and power of her own words and the effectiveness of her social posture. From a Thai point of view, it is the persuasiveness of this kind of theatrical performance—and not the truth or falsehood of her words and the realities that they reflect or conceal—that is perhaps most important. Even her occasional touches of seemingly genuine self-effacement and honesty contribute to the overall effectiveness of the performance. At the end, the author simply refuses to resolve the question of truth or falsehood and leaves it both to his characters and to his readers to make their own judgments. That these judgments should be as attentive to the quality of Madame Lamhab's stagecraft as they are the question of her integrity is underscored by Bunmyy's final remark, "Isn't it good that there is a person like Madame Lamhab?" She has given us all a lesson in the problematic nature of the verbal world.

Some lesser points in the story should perhaps be noted. Madame Lamhab's initial confusion about the interview would not be unusual in any society. However, in Thailand this kind of confusion is particularly true to life. In novel encounters with strangers many Thai are likely to feel a tinge of anxiety about the purpose of the encounter and their ability to gain control over it so that it will move along in a manner that is most satisfying or advantageous. Confusion often ensues from both the desire to understand what the situation is about and the anxiety that one might not understand. While Thai rarely take such confusion seriously, they do recognize that it occurs—in very much the way Madame Lamhab experienced it. In the same vein, Bunmyy's sudden switch from the subject of the interview not being "about court matters or legal cases" but rather about the homely issue of Madame Lamhab's age, while extraordinarily abrupt, is ordinary Thai conversational style. It is a simple way of saying, "There is nothing to worry about. Let us get onto something with which you are comfortable and are sure to know." Later in the account, Bunmyy is portrayed as a somewhat overzealous reporter who permits his own suppositions and prejudices to dominate the direction of the interview. While this portrait is not unrealistic for some Thai newsmen, it is unclear whether the author has done this because he wants to be felicitous to what actually occurs in real life or because he wants to take a satirical slap at his colleagues in journalism. In either case, the description is as as culturally and psychologically accurate as his description of Madame Lamhab.

Finally, English readers should note that although this story is included here because of the author's sensitivity to the nature of those who try to be *phuu dii* and the importance of this concept in Thai ideology, it was written for very different reasons. From a Thai point of view, its aesthetic purpose is not to describe a *phuu dii* ("we Thai all know about that") but rather to point to some of the psychological and interpersonal dimensions of corruption. In the same vein, readers should not misunderstand the author's intent regarding Bunmyy's use, and Madame Lamhab's ignorance, of the English term "women's lib." In Thai, the purpose of these words is to underscore Bunmyy's big-city pretensions and Madame Lamhab's down-home qualities. In this context, "women's lib" is simply one more in a series of short-lived American fads to enter the country for the titillation of the urban elite, while Madame Lamhab's candid acknowledgment of her ignorance is an integral element of her *phuu dii*ness. It is perhaps true that as the story progresses the "women's lib" issue does have a deeper meaning, that is, while Madame Lamhab says she is interested in being only a supportive wife, the substance of her remarks demonstrate that she and all the other women she cites exercise extraordinary power over their husbands in order to achieve their own ends. However, once more this is something that all Thai "know" and for which they do not need an American catch phrase as a reminder.[1]

For biographical comments on the author, see "Lord Buddha, Help Me?"

"I don't know what you're talking about sir"

NOTES

1. A Thai analyst of these materials dissents from this view and suggests that the "women's lib" phrase actually adds a more subtle and significant element to the whole story. This scholar suggests that strictly speaking Madame Lamhab does not fulfill the qualifications of a model *phuu dii,* that is, a "real *phuu dii*" would be considerably more muted, evasive, and less persuasive than Madame Lamhab. Even if she were as clever as our heroine, she would not display her cleverness directly, but would instead deflect Bunmyy's questions and present herself in a more politely ambiguous way. This analyst argues that what the author has done is to create a modern *phuu dii*, a woman who has in fact been liberated by a "women's lib" mentality, and that the allusion to "women's lib" at the beginning is to suggest a category for understanding her extraordinary character.

This was written in 1971 IN AMERICA ... influence of the "?'s lib" movm.

Madame Lamhab
Wife of a High-Ranking Officer of Phayao District, Chiengrai Province

SUCHIT WONGTHED

PLACE: Living room or game room of an old two-story house built by
the government for high-ranking officials of Phayao District,
Chiengrai Province.
TIME: Thursday afternoon, May.
INTERVIEWER: Mr. Bunmyy Chonnabod, a reporter from the great
capital city of Bangkok.
INTERVIEWEE: Mrs. Lamhab Sunthornsarathit, honorable wife of
Mr. Thawaan Sunthornsarathit, an official of the rank of chief of
section in the district administration.[1]

LAMHAB: I'm sorry to have kept you waiting, sir. I was preparing some
food for tonight's dinner party in honor of the director general,
who will be arriving later today from Bangkok.
BUNMYY: Oh, that's all right, ma'am. Have you finished everything?
LAMHAB: No, not yet, but my children will be able to handle it. I've told
them what has to be done. Well, what can I do for you?
BUNMYY: I'm a correspondent from Bangkok, ma'am. My editor sent me
here to interview you, Madame Lamhab. I arrived in Phayao last
night, ma'am.

From *Chaawbaan Monthly* 1, no. 8 (July 1972).

1. The meanings of the names of the characters are not arbitrary. "Lamhab" is
the name of the heroine of an ancient Thai folk tale, later reworked into a major
nineteenth-century literary work. In all versions, Mrs. Lamhab is portrayed as a
sweet, proper lady who is oblivious to a world that is falling apart around her;
few Thai parents would actually give this name to a daughter. Although Mrs.
Lamhab's surname means "beauty in all directions," her husband's first name suggests a man of considerable wealth. "Bunmyy" means "meritorious hands," but in
this context his surname, "Chonnabod," means "up-country hick."

LAMHAB: Interview me? What matter could be so important that you
    would have to travel all the way up from Bangkok to see me? I
    haven't done anything extraordinary.

BUNMYY: It's about women's lib, ma'am.[2]

LAMHAB: About what, sir?

BUNMYY: Women's lib . . . women's liberation, ma'am.

LAMHAB: I don't know what you're talking about, sir.

BUNMYY: It doesn't matter. This interview is not concerned with politics
    or with any legal issues or court cases, and it's not concerned at all
    with particular people. It's only about the routine work and gen-
    eral activities of Madame Lamhab. Can you chat with me about
    these matters? I hope you don't mind if I take notes. Since I might
    not to be able to write everything down, may I also ask your per-
    mission to tape-record our conversation? Tape-recording is also a
    perfect way to get all the details, so that when I write up the inter-
    view there won't be any mistakes. If there are errors, I can always
    check back with the tape. It also means that at any time you
    would be able to object to what we print and require us to make
    corrections.

LAMHAB: I understand what you're saying, sir. Even if it did concern pol-
    itics, I'd be happy to talk with you. But I'm really quite ignorant
    about court matters or legal cases, because I can't really think of
    any case that I have ever been involved with.

BUNMYY: There's nothing of the kind here about court matters or legal
    cases. Madame Lamhab, how old are you?

LAMHAB: Thirty-six, sir.

BUNMYY: Where did you receive your highest degree, ma'am?

LAMHAB: At the Dao Grachai School of Dressmaking in Bangkok, sir.

BUNMYY: Didn't you attend a university anywhere, ma'am?

LAMHAB: I only completed the tenth grade, sir.

BUNMYY: Have you been married to Mr. Thawaan for a long time,
    ma'am?

LAMHAB: Over ten years, sir.

BUNMYY: I suppose you've been living here for several years, ma'am.

LAMHAB: Three years, sir.

BUNMYY: Before coming here, where did you live, ma'am?

LAMHAB: Bangkunthien. That's on the Thonburi side.

BUNMYY: Oh my, what a pity! You've had to leave Bangkok and come up
    here to live. I suppose you must have had some problems, and
    that's why you came up here . . . because there isn't a person who
    would not want to stay in Bangkok. Madame Lamhab, didn't you

---

2. This and the following line by Bunmyy is said in English, not in Thai translation of the English.

ever try to use some influential contacts to . . . ? You know what I mean. . . .

LAMHAB: You misunderstand. I did use influential contacts, to the maximum extent. I approached the thing through the Director General of Administrative Services whom I asked to send my husband here —because I hate Bangkok.

BUNMMY: Wasn't Mr. Thawaan very angry, ma'am?

LAMHAB: Well, we quarreled for several days, but Mr. Thawaan finally gave in. You know, Mr. Thawaan received his degree in political science. He knows the kinds of problems we have in our country very well.

BUNMYY: What were your reasons for wanting Mr. Thawaan to come out here? I'm rather curious.

LAMHAB: There were no specific reasons. I was only thinking about trying to find a way to get out of Bangkok and to live somewhere in the provinces that would be remote from Bangkok. Right at that time, the Department of Administrative Services was looking for someone to come out here, so we agreed. I don't like the idea of government officials being holed up in Bangkok. There is no honor and integrity in working there. The truth is I really didn't want my husband to be in government service. He's had many opportunities to work for private firms that have offered him high salaries. But my husband loves government work, so I didn't protest. But when we got married, I asked my husband never to become an official who does nothing[3] and never to be corrupt. No matter how difficult or smooth things are, no matter how rich or poor we are, I want him to be clean. And wherever we are, I want people to pay us respect—a respect that is sincere, not the kind of respect where people raise their hands to their foreheads but where in their hearts they curse our ancestors.

BUNMYY: And what about living in the provinces, ma'am?

LAMHAB: I don't have any knowledge of administration, but I remember the words of my husband when he was chatting with some friends right after their graduation from the Political Science Faculty. They were brimming, as they say, "with fire and ideals." They had the idea of coming out to live with the people in the rural areas and to develop them. I agreed with them completely, because the place where I was brought up was also in a rural area, barren and desolate. It is in Chantaboon Province, close to Cambodia. I can visualize my parents, my family, and my acquaintances there, and how they are now. I had a great deal of trouble from the dishonest government officials who were there. One of my uncles is now in

---

3. Literally, one who acts like "a dried up, leftover ghost."

prison on the charge that he stole some water buffaloes. But the truth is he never did. It was all because the commune headman didn't like him and wanted to get rid of him. It was because my uncle farmed a piece of land that was very fertile and produced high yields.

BUNMYY: So these are the reasons you thought your husband should come out to live in the provinces?

LAMHAB: I just can't stand seeing my husband yield to the whims of superiors, whatever the reason. Even though I'm just a girl from the country and have only studied dressmaking, I can't tolerate my husband becoming an official who acts without integrity and honor. I may have had stronger feelings than my husband when he gave his oath—on his graduation day, before His Majesty—that he would work faithfully and loyally for the nation. That's all. My husband must have an honest reason for every single action that he takes. If he doesn't, I will see to it that he does.

BUNMYY: And if Mr. Thawaan does not yield to you?

LAMHAB: I won't yield to him either.

BUNMYY: What does that mean, ma'am?

LAMHAB: My parents are poor, but they constantly taught me to be honest—that whatever happens to me, I have to live in this world with my head held high, as a person of substance and not as someone who is afraid of being disparaged by others. There's no need to talk about the wives of those high-ranking officials, those highfalutin ladies with their airs and money. If they became wealthy through corruption, well then, it's a pity, and they deserve only scorn. However, if I have only one husband, and that husband happens to be corrupt, I think it would be better for us to go our separate ways than to have me become an accomplice. I believe in the words of my parents. And I am afraid of the future: if our children have parents who are corrupt in their official duties, they would suffer the consequences of the things we would bring upon them but for which they are not responsible. They know nothing about it. I'd rather be a woman who has been rejected by her husband than the wife of a corrupt official.

BUNMYY: Which of these two things is more embarrassing to you?

LAMHAB: In my opinion, I must say that being the wife of a corrupt official is the greatest shame. To be divorced from a dishonest husband is more a cause for honor than a cause for shame.

BUNMYY: Excuse me, ma'am. Please don't take this as an insult. But has Mr. Thawaan ever done anything that suggests that he could have been involved in something dishonest?

LAMHAB: On several occasions the owners of companies bidding on the construction of government buildings have tried to put some money in envelopes and leave them here pretending that they have forgotten them. I'm not without some knowledge of what this means and what its real purpose is. I always caution those people not to forget their things and never—absolutely never—to leave them in this house. I've always said this in a voice loud enough for other people to hear so that they would not try to disparage my husband by saying that we were poorer than other people. Maybe we don't have as much money as others, but we are honest, and we are rich enough in honesty. I don't interfere with my husband's work and duty, but I do have the right to preserve my husband's honesty. It's as important as life itself.

BUNMYY: But Madame Lamhab's husband might be accepting bribes somewhere else—in places and from people you've never seen.

LAMHAB: Well, that's something I can't do anything about. But you must believe me when I say that a husband and wife who have lived together and eaten together for more than ten years probably know each other's heart pretty well.

BUNMYY: Excuse me, Madame Lamhab, but how many children do you have?

LAMHAB: Three children, sir. My eldest son is attending a university in Bangkok. He is advanced for his age and is a very bright student. The other two children are here.

BUNMYY: Do you bring them up yourself, ma'am?

LAMHAB: I wouldn't let anyone else bring up my children.

BUNMYY: Perhaps you should hire some servants to help out?

LAMHAB: Where would the money come from? And I don't want my children to turn into little snobs, giving themselves airs, spreading their fingers,[4] and becoming like those other children who have been raised by maids.

BUNMYY: What do you think about coming out to live here?

LAMHAB: What do you mean by that?

BUNMYY: Well, I mean do you like Phayao? What do you think of the people here? Is there anything around here that makes you uncomfortable?

LAMHAB: It couldn't be more convenient or more pleasant than it is here. You probably know that Lake Phayao, which is located here, makes the weather cool and comfortable almost the whole year around. You probably already know what the people out here, in

---

4. In traditional Thailand, the daughters of royalty and nobility were trained by nannies to stretch their forearms, hands, and fingers as expressions of beauty and delicacy. Fingers that were nimble, soft, and free of all evidence of physical labor were particularly favored. The spread fingers of women in Thai classical dance is perhaps the best known expression of this symbolism.

this part of the country, are like. As for myself, I have no concerns or anxieties whatsoever. I have loads of friends and neighbors because my husband is a high-ranking official. The people here know each other well and they know who he is. I am so proud of the fact that my husband is so honest and fair. People raise their hands wholeheartedly to pay respect to me, so I pay respect to them with a pure heart. Everybody knows how poor our family is and everybody knows how much money we have in the bank.[5]

BUNMYY: Has anyone ever asked you or your husband to use your influence?

LAMHAB: Yes. But my husband wouldn't do it. And had he done it, I certainly would have never lived with him or eaten with him again. Some people have come to us asking us to use our influence to get their child admitted into the district government school for advanced students. I told them that even my middle daughter has to attend a private school because she is not as bright as other children and could not pass the entrance examination. I told them to go find someone else who might be willing to use their influence. This house has no influence and has no thought of looking for any.

BUNMYY: You must feel put upon by all those people who come to you with requests for favors or who try to reach your husband, as they say, "through the back door."

LAMHAB: Well, Mr. Thawaan has a back door. But I'm that back door, and I'm the one who decides whether it will be closed or open. I open it only to lecture them. I open it so that people will come and sit and listen to what I have to say to them or, in other words, to scold them.

BUNMYY: But don't they get angry?

LAMHAB: I always let them know that they shouldn't be angry, because in approaching me for that purpose they made me angry. But if we understand each other, then there won't be any anger anymore.

BUNMYY: What is your strategy for making your husband a good civil servant?

LAMHAB: I don't have any. But I've never tried to wheedle my husband into buying me a diamond ring. I don't have one. I don't want the wives of the officials who are subordinate to my husband to come and wait upon me because they want something; I only want to be with my children. I don't want to have a car so I can sit there craning my neck and showing off my diamond necklace, because I don't have a diamond necklace and I don't want one. I don't want a teak house as long as I don't have enough money to have one

---

5. This is a turn of phrase, not a statement of fact.

built for me. Whenever I'm invited to play cards or gamble, I say "no," no matter who invites me. I have never made a great donation to any temple in order to have my name inscribed up there; I only go to temple fairs where I help out with a sincere heart, sometimes collecting small donations. I don't really care who comes from Bangkok or who goes to Bangkok. Even if it is some big shot from some department or ministry, I'm not interested. If he wants to stop by at my house to eat rice and fish with us, it's all right with me; but he'll have to eat the same food I eat. If he wants anything more extraordinary, he'll have to go buy it for himself at some shop in the market.

BUNMYY: There must have been some instances when big shots in the department or ministry gave you a hard time.

LAMHAB: I don't pay attention to such things, because if I did, I would probably have to say there were some instances. So, if I don't think about them, I feel more comfortable. But my husband always asks me why he is never promoted and why his salary stays the same.

BUNMYY: And what do you say?

LAMHAB: Well, I tell him that his work still isn't good enough. He has to work harder. He has to bring more development to Phayao District. He has to mobilize all his skill and strength for this purpose —even though the truth is that high-ranking officials really do not want people who work well as much as they want those who work some and bootlick some. I don't want him to think that way, and I don't want it to be that way. My husband understands the thing well and he has staying power.

BUNMYY: It must be because of you, too.

LAMHAB: But it is more important that my husband himself be that way. However, the wife certainly has some role in making the husband be whatever he is. When I was in Bangkok I saw many cases where husbands could not resist their wives. The wives kept pushing them to do this and to do that; to get their wives this and to get them that. So it was necessary for the husbands to do some things to satisfy their wives' desires; and once they did those things, it was necessary for them to continue. I couldn't stand being that kind of wife. The Thai nation does not belong only to me, sir. Neither does it belong to any other single person. The only thing that a woman like me can do is to give moral support to my husband, because the only power I have is the power in the family, and that's only a little power.

BUNMYY: Do you have anything else to say to me so that it can be presented to the public in the newspaper, ma'am?

LAMHAB: If you have nothing further to ask me, I have nothing further to say, sir.

PLACE: Office of the editor in the great capital city of Bangkok.
TIME: Monday morning, May.
INTERVIEWER: Editor.
INTERVIEWEE: Mr. Bunmyy Chonnabod, a reporter.

EDITOR: I read your report and listened to the tapes of your interview with Mrs. Lamhab Sunthornsarathit. It's fine. But I want to know the truth: when I sent you to Phayao, did you really go to Phayao and interview the real Madame Lamhab or did you sneak over to Chiengmai and interview some other woman for me? What woman, I don't know.[6]
BUNMYY: What do you mean? How could you say that, Editor?
EDITOR: You better answer me first!
BUNMYY: Of course, I really went to Phayao. I've already sent my bus and railway tickets to the business office for reimbursement.
EDITOR: And the person you interviewed: was it really Madame Lamhab? Are you sure that it was the wife of Mr. Thawaan Sunthornsarathit?
BUNMYY: Of course! Sure! Why the hell would I make up a story like that?[7]
EDITOR: Watch your language when you're talking with your editor. And don't tell me later that I haven't warned you. Okay, it's not important. Look, I want you to read this text of a long distance phone call from our stringer in Chiengrai.

PHONE CALL FROM CHIENGRAI CORRESPONDENT:

Mr. Thawaan Sunthornsarathit has eaten[8] the national forest reserve at the foot of Kiiwmaudom Mountain in Phayao District. No other details as yet because all local officials refuse to say anything. Ask that you do further research at Land Department Headquarters or other relevant government agencies. Await immediate instructions on how I should proceed.

---

6. This is a teasing, if ambiguous, allusion to the possibility that the reporter visited some coy beauty and/or prostitute in Chiengmai—both of which the city is famous for in the Thai popular imagination. Chiengmai is located some 225 km. west of Phayao.

7. Literally, "to grab and hold up a cloud—for spear's sake!"

8. While the "eating" of government property was traditionally the legitimate prerogative of royal officials who ruled an area, in contemporary Thailand the phrasing is virtually synonomous with "official corruption."

EDITOR: Well, what do you say about this?

BUNMYY: I pass.

EDITOR: You can't just pass. You've got to give me your opinion.

BUNMYY: I've done my job. I interviewed her, and what you do with it is not my business.

EDITOR: Damn it! What the hell am I going to do? Help me think, for heaven's sake! Why the hell does there have to be a person like Mrs. Lamhab in this country? Is this what she really thinks or was she just talking?

BUNMYY: An editor doesn't have the right to ask whether it's one way or the other. That's what she said so that's what we have to publish. Isn't it good that there is a person like Madame Lamhab?

EDITOR: What a bloody pain in the butt![9]

---

9. In Thai, *puad kabaan chiphaaj, kabaan* meaning literally, "crown of the head" and *chiphaaj* being a four-letter expletive that is otherwise untranslatable.

Big Shots and *Likee*

Introduction

The following homily on the real and fanciful world is included in this volume for a number of reasons. First, in its brevity and directness, it is an excellent example of Thai didactic writing. Unlike many of the other selections, it does not plead, whine, scold, or use ironic endings but merely lays out its message in simple, unpretentious prose. This is the way most Thai *actually* communicate in the real world—something that is easy to forget in a book like this where so much of the material is dominated by literary convention and affectation. Second, for all the simplicity of the prose, the metaphor the author uses—*likee* or *yikee* (the terms are interchangeable)—is in fact rich in associated meanings, and one wonders whether, in addition to his manifest message, the author does not also mean to stimulate his readers into a more subtle consideration of the links between the real and imaginary worlds.

Likee is traditional Thai folk drama performed by travelling troupes—usually at temple fairs or at parties celebrating special occasions. While the plots of *likee* stories are highly traditional, the essence of a performance is the use of contemporary themes and local color in a comic, ad-libbed, and often scatological way. Thus, good *likee* has to be related to the realities of the immediate social situation and be expressed in the most down-to-earth language. Further, although the characters are high-born and the costumes brilliant, *likee* turns on cutting down to human size all that is grand and pretentious, often including "government officials who are big shots." Equally important, the audience plays a direct role in every performance by loudly approving or disapproving the actions of the characters as well as the originality of the performers.

The point is that while *likee* is very much about a make-believe world, it makes sense and has relevance only in terms of the here-and-now real world. *Likee* is in fact an aesthetic representation of the blurring of the two worlds. The other side of the metaphor partakes of precisely the same logic; that as much as big government officials are of the real world, they have many of the same pretensions and postures as *likee* characters and to that extent are theatrical creations of Thai society. Certainly, like *likee* performers they are role players, and like their counterparts, they too "will ultimately reach the day when their roles must change. . . . They will have to come down and live together with the general population."

This last point, although seemingly so obvious, is in fact quite provocative. This is the only instance we encountered of a Thai author explicitly addressing the question of what happens to the powerful when they no longer have power. The author's intention here is not to evaluate or caution but merely to provide some realistic time perspective on the human career or perhaps a Buddhist sense of the ephemeral nature of all things. But for a Thai audience, the point is important—if only because it is one that is rarely raised to the level of consciousness.

The author of the essay is a professor of history at Thammasat University and is perhaps best known for his English-language work, *The Rise of Ayudhya: A History of Siam in the Fourteenth and Fifteenth Centuries* (Oxford University Press, 1976). He received his Ph.D. at Cornell University and has been a visiting professor at the University of California, Berkeley, and a scholar-in-residence at the Center for Southeast Asian Studies at the University of Kyoto. For a period of time he was also vice-rector of Thammasat University.

The context of the piece is also significant. Although originally published as a newspaper special feature, it was reprinted in a collection of the author's essays published on the occasion of the cremation of his father. "Cremation books" are published in limited numbers and are distributed as gifts to guests attending the funeral of the deceased. Although the substantive portions of most cremation books are stock items—selections from the Buddhist canon, patriotic essays, famous poetry—often members of the family of the deceased will prepare a more personal and unique book to honor their relative. Such was the case in this instance.

Big Shots and *Likee*

CHARNVIT KASETSIRI

Many of us have probably seen *yikee* and have been amused and enchanted by it, enchanted in the sense that the stories are about dream worlds—make-believe places of luxurious grandeur where there may be some suffering and misery but where in the end there is only happiness and good fortune.

In the *yikee* cast the characters usually are royal lords and ladies. They are men and women of great merit and high rank, and following the plot of the play, they will achieve happiness and live happily ever after.

There is one element which the *yikee* cannot do without—the audience. A *yikee* audience is significantly different from the *yikee* characters in that it is comprised of the most ordinary, commonplace people. Some have no education and some have only a little. However, the majority are dressed simply, and they are nowhere near as well-off or blessed as the characters they are watching.

The fact is that there is an enormous gap between *yikee* characters and *yikee* audience. It is the gap between the world of dreams and the world of reality. It is the gap between two different styles of dress and two different social ranks.

Simply stated, *yikee* characters are representatives of wealth, power, good fortune, and grand status, while the members of the audience are only ordinary villagers.

When a *yikee* has ended and the actors and actresses step down from their stage, their station will be immediately altered. They will be transformed from people of merit, from being heroes and heroines, into mundane villagers whose mode of dress and social position are not very different from that of any other villager.

First published in *Prachachart* Newspaper, November 7, 1972; reprinted in Charnvit Kasetsiri, ed., *Thaa Than Maj Pen Suan Nyng Khong Kankaeae Panhaa Than Kau Pen Suan Nyng Khong Panhaa* [If you are not part of the solution you are part of the problem] (Bangkok: Phikkhaned Publishing Co., 1975).

The gap between *yikee* characters and *yikee* audience is reminiscent of another gap which exists in reality. This is the gap between government officials (particularly those who are big shots or otherwise of high rank) and common villagers.

Big government officials are similar to the protagonists of *yikee* stories. They have good fortune, power, and great esteem. While they hold their positions, other people look up to them with admiration, awe, and veneration. Official cars and drivers await them, and they are showered with gifts of every kind.[1]

In short, they sit surrounded by people, fore and aft, who, waiting on their words, make their every wish happen.

The common people, on the other hand, are very much like a *yikee* audience. They have no power, no great fortune, or great esteem. Most of the time, they are only onlookers with almost no right or even voice to persuade those great men to attend to their wishes.

In sum, the gap between big shots and common people is similar to the gap between *yikee* characters and their audience.

But most big shots, no matter their rank, will ultimately reach the day when their roles must change. And when that time comes, they will be no different from those who play the leads in *yikee* stories.

They will have to come down and live together with the general population. The eventual end of power and fortune, whether it is a result of normal retirement or of political pressure, will suddenly deprive these great men of the attention and pandering that they were accustomed to for so long. The swarms of retainers will thin out. The official cars and residences will disappear, as will the heaps of gifts that they used to receive.

The gap discussed here is one of the prevailing problems of society. It is a problem between government officials and the common people. Whereas the gap between *yikee* characters and *yikee* audience does not need filling or bridging because it exists only in a make-believe world, the gap between government officials and the common people does require bridging, a bridging that is absolutely necessary because it exists in the real world.

---

1. Literally, "pork, mushrooms, ducks, and chickens."

Paradise Preserved

Introduction

Khamsing Srinawk, the author of the following selection, is widely acknowledged as Thailand's most accomplished short-story writer. He is the only creative writer in the nation who has had a collection of his work translated and published outside the country by a major international press (*"The Politician" and Other Stories,* Oxford University Press, 1973). "Paradise Preserved," written later, is presented here as much for what it says about the author and Thai narrative style as for its descriptive content.

Most of Khamsing's earlier work focused on the character of villagers: their pathos and credulity, their wit and occasional greed, but always their essential humanity. In fact, Khamsing is virtually the first Thai writer to give peasants a literary reality, instead of viewing them, as almost all preceding Thai writers had, as merely adjuncts or part of the scenery of upper-class and middle-class life. (See his "I Lost My Teeth," elsewhere in this volume, as an example of this concern.)

In "Paradise Preserved," Khamsing expands his horizon and describes a person who, although one of the most important and recognizable psychological types in Thailand, has never before been crystallized in the indigenous literature. The hero is very much a "modern" Thai, a member of the lower middle class, who takes advantage of every opportunity in his rapidly changing world to "make it." In an environment so rich in opportunity, the numerous changes he makes in his career seem in no way unnatural, either to himself or to the narrator. If he is an interesting person it is because of the unique nature of the work he undertakes and not because he moves from one job to another. In the few lines the author gives him to speak for himself, he comes across as an ordinary chap— relaxed, likable, with the typical personal and family problems of anybody in his position.

However, from a Thai point of view these same problems suggest that, for all his opportunism, the hero is also a victim of circumstances. In order to house and feed his growing family he left the security of his job of twenty years to serve and to become subject to the whims of the gods —the descendants of Mars—officials who demand bribes and politicians who wield power. There is in all of this a sense of his doing things that he must to succeed but that he would prefer not to. His essentially plaintive position is expressed in the words of resignation he uses with the narrator.

Toward the end of the story, the narrator's attitude toward this "lowly man" turns to scorn, but the scorn is obviously directed against what he does, and the system that supports his doing it, rather than against what he is as an individual. There is no doubt that, the narrator's bitterness notwithstanding, the majority of Thai readers would be likely to consider the hero's good fortune more a cause for admiration, even envy, than a cause for condemnation. But the whole thrust of this story is so intensely cynical that not even this ultimate irony should come as a surprise, perhaps not even to the author.

To the Western reader, the narrator's unexpected anger at the end of the story gives it a perplexing, jarring quality—as if the author had suddenly changed his terms of discourse from literary description to ideological commentary, with the result that, in English at least, neither aim is effectively fulfilled. To most Thai, however, such unanticipated shifts of viewpoint or mood are by no means unusual. Although perhaps less obvious, several selections in this volume contain similar narrative surprises: in "Grandma" there are no transitions to mark the changes in time; in "Lord Buddha, Help Me?" Maha Boonman's excursions into political aphorism seem both out of character and contrived; in the two essays by M. R. Khukrit Pramoj the final paragraphs seem to be shaped more by a lack of space or by uncertainty about how to conclude the commentaries than by any obvious expository purpose. These narrative styles probably derive from and are sanctioned by the precedents of Thai classical writing, which was also transitionless and episodic.

However, in the case of "Paradise Preserved," the surprising confounding of literary description and political advocacy has a deeper personal meaning. Khamsing is himself a "modern" Thai. Born in 1930 and reared in a village in northeastern Thailand, he has been at various times a peasant, journalist, forest ranger, lumber mill foreman, research assistant to foreign scholars (including the editor), and travelling sewing machine salesman. During the past two decades, he has also been a world traveller (one year in the United States and shorter visits to France, Germany, Israel, and Ivory Coast), a creative writer, a highly successful modern dairy farmer, and an unsuccessful politician. The last is the result of his failure on two occasions to be elected to parliament on the ticket of the Socialist Party of Thailand; each time he financed his campaign by selling one of his cows.

Lately, Khamsing has experienced personal uncertainty about what he really is, what he wants to do, what he can realistically accomplish, and most important, what the value or use of his writing is. Such issues are of concern at one time or another to many serious Thai writers. But for Khamsing, they are particularly acute, mainly because of his maturity and his keen awareness of not only the power but the limits of ideas and words to alter history; the capacity of politics (including socialist politics) to dehumanize people; and his own indecision about whether to respond with detachment or rage to the injustice, fraudulence, and manipulation that he sees everywhere in his society. While it is the detachment that stimulates his literary impulses and the rage that stimulates his political advocacy, it is his indecision about which is to be valued highest or pursued first that leads to the kind of bifurcation and ambivalence that is so patent in "Paradise Preserved."

Historical events in Thailand have done little to resolve his ambivalence. Immediately after the coup d'etat of October 1976, he fled the country for his own safety and lived in Sweden with his wife and three children. He returned to Thailand in 1980, resumed a quiet life, and completed his first novel, *Maeaew* [Cat]—a metaphor for Thai society.

Whatever position Khamsing ultimately assumes in the history of Thai writing, he has already had considerable impact. Many of the other writings on peasants in this book have been self-consciously modeled on his precedents. Although some of them may be more poignant or beautiful than Khamsing's work, none is his equal in the crisp and precise use of language or in his felicity to the realities of the underside of Thai life. "Paradise Preserved" may be disappointing to Westerners because it is aesthetically disjointed and because its hero is never fully fleshed out. But these few paragraphs say more about the human consequences of the ten-year American military presence in Thailand and about the importance of the flunky—that character who holds the Thai political and social system together and who keeps it functioning smoothly—than anything else that has been written in the Thai language. Its ideological message notwithstanding, it is the simple act of transforming the flunky from a "nothing"—which is the way most Thai view him—into a literary figure that gives this story its significance.

Paradise Preserved

KHAMSING SRINAWK

And so it is. Paradise is still preserved in Thailand. At least that's the position of the prominent experts who participated in a panel discussion on Thailand's economic problems at Chulalongkorn University auditorium at the beginning of this month.

The reason why there are many things in society that seem a bit uncertain and shoddy, the respected panelists explained, is because our Thai gods have not been very good. While I sat there and listened, I hesitated to agree with them wholeheartedly. Thinking of the pale faces of friends from various walks of life that I observed almost daily, the paradise to my mind had already been lost. But though I am not a ready believer, those experts seemed to be more impressive than house lizards or geckoes.[1] And after having observed the ways and means of my own friends and other people, I began to agree with the experts' opinions—especially the part that referred to the gods. At least I had to admit to myself that I had witnessed various happenings that supported such ideas.

One case was that of a former neighbor whose fate almost turned him into a brothel owner. But, by the skin of his teeth, some god had managed to save him.

In fact, it seems that still another angel has been born in Thailand.

The story goes like this. The neighbor friend was originally a schoolteacher. He worked diligently at this profession for twenty consecutive years. His fortune was what might be expected for an ordinary government official of his age. He had a house of his own. As he had more children, his house came to be too small and crowded, and his family

Published originally in *Sangkhomsaat Parithat* (August 1973); reprinted in Khamsing Srinawk, *Khamphaeng* (Bangkok: Puthuchorn Publishers, 1975). Abridged.

1. This refers to a traditional Thai belief about the cries of a house lizard or gecko being omens of misfortune if uttered when one is leaving one's house.

expenses increased every day until he had difficulty making ends meet. Finally, thinking about the problems he faced, he considered looking for a new livelihood. He decided to resign from government service in order to collect his retirement bonus. He calculated that it was sufficient to build a rather large house for his family. He then applied for a job on an American military base.

Compared to the old job, his new income was rather high, and he expected that his household would turn into a paradise overnight. At the same time, the town he lived in was booming. It was exploding with life and color. But along with this, the cost of living also boomed, and the paradise that he thought would be coming over the horizon seemed to be receding into the distance. However, because of the familiarity and sensitive understanding that he had developed toward his new friends (in fact, masters or gods) he was in a better postion than most. So he divided his big house and rented a room to one of his new friends.

After a while, the manner in which this friend spent his leisure time at home made my old neighbor rather uneasy, since his children were just entering puberty. He could evict his new friend, but then, he could also use the rent. In the end, he took his wife and children back to their old small house, leaving the big house as a gathering place for the descendants of the god Mars and the angels from the nearby hamlets.[2] So my teacher friend, a lowly man, had the privilege of owning a carnal paradise.

All was well until the time of the withdrawal of the gallant American troops. My friend's paradise plunged downward in this new era. We met occasionally. When I mentioned the changing situation, his look was serious. But there was a trace of a smile on his face—not the original gleeful smile—but still a smile. He said—as if he were presenting an advertisement (mainly to himself)—that the situation was not yet critical. A lot had already left but new ones had also arrived. Would an ally let an ally down? His voice was sure and firm. His big house still had tenants, one after another. The girls were there all the time to attend to his business interests. It was not until our ally began to close down its bases that the happiness and contentment on his face disappeared completely. In this situation of panic and disorder, it is hard to say in which part of the Dharma[3] my friend took refuge—to control himself so that, without hysterics, he could endure the sight of his own paradise crumbling down in front of him.

Many months later, we met again. This time he was driving a black

---

2. In the original Thai text, "Jupiter," written in transliteration of the Western name, is used instead of "Mars."

3. Buddhist canon or belief.

license plate taxi transporting passengers up the hill.[4] He dropped by to visit and talk about his demise.

"The young ones had to leave school. The oldest one finished vocational school, but she can't find a job yet, and she's behaving as if she hates home," he said talking of his children.

I asked about the house he rented out. He shook his head. "It was closed down," he said. "In fact, I didn't do it. The authorities did. I could have kept it open if I was willing to pay them off regularly, but I didn't think that was worthwhile pursuing. So now I'm trying this." He meant his taxi. "But there's hardly anything left after you have paid for daily and monthly queue fees, fees to those who operate the depots, toll charges, and also service charges, for the 'gods'.[5] I am now applying to get back into the civil service."

It is true what the experts say. There are gods in Thai society. The last time I saw this friend of mine, he had changed so much—but only for the better. His thin face was now filled out and beaming with the signs of well-being. When he talked, his voice was vigorous with a ring of authority. He was a new man.

The change was very much a surprise, but if you looked deeper at the cause, it was not so surprising, because in this society of ours power comes from mysterious sources.

My friend related to me that his running around for readmission into government service had brought him into close contact with an important person who could be counted as a kind of god—a member of parliament (from the "Can-Do-It" Party).[6] Those who have ever believed in the moon and the stars would claim that it was my friend's lucky star that was guiding him, since at the time he went to see the MP, the MP was planning his campaign for the upcoming election.

As it happened, my friend was rather gifted at the art of rhetoric. At least that was the result of his having to use it in his work with schoolchildren for twenty years. This gift probably gave the honorable representative the idea that my friend could be useful in his next campaign. His application for readmission into government service was accepted with no difficulty whatsoever.

Every time I think of the story of my friend's life, the words of an author I once read come to mind. He said simply: "Life is a journey." I am

---

4. A "black license plate taxi" is an illegal taxi; legal taxis carry yellow license plates. "The hill" leads up into the Khorat Plateau, the beginning of Thailand's northeast.

5. In this instance, any official who can pull his weight.

6. The fact that this is the slogan of the Social Action Party, in power during 1975–1976, is fortuitous. (See the story, "A Day in the Life of Pat.") The "Can-Do-It" Party did not come into existence until well after this story was first published.

not sure whether my teacher friend has read these words, but the way he has been carrying on seems to indicate that he knows them by heart. Since that day he found his new path—which took him, carrying a file, from the MP's house to his new office in his government department—he has made scores of journeys of the same sort. (Of course, the journey of a lackey is an ageless journey.) The distance he has travelled back and forth from his office to the MP's, carrying letters of authority to departmental offices, schools, and universities (seeking admission for certain students) would probably measure half the length of the continent. The more he travels the more firm is his place in the inner circle and the more power is bestowed upon him.

Being the MP's man, he is now respected and feared, in and out of the district. If his town were a town of animals, this friend of mine would have the status of a crow who picks at the wounded backs of a society of cows. But since his town is populated with humans, he has the status of a superman. At this point I would be content just to call him "the shadow of the privileged class."

A Telephone Conversation
the Night the Dogs Howled

Introduction

The following bit of political satire touches upon one of the most important and least analyzed domains of Thai experience—the belief in the power of supernatural spirits, and of the supernatural world in general, to play a role in human affairs. It is important because those who believe in such power believe it profoundly and unquestioningly. It is little analyzed because most Thai do not know who believes and who does not believe and, more significantly, because they hold that matters of faith are totally personal, beyond the influence of either logical or interpersonal disputation. Of course, the vast majority who do believe cannot understand how the very few who do not would dare not, but they would also consider that to be the latter's problem.

None of this is to deny that there is a great deal of commentary about the supernatural. But most such discussion assumes the reality of the supernatural world and addresses mainly tactical questions of the effectiveness of the human response: Which seer or shaman is better than another? What kinds of rituals are most effective? What times, places, or decisions are auspicious or not? (See Tambiah 1970; Terwiel 1975; Textor 1973; Thongthew-Ratarasarn 1979.)

In this story it is unclear whether the author means to mock Pramarn's presumed belief in the supernatural (for most Thai readers, a safe presumption), his effectiveness in dealing with it, or perhaps both. In a sense it makes no difference, since either notion provides sufficient basis for implicating Pramarn in a real historical event and for suggesting that what actually happened resulted directly from what he wanted to happen. In the supernatural world wishes and actions are frequently indistinguishable.

The actual circumstances surrounding this tale concern the formation of the Thai Cabinet after the April 1976 election and Major-General Pra-

136

marn Adireksarn, leader of the Chart Thai Party and former defense minister in M. R. Khukrit Pramoj's coalition government, losing that post to General Kris Sivara—the military hero of the 1973 Student Revolution and indisputable leader of all the Thai military. Pramarn was left with the lesser position of minister of agriculture in the new coalition government formed by M. R. Seni Pramoj's Democrat Party. However, almost immediately after the formation of the government, General Kris inexplicably entered the hospital and even more inexplicably died. The causes or circumstances of his death have never been adequately explained. This story was published within a fortnight of the death.[1]

There are a few elements of the story that should be noted. The allusion to textile stocks refers to Pramarn's successful career as a textile manufacturer. Dogs that howl at night are assumed to be howling at malevolent supernatural spirits in search of human prey. The former prime minister, Field Marshal Thanom Kittikachorn, in office for more than a decade, lost his power and was forced to flee Thailand in October 1973, just a short time after receiving some reassuring advice from an astrologer who had studied in India.

It is ironic that in contrast to Thanom and despite the anxieties attributed to him here, General Pramarn went on to be a politician of considerable influence in Thailand. In 1981, he was the kingdom's deputy prime minister.

Finally, it should be noted that the *Luang Phauau* cited here is in fact a real monk from Wat Suthat who at the time was famous for maintaining a large following of astrological clients among military leaders and politicians and for his own keen attention to entrepreneurial matters. Thus, the story is also a satirical, if realistic, slap at those monks who would exploit the moral power of their religious positions.

Although the story is unsigned, the author is known to be a British-educated Thai economic journalist who in the decade between 1966 and 1976 had a major impact on the Thai intellectual world. With several colleagues at *Sangkhomsaat Parithat,* he became a critical figure in bringing the realities of the Vietnam War to the attention of the Thai reading public. Later he created *Chaturat* as the nation's most reliable and respected news weekly. After the coup of October 1976, he was jailed for a period of time and then lived in the United States with his American spouse. He returned to Thailand in the early 1980s and revived *Chaturat* as a general interest magazine aimed at the Thai upper-middle classes. He is also the author of another story in this volume, "A Day in the Life of Pat."

NOTE

1. The most frequent (if contrasting) explanations of his death were: (1) the seemingly healthy and active general entered the hospital because of exhaustion, and one of his enemies arranged to have the plug literally pulled on his life support system and (2) that he died of a heart attack from overindulging his passion for sticky rice and mango. The latter is so widely accepted that General Kris has become a familiar symbol for cautioning older people about the dangers of gluttony.

A Telephone Conversation
the Night the Dogs Howled

"This is Wat Suthat. Holy Father is speaking."[1]

"This is Pramarn, sir."

"Which Pramarn? Oh, . . . Pramarn the pork butcher, isn't it? I already sent the boy with your horoscope. Didn't you get it?"

"No, Holy Father. This is Pramarn the minister."

"What's the matter? Why are you phoning so late at night?"

"It's like this, Holy Father. I would like to make an appointment to make merit at the *wat*."

"So, . . . why are you calling me so late at night like this? You could send *Khunying*[2] here tomorrow to do it for you. That would be fine."

"No, no, Father, it's not like that. The thing is . . . today I received some news that wasn't very good. I feel that I must make merit and feed the monks quickly. The sooner the better."

"What's the problem, *Khun* Pramarn? I already examined your horoscope and it said that your big undertaking of last week would be successful. It said that your enemy would certainly meet his fate. There would be no difficulty about that, although the resolution might create a little fuss in the national political situation. C'mon, I'm no amateur in this field. I've had long experience in doing horoscopes. Like I told you, I examined 'Nom's,[3] and no matter how many times I warned him, he

From *Chaturat* 2, no. 43 (May 4, 1976).

1. In the Thai text, the title *Luang Phauau* is used. It has a number of meanings: a monk with supernatural powers; a monk who is particularly venerated or loved; Holy Father. In other contexts it also means "Buddha images."

2. A royal title bestowed upon women for service to the nation. Although a highly valued honorific, many wives of high government officials possess the title.

3. A clear allusion to former prime minister, Field Marshal Thanom Kittikachorn.

didn't believe me. Instead, he went to see the astrologer who had studied abroad. Of course, it was a bloody disaster."

"No, no, Holy Father. I really believed you. That's why I followed your advice and did just what you told me. But I never thought that things would turn out one hundred percent . . . exactly as you said they would."

"And why not? Is someone pushing you again for the minister of defense post? Come on, don't take it! Do you hear me? Your horoscope says that you should be retreating during this period. If you persist in stepping up again to the same position it will be disastrous."

"Holy Father, listen to me first. I did not say that. The thing is . . . that damn enemy of mine really met catastrophe, just like you said he would. I'm afraid of the ghost that's going to be haunting me."

"Hey, is that true? Don't you be kidding me now."

"Of course it's true. Why would I lie to you?"

"Okay, let's be cool. Let me think first about what we ought to do."

"Don't let it take too long, Holy Father. The dogs at my house are already howling."

"Let's do it this way. When you come here tomorrow . . . according to your horoscope you ought to bring an offering of two hundred and fifty thousand *baht*. But to make sure the bad luck is really defused, it should really be five hundred and thirty thousand, plus two thousand shares of textile stock.[4] That will guarantee perfect results. . . ."

---

4. Approximately US$12,500 and US$26,500, respectively.

2

Nothing Is Immutable:
The Internationalization of Thailand
and the Development Ethos

Fulfilling One's Duty
The Enchanting Cooking Spoon
Getting Drunk Abroad
Naaj Aphajmanii
I Am a University Student
Social Work
Headman Thuj

Fulfilling One's Duty

Introduction

Although somewhat awkward in its exposition, this little story about fulfilling the obligations of one's social role touches upon some of the central issues of contemporary Thai life.

First, it should be understood that for all his attractiveness, the hero, Kham, is as much a social type as he is an interesting and provocative personality. He is almost a perfect *nagleeng,* the hoodlum-protector found in almost every Thai village: a man who is physically and emotionally tough, who speaks his feelings from his heart, whose word is his bond, and who, although not above the use of guile in his interpersonal tactics, is a man of deep principle.

It is this last quality, however, that points to the limitations of his heroism. For despite his integrity, he is also inflexible and unrealistic. When these qualities are linked to his inherent aggressiveness (the *sine qua non* of the *nagleeng*) his denouement is inevitable.[1] It is the combination of these attributes that makes him such an attractive and interesting person but not necessarily one to be admired. In fact, if there is any psychological lesson to be drawn from this story it is not that men of principle are admirable or heroic but rather that they are subject to the same unknown forces and ironies that determine the fate of all people. Kham is completely a man of human proportions—reliable, tough-minded, and constant—but who, by virtue of these very traits, is incapable of heroic status. To possess the latter he would either have to be born with it (in terms of *karma* or *phromlikhid*) or be supernaturally endowed.[2] (Particularly favored in recent times is the hero who has the power to stop bullets from leaving the barrel of a gun.) These extremely high standards may well be the reason why modern Thai recognize few heroes in their public life.

In this volume, most of the fictionalized "heroes" *(wirachon)* are really demi-heroes—men who are morally good (the Billy Budd character in

"Relations With Colleagues"), valiant (*Nok Khun* Thauaung in "Oh! Temple, Temple of Bot!"), or principled (as Kham is in this narrative), but who are themselves overcome by large historical forces or by their own fate. At best, they effect history only as martyrs or as people whose actions might have some personal, but unknown, karmic consequences. All are denied the satisfaction of enjoying the consequences of even their limited heroism in this life.

Of course, for normal human beings the pleasures of life are meant to be more prosaic, and this is the real moral message of this story. For Kham, the richest satisfactions come from accepting and fulfilling the requirements governing the performance of his various roles. He is a man very much at one with his social order—which is not without its irony, considering that it is this same social order that has tried to deprive him and his colleagues of their land and livelihood. But in Thailand this is an ordinary problem, and Kham handles it in his own special way: he knows exactly how to wag his finger at a government official and how to get that official into a posture of cajoling him into being socially responsible. For a *nagleeng,* the theatrics of this kind of scene can be exquisite.

The key to Kham's character is his sense of theatre. Like Madame Lamhab, M. R. Khukrit Pramoj, and many other Thai, he knows that, irrespective of underlying substance or even truth, a good performance defines one's talent and social character, one's capacity to influence others, and can in the acting out even fulfill one's richest fantasy or noblest image of oneself. Whether this concern with a good performance can also impel men to act out their own deaths is the dramatic—or the more cynical modern Thai might argue, merely the melodramatic—question of the story.[3]

There is another level of the story that has little to do with Kham's dramatic performance or even his character. In fact, for many Thai readers the central issue is not the psychology of Kham, but rather the overwhelming power of the historical force that determines the behavior of everybody. It is not only Kham, his boatmen, and the confused villagers who defer to the inexorable power of technological change but the engineers as well. If Kham's fate is to be first a victim of the dam, then its agent, and then again a victim, the fate of the engineers is to create the dam but to have no control over the consequences of their creation. The narrator may feel despondent about what his venture has done to the villagers and even dream of blood pouring through sluices, but in the end he too is merely fulfilling his role in the larger historical drama—perhaps not with the élan of Kham, but as a dutiful civil servant who believes there is at least some good in the enterprise. His awareness of the inherent paradox of the enterprise, and perhaps the paradox of all technological change, is expressed clearly in the sentence, "But when such happiness belongs to the majority, it is often bought at the expense of the minority." From this point of view, the entire story is essentially a modern parable to traditional Thai fatalism.

The author is a career engineer born in the early 1940s who wrote the story while serving on a dam construction project with the Electricity Generating Authority of Thailand. He was born and brought up in Srisaket Province in Thailand's Northeast and studied engineering at Chulalongkorn University, where he was also heavily involved in university literary circles. He currently holds a high administrative position at the Sirikit Dam in Uttaradit Province.

NOTES

1. Paitoon Khruakaew, a Thai sociologist-politician who has attempted to codify the major characteristics of his society (1970), speaks of the *cid-caj nagleeng* (the *nagleeng* temperament) as one of the nine most important "values" of Thai culture. He cites three components of this value: "manliness," "sportsmanship" (a combination of the desire both to follow the rules and to take risks), and "benevolence" (taking care of one's followers). Also, the characteristics of the *nagleeng* that are emphasized here are different from those of a *nagleeng hua maaj* (a "wooden-headed *nagleeng*") who is a brutal, charmless, unadulterated thug.

2. *Karma* is the proportion of merit to demerit accumulated in past lives and brought into this one. *Phromlikhid,* or "lines of one's fate according to Lord Brahma," is a Hindu-derived doctrine of predestination. The notion of *upanidsaj,* or one's genetically given character, is part of the same semantic field.

3. Geertz's *Negara: The Theatre State in Nineteenth-Century Bali* (1980) provides persuasive evidence that this has been happening recurringly in Bali since the fourteenth century. It should also be noted that there is no hidden cultural meaning (although there may be a great deal of psychological meaning) to the dual symbolism of Kham's death, e.g., that he took his own life in fulfillment of its theatrical appropriateness and that he did this by presenting himself to someone who was exactly like he had once been.

Fulfilling One's Duty

Banthid Chumnikaaj

The vast area of land, altogether about two hundred and fifty thousand *rai,* spreads far and wide before us.[1] Its boundary in the distance is the Phaankam Mountains. The mountain range is being blasted apart where a small stream, the Phong, cuts through a narrow canyon. A dam eight hundred meters long with a core of clay is being built there. It will connect the mountains on each side, and the land before us will be turned into a man-made lake. Surely man can conquer everything. He can conquer the water, the earth, and he can even try to conquer the universe. But there is one thing he is incapable of conquering . . . the despair of the human heart.

I can't really guess whether you will feel or understand the kind of despondency that I have felt. Peace and happiness usually arise out of what started as trouble and difficulty. But when such happiness belongs to the majority, it is often bought at the expense of the minority. Every time a family, one after another, had to tear down its house and herd its animals and carts away from the area being flooded by the rising reservoir, every face would turn back to look at the land of his past. Each one carried a look that no other person could possibly read but which expressed feelings that reverberated within each of their hearts. Some families who received compensation for their land had the opportunity to move into the new community provided by the Department of Public Welfare. Some had long-standing problems about their land: the title deed indicated that they had ten *rai* but when the land was measured it was in reality only seven or eight *rai.* So payment had to be held up. Nobody could be held responsible, except maybe the officials from the Land Department who had done the original survey. Worse yet, some families did not have a title

From Suchart Sawadsii, *Laeng Khaen: Ruamryangsan Ruan Samaj Khong Thai* (Bangkok: D.K. Publishers, 1975).

1. One *rai* equals .40 of an acre. Thus, the area is one hundred thousand acres.

deed or even a squatter's land use certificate for the land upon which they had been making their livelihood for so long.[2] All we could do was feel sorry for them and quietly offer our sympathy. Their sad and worried faces showed repeatedly that they did not understand the situation. From one face to another, from one bewildered stare to another, there was only a look of innocence, devoid of any dishonesty or corruption.

I became more susceptible with every moment and more emotional about everything that was going on. I met a few families who had settled on the edge of the reservoir at the 175-meter level which, of course, would not be spared when the water reached its full height at the 182-meter mark. We asked them to move back from the reservoir area, an area that had been taken by eminent domain and assigned to the Northeastern Electrical Authority.

"Wherever we live, we're pushed out. Wherever we live, we're pushed out." These words still echo in my ears, ". . . as if we weren't human beings."

"But this area will be flooded," said Sukri, a field officer.

"Been living around here since I was born until I'm now ready to die in old age, and it has never flooded up here before," said the man as he picked up his son from the *paakhawmaa* cradle tied between two wobbly wooden house posts.[3]

"After we leave here, where do you expect me to go and starve to death?"

"The Department of Public Welfare's community, of course."

"I asked them, but they wouldn't let us move in. They said that I didn't have any papers to show that I was eligible." We left him hoping only that when the rains come and the water level gradually rises, nature will force him to move. "I only hope that the water won't suddenly sweep down in torrents. If that happens, I won't be able to forgive anybody, even myself."

By the beginning of the year, the villages of Phu Wiang, Non Singa, and Nong Rya would be under water, and in the far distance Non Sang would be an island high on the water. What was most troublesome to us

---

2. By Thai law and long tradition, virgin or unoccupied public land that has peen cultivated for ten consecutive years becomes the property of the cultivator. However, to be eligible for a title deed the original squatter must have had a land use certificate covering the preceding ten-year period.

3. The *paakhawmaa* is a simple rectangular cloth, usually in colored checks or plaids, that is the most frequently used item of the Thai peasant. Either worn or within arm's reach, it is used variously as a loincloth, belt, turban, rope, bath garment, and here as a cradle. No male Thai villager would ever be without one. It might also be noted that the seeming incongruity between the speaker's old age and the existence of a baby son would go unnoticed by most Thai readers—either because such paternity is not infrequent or because the whole situation would be read as normal village hyperbole.

was that while construction was still going on, there was a flotilla of small boats moving throughout the reservoir area. In the beginning, we permitted only the twenty boats that were originally there. Later we regretted having given them permission because more boats were built for transporting things around the dam area, obstructing the ongoing construction. We were forced to forbid them in the area even though we realized that the people operating the boats were those whose rice fields had been flooded and for whom operating the boats was a new way of making a living, helping them to make ends meet.

In the local newspaper of Khon Kaen Province criticism and complaints against our work began to appear. "People have been coming to me constantly with complaints," the editor told me. "Even though I agree with the government, I have to show them that I'm on the people's side, acting as their loudspeaker. Otherwise, I would just be breaking my own rice pot." All we could do was wait for the dam to be finished so that the Harbor Department could take over and control boat registration and the water traffic system.

While we were waiting for the problem to be straightened out, the incident with Kham occurred.[4] What I most clearly remember is the way he came walking into our field office one afternoon. He was a robust fellow, packed with muscles, arrogant in bearing. Following him were two other boatmen with that compliant and fearful look so common to villagers. They had been pushed around, generation after generation, by so many different "bosses" that by now they were completely cowed.

"How come we can't run our boats?" The first question he threw at us made Rampherj, the public relations officer, squirm uncomfortably.

"I would like to explain to you so you'll understand . . . ," Rampherj paused and went on, ". . . that we did not prohibit it. We only asked you to do us the favor of keeping boats one kilometer away from the dam."

"I don't understand. Why can other boats run and ours can't? The fact is that we're from Ban Sawang, and our boats always ran in the old reservoir. How come there are exceptions? How much money do you want, Mr. Engineer? One or two hundred *baht* a boat? I'll find it for you. All we want are the same rights as everyone else."

"It can't be done."

"All right, Mr. Engineer, what if I do it anyway?"

"I'll have to order the guards to arrest you."

"Arrest!" Kham repeated with a tone of mockery.

"I'm only doing my duty, Kham,"[5] Rampherj said, sighing heavily.

---

4. The author's selection of the name "Kham" is probably not arbitrary. It means "buttress" or "brace."

5. The use of only a first name with no "Mr.," title, or honorific is not unimportant. It means to suggest familiarity and also friendliness and is thus intended as a leavening to the situation. It also contains an underlying tinge of a put-down.

"We're also performing our duty." Kham pointed his raised finger around.[6] "You, Mr. Engineer, have your duty to try to arrest us and take us to be fined or to be put in jail. Your duty is to follow the orders of your boss so that you can continue to get your monthly salary. I also have a duty. My duty is to feed my own mouth and stomach. The duty of boat-running is to prevent us from starving to death. Everyone has his own duty."

"Kham, can't you wait and postpone this duty of yours a little longer?" I injected into the argument. "Just wait until the dam is finished, and the Harbor Department will get involved and will operate things around here. Then, we wouldn't prohibit anything."

"The duty of our people is to struggle for survival. Our duty is not to wait around to die and starve. You engineers may have never had any difficulty in making a living. You have your salaries. You have your houses. Your stomachs are always full. How would you know what to do when people's stomachs are empty?"

"Kham, you finished the seventh grade and have already served in the army, haven't you? Now that you've already done your duty of serving our country as part of the fence protecting the nation—don't answer yet.
. . . When Kham was a soldier, Kham was willing to serve our country with Kham's blood, flesh, and life. Now we're asking Kham to do the same thing again for our country. I'm not just carrying on with slogans and sweet-talk. Can't you see for yourself that during the first ten days of this month the water level has been rising rapidly? It's gone up a meter just during this period. What about tomorrow or the day after tomorrow? It will be even high and higher. Haven't you seen that we've cleared about ten thousand *rai* of forest, felling how many hundreds of thousands of trees? Our forest clearing had to burn huge stumps and drag as many logs as possible away from the reservoir area. We don't know how many logs have had to be burned, even though they're extremely valuable. As the water level rises, some of the stumps and logs the crew didn't get out will float with the current and hit the dam. This huge dam which is being built to store water for irrigation and the generation of electrical power could at any time be damaged, and then hundreds and hundreds of millions of *baht* will go down the drain. Think about it: If the reservoir is full of boats, how can our work of sweeping up the stray logs be done efficiently? It's true that running boats is your profession. But Kham, think of the millions of people whose professions will depend upon the power generated by this dam."

Rampherj's words provoked Kham into a long silence.

"But it won't matter if I run a few more boats. If you want to arrest me, go ahead and do it . . . until you finally give up. There are so many

---

6. This is very explicitly a gesture of pride and challenge.

boats, you engineers wouldn't know which one has a license and which one doesn't."

"Kham, why are you so stubborn?" Sukri said to himself wearily.

Kham and his men left. Sukri and Rampherj discussed the steps that had to be taken. I rushed back to Bangkok. And in Bangkok I read the news about the shooting of a high-ranking police officer by communists in Nakae District.[7] This news made me feel very uneasy. One thing that has been brought home to many developing countries is that a great wave of general discontent among the people is often set off by small eruptions here and there.

I feel apprehensive all the time. I am apprehensive about the possibility of little incidents turning into major disasters. I am so cowardly that my eyes turn white at the mere suggestion that there might be bloodshed.[8] I began to imagine the vast reservoir behind the dam filled to the brim with blood, blood flowing over the top to turn the wheels powering the generators, blood pouring through the sluices at the rate of twenty-five hundred cubic meters per second. Blood and more blood everywhere.[9]

I again returned to the Phongniip Dam. The train arrived at Non Phayom Station just as I was getting up, so I was still drowsy when I got off the train. Sukri had driven to the station to meet me. In the Land Rover we sat quietly for the forty kilometers. Just as we were entering the campsite, I asked about Kham. Sukri only smiled and shook his head. We said nothing else to each other.

At the gate, one of the guards reported that they had caught three boats operating illegally. I immediately thought of Kham. As we turned toward the police station inside the camp, I became more certain that I would be meeting Kham there, Kham with his arrogance and his special ability to infuriate people. His talent for leadership made me feel even more uneasy. I imagined him going back to his village, inciting his friends and neighbors with his heated arguments, and impressing his family and relatives with his stormy indignation.

I glanced around uncomfortably, looking at the boatmen who had violated the regulations. In their faded black clothing they looked like a cluster of plants that had withered in the hot sun. I let out a sigh of relief. Kham was not among them.

"The guard handed them to me this morning," reported the police cor-

---

7. Located in Nakorn Phanom Province in the Northeast, Nakae was the first district in Thailand in which some villages were effectively controlled by communist revolutionaries.

8. An idiom suggesting that the fear is so great that the pupils roll into their sockets, leaving only the whites of the eyes.

9. This image of flowing blood might be modelled on a well-known omen appearing in the pre-Bangkok Thai classic *Phra Lauau,* in which rivers of flowing blood and flowing water symbolize the hero's speculations about his destiny.

poral. "This guard is great at arrests. He pulls them all in, favoring nobody."

I spent the whole week going back and forth between the smaller power stations in Myang Phon, Sarakham, Udorn, and Khon Kaen. Whenever I got back to camp to spend the night, usually exhausted, I heard about this guard and the dedication with which he was going about his duties, arresting trespassers who had torn down official signs, people who had been fishing illegally in front of the dam, those who had smuggled their boats into the prohibited area of the reservoir. He was forever prohibiting and arresting. Each time I heard about this guy, I shuddered and closing my eyes tightly covered my head with the bed-sheet.

Late one night, a little after one o'clock, Sukri came rushing in and dragged me from my bed.

"Kham's been shot." He was struggling to catch his breath. "He's lying out there in front of the camp gate. Help me get an ambulance to get him out of here fast. I have to get over and report it to the chief first."

I thought, "He must have been sneaking his boat into the area again." On second thought, "Maybe this will serve him right, the stubborn fool. They told him that he was forbidden to bring his boat in, and he didn't listen. This time he probably had a big quarrel with the guard."

But my morality had to respond to the situation, so I awakened the nurse and driver and ran out to the gate.

Kham's face was deathly pale and his khaki uniform was soaked with blood. It was dark red, almost black, flowing down like water from a spring glistening in the light.

I ordered the guard and the nurse to lift Kham up into the ambulance. He lay still, with almost no movement, while the nurse pressed gauze to the open wound on his chest to staunch the flow of blood. The headlights of the ambulance shone brightly and the siren screamed through the night as we drove along. I sat beside him listening to his delirium alternate with his groans.

It was not long before his eyelids became heavy and narrow as blood poured from his nose, ears, and lips. Just as we turned onto Friendship Highway, his last moment came.

"Kham was a good guard who performed his duties extremely well," Sukri told me. "I called him to become chief guard after you had gone back to Bangkok last time. He was a man who was always deeply loyal to his duty, whether it was the duty of a boatman or the duty of a guard."

He was shot by a boatman with whom he used to run illegal boats and whom he later caught. The man shot him while the guard was being changed.

Goodbye, Kham. Farewell.

I will never forget his last faltering sentence: "Everyone has his own duty, Mr. Engineer. It goes with the position and with the *Khoon* mask that he has to wear.[10] A person may be forced to ambush and shoot somebody . . . in order to prove that his duty's fulfilled."

---

10. This is a reference to classical Thai dance, where every character wears a mask that defines his role. *Khoon* contrasts with *Lakhoon,* where the major characters wear no masks and have considerably greater freedom of expression.

The Enchanting Cooking Spoon

Introduction

Although it has some of the attributes of an upper-class soap opera, "The Enchanting Cooking Spoon" is both culturally and psychologically the richest essay in this volume. While it was written principally to document the changing nature of the role of Thai women and the conflict between old and new cultural standards, it simultaneously addresses several other equally significant themes of upper-class life. Among these are the miscommunication between spouses; the consequences of foreign education; the nature of familial responsibility; the *noblesse oblige* assumptions of *phuu dii* and the uncertainties about such assumptions in a society that has become increasingly equalitarian; the cycle of boredom and excitement that pervades every part of Thai emotional life and that influences major decisions; the constant attention to social ritual; the cultivation of verbal confusion and the high tolerance for things that may make little verbal sense; and the perennial threat of the "other woman."

In addition to being thematically complex, the story is extraordinarily felicitous to the tone and quality of upper-class life, mainly by using an idiom that stylistically is similar to that actually used by members of upper-class society. In this sense, the formulaic and ritualistic elements of the story are not merely literary inventions. When members of this class speak of "a good husband" they think immediately of a man who, like Praphon, is constantly arranging things for his wife and their friends. Similarly, those who have attended foreign universities do conceive of "the many hundreds of books" they have read as a principal source of their sophistication. And notwithstanding Praphon's protest, most members of this class *still* think of the ideal Thai wife in terms of the cooking spoon metaphor.

It is as a psychological statement that the story is most complex and revealing. At its most obvious level, it is an account of a woman caught between the traditional role definitions of her culture and the modern definitions of her husband and, because the two definitions are irreconcilable, being unable to fulfill either in a personally satisfying way. While contemporary Thai society provides many variations on this kind of conflict, the details of the scenario laid out here make complete cultural sense and are in no way unusual. However, at a more subtle level the story is also an account of the husband being caught in the same conflict and, although he is unaware of it for most of the narrative, his being the cause of his wife's double bind, that is, by wishing and goading her to be as much a modern woman as he is a "fully modern man"—mainly by having her serve as one of his intellectual adversaries. Not being able to escape his own orthodox male chauvinism, he also treats her as (and, of course, marries her because she was) the embodiment of the traditional feminine ideal.

That a man of Praphon's wealth, status, and worldly experience could even have such a conflict, and actually come close to acknowledging it, transforms what might otherwise be an engaging but banal story into a statement of literary and ethical originality. In fact, from the point of view of traditional Thai male morality, Praphon's awareness of the conflict represents a redefining of the meaning of male sophistication. From a Western point of view, it could be argued that Praphon's alternative perceptions of his wife's role (a cooking spoon versus a debating partner) are simply different expressions of his own underlying narcissism and that his "conflict" here is really no conflict at all. However, narcissism (defining the woman primarily in terms of her value to the male self) is such an unquestioned attribute of the Thai male's orientation toward women that although the argument may be true, it was probably irrelevant to the author's formulation. Praphon's final speeches—which from the author's point of view represent his moral redemption—virtually ooze with male self-concern. It is a self-concern modified by insight, but nevertheless self-concern. For this reason alone, the character of Praphon represents a superb portrait of the psyche of the upper-class Thai male—or at least of one of his more significant attributes.

There is another, equally subtle level to the story, one that has more to do with the relationship between the two principals than with their individual characters. Throughout, Phachongchid complains that she does not understand the meaning or intent of Praphon's words. Although some of her confusion may be self-imposed, clearly there is merit to her grievance. In places, Praphon speaks in riddles ("Everybody must lack something. Just let's not lack the most important thing.") In others, he attributes things to her that obviously are projections of his own interests, not expressions of hers. In still other places, he plays Socratic games with her, perhaps to instruct her but more clearly to twit her or to dramatize his own self-importance (asking for a test of the meaning of "social order"). And through much of the second half of the story, he struggles to bring order and clarity to his own reasoning, as much for himself as for his wife. Indeed, although he explicitly asks her "not to take the things I say too seriously," he cannot stop himself from running on at the mouth —if only out of adoration for his own ideas or for the process of creating them.

What is intriguing about this verbal confusion is that while it is used aesthetically to create tension—and, in fact, is the literary device that makes the story possible—it is also presented as a culturally normal way for two people to relate to each other. Despite Phachongchid's complaints, neither she nor the author ever comment upon, recognize, or otherwise allude to anything unusual about Praphon's verbal style. At the descriptive level, it is obviously "interesting" behavior, but beyond that there is nothing about it that merits evaluation. It is as if the author simply perceives ambiguity, perplexity, and miscommunication to be as inherent to the marital situation as their opposites. Many Thai would say that she is probably right.

Some scholars have in fact argued that the Thai may have a higher tolerance for uncertainty and ambiguity in interpersonal situations than do other people. (See Bilmes 1975 for examples from real-life village situations that are very much in accord with the fictional examples provided here.) If this is true, it is probably not because they prize uncertainty as an end in itself, but rather because such uncertainty serves other, more psychologically important purposes—"important," at least, to the actors themselves. Thus, without passing judgment on Praphon's interpersonal priorities, his behavior demonstrates that for him verbal dueling and using his wife as a pawn were more important than communicating with sufficient clarity for her to understand—the alternatives being mutually exclusive. Similarly, it would seem that he was more taken with his own inner cognitive processes and with his attempts to transform these processes into coherent, socially meaningful thought than he was with his impact upon the person with whom he was dealing or with her actual responses. There is, of course, nothing fundamentally exotic about such behavior. It simply reminds us that any interpersonal relationship has a multiplicity of attributes and purposes and that there is no inherent reason why clarity of communication or certainty of meaning must be the most important of these. The latter are only a few of the things that may —or equally likely, may not—happen when people talk to one another.

There are a few other aspects of the story that should be noted. Notwithstanding Praphon's attempts to place himself, Phachongchid, and their *phuu dii* friends into the middle class, the evidence indicates that they are of the upper classes. The story is set in the late 1950s or early 1960s, and during this period only such people could have so readily become country squires, have graduated from Sandhurst or have received their medical degrees in the United States, have a grandmother who was a *thaanphuuying,* or have spent so much time partying (or at least talk as if they did). What the actual wealth of Praphon's circle of friends might have been is quite another matter. Praphon's foreign experience gave him an international perspective on the Thai class system, and his comments on the Thai elite not being "wealthy enough to do anything great . . . what Chinese or *farang* millionaires do" were probably correct. By having him refer to himself and his circle as members of the middle class, the author might have been trying to suggest that in terms of actual wealth, and perhaps social values, Thailand's *phuu dii* were essentially at the same level as the middle class of other societies. Of course, the critical factor here may have simply been the tendency that all Thai have, villagers as well as *phuu dii,* to level themselves off and to give themselves a middle position whenever discussing their own status.

Finally, it should be noted that although some of the details of the story are dated (nowadays even rural Thai relax in front of television, not radio) and the hero's character might be considered a bit quaint (few Thai men would now identify with Praphon's fetish for intellectual encounters with his wife), the basic issues that the story addresses are still critical to the experience of many members of the Thai elite. Thus, for all the prestige they enjoy for having been educated abroad and for being "fully modern men" (and women), there are numerous Thai who, like Praphon, have paid for their prestige by being unable to communicate with their spouses, by being bored with their friends, and by feeling a sense of malaise about their culture. This is not to suggest that most Thai would deny that it was worth the price. On the contrary, it is simply to reinforce the author's contention that there is indeed a price—a price that involves the most subtle dimensions of one's identity and of one's relationships with loved ones.

Another basic issue, one perhaps that the author never intended but that emerges with unmistakable clarity, is the frivolity, self-indulgence, and essentially uncreative nature of the lives of the two principals. Of the two, Praphon—who tries to be reflective about everything—feels more uncomfortable about it and responds with more ambivalence. But neither he nor Phachongchid ever really come to terms with understanding the social basis of their "boredom" or what they can realistically do to remedy it. If Praphon is to be believed, his love and respect for his wife, and his emerging awareness of the constraints placed upon her by her background, would prevent him from doing very much to significantly alter their lives, if only to avoid adding to her burdens. Thus, as in the description of their relationship with each other, the author has recognized and laid out a problem but has not provided us with any easy answers.

The author, M. L. Boonlue Kunjara Debyasuvan, was for several decades and in a variety of roles a leader of Thailand's intellectual community. At various times she was a writer, teacher, intellectual celebrity, educational administrator, cultural innovator, and even a social symbol. Born in 1911 into one of the nation's most distinguished families, she was the youngest of the twenty-five children (sixteen girls and nine boys) of *Chaw Phya* Thewes—officially the equestrian of King Chulalongkorn and the companion-protector of the crown prince but more importantly the king's most trusted equerry and closest personal friend; the two would often steal out of the palace in disguise and join other customers in the noodle shops of Bangkok's Raachawongse area. Her mother died when she was four, and she was raised by a brother ("with whom I constantly argued") who was thirty-one years her senior. However, she considered the two most influential persons in her life to be her father ("who taught me to be a rebel") and her uncle, Prince Narisara Nuwatiwongse ("who encouraged us to ask questions that Thai children do not ask.") The latter lived in her father's compound while she was growing up and during his lifetime was considered to be Thailand's greatest composer, dramatist, and architect—his most acclaimed design being Bangkok's Marble Temple.

Boonlue's older half-sister by six years was Daukmaajsod (M. L. Buphaa Nimanhemin), who is generally viewed as the most influential female author of this century in Thailand. In numerous novels and stories, Daukmaajsod virtually institutionalized the concept of *"phuu dii,"* so that in a very real sense the normal Thai use of the term came to follow her artistic formulation. Although Daukmaajsod had spent her formative years living in the palace, she and Boonlue became close friends after the latter reached young adulthood, and they maintained their closeness for the balance of their lives. Boonlue was to have a more varied career than her sister and also did not begin her own creative writing until much later in life, but being sisters, the two have been constantly compared. The prevailing critical view is that while Daukmaajsod had a much greater impact on the taste and imagination of her readers (mostly middle- and upper-middle-class young women), Boonlue's work is considerably more mature, subtle, and realistic and thus represents a more authentic record of the actual nature of upper-class life.

Boonlue received her early education at a convent school in Bangkok, and after her father's death, when she was eleven, she went on to a convent in Penang, Malaya. She has said that these experiences not only provided her with a solid grounding in English, which remained a lifelong professional interest, but also provided her with a sense of challenge and inquiry: "the nuns challenged and intensified my belief in Buddhism and taught me the necessity, and also the pleasure, of examining things that most Thai never question." She later graduated from Chulalongkorn University and received a fellowship from the American Association of University Women to study at the University of Minnesota ("which were the happiest years of my life"), where in 1950 she was awarded a master's degree.

Much of Boonlue's professional life was spent in the Ministry of Education where, decades before it was popular, she essentially created the teaching of English as a foreign language and where she also served as a teacher, teacher supervisor, principal of a college of education, and held other high administrative posts. However, she was keenly aware of the fact that she never reached the top of the bureaucracy: "My family background and sex prevented it. We were brought up by men who taught us to speak our minds and to give and take criticism without feeling threatened. The modern Thai bureaucracy does not operate that way. Because a woman has to speak louder and more firmly in order to be heard, I was always getting into trouble with my superiors. I think that if I had either learned to keep my mouth shut or had been a man, I would have been a minister twice over." It is no accident that Boonlue's own favorite character in "The Enchanting Cooking Spoon" is Chaarinii.

If her forthrightness got her into trouble in the bureaucracy, it clearly served a very different purpose in her public life. Together with M. R. Khukrit Pramoj, whom she considered one of her most friendly adversaries, she was for years one of Thailand's major intellectual celebrities, serving as a panel discussant, commentator, and lecturer on matters of cultural import. This role and her numerous writings resulted in her being called the "Margaret Mead of Thailand." However, unlike her American counterpart, her royal title and associations also made her into a symbol of a vanishing social type—the self-confident and outspoken aristocrat.

Boonlue wrote numerous short stories, some major novels, translated Thai fiction into English and English literature into Thai (Sir Walter Scott's *The Talisman,*) and authored numerous essays on the culture of the English and Thai-speaking worlds. After a trip abroad and a lengthy illness, Boonlue passed away in June 1982.

The Enchanting Cooking Spoon

"Boonlue"

My parents, at whose feet I pay respect and whom I love most deeply,

Your child has started this letter several times, but I have not been able to finish it. I have torn up and thrown away all my earlier efforts. I could not send them. But now I can no longer hold back. I can no longer stand living with Praphon, because there is absolutely no way that we can get along—absolutely no way. And there is absolutely no way for us to reach an understanding with each other. Therefore, your child is writing you about this—so that you will know. And I also want to tell you that your child does not blame you for this, because in bringing me up the two of you always had the finest intentions. It is a result of my own kam.[1] *But I do not understand. I do not understand at all. Father dear, Mother dear, I do not understand at all. . . .*

"Could it be the way I was brought up? My education? Maybe that's it. . . .

As she dwelled on all of this, several more tears came to her eyes and dropped onto her cheeks.

"Is it possible that Phachongchid had too little education to become Praphon's loving wife. If that's the reason, my father and mother were the ones to blame. Because when Phachongchid finished her secondary education, there was a long discussion on whether or not she should go to the university. Father and Mother were the ones who decided so confidently that Phachongchid need not further her education at the university level. They decided instead that she should study those things that a

---

Abridged from *Chaak Nyng Naj Chiiwid* [Scenes from life] (Bangkok: Prae Pittaya Publishing Co., 1964).

1. *Karma,* the proportion of merit to demerit accumulated in past lives and brought into this one.

woman should know, such as how to be a good housewife and home-maker. Father and Mother always said—they said it so the relatives, Pha-chongchid herself, and everybody around her would hear—'An enchant-ing cooking spoon can charm her man until the day he dies.' "

After the decision had been made, Phachongchid had tried to study and to learn all those things, every single thing, that her father and mother wanted her to learn—from her parents themselves and from the teachers her parents found to instruct her. Eventually she got the reputa-tion for being the very best homemaker there was.

To quarrel with her husband was something that just could not hap-pen. It was simply something that could not arise in her kind of life, even if she and her husband were to separate and go their different ways and she had to leave behind her three-year-old son—which was precisely what she was now planning to do. Phachongchid and Praphon would not quarrel with each other, because Phachongchid would never argue with the man to whom she was married.

When it came to quarreling the whole thing was strange. Praphon did not understand, Praphon who was also a most well-bred person, just like Phachongchid. He did not consider quarreling between a husband and wife as anything terrible. When Phachongchid said to him, "All right, okay . . . let's not quarrel. I'm not going to argue with you," his response would be, "But why? We are husband and wife. We ought to be arguing. Not to argue is unnatural."

But Phachongchid would not argue with him. She kept her disappoint-ment to herself, secreted in her own heart. As each day went by, her inability to understand him increased.

"*Khun* Praphon, dear, don't you believe that adultery and taking some other man's wife as a lover is immoral?"

"To have a lover and to be a lover is an individual matter. It depends on the couples. It depends on the circumstances . . . on the story. Some-times it is a bad thing. On other occasions it is a good thing."

She saw Praphon's face change from being cool, calm, and expression-less into the face of a person brimming with attentiveness. His eyes opened wide and gleamed as if filled with the pleasure of the exchange, the pleasure of being able to talk back and forth. So Phachongchid dared to go further.

"Is it really possible for it to be considered a good thing?"

"Why can't it be?" Praphon answered. "If the love they have for each other is pure, then it could be called a good thing."

"Who? Who is that? What people love each other purely? Is it possible to call adultery something pure?" Phachongchid responded in disagree-ment.

"But sometimes people meet their eternal mate[2] at the wrong time. She is already married and with a husband. What can they do?"

He fixed his eyes on her, as if inviting her to continue the controversy. Seeing his eyes Phachongchid came to her senses. She realized that it was not part of her duty to disagree with him on this kind of issue. But she was still very disappointed in him for taking this attitude. She could no longer keep it inside of her, so she said, "All right. Let's not disagree. It might turn into a quarrel. But I'm concerned with what my friends might say, particularly Adcharaa.[3] She is a person who takes the things she believes in very seriously."

Praphon looked as if he were not very happy about what his wife had just said. Ignoring her comments on her friend, he responded, "Why? We're husband and wife living together. We're supposed to quarrel."

Phachongchid said nothing, but she thought to herself, "I have never ever quarreled with him, and see how little he loves me. If we had a real quarrel, he might leave me and go find another wife. I am sure that at this time in our lives the only thing that keeps us together is our son, the one person he loves as much as he loves his own life."

Phachongchid's thoughts ran on so quickly, almost like lightning. All the different events in her life crowded her memory. They were more vivid than they had ever been before.

Her mind went back to the time before Praphon had come to ask for her hand in marriage. . . . As time had been going by, so had many of

---

2. The original Thai here is *nya khuu thaeae* (literally, "genuine flesh and blood mate"), which has reference to the notion that the couple have been lovers and/or husband and wife in continuous previous existences. Many Thai use this same metaphor to explain the state of old maidhood, e.g., that the woman is simply out of phase with her *nya khuu thaeae* and is patiently waiting—if necessary, until her next life—for him to appear.

3. Adcharaa is a character who exists only as an occasional verbal allusion and whose role has been omitted from this abridged translation. She is an unmarried, physically unattractive, old classmate of the heroine who is going overseas for an advanced degree and for whom Phachongchid and Praphon are planning a going-away party. It is these very qualities, however, that make her a critical symbol of elite female life of this period.

On the one hand, the party is for Adcharaa virtually a *rite de passage* into old maidhood and thus an expression of her failure to fulfill the normal expectations of the women of her class. The author writes: "Those friends who had been successful in life—that is, those who were able to find a husband, have a beautiful and comfortable home, and a car in which to go around—all felt that they had to make Adcharaa realize that they did not desert her simply because she was not successful. 'Not being successful' meant 'not being able to get married.' And her classmates were happy that Adcharaa was able to have at least one kind of success that gave her happiness, although they realized that the very scholarship that

the desirable men. They were marrying Phachongchid's friends or relatives or those whom Phachongchid knew only by name. And some married young women whose names Phachongchid had never heard before.

It was all done in whispers. When certain things came to pass—where there was a young man of sufficient wealth, the off-spring of people of the same class and circle as Phachongchid, someone who had perhaps completed his education abroad or had already been given one of the more desirable posts in Thailand—some of the senior members of the family would come and whisper such facts into the ear of Phachongchid's mother. Mother would then whisper them to Father. In some cases, Mother was agreeable, but Father was not; in other cases, it was just the opposite; and in still other cases, the young men indicated that they did not find Phachongchid quite to their liking. One young prince said that she was too tall. Another gallant, a captain who had graduated from Sandhurst, said that she did not dance too well and was not a good conversationalist. And still another, a physician with a degree from America, said that both her parents were snobs who turned every chance meeting into a formal ceremony. And there was still another physician from America who sent a go-between to ask for her hand. After Luang Phithuk, he was the second one to push his suit this far. But Phachongchid did not find him to her liking, mainly because his manners were too modern.

As each year went by Phachongchid got older. Her mother began to consult astrologers more frequently about Phachongchid's situation. To her, it was incredible that her only daughter could not find a husband—a

---

signified her success would in the end greatly reduce her chances for their kind of success."

On the other hand, Adcharaa's experiences and opportunities represent for many Thai women all that is exciting in life: going off to foreign lands and being literally "a woman of the world," developing one's own talents, being free of family (particularly spousal) responsibilities and cultural restraints, and also being the pride of one's family of birth. In these terms, Adcharaa is a direct contrast with Phachongchid but is also almost a female Praphon: she is about to partake in a lengthy foreign experience; she is a person who "takes the things she believes in very seriously"; and she is also a person whom the parochial Phachongchid thoroughly misunderstands.

Another character who is alluded to in this situation is Luang Phithuk, an old admirer of Phachongchid's whom Praphon wants very much to invite to the going-away party for Adcharaa. That a husband should wish to invite one of his wife's old admirers to his own home is most unusual and further underscores Praphon's unique personality. Luang Phithuk is a man who himself "stole" another man's wife and is now most happily married to her—providing strong evidence in support of Praphon's arguments on the feasability of adultery. Finally, it turns out that the "stolen wife" is known both to Phachongchid and to Adcharaa, having been one of their secondary school classmates.

daughter to whom she had given the finest education and training, whose wealth was so appropriate to her status, and whose face and figure were no less charming than that of any other woman in their circle of relatives and friends.

It was just when Phachongchid herself was becoming more concerned about the astrologers' interpretations of her horoscope that Mr. Praphon Bunyalak returned from abroad. At the time, Phachongchid was a full twenty-eight years old, going on twenty-nine. In just another year she would be thirty. In the Thai way of counting this is the age at which you can no longer fool yourself that you have not become an old maid.

Praphon was already thirty-five years old when he returned to the land of his birth. During his many years abroad he had lived in different and strange places. He had first gone to study in Switzerland and in France. And later he was in Italy on government service. When the war began he was in England attending a conference, and he later spent the war years in America.

Unlike most men who had lived overseas for several years, Praphon had returned home without a foreign wife. Relatives, older friends, and those of his own age—all those with good will—tried their best to have Praphon meet Phachongchid and get to know her. They also tried their best to let him know her virtues—all of them—and also they tried in every way to prevent him from meeting anyone younger than Phachongchid who might have a chance to capture him or to divert his attention away from her. . . .

Phachongchid remembered that during the early period of the Phachongchid-Praphon project it was her father's oldest brother, the one who loved her so much, who served as chairman of the Operating Committee and that his wife was probably the chief strategist. Another uncle was vice-chairman, and there were several others who also served on the committee.

The uncle began the operation by coming to see her father and whispering into his ear, "*Thaanphuuying*'s grandson has returned.[4] He doesn't have a *farang* wife. She wants someone to help her find a good wife for him. She doesn't want any of those modern girls."

"Our group . . . we don't know very much about her . . . ," Father said.

"They say that she's an absolute snob," Uncle replied, ". . . and yet she's not so rich. But she's not so poor either. But our little one is no

---

4. *Thaanphuuying* is the highest official title that the king of Thailand confers on women for their contributions to society. However, since most *thaanphuuying* have in recent years been largely wives of prime ministers and deputy prime ministers, the title has become more descriptive of the husband's social rank than of the wife's social contribution.

longer very young. And the guy has never been married. This kind of match is hard to find, hard to find . . . something like this. . . ."

Phachongchid knew that Praphon's thirty-five years in no way lessened his value in the marriage market of Thailand's royal capital, if only because his advanced age gave him a proportionately higher rank in the national bureaucracy.

The efforts of Phachongchid's relatives and friends were fully satisfied. The older member of Praphon's family who had represented the groom's interests had come to Phachongchid's father and mother to ask for her hand.

During all the phases of the negotiation—from the time they first knew of each other, through the occasion of asking for her hand, to the beginning of their actual engagement—Praphon never did anything to make Phachongchid waiver. She was certain that she would be successful in her marriage because almost all her older relatives reminded her of what she was. Her uncle often said to her, "Whoever gets you, my little one, will fall hard—that's for sure. A girl who fries noodles like you—you're out of this world!"

Other relatives used to say, "When Phachongchid raises her children, no one will dare to be critical."

And male in-laws would often praise Phachongchid for possessing precisely those things that their own wives lacked.

On one occasion, just two weeks before her hand was asked for, Praphon himself had a fleeting moment alone with her, and told her, "You are truly beautiful, *Khun* Phachongchid. From whatever angle I look, I see only beauty. . . ."

Shortly before the engagement ceremony, Phachongchid's father and mother invited Praphon to their home for dinner. It was to be just the four of them: Father, Mother, Praphon, and Phachongchid.

Phachongchid had carefully prepared all the with-rice[5] dishes and the dessert, had arranged the dining table, the living room, the recreation room, and the patio, had trimmed all the flowers in the garden, and had done everything to make the house a place that was pleasant to the eye and to the heart. And then she dressed herself carefully, not to be too beautiful but to be beautiful in a way that was flawless. Everything that Phachongchid did was done with grace and proportion. To glance at it was to see its beauty. To scrutinize it was to see its suitability. That night everything was felicitous to the occasion.

---

5. The staples of the Thai diet are divided into two major categories: "rice" and "with-rice," the latter including all curries, meat, fish, chicken, cooked vegetables, shellfish, condiments, and soups. "Fruits" and "sweets" (or "cakes" and "desserts") represent minor, independent categories.

It was at the dining table that Praphon commented on how delicious all the with-rice dishes and the dessert were and how beautifully the flowers had been arranged. And when there was an opportunity, he let her know with a whisper how attractively she was dressed. But when dinner had been finished and the four of them had moved into the patio, her mother walked out, soon returned, and beckoned Phachongchid to leave with her once again, saying that Father and Praphon should be left alone for a suitable period of time. When the suitable period of time had elapsed, her mother returned to the patio, calling to Phachongchid, "Why have you been gone so long?"

When Phachongchid returned to the patio, the four were together momentarily, and then the parents sneaked out, leaving their daughter alone with Praphon—just the two of them. This was something that had never occurred before, at least so obviously.

On this first occasion that the two were together—alone and face-to-face—so that they might become better acquainted, Phachongchid began to learn some surprising things about Praphon.

At first, he was talking to her about the most ordinary things—movies, novels, parties that they had both been to, and then, at some point, he began talking about married life.

"It seems to me that you and I don't have to beat around the bush anymore, being so formal with one another. It is now well known that we're going to be married. But we haven't done anything that really binds us together. Therefore, before we're tied to one another I would like to know your ideas and how you think about marriage and if there is anything about marriage over which we basically disagree."

"What kind of disagreement could we have?" Phachongchid asked with astonishment.

"Oh, there might be some things. For example, . . . let me give you an illustration: What are your moral views about marriage? Do you think that a marriage should allow divorce?"

"Eeee . . . ," Phachongchid cried out, unaware of what she was saying. She continued: "Do you mean a woman and a man who have already been married? That they ought to be divorced? Is that what you mean?"

"All right. . . . If you want to begin with that subject, we should talk about it."[6]

"Obviously there should be no divorce," she answered.

"There should be no divorce at all? Divorce, separation, is something that should never be done at all—is that what you mean?"

"Oh, . . . for some couples it is necessary," Phachongchid answered.

---

6. Praphon's assignment to Phachongchid of the responsibility for initiating discussion on this subject is even stronger in the original Thai than it is in English.

He immediately indicated his satisfaction with a smile. "That means: Some couples can divorce, and some couples should not divorce. Is that right?"

Phachongchid did not think that this was the kind of problem that should ever be raised, but when she saw his bright smile, she smiled too.

"All right," he said, "On this matter we think precisely the same. Now, this concerns you directly. If you were married, could you contemplate divorcing your husband?"

"What? Why should I contemplate something like that?"

"No, that's not right. I'm not speaking clearly. What I mean is that, as far as you're concerned, if you had a husband with some terrible flaws, if he were a bad person, and if you found this out later, after you were married, would you divorce him?"

Phachongchid stared at him in puzzlement. She examined his face carefully and then diverted her eyes. "What is he beginning to confess?" Her heart started to palpitate. "Is he going to confess that he has a foreign wife, a child hiding in some foreign country?"

He looked at her in a stoical way, as if he had no hidden motives.

She gathered her courage and looked him straight in the eye. "What are you planning to do? Or what have you done?" she snapped.

"That's right!" he said with satisfaction. "That's an answer I understand."[7]

He then changed the topic of conversation and began to talk of travel, a house that he thought of building, and other subjects that were not important to Phachongchid, leaving her to mull over the meaning of his words until he was ready to leave.

It was not more than a week after this discussion on divorce had taken place that the ceremony of the engagement of Praphon and Phachongchid was celebrated. And on the very night of the engagement Phachongchid was once more faced with the puzzlement of Praphon's character.

One of the things about Phachongchid's home was the fact that when people came to dine they never failed to carry on about how the food there captured their attention and demanded their admiration. But when some people began to congratulate Praphon over the fact that he was about to marry a homemaker of the highest rank, Praphon solemnly spoke out: "It should be understood that I'm not marrying Phachongchid

---

7. Although the meanings here are not explicit in English, they are very clear in Thai. Phachongchid's response is (and is correctly perceived to be) one of annoyance and hostility, rather than inquiry. To a Thai reader this suggests that with the proper provocation, the wife could reach the point of divorcing him—which is the very answer that Praphon wants to hear.

because she happens to be a cook of the highest rank. If I were the kind of person who were preoccupied with his stomach I would go out and hire a good cook. It would not be necessary to make an investment equal to the one I'm now making."

A little later, when they were alone and able to chat, Phachongchid turned to Praphon and asked, "Excuse me, dear, but I would really like to understand something. What is the meaning of that word 'investment' that you used earlier?"

"Oh, my . . . ," he said laughingly. "Don't you see? The cost of the love nest, the engagement ring, and the Chinese banquet for the wedding party . . . because if it's not arranged that way the bride will get all involved in the kitchen doing the thing herself, and she'll forget all about the groom."

"And what did you mean about 'hiring a cook'?"

"Well, . . . it's impossible to hire somebody to be 'the perfect wife,' "[8] he again laughed in a bantering way. . . .

Two weeks after the engagement ceremony Praphon caused his fiancee to tremble and to shake—but in a good way.

That night the moon was full, and it had showered its silver rays throughout the garden. Beneath the great magnolia tree that had been planted by Phachongchid's great grandfather, Praphon enveloped Phachongchid's body in his arms and, without giving her time to answer, asked her: "Does it violate tradition terribly if I do it? I am going to kiss you." And then without hesitation he did exactly what he said he was going to do. Phachongchid's entire body trembled, like the body of a baby animal which had encountered an animal other than her mother for the first time.

She was surprised by her own feelings. She felt good all over—in a way that was beyond words to describe. But her upbringing helped harden her heart, and she answered, "Wouldn't it be better not to violate tradition too often?"

Praphon knew that what he had done had created great conflict within her, and he did not want to make her feel that way too often.[9]

But as their wedding day approached, Phachongchid gradually let her feelings of fear be replaced by her feelings of pleasure, until one day, about a month before the wedding, Praphon noted: "People told me that

---

8. "The perfect wife" here is *"sri pharayaa,"* which has several specific connotations: a perfect homemaker, conversationalist, beauty, lover, mother to one's children, and also someone whose inherent quality it is to advance her husband's career. During the 1950s, the term was used by the Thai press to mock the overly helpful wives of national political figures.

9. The Thai here is as clear as the English in suggesting that Praphon thought it was perfectly all right to make her feel that way from time to time.

I would be marrying an angel. But the truth is, you're just a normal woman.[10] Isn't that right?"

Phachongchid's heart fell. Once more, he was saying something that she did not understand.

"What do you mean by that?"

"Oh, . . . you're looking for the meaning again. You just love to ask questions, don't you? You want me to pick my words and phrases so they describe everything perfectly. What I mean is that you are the joy of Praphon's heart. You are the essential thing of Praphon's life—that's all. . . ."

Phachongchid sighed heavily to herself. His explanation did not make her bloom with pleasure. She rationalized that if she were a real angel she would have to be in a place that was beyond his reach, and that was something that could never be. He did say that the joy she gave him was just right. And since this was sufficiently on the positive side, she decided to stop her nagging. She remembered that she had been taught never to bore a man with arguments. A man does not want to argue with a woman he loves. If he wants to argue, to sharpen his wits or for some other reason, he will go do this with his male friends. A woman is the one who gives him happiness. When he comes to see a woman, he comes to obtain happiness. . . .

One day a bit later he and she went to a luncheon that had been arranged at the home of one of his cousins. That particular cousin was known to be a warmhearted person, and it was with sincerity that she welcomed Phachongchid into her home. She spoke in a soft, endearing way. But her food, particularly her with-rice dishes, had no taste at all. Phachongchid, however, noticed Praphon partaking of the food without difficulty, taking suitable amounts, and later complimenting the hostess, telling her that everything was delicious—all of this being done in the same manner that was first used with Phachongchid.

Since their engagement, Phachongchid and Praphon had gotten into the habit of having dinner together every evening. And that night, when they were chatting after their meal and the opportunity had presented itself, she asked him: "*Khun* Praphon, dear, at lunch today—were you really able to eat that food? I saw you passing out the compliments. . . . Or were you just pretending?"

"To say that I was 'just pretending' is not right, because my reason for saying those things was to make the hostess feel good."

---

10. Here the Thai is in fact ambiguous. The original term, *thammadaa*, can also mean "common" or "undistinguished." Thus, whatever Praphon's motives, Phachongchid is not totally amiss in considering the phrase an adjectival comedown.

"Does that mean that whatever you eat, no matter how bad it tastes, deserves a compliment? Is that what you're saying?"

"When someone invites us to their home to share a meal with them, we compliment them. We do it because we feel grateful to them for inviting us. They have a good heart and are being generous to us. We're not complimenting their expertise at cooking. 'Expertise' depends on the individual's viewpoint—on each person's mouth and tongue. If it's right for a mouth and tongue, it's called 'expert cooking'."

"And when you eat here—if the food is not too good, do you compliment me, too?"

"In this house, there is nothing that is not delicious. When I'm with Phachongchid, anything and everything is delicious."

Phachongchid did not dare to nag him more than that. So she turned the conversation to other things. But later that night something happened as they were saying goodbye to one another. She was standing near the driver's door of his car when he turned on the lights and started the motor. He then reached out, kissed her hand, and caressing her long, soft, round arm, he looked into her eyes and said, "Phachongchid, don't pay so much attention to food and to eating. It's not the most important thing in life. . . ." Letting go of her hand, he then drove off.

Phachongchid brooded a long time before falling asleep that night.

What does it mean? There were all those words of advice and instruction that she had been given by her elders, her family, and her friends—all those people who knew her. Were they all wrong? Or was it because she did not have the ability or talent? Were all those compliments merely words to express feelings of kindness?

She had the feeling that she lacked something that Praphon wanted, but she could not identify what that something was. Every time she asked him for the truth, his answer indicated he loved her, but it was never about the thing she wanted to know.

She remembered the day she had a chance to ask him straight out, "Praphon dear, what is it that I lack that you want?"

His way of answering her was to express his love and desire passionately, and to say, "Everybody must lack something. Just let's not lack the most important thing."

? ? ? ? ? ? ? ?

When they were first married, Phachongchid's various doubts and confusions were temporarily forgotten. This was because she and Praphon were so involved in expressing their deep love for one another. But as the days passed, Phachongchid became aware that Praphon's admiration and pleasure in her were something less than absolute. His behavior suggested that he was accepting about the things he had and that his luck, his good luck, was about the same as that of any man. He was an affable husband who tried to please his wife some of the time. But he was also bored with his way of life. And many of the things which interested or excited him, Phachongchid did not consider important.

For example, one day the two of them went on an outing to the seashore at Samut Prakan where they happened to meet an official who was responsible for recruiting bright village children into provincial secondary schools. On their drive back to the city, Praphon talked constantly about this subject. Sitting beside him, Phachongchid let him carry on, always contributing enough "yes, yeses" and appropriately timed questions to fulfill the rules of being a dutiful wife.

The opposite also occurred. Phachongchid could not avoid noticing that Praphon's whole disposition changed whenever she and her friends got together for a party. It was so obvious that she had to tell him, "It seems that these kinds of parties are not very much fun for you. If you don't want to go, you don't have to. I'm not going to say anything."

"These are parties you have to go to—because we live in the same world with others. Not to associate with others at all is something that cannot be. . . . When they are having fun, we have to join them in their fun. When they are grieving, we have to join them in their grief."

"But you're so bored with these things. . . ."

"I appreciate your cautioning me. I have to improve somewhat the way I behave—because that too is a social problem."

After that, Praphon demonstrated his pleasure in all kinds of social activities. He became the central figure, rather than a mere on-looker, in arranging things like birthday parties. He took charge of the task of organizing the group, of printing invitations, of making the guest list, of delivering the invitations, and the like. And if it were a cremation, he did even more to make himself useful to the host—until the word had gone out to all that Phachongchid had the nicest of husbands.

Finally, one day she could no longer hold back her curiosity, and she asked him: "Praphon, dear, what is the real reason you're running around, pulling strings everywhere, and helping everybody?"

"To cure my boredom. It's better than sitting around bearing the boredom. Beside that, I'm doing people favors.[11] I still am indebted to you for cautioning me that day to improve my attitude."

Phachongchid was enraptured. She felt the same way she felt when she smelled the scent of flowers being carried through the quiet night air. But then she continued: "How about here? Is there anything in this home that bores Praphon?"

"I'm bored with the way of life of our group," he answered.

Phachongchid's feelings changed. She felt as if she were lying all by

---

11. The term for "favors" here in *bunkhun,* which simultaneously means "creating obligations."

herself, deep in the night, and suddenly heard the sound of footsteps sneaking up the stairs.

"Who and how?" she asked immediately, almost without thinking.

"Our group. We *phuu dii* Thai, we who call ourselves 'the *phuu dii* class,' "[12] he answered. "I'm not asking any of us to be anything in particular. I'm just asking that we be something—at least something."

"My goodness, . . . I would like to hear your explanation," she cried out, despite her efforts to control her feelings.

"Our group. . . ." He changed his train of thought, as if a special interest had suddenly entered his awareness.

"Our group is not wealthy enough to do anything great. Neither can we do what Chinese or *farang* millionaires do. But we're not poor enough to know how difficult life in this world can be. For us, life is good, food is good. . . ."

Phachongchid completely forgot the commandment that good wives should never let their husbands realize that they are being contradicted. She said, "Wait a minute, wait a minute. Do you believe that in this world there should not be people who live well and eat well? Should there be only the extremely rich and the extremely poor?"

As he answered her, the expression on her husband's face began to carry the attitude of someone playing a game, thriving on its fun. "Oh, oh. . . . We're getting at it, we're getting at it. I didn't say that!" he said with a smirk on his face. "I said 'the *phuu dii* Thai class' is just like the middle class in other countries. They maintain the status quo.[13] I did not say that the meaning of '*phuu dii*' was bad—not at all. The 'middle class' could be said to be the backbone of society. If there were no middle class all kinds of jobs necessary for society would not exist. But to be a member of the middle class is to be bored."

His response made her so unhappy that she was unable to ask him any more questions. For one thing, he used words she did not understand. Second, even if she understood these words, she knew that she did not grasp what he was driving at.

"Go ahead, go ahead," he said.

Instead of answering, she forced a smile and buried her face in his arm.

He embraced her tenderly, with love and care, and then said, "Right now, I can't yet do what I want to do to relieve my boredom, because my grandmother is terribly old. . . . If I tried to change our way of life or do some other kind of work or do something out of the ordinary, it would

---

12. To be a *phuu dii* is to be well behaved, proper, civil, disciplined, self-confident, and to conform to some ineffable elite standard. The term is used both as a personal and class attribute. See "Madame Lamhab" for a more detailed description of one type of *phuu dii*.

13. This is written as a Thai transliteration of the Latin in the original Thai text.

speed up her death, and that would be a terrible sin. But Phachongchid, dear, when her death finally does come, please don't let me be disappointed in you."

These words filled Phachongchid with a great sense of apprehension. Later, when Praphon's grandmother did become ill, Phachongchid tried her very best to nurse and to care for her in order to prolong her life, if only to give herself more time to figure out what Praphon had meant.

"What will he want to do? Why did he speak in such a perplexing way? He spoke of the people who have and the people who don't have, just like a Communist. But Communists are not likely to have that kind of gratitude toward their grandmothers. . . ."

As it turned out, Phachongchid's nursing efforts were unsuccessful, and Praphon's grandmother died. The numerous children, nephews, nieces, and grandchildren were surprised by the fact that she left everything to Praphon.

With great care and anxiety, Phachongchid saw the situation develop. Her heart pounded and felt suspended in air as it became clear that Praphon was now a small millionaire. All of the grandmother's property had become his alone. Nothing had to be divided and nothing had to be shared with anybody.

But Praphon surprised her again. After the old woman's cremation had taken place he arranged to divide the property among all those other relatives who had contributed to his grandmother's being able to live her life in happiness. There were two unmarried aunts, two grandchildren beside himself, and three of grandmother's lifelong servants. He made all his own decisions, despite the criticisms he received—both from those who agreed with his views and those who did not.[14]

Phachongchid continued to watch the situation, wondering what he would ask her to do or to sacrifice.

But when the critical moment came, when he approached her with his

---

14. As is suggested by the "surprise" of the numerous relatives, this kind of inheritance situation is not typical. In most inheritance cases (e.g., where neither the donor nor the heirs are wealthy) property is awarded alternatively to: (1) the child who has cared for the donor in his or her dotage; (2) the youngest child, usually the youngest daughter; (3) all or most of the children, equally divided, with perhaps some preferences based on emotional considerations or on the varying economic needs of the children. Grandchildren usually are not primary beneficiaries. Too, the donor usually makes all his choices bindingly explicit (sometimes in a will) prior to his death.

With increasing wealth, the stakes become increasingly complicated, and the kind of situation described in the story, although rare, becomes increasingly possible. Although there is no clear evidence of what motivated either the grandmother or Praphon, most Thai readers would agree on the likelihood of some of the following. The grandmother willed all the property to Praphon with the

dream, she almost burst out laughing. Now she knew how stupid she had
been. It made sense that Praphon had sometimes been bored with her.

What Praphon had finally asked her to do was to go live with him
upcountry. He had asked her if she would do it. He would like to be a
planter, and he was going to ask if his transfer to a provincial post could
be arranged. He wanted a large spread of land on which to try his hand.
He was not ready to give up his government position because he was not
sure whether he would be successful in agriculture, and he did not want
to commit himself to it as a career. He wanted to learn gradually and to
try it gradually. If he could acquire the knowledge and if he had the ability, he might change his profession and become a plantation owner or
agriculturalist.

Phachongchid responded to his request with pleasure. This would give
her the opportunity to display her genuine abilities, to show Praphon
that she was not merely a cute decoration or the helpless baby of her parents, uncles, and aunts. She would be a homemaker of many talents, the
finest mistress her country squire could possibly want. She was not
merely someone who lolled around the house trying to stave off her
boredom. . . .

Praphon's colleagues and supervisor congratulated him when they
heard about his decision to move upcountry; it was rare to find someone
of his calibre and training who was willing to move out to the rural areas.
He was assured that it would help his advancement in the bureaucracy
and that he would be promoted faster than if he had remained in
Bangkok.[15] The only people to object to this plan were Phachongchid's
relatives and friends. But he paid no attention to them.

Phachongchid, Praphon, and their little one transplanted their entire
household to their new home in the country. Praphon had found land
easily because he knew how to contact and to deal with people of every
class, age, and background. He had bought a car that was suitable to the

---

implicit understanding—but with no explicit instruction—that he distribute it
according to his own judgment after her death. He was under profound moral
obligation and some social obligation, but no legal obligation, to do so. The
grandmother reassigned the responsibility to Praphon for any number of different
reasons: she wanted to avoid being the object of anger or hatred from disappointed claimants; she wanted to express her power or whimsy toward her heirs;
she did not trust herself to make wise decisions in her old age about such important matters; she simply did not want the trouble or aggravation of making the
decisions. Finally, Phachongchid's nursing of the grandmother probably played a
role in the trust that the latter extended to Praphon and also in Phachongchid's
expectation that the bequest was solely for them, e.g., since in caring for the
grandmother in her dotage she had fulfilled the role of the most likely beneficiary
it was reasonable for her to think (as a person so dedicated to proper role performances) that she and / or Praphon would be selected as the actual beneficiaries.

country roads, and then he had his house built—approximately seven kilometers from the district seat but in a site that was not isolated.

During their first year out in the country Phachongchid was so much happier, even though she missed her parents and friends a great deal. But her heart was focused on her husband. She now had the opportunity to show fully her love and loyalty to him. And every morning and night he indicated that he had the disposition to express his deep love for her.

He and she sat and discussed matters concerned with the new house; how to set a good example for all the local people who were coming by to visit and sometimes only to look; how to live comfortably, but economically, and also in a way that was suitable to local environmental conditions. They discussed the small generator for electricity; the pump for bringing water up into the house; the kind of toilet that would be most appropriate for their situation; the making of a verandah for dining; where the best locations were for writing, reading, and listening to the radio; how to keep food for longer periods; how to care for workers when they become ill, how much to pay them, and also how to treat them so as to win their loyalty.

He and she cooperated closely in everything. She was totally absorbed in her new life. She was particularly good at the most essential jobs. Praphon was constrained to praise everything she did, and he praised her sincerely, not out of politeness. And her talent at cooking was displayed fully, as she used local greens and deer, boar, and meat of other local wild animals to create dishes that teased the nostrils and the eyes, and that Praphon ate with keen appetite. Praphon often returned home with guests. And when these provincial guests expressed their admiration for Phachongchid's cooking, Praphon beamed with pleasure—a genuine pleasure, not a mock pleasure—because Praphon believed that the people in the provinces were really impressed by things that were unusual and new and that if they were not honestly excited by something they would never pretend that they were.

But Phachongchid's and Praphon's lives gradually became routine. Custom and order took over. The excitement they had known slowly

---

15. Thai bureaucrats are of two minds on this matter. On the one hand, in the early 1960s, at the height of the Sarit regime and the burgeoning of the "national development" ethos (e.g., the approximate period of this story), bureaucrats sometimes actively sought rural posts as a means of proving their mettle—and, indeed, such service sometimes did result in rapid promotion. On the other hand, all Thai bureaucrats believe that in addition to proving one's merit, one has to be visible, available, and have the proper liaisons that expedite or create one's promotion—and that all such things can occur only if one is located in Bangkok. In this story, Praphon's visibility and social identity are already so secure and well developed that he need not give them great attention. In fact, his desire to assume the role of country squire is a clear expression of his belief that he is above such matters.

faded away. Phachongchid herself began to feel bored. The few faces that she saw in the provinces were always the same. And the stories that Praphon brought home from the office for her to hear were about things that she did not consider very exciting. And when she looked at Praphon she noticed that he seemed to be getting bored too. When the two were together in the evening he would listen to the radio or read, and then he would give her his analysis and criticism of this material. And she would listen, maybe asking a few questions to try to demonstrate her interest and agreeing with almost everything he said. But she noticed that his analyses and criticisms were being offered less and less frequently, and he sometimes complained that perhaps it would be better for him to train himself as a writer rather than as a speaker.

And it was then that Chaarinii entered their lives. The anger and dismay that this event created in the heart of Phachongchid were really beyond description—because it showed her so clearly how Praphon had changed.

In his outward behavior, he was in every way very much a good husband, even in the time and place that husbands and wives are closest to one another, doing their secret things. But Phachongchid was convinced —she could not avoid seeing—that Praphon had changed since the start of his friendship with Chaarinii. The change was revealed in his obvious happiness, a happiness that followed the friendship like a shadow.

Praphon was a happy man. However, Phachongchid's husband was a happy man not because of his enchanting cooking spoon, but rather because of another woman, a woman who was no prettier than Phachongchid (except that Praphon's eyes did not see things the way most men saw them); a woman who possessed no qualities superior to those of Phachongchid (except that Praphon's viewpoint on such things departed from those of most people); a woman who was no more youthful than Phachongchid (although viewed chronologically, she was her junior by two years) and who, even though she was younger, hardly seemed it because her skin and complexion were so unappealing; and a woman who, if you considered her taste in dressing, would, on a scale of 100, rate in the lowest "decile"—to use one of those words that Chaarinii was always using and which Praphon would repeat and laugh over, sometimes with Chaarinii and sometimes by himself. (He laughed by himself when Phachongchid could not understand what was funny.)

Looking back, it is obvious that at first Phachongchid viewed the relationship between Chaarinii and her husband with perplexity. Later this changed to surprise and fear. Soon afterward it turned to fury and pain. And in the end, it finally turned to hopelessness.

Phachongchid herself was the person who brought Chaarinii into Praphon's life. Chaarinii was the first cousin of Adcharaa, Phachongchid's old schoolmate. About two or three months after Chaarinii had moved to the province, Adcharaa, who rarely wrote her friend, wrote Phachongchid from abroad, asking her to look after her relative: ". . . Not knowing anybody, she may be very lonely. I'm the one who encouraged her to move upcountry. Could you be friendly to her? She's an honest kid and she's a lot of fun. You'll also lose your own loneliness. . . ."

Chaarinii turned out to be a barrel of laughs. She could see the "funny" side of everything, and Praphon saw the same funny things. Phachongchid was the only one who could never see what was funny.

Chaarinii did everything that Phachongchid was trained not to do. It did not make any difference what Chaarinii was talking about or to whom she was talking; if she disagreed, she would let that person know. If she were talking with a man, she would be more likely to disagree and to disagree without modesty or inhibition. And she much preferred to converse with men than with women. Most of the single men in the province—and there were not many of them—who had the same educational background and who were of the same social status and were able to chat with her, did not want to. It was the married men who wanted to, especially Praphon. And Chaarinii was particularly fond of talking with him; in fact, she loved to talk with him more than with any other man. Toward Phachongchid, Chaarinii always expressed respect, as if she were an older sister. Chaarinii never disagreed with Phachongchid. In fact, Praphon used to say that "if Chaarinii has not disagreed with a person it means that this person is not a worthy opponent for her disagreement." Phachongchid kept her feelings to herself for several days. In the end, she could not hold them back, and she found a chance to tell Praphon that Chaarinii had never disagreed with her.

"Is that right?" he asked. "You're a person for whom she seems to have genuine respect."

"What? You always said that if Chaarinii did not disagree with somebody it was because that person was not worth it or because that person did not come up to standard or something like that. . . ."

Actually, of course, Praphon used the English word, "not *worth* being an opponent for her disagreement."

"I remember, I remember," he said with a happy look on his face. "With you, it was probably because you might not talk of things about which she had to disagree."

"What are the subjects about which she has to disagree with other people?"

"They're subjects that do not concern personal matters. Chaarinii is a person who is mature for her age. When I'm talking with her, I feel years younger. When I'm talking with our friends in Bangkok, I feel like a very old man, and in the end, I just have to stop talking with them."

"I saw you talking with people everywhere. It didn't make any difference where we were . . . what parties we were at. . . ."

She began to feel that this was the kind of disagreement that Phachongchid should never have with her husband, if only because to argue like this was to be just like Chaarinii. Before meeting Chaarinii she would never have disagreed with her husband, because she believed it was not the proper way for a good wife to behave. Now she had a better reason.

So she changed the entire tone of her words, lowered her voice, and added to her response, "Is that right, Praphon?"

"You're talking about Bangkok . . . ," he continued. "In Bangkok, I chitchat with everybody, but I rarely talk with them. There are not many people with whom I can talk. One of the few people I can talk with is Luang Phithuk. But I noticed that you were not very comfortable talking with him. So I never invited him to our house. When we did meet, we had good discussions. . . ."

"You still have not told me anything about the subjects that Chaarinii enjoys arguing about with other people." Her voice began to rise and to sound more demanding, in spite of her best efforts to control herself.

"She enjoys talking about our Thai society. She's unusual. There are not many Thai men who take an interest in the social order, in the life of people in society. But Chaarinii is a woman who has an interest in broad subjects like that."

Phachongchid would have liked to ask him more, but she felt the pain in her throat from trying to control her voice and she knew that if she lost control tears might begin to fall. So she began her movements of distraction. She reached for the rice bowl and ladled out a large portion for her husband. Instead of talking with him she began to move things around the table, putting each thing in its proper place on the table—the table that was located on the verandah, the place where wives "chitchat" with their husbands.

It was Praphon's practice to bring Chaarinii home with him for dinner about twice a week. She would meet him at his government office, they would drive out to the house, and after dinner he would drive her back to town.

As was her style, Phachongchid would always welcome Chaarinii into her home and she would do so in the manner of a *phuu dii,* concealing her own anxieties within her heart. She knew very well that the quickest way to alienate her husband's affections was to show her jealousy and possessiveness.

The period before, during, and after dinner was marked, as usual, by polite conversation. Chaarinii described the children in her classrooms, the naughtiness of the young ones; the stubbornness of those in the middle grades; and the timidity, embarrassment, awkwardness, and the errors of judgment of those in the higher grades. As usual, Praphon listened to all of this with interest. And the conversation would go on, focusing on the parents of the children or on the causes of the children's characters: Why was one child timid? Why was another one so stubborn in his obvious refusal to use his reason? And at the end of the discussion, Praphon turned to Chaarinii and nodding toward his wife said, "Hey, Chaarinii. Your older sister here wants to give you a test, or maybe I'm the one she wants to test. She told me earlier she wants to know the meaning of the concept 'social order.' I told her to examine you on what it means."

When she heard this, Phachongchid felt so humiliated that she arose from her seat on the verandah. She was confused by his making fun of her. Why does he have to use this way of showing her that she is so much more stupid than he is.[16] She never, simply never, tried to make herself his equal in matters of knowledge. She was not the type of woman who tried to put herself up as knowing anything as well as her husband. She made herself his disciple in everything she did not know. If she were too stupid to be his wife, it might as well mean the end of the marriage.

Phachongchid heard Chaarinii's voice trail her as she headed toward the bedroom.

"Oh, *Phii* Phachongchid,[17] what a question. . . . I can't answer that. *Khun* Praphon, how would you answer it?"

"What criterion, what principle, do you want me to use in answering the question?" Praphon responded. "But if I. . . ."

Phachongchid did not hear anything more because she had entered her bedroom and bolted the door.

She had been lying on her bed for about a half an hour when off in the distance she heard Praphon say, "Aaww. . . . Where has Phachongchid gone?" And then she simply heard the sound of their continuing conversation.

She called upon all her discipline to suppress her turbulent emotions, opened the door, and returned to the verandah to rejoin the conversation —or to express it more accurately, to sit there quietly while the other two talked.

Later, both Praphon and Chaarinii asked Phachongchid to go with them when Praphon had to take Chaarinii home. Chaarinii noted that there was a full moon and that Phachongchid might appreciate the cool night air; also, Praphon would then not have to drive back from town by

---

16. The grammar here is explicit in attributing some stupidity to Praphon.

17. *Phii* is the kinship term for older sibling. It should also be noted that the reason for Phachongchid's flight is not as obvious in Thai as it is in English. Phachongchid could well have left the verandah—without providing any anticipatory cue whatsoever—because she has to go to the bathroom, the kitchen, or anywhere else for any number of different reasons. A perceptive participant in the situation would have observed that she left out of a sense of personal pain; less perceptive participants would have either ignored the question of her motivation or offered less emotionally loaded reasons. Leaving the field without a cue or explanation occurs constantly in Thailand.

himself. But Phachongchid rejected their entreaties. After they left, she immediately went up to the bedroom and got into bed where she lay alone. Much to her surprise, Praphon returned in less than half an hour. She pretended to be asleep when he came up the stairs.

Praphon customarily arose at dawn to begin his day's work. However, this morning he did not get out of bed. Instead, he moved himself closer to his wife. When she opened her eyes, he kissed her tenderly.

"Last night, *darling,* what were you angry about?"

Phachongchid immediately snapped her eyes shut. The *farang* word, *"darling,"* cut through her ears. It was a word that Praphon had often cited as a word he should try to use—it was modern and popular— although he himself did not really like its strange sound. She tried to remove his hand from her.

"When you're angry like this, my little mouse, you're at your most adorable," he then said.

Phachongchid was even more miserable, almost to the point of not being able to hold back her tears. She knew that she was the kind of person her parents brought up to be "an adorable little mouse," not a person who was an adult, a person who understood the world as Chaarinii did. She lay there silent and rigid, and no longer tried to remove his hand.

Praphon sat up and assumed the voice he used at work. "Phachong-chid, . . . *Khun* Phachongchid, let's talk about something. . . ."

She sat up, too. She collected herself and looked straight at him so that he would know that she was an adult, too. Seeing the look on her face, Praphon became somewhat sad, as if he understood what she was trying to do.

"Phachongchid, . . . you don't like Chaarinii, do you? Why? Is it because of me or is it because you yourself don't like her?"

"I don't have any feelings toward her," Phachongchid answered.

"Chaarinii likes you. She respects you. Don't get her wrong. I'm speaking to you like this because I respect you, too."

Phachongchid immediately turned her face away and got up from the bed. She didn't want his respect. She began to realize what was happening: at one moment he treated her like a child, and a moment later he turned her into an object of respect. What was this all about?

Praphon heaved a large sigh that was intended for her ears. "I must be a very bad husband. What can I do to make myself into a good one— other than making myself into one of those proper dudes, one of those brainless dandies of Bangkok?"

She suddenly turned her face toward him and almost forgetting everything she had been taught, she said, "It's me. I want to know how—what is it that I can do?—to become your good wife?"

"You're the very best wife that I could ever find . . . ," Praphon answered.

Phachongchid noticed that after saying "ever find," he was going to say something more, but hesitated.

"Why don't you finish what you were going to say? Go ahead. Finish what you want to say," she responded.

"I'm finished," he said. He got up and took her in his arms so quickly she could not run away. "My sweetie, . . . don't you know your husband's heart . . . at all?"

Phachongchid wanted to say "I don't understand at all. I don't really understand," and she wanted to tell him about all her perplexity and doubt—from the very first time they talked till now, when his son was already three years old. But she was always stopped by something inside of her whenever she was close to his flesh. The love within her that she held for him was always stronger than her thoughts and doubts. So she went on being a wife who did not really understand him.

From that day on, Praphon drifted away, little by little, from Chaarinii. He busied himself increasingly in the work on the farm. Then one day Chaarinii came out to see them. A friend had given her a ride. She had come to say goodbye. She had asked to be transferred to a teaching job in another province.

"We'll miss you terribly," Praphon spoke out. And simultaneously he looked at Phachongchid's eyes in a plea of support.

Phachongchid forced out a slight smile and asked, "Why are you leaving?"

"Oh, . . . for the sake of doing it. For the change. Maybe I'll find some new things."

And then, as if they could no longer control themselves, Praphon and Chaarinii looked into each others' eyes sadly. Phachongchid forced herself to make two or three more polite statements, and Chaarinii departed.

Chaarinii had gone. Her rival had left. The danger had vanished. Men are like that. All men go astray sometimes.

But she had won!

She thought, "Let's not stir up any trouble." And as she thought of her success, she glanced at her husband, who was lying in his chair in front of the radio. His manner and his expression showed his boredom, the boredom that resulted from their being left to themselves, just the two of them together.

Her thoughts continued. "There's no sense in suggesting that we go anywhere. He's bored when we go to Bangkok. He's bored here. He's bored with me. When Chaarinii was here, he was lively and enthusiastic. He saw the humor in everything." She tried to suppress her feelings and her awareness. "I'd better keep my mouth shut and not have thoughts like these. He'll forget. Men aren't steady in their passion. He loves his son; that's good enough! He stays with me because he loves his son. The other woman's gone: out of sight, out of mind. . . ."

But at the bottom of her heart Phachongchid knew that the words "good enough" were really not good enough and that she was a wife who was not able to make her husband happy. And the reason she was not able to make him happy was not because of any mysterious ailment that nature had imposed upon her body or passions. Rather, it was because, as the old saying expresses it, "a strand of hair had blinded her view of the mountain." How could she be made to know? How could she be made to understand? She had asked him straightaway, "How can I make you happy?" But he told her nothing that could shed any light on her question.

Then one night something happened. Phachongchid was not the one who initiated it. As was usually the case after dinner, Praphon was lying in his easy chair in front of the radio. Phachongchid was sitting knitting a sweater for the coming cold season for her son. He was chitchatting with her about things—their hired hands, their crops, their child—and when he had covered all the familiar subjects, he stopped talking. And as was his custom, he turned on the radio to listen to the news. When the news ended, he turned the radio off, stretched himself way out, yawned, and heaved a large sigh. Phachongchid looked up at him and tried to control herself from raising the question she wanted so much to discuss—his boredom with her and his missing of Chaarinii. At that moment, Praphon spoke up.

"How about our going back to live in Bangkok? What do you think?"

Phachongchid's heart fell. She did not know whether to feel happy or frightened. Therefore, she denied any feeling, saying, "It's up to you."

Praphon sighed lightly and said, "The truth is, for people who are bored with the world, it is the same wherever they live."

"Who? Who is bored with the world?" Phachongchid's heart began to beat out of phase.

"Me. I'm the one who is bored. But the truth is, . . . it's wrong to say that I'm bored with the world. What ought to be said is that I'm bored with myself."

Thinking that she could finally get at the truth, Phachongchid quickly responded, "You have to explain whether you're bored with the world or bored with yourself."

"The things I want cannot be asked for. . . ." He continued, "I want Thailand to be something that it cannot be. I want the world to be something that it cannot be."

She looked at his eyes with interest.

"I lived in the *farang* world too long," he went on. "I've seen many places. So I'm no longer satisfied with anything."

"So the things you have—you're not satisfied with any of them? Is that what you mean?"

"That's right. But if things are to change, we first have to change ourselves. We can't expect others to change first."

"If you could do anything you wanted to do, what would you do?"

"Oh, . . . when I talk about that, I have to give a long lecture. A person who already has a wife and child cannot follow his own heart. The person with the greatest freedom is the person who doesn't have anything —the monk in yellow robes."

As he finished his sentence, he turned his body and face to the radio, and then changing his mind, he turned his face back toward her, lifted his head, and said in a voice just loud enough for her to hear, "But I must ask you not to take the things I say too seriously. Chaarinii used to say that when I talk I say things too generally and abstractly so that people who are listening to me often don't know what I'm talking about."

It was then that Phachongchid decided she could not give any more thought to the matter. She had tried to control the direction in which her brain would take her, but whatever she did, it constantly came back to one point: "He doesn't have freedom because he has a child. He cannot change his life because of the child."

That this thought—"he cannot change his life"—had embedded itself in her brain was even more apparent when she thought of Praphon playing with his son. She remembered what happened yesterday before Praphon went to work, after he returned, what he did during the evening, and even this moring. He would lift the child up on his shoulders and even over his head and romp and run around, and when his son directed him, he would become a horse crawling on all fours with the boy as the rider. And they always had things to talk about. He answered every question his son asked and they laughed and giggled in glee.[18] And Phachongchid felt that when they talked, their "talk" was real conversation, very much like the "talk" he used to have with Chaarinii, not the kind of "chitchat" he exchanged with Phachongchid.

She thought to herself: "What is the purpose of living together as husband and wife? Only to have children? He doesn't get rid of me because he loves his child. Is that enough? If I split up with him and let him find his happiness and allow him to marry Chaarinii, every one of them—my mother and father, every relative, friend, everyone I know—will think I've done the wrong thing. Everyone will blame me for having no tolerance, for being uncompromising. They'll say, 'Every man is like this. There's not a man who occasionally does not go astray, who does not let

---

18. This description immediately identifies Praphon's child-rearing practices as "modern" or "*farang*-like." It would be a rare Thai father who would "answer every question" he was asked or who would get down to the cognitive-emotional level of his three-year-old son. The traditional Thai father is an aloof figure of abstract honor and respect; for such a father to serve as his son's horse, even in play, is simply bizarre. For most pre-Oedipal Thai sons, the major source of their developing sense of personal value, and also their emotional support and attention, are siblings, grandparents, sometimes their mothers and their siblings, perhaps nannies and other servants, but almost never fathers.

his heart roam. But he has so many virtues. Where else could you find a man like this?' That's right. He is good, he does have a lot of virtues. But he and I, when we talk together, we don't communicate. We don't understand what the other one is saying. And he has already confessed that his happiness is with another woman. But there is his duty. There is his duty as head of the family. His duty is making him sacrifice his happiness. He used to tell me that some people meet their eternal mate at the wrong time, but because he loves his son so much he can make the sacrifice of giving her up. . . .

"Every one of those people would blame me. Were any of them ever in. . . . Did any of them ever fall into a situation like mine? Did any of them ever have to sit and bear looking at the sad and bored face of their husband for five years? And his sadness and boredom came before his love for Chaarinii. He had it with me even before he met Chaarinii. He was bored with everything connected with me, with everything that made me be what I now am. He was bored with my parents, my uncles, my aunts, my friends and their husbands, those spouses who call each other 'little mouse, older brother, or *darling*.' He was bored with life because he does not have what every person wants—freedom."

Early that morning Phachongchid came to her final decision. She stood and watched Praphon driving away from the house. Then she went upstairs to write the letter to her parents. She looked out the window and noticed the rising sun change the color of the sky and of the fields, and she saw the tall rubber trees waving in the morning wind. She realized that this was the last time she would be seeing this scene that she loved so much. She then thought of returning to her parents' home. She would not tell the real reason to anybody, simply pretending that she was there to relax and have a holiday. She would continue to stay there until people would begin to say that she was the child who was most adored by her parents, the one to whom her parents could never say "no." If people blamed her for being spoiled she wouldn't care. She hoped only that they would not ask for the real reason she was staying on, because they would never understand and because she could not stand their nagging for explanations. If they blamed her for not being a good homemaker, as someone who did not meet their expectations, she would not take any interest, because she's lost so much already: "If you're a loser in life, it does not make much difference if you've lost a lot or a little." She thought of her little one. Everything would be easy for him if she left now; he was still young. It is easy for little boys to get used to their stepmothers. And Chaarinii and he would be friends, because Chaarinii was a person who could "talk" with him, who could talk for a long time, and the two would happily play with each other.

Her reverie was broken suddenly by a servant calling from below: "*Khunnaaj*. . . . Mistress, mistress. . . . *Khunnaaj*. . . ."

She looked down and saw Mr. Bunchuaj, the foreman, carrying a little boy in his arms. The child was about three and his arm was covered with blood.

"What? What's happened?" she screamed in a high pitch, fearful that the child was her son. "Who? What's happened to him?"

"It's little Chan. He was bitten by a dog. He might have been tussling with the puppy, but it was the mother that bit him. There are deep bites. The jeep is off hauling wood, but the old car is working and can make it in to the hospital."

Phachongchid was one of the three people on the farm who could drive. She rushed downstairs and motioned to Bunchuaj to carry the little one to the car, and she drove off toward town.

It did not take long. In less than forty-five minutes she was heading home. But as she approached the house, her heart fell. She saw Praphon's car parked next to the house. She quickly parked her old car under the tree and hurried upstairs. She entered the bedroom. Praphon was lying on the bed, his face beaming with a broad smile.

"Why did you come back?" she barked at him.

"I came back to see my wife," he answered, as he got up and confidently gathered her into his arms. He then forced her to lie down on the bed, and to show her that he had seen her unfinished letter, he reached under the pillow and exposed the piece of white stationery. He bent over and hugged her tightly. Phachongchid did not resist because she was still so preoccupied with the surprise of seeing his beaming face.

"My lovely little mouse, . . . who are those people who said I married *Nang* Kritsanaa?[19] The truth is I married a woman, the woman I love. That's right, isn't it? . . . My wife, my beloved wife."

"It would be better if you said what you want to say so that it could be understood," Phachongchid said angrily. At this moment, her only feeling was anger. She felt she was suffocating—suffocating from his embrace and suffocating from not being able to do what she wanted to do. And she was angry at him for continuing to keep her in complete darkness about what he was thinking.

"I've told you already. Whenever you're angry, you're lovely! Okay, let's talk. For once, let's talk so that we understand each other. Why did you write a letter to your parents, a letter that's like a petition? Why didn't you ask—ask me? Why didn't you do your snapping at me—like you just did?"

"You're speaking Thai like someone out of the pages of history," Pha-

---

19. Following the Indian-Thai legend, Kritsanaa was the wife of Orachun who had four brothers and who in fulfillment of an earlier vow to his siblings shared her with them. She proved to be a perfect wife to all five men, and later poems about her five modes of marital perfection were written.

chongchid said. "Just now, you mentioned *Nang* Kritsanaa. I've never heard anybody talk like this."[20]

"I happen to be a modern man, a fully modern man," he argued back. "All right, let's talk. What is it that you didn't understand, . . . that you don't understand about me? Tell me. If you can stand listening to me, I'll answer everything you ask."

"If we start with what just happened . . . ," Phachongchid said nervously. And without thinking, she continued, "Why do you have such a grin on your face? Do you think it's a joke, that my decision to return to my parents' home is funny?"

"No, I don't think it's funny at all," he replied. "I was just so happy that *Naaj* Lek had gone into town today, that he had met me, and that he told me that little Chan had been bitten by a dog. I was afraid it might have been our own little one, so I decided to come home right away. You and I probably passed each other on the road. . . ." He stopped and stared at her. "When I got home and saw the letter, I was so pleased because I could see that my wife wanted to understand me, and when she couldn't she was miserable and helpless.[21] This was so different from what I had earlier thought—that you were not interested in understanding me. But if we are to talk to one another, you must be able to listen to the truth. . . ."

"I really want to listen. I want so much to know the truth." She was at this point finally able to move away from his embrace, sit up, and look straight at him.

"Let's begin with me. I'm so stupid. I don't understand my wife at all. I began to understand when I saw your letter. The words of your letter are helping me to understand a lot of things. . . ."

"Like what?" Phachongchid asked with the sourness of a juiceless lemon.[22]

---

20. Most Thai readers perceive a dual meaning in this misunderstanding. At one level, Phachongchid's misinterpretation of Praphon's literary allusion is obviously intended to be a demonstration of her ignorance of Thai literature and her general lack of learning; most reasonably educated Thai would have easily grasped and understood the reference. However, at another level, Praphon's initial use of the reference is clear demonstration of his indifference to the seriousness of his wife's mental state and his readiness, even at this late hour, to make light of her situation by dealing with her as a symbol or as a character in a drama. From this point of view, Phachongchid's literal, unsophisticated approach to Kritsanaa is a clear statement that no mere literary allusion will deny the reality of her turmoil and the pain that her husband's opacity has caused her.

21. The double meaning that is apparent here in English also occurs in the original Thai: that he is pleased over his wife's concern for him, and that he is pleased over his wife's suffering because of him. Any careful Thai reader would immediately perceive the sado-masochistic elements of this response.

22. This metaphor refers explicitly to the loss of good manners when discussing something with another person.

"I realize now why I love you. At first, I didn't understand myself at all. Every single time that you said or did something that made me miserable I was surprised by my own reactions: Why do I love this woman? Was I the same as every other man? Was I the kind of man who simply lays his eyes on a woman and falls in love with her? And who, when she doesn't satisfy a man, blames her for not knowing how to satisfy him? The kind of guy who, before falling in love, doesn't look to be sure whether she will be satisfying?"

"And now? What is it that you know now that you didn't know before?" Phachongchid had gathered her wits together sufficiently so that she could at least be polite.

"I love you because you're a person who is dedicated to your kind of beliefs—beliefs that could be called 'ideals.' At least you're committed—you're unwaivering—in your desire to be the very best homemaker there is. And you have studied and acted in accordance with your beliefs."

"All of which has no importance to you at all." Phachongchid's reply had a tone of absolute finality.

"Don't get me wrong. I think it's a very important matter, but as I've told you before, I don't think it's the most important thing in life."

"And what's the most important thing in life?"

"You first have to ask 'Whose life?' " Praphon replied. "For me . . . ahhh, . . . you're probably more than a little confused. But as I told you long ago, husbands and wives have to have the opportunity to quarrel. It has to be possible for them to argue about what is important. Who trained you not to quarrel with me? When I read your letter, I understood.

"My thoughts went back to the time I talked with your father before we were engaged. At first, I didn't understand him at all, and I wasn't interested either—because I was going to be married to you, not to him. It wasn't necessary for me to understand him. But now I know that I was wrong. 'To marry you' really means 'to marry your father, your mother, your uncles, your aunts, your teachers, your nannies, your wet nurses, your servants, your slaves. . . .' Wow! Gee! I married them all. And when you married me, it was the same. You married all the *farang* countries in which I lived, all my professors at the many universities I attended, my *farang* friends with whom I hung around and discussed things, and the many hundreds of books I read. . . ."

Phachongchid had been waiting for a long time to interrupt him but could not find an opening. Now, when he had stopped just long enough, she said, "My parents . . . my parents did not teach me by words alone. They taught me by example, by having me watch what they did, and by showing me how to do things little by little. They also found this teacher and that teacher; they took me to see this older one and that younger one. They never told me not to quarrel, but I was old enough to understand. . . ."

"You're still not terribly grown up. You still rarely use or trust your own thoughts. There are all those times that I've noticed—something I did not understand earlier, but which I now understand—when you have doubts about something, and when you want to ask or want to disagree, and when I've given you every opportunity. . . . And what happens is that you check yourself. Something enters your head to stop you. What are you thinking about that stops you from expressing your doubts? What's inhibiting you?

"As I just said. I've finally realized what's been going on. On that day that your father and I talked he told me that you were the very best kind of child. You were obedient in everything; whatever you were told to do, you did. Everything you did you always tried to do in the best possible way, even if you didn't fully understand.

"Do you think that your parents never quarreled with each other? If they didn't, they could not have loved each other for more than thirty years. But if they didn't quarrel with each other, then it violates my theory. . . ."

"My dear, can you talk so that a stupid person like me can understand you better? Wouldn't it be better to try to be clearer?" Phachongchid interrupted him confident that not even a person with an M.A. degree could understand what he was trying to narrate. Although she was not aware of it, it was the first time she had used the words "My dear" when speaking to him.

"Excuse me. I don't know how to express myself. I don't quite know how to speak in a way that is right for the time and place. The thing is— it would really be a good idea if you would try to make yourself understand what this is about, so that we'd finally have it. What I'm saying is . . . suppose that we people had a set of rules that applied to ninety-nine persons, but that didn't apply to one person. And suppose that this person is the most important person in our life. Oh, what a mess it would be. . . . Maybe your father and mother never quarreled with each other. But if they didn't, they must have been a strange pair. They were the exception to the norm. Or maybe they were normal. Who could ever know? But as for myself, I say that people who are married to each other have to be themselves. They have to be natural with each other.

"You were given a lot of advice and training. I knew that. But now I've added it up to see what it all means. You saw yourself as *Nang* Kritsanaa. Before I was married, people teased me about this, and even after we were married they would often say this about you. You knew this. You heard them. And I saw that you were not too happy about it. But it's true. You tried to make yourself the very best wife. To do that you used to ask me to tell you about your shortcomings. And I would answer that you didn't have any. But the truth is, I was wrong, too. I wasn't myself. My answer was in terms of your framework. I should have answered that for me you did have some shortcomings—because I did not want a wife who was a homemaker of the highest rank or a first-class child-rearer. I want a partner-for-life, a person with whom I can talk and play. The other things come afterwards.

"But instead you thought that men are interested only in eating and sleeping. You insult men terribly. . . ."

"What?" Phachongchid exclaimed.

"That's it. See! You don't know yourself. Most people are like that, they don't know themselves. . . . Now I've gotten it all out. That phrase —'an enchanting cooking spoon can take care of any marriage . . .'—I knew about that, too. That's the reason you were always shocked when I said, 'Food and eating are not the most important things in life.' Do you think a husband will love his wife only because she can cook well? That's not right. For every hundred men, there are a hundred reasons. Every person is different. That's what I say. . . ."

When he saw that she was looking at him with interest, he continued. "When I carry on like this . . . just talking on and on, I feel a little embarrassed and strange. And I repeat myself a lot. . . . I have seen a lot of the world. The vast majority of men like to partake in delicious food and love to sleep in comfort. That's certainly right. And there are also some who pursue only their sexual desires. Some men love women for only one thing, and for that thing they'll do anything; they'll let their precious angels stomp all over them. And there are some men like me who love to partake of delicious food and to sleep in comfort, but who want even more. That means that we're somewhat greedy. Men like this want their wives to talk with them. I've got a lot of problems. I want to ask and inquire about them. I want to talk them out with people, and I want people to talk them out with me. I want them to be able to stand listening to me when I answer their questions.

"This is my flaw, my shortcoming. When I talk, nobody can stand listening to me. If I had a wife who could bear listening to me it would be good. But she should be willing to listen to me, she should be able to bear it, not to please me and not because I'm her husband and she has to do her duty, but because the subject I am talking about is interesting. But if you're not interested, I'm not going to blame you. You'd be just another person who couldn't stand listening to me."

Phachongchid did not hear every word that he said at the end of his last speech because she could not immediately correct that part of her character that forced her to pretend to listen so as to please him. But she heard enough to satisfy her desire. What she wanted to do was embrace him tightly. But she was too embarrassed. She wanted to tell him that she could bear listening to him her whole life. But when she saw him get up and move as if he were going to turn his head away again, as he had often done before, she hurriedly grabbed his hand.

"Praphon said that Praphon has a flaw, an imperfection. Isn't that what you said? I might have one, too. . . ."

But Praphon interrupted her before the thought could be completed. He said, "At first, you overestimated yourself. You were certain that a man had to have a woman who was a good homemaker. But when you realized that I was not fulfilled by this, you began to feel that you were deficient. You are very acute and perceptive. That's because you are so intelligent. . . ."

Praphon and Phachongchid did not have the opportunity to consider and debate the various problems of their life any further because a small fist was knocking at the bedroom door. A tiny voice behind the door said, "Father, Mother—Chan has come home. He's wearing a big white cloth on his arm. Chan's not crying either. . . ."

Praphon said, "Ahhh . . . that little Chan. See. Look at that! Who would have ever thought that this little kid would have played such an important role in our lives. We ought to set up a special account for him called the 'Chan Educational Aid Fund' for the extraordinary favor he has done for us."

Then Praphon opened the door in order to receive the child who was even more important to their two lives.

Getting Drunk Abroad

Introduction

Of all the forces contributing to the "internationalization" of Thailand in recent decades perhaps the most unpredictable, at least in their ultimate consequences, were the *nakrian nauauk*—collectively, the thousands of young Thai who were sent overseas for training and education. The unpredictability of the *nakrian nauauk* derives from the fact that in addition to learning all those things they were supposed to learn to operate a modern society (engineering, cosmetology, medicine, pastry baking, police administration, economic planning), they also learned many other things—some of more dubious value and most of more complex dimensions.

Perhaps the most typical (if ultimately short-lived) characteristic of those who studied abroad was their diffuse sense of dissatisfaction with Thai society. For many, particularly those who had gone in the early 1960s, this took the form of returning to Thailand primed to put into practice their recently acquired expertise but instead being frustrated by the bureaucratic inertia and conservatism they felt they encountered. For others, the dissatisfaction took the form of having to relinquish the sense of discovery and personal liberation they had known overseas and being forced to readapt to the constraints of family and class obligations. And for many, as in the following story by Suchit Wongthed, the dissatisfaction took the form of feeling that they would not be able to follow the Western middle-class lifestyle to which they had become accustomed abroad or, perhaps more poignantly, of feeling a sense of shame about the conservatism and anomie of Thai life.

While the vast majority of the dissatisfied were eventually reintegrated into Thai society, there were others who never returned home and others who, having gone home, paid off their debts to their sponsoring agencies and soon re-emigrated to the lands where they had been educated. The repayment of debts was no small matter: those on government scholarships had to pay the equivalent of double their annual salary for each year they were overseas, plus 15 percent interest. It is said that the Thai community of Chicago, comprised mainly of well-paid nurses and their families, came into existence on this basis. On the other hand, the Thai community of Los Angeles, which is the largest community of overseas Thai in the world is said to be dominated by "second generation Yawaaraad," the children of Chinese who emigrated to Thailand and whose offspring went off to the United States for the same reasons that they came to Thailand. ("Yawaaraad" is the center of Bangkok's Chinatown.)

In the following story, the author-narrator is not at all sympathetic to the "problems" of the *nakrian nauauk*. Using a Thai rather than overseas perspective, he correctly points out that when the complaining Ph.D. candidates return home they will be considered "gods or close to gods" by most of their compatriots. Higher paid and supposedly more sophisticated, they will be in the best positions to mitigate the very problems they claim are the cause of their own disaffection. The argument on its face is so idealistic and so conservative as to seem almost patriotic in its motivation. In fact, to avoid the possibility that his position may seem too quaint to the normally cynical Thai reader, Suchit phrases these views as the blatherings of a drunkard, although in so doing he obviously is also giving voice to his own cynicism about the unreasonableness of Ph.D. candidates he has known.

From a Thai point of view, the most important attribute of this story is its extraordinary realism. Suchit is unique among contemporary writers in his ability to capture the subtlety, ambiguity, and purposefulness of Thai speech in informal situations and to show how such speech reveals the inner states of his characters. Anybody who has ever attended a party of Thai students abroad has met individuals who think and talk exactly like Messrs. Chicken, Egg, Buffalo, Snake, and Person. In fact, the language of these get-togethers is so perfectly stereotyped that, as the narrator suggests, one party is virtually a replica of every other.

It is perhaps ironic that in the two social science studies that have so far been done on the impact of the foreign experience on Thai students (Barry 1967; Palmer 1972), little is said about the kinds of issues that loom so large in this fictional account.

Getting Drunk Abroad

Suchit Wongthed

". . . Before, the people I hated most were those who would sneak out of our country to make their living abroad," said Mr. Chicken, screwing up his face in disgust.[1] "But now I'm beginning to understand that they have to do that . . . because if they had to return to Thailand, they wouldn't know what to do to earn a living."

"That's it. . . . That's right. That's just what I was going to say. Our country is really in bad shape,"[2] said Mr. Egg in agreement. He started on a long explanation involving all five rivers—the Ping, the Wang, the Yom, and the Naan—and he even included the Chao Phrayaa, although I'm not sure whether it's supposed to be part of the expression about the five rivers.[3]

I sat zonked out in the corner of a large apartment. Besides smoking the strongest cigarettes I could find in America, I was guzzling the worst wine I could find in the downtown area of this city.[4] The cigarettes were the closest thing I could find to tobacco rolled in banana leaves, and the

From *Sangkhomsaat Parithat* 10, no. 2 (1972).

1. All the names in the story follow the Thai alphabet, each letter of which has a standard name, e.g., as "a" is for "apple" in English, "k" is for "*kaj*" ("chicken") in Thai, although in Thai each letter and name is completely integral. Ordinarily, the meaning of the letter would be ignored in translation and appear simply as "Mr. A.," "Mr. B.," and the like. Here, however, the letter-name is obviously intended to say something about the speaker as well as to identify him.

2. Literally, "filled to the brim and running over with hopelessness."

3. All of this is a reference to the Thai metaphor "adding the fifth river," meaning "to annoy or to bore by running over at the mouth." Any Thai knows that the first four rivers flow into and create the fifth, the Chao Phrayaa. Thus, even to mention the fifth is to be redundant, self-evident, or superfluous.

4. "Downtown" refers to the narrator living a transient existence: sleeping in rented rooms or inexpensive hotels; eating in 24-hour cafeterias, using public transportation instead of owning a car, and the like.

bad wine smelled a little like the village-brewed white lightning I used to get at home.

The sounds of the unofficial seminar drifted over now and then from the group of Thai students on the other side of the room. They were mainly government officials who had been given scholarships to study in America. There were only one or two who had come on their own. Most of them were studying for Ph.D.'s that would take at least another two years to complete.

I felt like saying straight out that I was fed up with hearing the same damn saliva-gushing seminar that I had been hearing all the way from Bangkok. But I really didn't have the nerve to speak out. I wanted to tell them that this kind of discussion of Thailand's problems and constant bad-mouthing of Thailand was something that I had already heard from all the Thai students spread between New York and Chicago. There wasn't a single one who saw anything appealing about Thailand, not even the slightest bit appealing. But I didn't have the courage to say this either. Because even though they weren't altogether right, they really weren't altogether wrong.

"How about selling Thailand to the United States? How would that go? What'dya think?"

That's just what I said, and it was the perfect moment. People just looked at me and assumed that I was drunk on bad wine. So there was no necessity for them to comment on my observation. Also, it wasn't my intention that anybody should pick up on what I'd said and subject it to further analysis.

"Mr. Owl just graduated in engineering last year, but he didn't want to go home. He wanted to find a job here and work for a while so that he would have enough money to buy a car, a house, and something left over to lend out to make more money when he got back to Bangkok." Mr. Buffalo cited this case to endorse the first speaker's opinion.

"That's true. Back home, nothing happens without contacts or connections.[5] How could Mr. Owl go home now? Think of it this way: What would his government salary give him? Maybe barely enough to eat. And how long would it take him to get just a car?" Mr. Chicken argued again, quite reasonably.

Whiskey and I have never gotten along very well. And canned American beer, even though it is so much weaker than Thai beer that it seems tasteless to me, has always made me either vomit or become dead drunk. So that's why I have developed this thing for cheap wine. When I've guzzled a certain amount it gives me the illusion that I'm drinking home-

---

5. The phrase reads literally "playing the politics of parties and factions [and implying also families and friends] so passionately that the eyes and ears cannot be opened to anything else."

brewed lightning or 28 percent Rong booze. "Illusion," . . . what a beautiful sound this word has for humanity. All the truths in this world are illusions. I myself have never seen a Noble Truth,[6] which some people say really exists in this world. At least that's what the rumor is. I would very much like to see a Noble Truth, but I'm afraid that if I did I would never again be able to see an Illusive Truth. Although I suspect that the Noble Truth would provide much greater happiness than the other kind, I'm not really sure. . . . "Not totally persuaded" may be a better way to express it. And what if I make the wrong choice and discover that the Noble Truth doesn't really satisfy me? Could I retreat and still be able to discover Illusive Truths?

"Thailand's economic situation is really as hopeless as Mr. Chicken said," Mr. Snake observed with a look of dark solemnity. "In my opinion, the reason why Thailand has not been able to solve its economic problems is because the Thai people are afraid to take risks. It's not difficult to find loads of wealthy people at home, but very few of them are brave enough to take the risk of investing their money in our industry and business."

"I think Thai people do dare to take risks in business, but they don't want to waste their money paying for all those costs and fees along the way," responded Mr. Egg.

"That's right. All that proves is that they don't even want to take the chance of paying a bribe to make sure that their business will operate and run smoothly," Mr. Snake argued back.

"So you want the Thai people to get into the habit of always wearing a bribery belt, right?"

"No. I'm talking about taking risks and not taking risks," Mr. Snake replied, "because we've got to admit that back home in our country all kinds of business won't move without bribery. Foreigners who come to invest in Thailand realize this, and they're ready to take every kind of risk."

"I support Mr. Snake on this point," said Mr. Buffalo, talking with both hands. "Take, for example, Dusit District. . . ."

And then he came pouring out with all kinds of stories about this district official or that police officer who did such and such and such and such.

The temperature outside must have gone down to thirty degrees fahrenheit—below the freezing point—because I could see snowflakes drifting past the window. I sat there imagining all those Thai students in New York City who were probably talking about the last dirty election back home; the Thai students in Chicago talking about crime in Bangkok being higher than the combined crime of New York and Chicago; the

---

6. From the Noble Truths of Buddhism.

Thai students in San Francisco talking about the degenerate life of our high society and the craziness of our hot-blooded teenagers, while at the same time some Thai student in Los Angeles was drawing his gun and shooting into the ceiling of a bowling alley in Hollywood.[7]

I'm so fed up with all of this that I don't want to think about it anymore. If forced to reflect on it, it would come down to the fact that Thailand is like a decaying and disintegrating land in the twilight zone—ugly and terrifying. It reminded me of my childhood fantasy of communism, and of what Communist countries and people were like.

"I say that if we really want to solve our problems, we have to begin with the middle class," observed Mr. Chicken vigorously. "Don't forget that I divide us into three classes: the high class, the middle class, and the lowest class. The high class are the people with administrative power. The middle class are the educated people and people like us who have gone to study abroad. The bottom class is made up of farmers. There is no way to make the high class solve our problems, and there has never been a time in Thai history when such problems have been solved by the bottom class. Therefore, I can see our problems being solved only by the middle class."

"How are the problems going to be solved, I'd like to know," Mr. Buffalo interrupted.

"By contraposition."[8]

My heart leaped into my throat.[9] At that moment, my mind's eye saw a picture of deputy district officers and district officers, both those who were friends with the people and those who oppressed the people—all of them ready to be contraposed. The image of a district officer like Mr. Rabin Naanaakhun[10] appeared vaguely but then faded out. Perhaps there were difficulties with the transmitter or maybe they didn't use the international communications satellite in getting the image to me. Then I started to chuckle at the Red Chinese label that describes us as "the Running Dog Country." Are they right? No . . . no . . . , it's all too idiotic and crazy. No, I'm the one who is crazy sitting here brooding like this by myself.[11]

---

7. Whether justified or not, the Thai community of Los Angeles is associated with a myth of youthful lawlessness—at least in the minds of Thai in Thailand.

8. Mr. Chicken's answer in Thai is *patikiriyaa,* which is an esoteric bureaucratic term. While it suggests what he has in mind, but does not dare say (e.g., "By revolution"), it is essentially a pretentious bit of jargon that avoids answering the question. The next paragraph points to the narrator's interpretation of Mr. Chicken's meaning.

9. Literally, "jumped across and hit my right shoulder bone."

10. A highly popular district officer in the period the story was written.

11. The political meaning of these ruminations is as ambiguous in Thai as it is in English. They are obviously an expression of the author's cynicism, not his political position.

"What about you, Mr. Person? What do you say . . . , or are you already sleeping?"

Mr. Bell turned around to address me—"Mr. Person," or as we say, "Mr. *Khon.*" (The *"kh"* of my name is not the same as the *"kh"* in *"Khwaaj,"* Mr. Buffalo's name. But because the *"kh"* of my name has been declared obsolete, I've been forced to borrow the other *"kh,"* at least until King Ramkhamhaeng University does something about it.)[12] He then threw me a question: "Can we or can we not solve our problems by starting with the middle class?"

It wasn't that I was sleeping or even drowsy. And it wasn't that I was confused. It was just that after having our country's problems heaped upon me for more than six months I was now numb to such questions. Wherever I went, the only thing I encountered were the enormous problems of our country. There were simply too many for an onlooker, a student abroad like me, to handle. They just blew my mind.

"I think you're the group that doesn't dare to take risks." I just blurted this out without knowing what I was saying.

Everyone sitting there either moaned or laughed, and then somebody said: "Sir, you're missing the point. We've already talked about taking risks and not taking risks. I said that you were fast asleep, and look. . . ."

I was taken aback. I didn't think I could make such a stupid mistake.

"You people. . . . You're the ones who always draw your bow before you've seen your prey. You're like the rabbit who always thinks the sky is going to fall in on him.[13] I uttered only one sentence and you jumped to the conclusion that what I said was wrong. . . . I say that you're the people who are everything you said that others were. Look who is calling the kettle black.[14] You attack these people for not daring to take risks. You

---

12. Between 1938 and 1944, the then premier of Thailand, Field Marshal Phibun Songkhram, promulgated a series of regulations in an attempt to "modernize" Thai culture, requiring people to wear hats, forbidding the chewing of betel, and altering the Thai alphabet, including the deletion of certain letters among which was the *"kh"* for *"khon,"* or "person." The reference to Ramkhamhaeng University is an expression of hope that the spiritual descendant of the thirteenth-century creator of the Thai alphabet, after whom the university is named, will eventually rectify Pibulsongraam's adulterations. (See Numnonda 1978 for an excellent discussion of these events.)

13. After one of Aesop's fables, although in the American version it is more often a chicken.

14. The phrase in Thai is "You accuse others, but you [think you] are Inao, and you are the one who should be accused." While the meaning of this idiom is clear, its logic is ambiguous and perhaps even double-edged. "Inao" is the title and principal character of a dance drama, based on an earlier Javanese model, that was reworked by Rama I and Rama II. In some respects, Inao is the perfect, traditional Thai hero: a man who gets everything he wants by virtue of his charm, good looks, good luck, and the fact that he is the grandson of gods. Thus,

attack those people for not daring to invest and for letting investment fall into the hands of big-wheel foreigners, and government officials for being a bunch of crafty cruds, and you bitch about every single little thing there is. The picture you draw for me is that Thailand has turned into hell. But it's not true. Because if it were true, it would mean that the Thai now living in Thailand have committed the worst possible sins that have sent them all to hell. . . ."

". . . . If I told you that Mr. Snake's director-general was corrupt, would you, Mr. Snake, dare to try to determine the truth and gather all the evidence that would be needed? If you got the evidence, would you dare bring charges against your director-general? Would you dare come out on center stage and expose his corrupt activities? Sir, I don't believe that you would ever dare. You would be just like so many other government officials who would whine and plead. . . .

". . . You would say, 'Please understand . . . , I'm just a low-level official. If they use their power to jam it to me, I'll have to leave the civil service, and then how would I make my living?' You would be afraid to take even this simple risk. . . .

"Then, if you think about the fact that you at least have a bachelor's degree—which gives you a much better chance than people in the fields and streets, those who depend only on their own hands and feet to survive and to make a living—then you're twice as afraid to take a risk. Furthermore, think about it: now, you are all studying abroad. This time, when you go back home you'll all be considered gods or close to gods. You may feel that being students abroad doesn't mean anything. But the truth is that you have extraordinary advantages over people who have never received degrees and also over people who earned their degrees in Thailand.[15] You already have so many advantages, but you still wouldn't dare to take a risk. . . .

"Excuse me, Mr. Buffalo, you opened your mouth to say something. I know what you're going to ask me, but please don't. Because if you're afraid that you're going to starve, that your wife and children will have nothing to eat, that you won't make enough to live on, then it shows you're the worst coward in Thailand.[16] Why do I say this? Because the

---

to think of oneself as Inao is to suffer the flaw of overly esteeming oneself and therefore deceiving oneself. However, Inao himself had certain striking (but never fatal) flaws. He dealt with adversity not by facing it directly but by becoming ill or by depending upon his adopted brother or the gods to extricate him, which they always did. Since his good fortune always depended upon external circumstances, he never bothered to examine himself, his responsibilities, or his faults. Thus, to be Inao in this sense is to have the very same flaws that he did.

15. Those who enter the civil service with foreign B.A.'s do in fact receive considerably higher starting salaries than those with domestic degrees.

16. Literally, "the progenitor of all the cowards in Thailand."

civil service in Thailand never kicks anybody out. They're never willing to do that. Unless you're caught red-handed at corruption, you'll never get fired. Nobody ever gets fired. The worst thing that can happen to you is getting transferred to Maehongsorn.[17] But then you know perfectly well already, don't you, that one of the main reasons there is so little progress in the country is because educated people will never go outside Bangkok to work. So why are you afraid? . . .

"Or you can even resign from the civil service. So why all of this fear when you already have a much better education than millions of people in Thailand? If you want to fight, why are you so concerned about your son not having a TV on which to see lousy movies? Why are you so concerned about not having a fancy car to be paraded around in? Gandhi would never ride in a car because he felt that walking was one of the best forms of exercise. . . .

"Why are you so afraid about not having food fit for a Chinese emperor when cabdrivers in Bangkok have been feeding themselves on greens and grass and fermented fish from the beginning of time? Even when these things are more expensive, the cabbies manage. . . .

"So you want to solve the problems of society. What is there to be afraid of? It doesn't have to be as big a thing as taking your own director-general to court. You just have to be bold enough to voice your own opinion, to protest, and to write some pieces for a newspaper. This is one way of remedying Thai society, the system that all of you have been saying is rotten. . . .

"Now that you've been doing all this thinking about changing the system, are you bold enough to take the risk without being afraid that someone will jam it to you or that you'll be denied a salary increase? The only thing I see is that most of the students abroad who are extremists remain extremists only as long as they're outside the country. As soon as they get back home, they're afraid of everything. They're just like the flying squirrels who live in the trees and who are afraid the earth will disappear; so every time they think about the earth, they have to come down and make sure it's still there. But the tiger knows all this. So he lies in wait under the tree, grabs them as they come down, and eats in comfort. . . .

"All this—it refers to you people here. I'm not damning all students studying abroad. You were the ones who argued that the solution to the social problems of Thailand must begin with the middle class, whom you said you represented. But I say you are the ones who are responsible for spoiling much of Thai society. The most corrupt officials are your kind of people. Those who oppress the people the most are from your class. Or

---

17. A province in the far northwest of Thailand.

do you want to argue that those district officers and deputy district officers[18] have never gone to the university. . . .

"Hey, who's the guy who made me say all this?"

"I did. What about it?" someone answered.

"You're a troublemaker. Why did you ask somebody who's sloshed on
cheap wine to say anything?"

---

18. In the original Thai, the phrasing here is *naaj amphur, naaj palad khik.*
Although *palad khik* obviously refers to "deputy district officers," it is actually the
name of the wooden lingam that hangs from a string worn around the waists of
young boys; in other contexts *palad khik* is also a tattoo of a phallus appearing
on the thigh or forearm and the name of a nonphallic protective amulet worn by
men. Here, the image of the wooden penis clearly suggests not masculinity but
lifelessness or uselessness and, because it is also a child's "toy," immaturity. *Khik*
may have still another connotation—the sound of the embarrassed giggle of
young deputy district officers avoiding responsibility.

Naaj Aphajmanii

Introduction

The following play by Witayakorn Chiengkul is included in this volume because of its historical and social importance, not its aesthetic or intellectual merit. Completed two years before the 1973 Student Revolution, it is an extraordinary testament to the capacity of an author of fiction to anticipate and crystallize the changing realities of his society. However, as an aesthetic effort it is obviously flawed—perhaps even more in the original Thai than in this translation. Thai colleagues who have examined the piece say that in Thai the author's use of political rhetoric instead of ordinary human speech seems even more culturally unreal than it does in English, that the one-dimensional nature of his characters is more blatant, and that the cataclysmic quality of the prologue is even more out of phase with the rest of the play. They also say that these features might be explained by the author's "experimental and very modern style," particularly in the prologue, where he uses imagery that has no precedence in Thai literature.

Viewed substantively, however, the play is remarkable in the way it brings together themes that very soon after it was written came to represent central issues of elite Thai life. Thus, the play's historic importance derives from the fact that it focuses on a then "unthinkable" occurrence—the direct, overt expression of anger and hostility between a Thai father and his adult sons—and in so doing asserts that such things should be publicly acknowledged, discussed, and the reasons for their happening thought about. That the family discord should be over political differences—rather than over such homely matters as money, bad friends, or sexual peccadilloes—points even more clearly to the events that were to follow. That the particulars of the disagreement should concern environmental protection—years before the concept of "ecology" was even known to most Thai but also years after the need for such protection had become obvious, even dire—is almost apocryphal. Finally, that the family conflict should involve a reversal of moral roles—the two self-righteous sons berating their ethically uncertain father—is, from the point of view of the morality of the period, to turn the Thai value system on its head. Yet, just two years later that is precisely what hundreds of thousands of young men and women were doing. It was the reversal of moral roles in the actualities of the Student Revolution, later constantly rubbed in by the unending demonstrations of the 1973 to 1976 period, that led so inexorably to the obscene reactions of the October 6, 1976, coup d'etat. It is Witayakorn's identification of the moral arrogance of the young, the obdurate centurionship of the older generation, and the conflict that results from these positions as one of the central problems of contemporary Thai culture that makes his effort, for all its stylistic excess, a significant statement.

There are a few places in the play where, despite the overarching solemnity, some of the relaxing spirit of traditional Thai culture finds its way into the text, almost as a way of subverting the integrity of the characters' positions. It is not quite comic relief as much as it is the kind of ambiguity that Thai use to deal with the contingent nature of the human experience. Thus, after all the pretense of their ideological position has been marshalled, elaborated, and justified, the two sons take the final step of their emancipation by telling their father they are leaving his home. But quite independent of one another, both are careful to include in their leave-taking the words "for now." In Thailand, *no* ideological position is so pure as to be unaffected by the possibility of a change of heart or circumstance.

The character of the mother has some of these same qualities. Although her passive, old-fashioned, and naive manner suggests a mildly comic figure, she is for most Thai readers the most authentic character in the play. She is a person of human proportion, and it is the realism and gentleness of her lines that expose the pretense of the men around her—her husband's as well as her sons' and their friend's.

During the late 1960s and early 1970s, Witayakorn Chiengkul was among the most influential writers in Thailand, mainly because his work represented the most articulate renditions of the alienation of educated Thai youth. An earlier short story, "Novel of a University Man," first published in 1969, is considered to have played a direct role in the awakening and mobilization of university students which led, at least in part, to the revolution four years later. Written as a self-evaluation, the story is a diatribe against the irrelevance of a university education and the activities of university students in modern Thailand. The spirit of the piece is considerably less arrogant but more narcissistc than that expressed by the young heroes of *Naaj Aphajmanii*.

Born in Saraburi Province in 1946, Witayakorn came to Bangkok as a young man. He graduated from the Faculty of Economics of Thammasat University in 1969 and was for many years employed as a professional economist, mainly in the research and planning section of Thailand's largest bank. Later he joined the Faculty of Economics at Chiengmai University. Witayakorn says he started to write because of personal difficulty in communicating and getting on with other people, and as his writing evolved, it served to overcome his loneliness, particularly the isolation he felt about his own ideas and experiences. Witayakorn reads and writes English fluently, and several of his stories have been published in English, German, and Japanese translation. In his willingness to borrow and test foreign ideas and styles, he is widely recognized as one of Thailand's most innovative writers.

A Drama
Naaj Aphajmanii

Witayakorn Chiengkul

Cast of Characters

Aphajmanii, age twenty-five, phlegmatic, rather good-humored, a
   dreamer with somewhat long hair.
Srisuwan, age twenty-three, seemingly indifferent to things but
   extremely radical, serious about his ideas, long-haired.
Father, age approximately fifty, with the manner of a high-ranking
   bureaucrat who is serious about his condescending attitude.
Mother, age approximately forty-five, composed and placid, a typical
   Thai lady of past generations.
Mora, age twenty-six, although radical in some respects, he has a courteous and polite manner typical of those who have graduated
   from a domestic university.

From *Proceedings: Seminar on the Identity of Thai Society in the Future*. First
staged at The Siam Society, February 5–7, 1971, by the Committee for the Preservation of Fine Arts, Architectural Society of Siam. Bangkok: Committee for the
Preservation of Fine Arts and the Environment, 1972.

The title *Naaj Aphajmanii* and the name of the characters are taken from *Phra
Aphajmanii,* one of Thailand's great epic poems, written by Sunthorn Phuu early
in the nineteenth century. It is not clear, however, whether the author is using this
historical model to suggest the constancy of intergenerational conflict (and intra-
generational loyalty) or to suggest the changing nature of the Thai hero. In the
original, *Phra* Aphajmanii is presented as a physically delicate, sexually irresist-
ible hero who plays the flute exquisitely—his flute of course being his instrument
of seduction. An intensely passionate man, he weeps at the slightest provocation,
although usually in joy. In his narcissism, *Phra* Aphajmanii betrays his wife and
his son, Sutsakorn. However, Sutsakorn continues to love him, viewing him (as
almost all Thai readers do) as someone who is always above normal human sentiments, rules, and family responsibilities. It is these qualities as well as his successful use of his sexual prowess and narcissism that define *Phra* Aphajmanii's "heroism." *Phra* Aphajmanii's brother, Srisuwan, is a contrasting character—the
symbol of manly reliability, tough-mindedness, and reason and by virtue of this

Stage Directions

Lights out. Blank verse is being read from behind the curtain. As the verse begins, a dim light appears. A group of young men and women gradually appears from the wings on the right and moves quietly and solemnly across stage. Each person carries a placard on which are written such words of protest as "Where have all the sonklin *flowers gone?"[1]; "This country has no young people—only the aged and children"; "Better to fight in our own country than in other countries. But to end all fighting is best of all"; "End the rice premium once and for all. It makes the taste of rice unpalatable."[2] At center stage, a group of pallbearers carrying a replica of a coffin with the word "legitimacy" written on it moves toward the wings on the left. As the pallbearers pass off stage the recitation of the verse gradually ends. Blackout.*

Blank Verse

I have a dream
That one day all differences will disappear from this world,
When people of different colors will mix and be transformed into a single
        race,
When all the different languages will assimilate and merge into one,
And when all the Gods will rise up, join hands, and will publish their
        teachings in the same canon.[3]

---

steadiness, a person who is ultimately understandable but not "heroic." Mora, a minor character, is one of three Brahmans who encountered *Phra* Aphajmanii and Srisuwan after they had been expelled from their father's home. Skilled in the ways of artifice, he is also the character who could weave from grass a vehicle that could traverse both land and water.

1. Like calla lilies in the United States, *sonklin* flowers *(Polianthes tuberosa)* in Thailand are associated with death. At cremations they are the flowers most frequently arranged around the coffin. The protest phrase itself is borrowed from the American Civil War song that became one of the most popular antiwar songs of the Vietnam era.

2. The "rice premium" is a tax imposed upon all rice exported from Thailand and for years represented the major source of income of the Thai government. Many have argued that elimination or reduction of the rice premium would result in higher incomes for Thai farmers, while others have said that only middlemen such as millers and shippers would profit. In the late 1960s the premium reached a tax level of 43 percent. In recent years, the tax has gone down as revenues from import duties on foreign goods have gone up.

3. The imagery of this stanza combines the rhetoric of Martin Luther King, Jr., with allusions to the Thai Buddhist conception of the pre-Nirvanic millennium, e.g., that period in some future existence when all men and all women will look the same, when spouses will not know each other, when everything will be shared, when there will be no pain, and when four magical trees will provide

When one day science will absorb nature,
And science itself will be transformed into part of nature,
When the real and ideal will mix and merge into one,
And when that which has shape, taste, smell, sound, and touch will be
       no more.

When hunger, sickness, and suffering will be no more,
When there will no longer be poems written, songs sung, or pictures
       drawn for anyone to admire,
When the rich, the influential, the tyrannical will no longer oppress any-
       one,
Because the engine of life will have turned so madly that it will finally
       drift off from reality.

When the atoms of the devastating bomb dance throughout the universe,
Floating in the atmosphere and penetrating down below the earth,
Startling even the relics of prehistoric skeletons.

When the holocaust[4] floods the entire world,
Boils the oceans until they have vaporized and been dessicated
Leaving only emptiness—all in the wink of an eye.

Let the mass of mankind be damned so that they will have learned the
       price of their infatuation,
Let hatred destroy them totally, down to the marrow of their bones,
So that they will learn to treasure the love they have lost.

May the bullets that pierce their chests teach them how cheap are the
       medals awarded to them for bravery,
May the knives that pierce their hearts demonstrate to them the empti-
       ness of their flag,
May the shrapnel in their eyes help them to see the worthlessness of glory
       and honor,
And may the atom that rots away their skin teach them to understand
       fully the meaning of what is called "A Better Life" and other
       absurd mottoes.

---

food for all. This conception of the millennium, however, never addressed questions of race and language, if only because such issues were never salient in traditional Thai Buddhist thought. The Thai term for this millennial period or condition is *Yukh Phrasiian*. It must be emphasized, however, that *Yukh Phrasiian* and
the millennial concept itself is not an important, or even widely known, category
of Thai cosmology.

   4. The concept of a "holocaust" is essentially alien to Thai thought, if only
because such thought recognizes not a termination to things but only eternal
change and modification.

May all the stars sing an elegy to the world so that human beings might
     become aware of the beauty and harmony that they have for-
     saken.
May the bright fire on the great grave burn eternally[5] so that mankind
     will at all times value living and regret the loss of life.
And let the dust record this last part of history so that the spirits of the
     dead will be able to relate the story forever after.

ACT I

[*A living room with four or five chairs. (Use ordinary crates or boxes if
props are not wanted.) Two sets of jackets and neckties hang from the
chairs, and on the floor nearby is some luggage with airline baggage tags
hanging from it. On the wall is a giant television set (painted directly on
it as a symbol) or some other object that reflects the modern lifestyle of
this household. As the curtain rises,* APHAJMANII, SRISUWAN, *and*
MOTHER *are sitting down.* FATHER *is walking back and forth, as if he is
still excited about his sons' arrival but unable to begin talking about what
is on his mind because of the estrangement he feels from the long separation.* MOTHER, *with a suggestion of a smile on her face, observes her
sons with admiration and waits for* FATHER *to begin the conversation.
The sons also feel the estrangement, so* APHAJMANII *takes out his harmonica (or any other type of modern instrument[6]) and tries to play it
softly while* SRISUWAN *skims through the pages of a newspaper. Other
than* MOTHER, *no one really pays any attention to anyone else.*]

FATHER [*stops pacing and stands in front of* APHAJMANII]: All right.
     . . . Do you want me to make an appointment for you tomorrow
     with Mr. Chiw or do you first want to take a few weeks off to rest
     up?
APHAJAMANII [*looking surprised*]: Who is Mr. Chiw?
FATHER [*slightly disappointed*]: What? You don't know the name of the
     biggest businessman in Thailand? He is number one. You should
     know that he is the person who can make anything happen. Once,
     when parliament was in such a mess that some influential people
     wanted to dissolve it, the first person they went to see was Mr.
     Chiw. When Mr. Chiw told them that the money market was tight
     and that it would not be easy to find the money to throw into a
     new election, all talk of dissolving parliament just stopped.

---

5. The image of a grave with an eternal flame has no precedent in Thai culture.
Most Thai readers perceive it as being linked somehow with the grave of John F.
Kennedy.

6. Since harmonicas are rare in Thailand (and flutes and mouth organs are not)
this is meant as a contemporary equivalent of *Phra* Aphajmanii's flute.

[APHAJMANII *listens to his father in a casual, indifferent way.* SRISUWAN
looks as if he is disgusted, while MOTHER *sits and observes the reactions
of her children.*]

APHAJMANII: I still don't see what any of this has to do with me.

FATHER [*irritated*]: You're not as sharp as I thought you would be. How
can you start off in your career as a businessman if you're not
quick to take advantage of an opportunity to meet a real big shot
like this?

APHAJMANII: I still haven't said that I want to be a businessman.

FATHER [*surprised*]: What? But I sent you overseas, across the water, to
study business administration, didn't I? What good would there
be in not working in the field you studied?

APHAJMANII [*collecting himself and replying calmly*]: I wasn't there to
study business administration, Father.

FATHER [*both astonished and angry*]: You didn't study business administration? Are you telling me that you brought absolutely nothing
back with you while I was so heavily involved in risking my government position, a position which for so many years I fought so
hard to reach?

APHAJMANII: I didn't ask you to invest that much just for me. I was only
a child then, and I didn't know which end was up.[7] You were the
one who arranged everything in my life for me.

FATHER [*getting louder*]: Are you accusing me of having become corrupt,
even though I was doing it all for you?

APHAJMANII [*tries to hold his temper and does not answer.*]

MOTHER [*turning to* FATHER]: Oh, . . . take it easy in what you're saying. It's all right. We should give our son a chance to explain himself. After all, he's not a child anymore. [*Turns to* APHAJMANII.]
Now, my son, why didn't you tell us about this before? You
should know that it's also your fault, at least in part, because you
misled us all this time.

APHAJMANII: I admit that in that respect it was my fault. But during that
period I was busy all the time. And I knew it wouldn't be easy to
write to Father and Mother to explain the whole thing clearly. So I
thought it would be better to wait until I got home where I could
explain it to you directly.

FATHER [*having calmed down a bit, changes his attitude from anger to
sarcasm*]: So you were terribly busy? I suppose you were busy
hanging out with others smoking marijuana. I suspected this
when I first saw the two of you at the airport and saw the kind of
haircuts you had and the way you looked.

---

7. In Thai, literally, "the difference between what was deep and shallow, thick
and thin."

SRISUWAN [*in a tone that suggests he wants to explain*]: Father, long hair
   or short hair doesn't mean that a person is good or evil.
FATHER [*turns sharply*]: Don't interrupt. I wasn't talking to you.
SRISUWAN [*turns deep red, stands up immediately, and grabs his luggage
   as if to leave the room.*]
FATHER: And where are you going?
SRISUWAN [*shrugging his shoulders*]: Well, nobody wants to talk to me.
FATHER [*feeling trapped, but trying to save face*]: All right. Why don't
   you first go bathe and get cleaned up. When you're finished, come
   back. I have something to talk to you about too.

[SRISUWAN *picks up his luggage and walks toward the right wings, not
paying much attention to his father's final words.*]

FATHER [*turning around, he drops himself on a chair in front of* APHAJ-
   MANII]: All right. I'll give you a chance to explain. What do you
   have to say?
APHAJMANII: I began to see that the business world does not fit with my
   character. I realized this when I got there and could see with my
   own eyes how real business over there operates. The lives that
   business people lead are not very different from the lives of race-
   horses. They may gain acceptance, people may try to please them,
   they may have a good standard of living, but there is not much left
   in their lives because they've used everything up in their endless
   racing against each other. They are always hungry and thirsty.
   They don't know what it is to be sated. They may be able to
   increase their own consumption and the consumption of other
   people, but they cannot make the world any happier. They are
   only good at making people want to consume more than is necessary. They are rapidly destroying all our resources, producing
   more garbage to fill the entire world, and polluting our water and
   filling the air with filth that is decaying our cities. The death rate
   is increasing because of new kinds of bacteria and our bodies are
   becoming more vulnerable. Therefore, I got the idea that at the
   present time the problems of the world are not really based on the
   fact that there is not enough development but rather are based on
   the fact that what we do produce is not distributed with sufficient
   fairness. If the people in the countries that are already well developed understood these problems and became less selfish, there
   would be less tension and more hope in the world.
FATHER [*disappointed and appearing enervated*]: I worked hard and sent
   you to be educated in the United States in order to learn this?
APHAJMANII [*still much too involved in his own disquisition to indicate
   any understanding of his father's criticism*]: Don't give up hope,
   Father. I'm still not discouraged by these problems. Although I'm

only a small, unimportant person who specialized in environmental studies, I'm still young enough and I still have enough time ahead of me to disseminate my ideas. It may take some time, but if human beings are really intelligent creatures, they should be able to help themselves and their fellow man from committing suicide throughout the world and insuring that this species is preserved.

MOTHER [*puzzled*]: Son, what did you say you studied? I've never heard that name before.

APHAJMANII: Environmental studies. It's the field that's concerned with preventing the destruction of the environment and things of that kind, a subject that is not yet widely talked about in Thailand, because we're still only in the early stages of industrial development. However, as time passes, it will become a bigger and bigger problem, and people will turn and listen to me more and more.

FATHER [*mockingly*]: Who will hire you? Don't forget, this isn't America. Thailand's problem is to find ways to develop and to grow more rapidly, not to bring growth to a standstill.

APHAJMANII: That's looking at the problem only from a short-term time perspective. If you look at it in long-term perspective, you can see that we still have a considerable advantage that America doesn't, because we still have the opportunity to prevent problems before they arise. At the present time, America is being forced to spend a tremendous amount of money fighting environmental problems that have already emerged. More than that, they're not sure whether there is still time to solve some of these problems; it may already be too late.

SRISUWAN [*pokes his head in from the wings on the right and says*]: Can I come in and join you now?

MOTHER [*turns to smile*]: Come on in, son.

[SRISUWAN *walks on stage, sits down, stretching his legs out comfortably.*]

FATHER [*turns, glances at* SRISUWAN, *then turns back to* APHAJMANII]: Let me ask you again: With this head of yours, how can you possibly find a job? At this time, in our country, there is nobody here who is as farsighted as you are. Every person thinks only of himself—that's it! Have you been away so long that you've forgotten our proverb: "To know how to survive is the greatest good"?[8]

APHAJMANII [*smiling contemptuously*]: I haven't forgotten it. But I think

---

8. This aphorism is perhaps the most famous phrase in Thai literature. It represents advice given *Phra* Aphajmanii's son in the original *Phra Aphajmanii.*

it should be considered more a "con-verb" than a "pro-verb"[9] because the only thing it teaches us is to be completely selfish all the time. That's the reason why Thailand has until now lagged behind other countries.

FATHER [*becoming irritated*]: That's an outrageous insult to your ancestors! Whatever they were, they protected and preserved the nation for thousands and thousands of years—until now for your generation.

APHAJMANII: Father, stop dwelling on the past. Other societies have been able to prevail for thousands or ten thousands of years, just like us. The problem is not how long we have existed but how well we have been living. How much happiness and satisfaction have the majority of the people in society had?

FATHER [*appearing dissatisfied, he stands up, paces back and forth, searching for a counterargument, and finally turns his attention to* SRISUWAN]: And what about you? I guess you're just as far gone too. You sure don't look like someone who has been trained at a military academy.

SRISUWAN: You didn't make a wrong guess.

FATHER: Did they kick you out?

SRISUWAN: No, I quit. Being in that place was just like being in a community for the retarded.

FATHER: Do you think you're a genius or something?

SRISUWAN [*shrugging his shoulders*]: No. I just didn't want to waste my time studying those absurd subjects. The next step that human beings should take in their progress is to find ways to develop justice, to make people understand and be sympathetic to each other rather than to develop ways to pursue war more efficiently. Not only will we not have to waste time preparing to fight and kill each other but we may utilize the surplus time and resources to help find solutions to the problems of the polluted world and things like that.

FATHER [*dropping into a chair and turning to speak with* MOTHER]: So look—all my sons have become saints.[10] Maybe I'm the only sinner left here. And what are your thoughts on all of this?

MOTHER [*comfortingly*]: Don't lose hope yet. Young people are like

---

9. This is the only place in this volume where the English language might permit a play on words ("con," to swindle or to be against) that is identical in meaning to the play on words of the original Thai. *Thuphasid* in Thai is like "converb" in English in that it has absolutely no meaning. However, it is as perfect an antonym to *suphasid* as "converb" is an antonym to "proverb," the latter being the perfect translation for *suphasid*.

10. There is no "saint" category in traditional Thai thought. Here the term *nagbun* is a direct borrowing of the Western concept.

this. Wait till they have children of their own and wives for whom
they have to be responsible. Then their ideas will probably
change.

SRISUWAN [*annoyed*]: Mother, don't talk like that. I'm fed up to here
with hearing this kind of justification. The point has nothing to
do with people of one generation thinking one way and people of
another generation thinking some other way. The whole thing
depends only on what you really believe. Father and Mother, if
you have believed only in the truth of those things that have
proved useful just to yourselves, you'll never be able to understand the truth of all those other things that exist around you.

FATHER [*frowning and raising his voice*]: So now the child is teaching the
parents, huh?

SRISUWAN [*with restraint*]: Again, it's not a matter of seniority, sir. It's
only a mater of logic. The whole world has changed. How can we
cling to the old and obsolete rule of seniority that uses the age of a
person as the basis of judging whether something is right or
wrong?

FATHER [*angry*]: Now you dare to argue with me! Just because you've
been abroad to study, you think you're so well educated, huh?

SRISUWAN [*beginning to lose all patience*]: Father, try to be reasonable! It
has nothing to do with studying abroad or studying anywhere,
damn it! I'm only trying to tell you that I think I have the right to
express and explain my beliefs, that's all.

FATHER [*so angry that he jumps up trembling*]: Stop it! Shut up! Close
that crafty, insolent mouth of yours! Don't forget the fact that I'm
the one who has fed you and supported you—right to the present
day.

[SRISUWAN *bites his lip and looks elsewhere. Everyone remains silent.*
SRISUWAN *stands up and starts to walk slowly toward the right wings.*
FATHER *drops down on the floor, burying his face in the chair, as if he
were sobbing softly.* MOTHER *looks at him with concern and anxiety. A
door buzzer sounds from the wings on the left.*]

APHAJMANII [*speaking to* MOTHER]: I'll get it.

[APHAJMANII *walks out the wings on the left. Curtain.*]

ACT II

[*A porch on the front side of the house with three or four chairs. (Crates
or boxes may be substituted.) As the curtain rises,* MORA *is waiting,
looking toward the wings on the right.* APHAJMANII *walks out from the
corner of the wings and they greet each other with smiles.*]

APHAJMANII: Well, how goes it?

MORA: And what about you?

APHAJMANII: Oh, there's trouble. We're having a bad time. My father's having a fit. I don't know if there is any way we can get through to each other to reach some understanding.

MORA: It won't be easy. Our rigid feudalistic system doesn't let people escape that easily, particularly those who've lived more than two-thirds of their lives under it.

APHAJMANII: I'm worried about that, too. But let's not talk about it. You still haven't told me how things are with you.

MORA: Well, so-so. My new job is a bit better than the old one. Now I have a chance at least to write about the things that have been on my mind. I was really an idiot for having wasted all that time in teaching. You just can't do any serious teaching in this rotten system and dishonest environment in which we're now living.

APHAJMANII: Why? If you have something to offer that others can't, people should be interested in reaching out for it, at least for some of it.

MORA: You're right. They might be interested in knowing some of it, but even before beginning, they have already been warped by the outrageous examples of society, by the wasteful, extravagant environment, and by the senseless mass media which all work together to corrupt and mislead them. I tell you, there is no way to correct these outrages by working from inside the system. There are always obstacles here and barriers there. And some of these obstacles are absurd, the kinds of things that can drive you completely out of your mind.

APHAJMANII: Don't you think there is still time to create a new kind of population? What about our intellectuals? Can we still place our hopes in them?

MORA: Oh, . . . that's more difficult than anything else. Our intellectuals come only from wealthy or middle-class families. Living such comfortable lives, they choose to believe only what they want to believe—and that's in living comfortably.

APHAJMANII: Well, what can people like us do then?

MORA: All I can do is what I am doing now, and that is to try to protest from the outside. As for the rest, we'll just have to wait for a really massive change to occur in society. I believe that this will have to happen someday. The system of privilege, the system of influence, and the system of corruption that exists in the present situation are all factors that will hasten the collapse of society in the near future.

APHAJMANII: When that happens, there will be chaos—and not just a little bit.

MORA: Certainly. There is no kind of change that does not cause pain.

[SRISUWAN *appears from the right wing, carrying his luggage. He greets* MORA.]

APHAJMANII [*looking at the luggage*]: Where are you going?
SRISUWAN: I have to go somewhere. I need time to get some peace, and if I stay here there is just no way that's going to happen.
MORA: Do you already have a place to go?
SRISUWAN: Not yet, but it won't be difficult. I've done a lot of hitch-hiking in the past, so it shouldn't be a problem.[11]
MORA: If you still don't have any firm plans, you can first stay at my house. Right now, I'm living by myself in a rented place. It's nice and quiet, too, and I'm seldom even at home.
SRISUWAN: All right, maybe I'll drop by. But what are you doing now, older brother?
MORA: I'm working for a publisher trying to produce a journal. It's not too bad. Hey, if you're interested, you could come and help us out. There's hardly any pay, but if you're interested in doing something satisfying, it's worth a try.
SRISUWAN: All right. But let me get settled first. I certainly have things to write about. There are a hell of a lot of things around that go against my grain.[12]
APHAJMANII: So you're going to leave me here to face everything by myself?
MORA: If you want to come along with us, that's all right, too. But what would your father say if the pair of you go?

[FATHER *walks out from the right wings.* MOTHER *follows at a distance.* MORA *raises his palms to pay respect to* FATHER *and* MOTHER *respectively. They both acknowledge the greeting absentmindedly, because their attention is focused on* SRISUWAN. *Everybody stands without moving, except* APHAJMANII, *who remains sitting quietly. For a while, everything remains silent because each person is waiting for someone else to begin the conversation.*]

MOTHER [*speaking to* SRISUWAN]: Where are you going, son?
SRISUWAN: I just want to go away somewhere. I didn't want my return, on the first day, to begin with a quarrel.
FATHER [*lowering his voice, but still maintaining his earlier stance*]: Don't accuse me of being the one who started the argument. You

---

11. Hitch-hiking is alien to Thailand. Even the term for it—"waving at a car and depending on the driver to go somewhere"—is an awkward, strange-sounding construction.
12. In the original Thai, "that go against my ears and eyes."

two were the ones who let me go around talking and bragging about you with all kinds of people.

SRISUWAN: I don't think it is only that, Father. The real issue concerns differences in all our basic ideas.

APHAJMANII: Oh! I just realized that the real reason you're angry is because you're afraid of losing face. You're not really worried about our future as much as you're worried about your own image.

FATHER [*getting angry again*]: So you're trying to start up again with me?

APHAJMANII [*becoming amused*]: No, I just remembered something, that's all. Children don't have the right to argue with their fathers. Hasn't this been one of the oldest traditions of our culture—from the very beginning?

MORA [*beginning to feel awkward*]: Maybe it would be better if I came back some other day.

APHAJMANII [*immediately interrupts*]: No, you don't have to leave yet. There are no secrets here. There is no reason why our generation should be concerned with etiquette any more when all earlier generations used etiquette only as a means to justify and rationalize their own hypocrisy.

FATHER [*trying to control his emotions*]: I think that we should end all this rhetoric and start to talk seriously. Mora, you can stay. Maybe your human language will be able to get through to these two monkeys.

[SRISUWAN *gives a secret smile to* MORA *who is trying to conceal his own smile.*]

SRISUWAN [*with a deadpan manner*]: Well, why don't you sit down, Father. That will be the best position for you to say what's on your mind.[13]

[FATHER *looks at* SRISUWAN'*s face to see whether* SRISUWAN *is putting him on, but when the face shows no cause for suspicion,* FATHER *sits down—hesitantly. Gradually the others follow suit.*]

FATHER: All right, now tell me what you two intend to do next.

APHAJMANII: I'll try to find out whether any agency or university wants

---

13. Since Srisuwan's statement is a suggestion that the father reduce himself to the spatial and social level of the son, the statement is clearly meant to be facetious. However, since it is simultaneously a suggestion that the father and son be spatial and social equals, it is also supportive of the father's statement that they "talk seriously."

somebody who specializes in my field. I'll go on from there—
working and trying to disseminate my ideas even further.

FATHER [*turning to* SRISUWAN]: What about you?

SRISUWAN: I don't know yet.

FATHER: What do you mean, you don't know yet?

SRISUWAN: Well, I just don't know what I can do yet in a society that is as
deformed as this one is. To put it simply, I don't know yet what
I'm going to do because I'm afraid that if I decide too soon—without the background and without knowing the difference between
heads and tails[14]—I might become somebody's instrument and be
exploited. In times like these, social scientists like me are easily co-
opted and tend to become the servants of the groups holding political power.

MORA: As a matter of fact, I just told him that in the meantime he could
work by helping out at our publishing house.

FATHER: Are you talking about *The New Way* magazine? I think the
authorities will be closing it down one of these days. If it's forced
to close, what will all of you do?

MORA: Well, they won't be able to kill our thoughts that easily.

FATHER: I must speak frankly and tell you that I don't agree with you at
all. What's happening that you have to go around challenging
society to this extent? Do you think you can reform society merely
with writings? With the printed page? That day will never come.
Why don't you people do something that is easier and that will be
of greater benefit to yourselves?

MORA: I don't want to argue the point. It would be better for Srisuwan
to make up his own mind.

SRISUWAN: I'll probably go and help older brother Mora, working on the
project mentioned earlier.

FATHER: But didn't you just say that you haven't yet made up your mind?

SRISUWAN: But I just did—this very moment.

FATHER [*irritated*]: So you want to challenge me, right?

SRISUWAN: Father, your words are really meant to bug my ears, aren't
they? I'm more fed up with your warnings and worries than anything else. It's the same with all you older people. Let you be the
last person from whom I'll ever hear this. I don't ever again want
to be brainwashed by anyone.

FATHER [*mockingly*]: So you think your generation is so exceptional,
huh?

SRISUWAN: I still have the right to think this way, because whatever happens, my generation still has the time to prove itself, while your
generation has already proved that it has failed completely.

---

14. In the original Thai, "the difference between north and south."

FATHER [*getting irritated*]: So you're beginning to preach to me again?

SRISUWAN [*not giving in*]: I'm only trying to express my ideas about the people of your generation so that you will know what they are, that's all.

FATHER: Didn't you ever give any thought to how you could have come to where you are now, to the present day, if there had been no people of my generation?

SRISUWAN: Now you're going back to looking at the thing from the point of view of expressing gratitude. To me, that is one of the most pitiful cultural characteristics of a backward society.

FATHER [*angry*]: Well, why don't you people go ahead and start a new cultural revolution?

SRISUWAN: Oh, we'll certainly do that, if we're in a position to!

FATHER [*getting angrier*]: Why don't you just seize this house, throw me out, and kill me?

MOTHER [*frightened*]: Oh, my goodness, how can you talk like that? Maybe it would be better if we set this subject aside and talk about it some other day.

SRISUWAN [*trying to suppress his anger*]: Mother, it's better to discuss it today so that we no longer have to keep it hidden in our hearts. I don't quite fulfill the image of the ungrateful wretch that Father has been trying to draw, in order to gain some sympathy. It's just that I can't express how sick and tired I am of having to listen to this kind of perpetual dunning to repay a debt of gratitude.

FATHER: You don't have to excuse yourself. I no longer hope for anything from you.

SRISUWAN: I don't want anything from you either, other than for you to understand me.

FATHER [*angrily*]: I don't want anyone to preach to me in the house I built myself, that I got with my own sweat, energy, and brains. And I don't give a damn which hell you go to!

SRISUWAN [*stands up angrily*]: Sure! Of course! What makes you think that I'm the kind of person who could stand living in a place where I'm not wanted? [*Snatching his luggage and turning to* MORA.] I'll drop by at your office later. [*Turning to* FATHER *and* MOTHER.] I'm leaving for now.

[FATHER *sits downcast.* MOTHER *has tears in her eyes, and moves as if she is going to get up to stop* SRISUWAN, *but she doesn't.* SRISUWAN *walks out stage left.* MOTHER, APHAJMANII, *and* MORA *follow him with their eyes. All remain silent for a while.*]

APHAJMANII: I feel that what Father did wasn't very fair.

FATHER [*unable for a moment to find his words, looks up, having still*

not recovered from his anger]: And do you think that what your
younger brother did to me was very fair?

APHAJMANII: You shouldn't think of it in terms of striking a bargain.
After all, you're a father, not a salesman.

FATHER [*his fury rising again*]: So you too are spoiling for a fight, huh?

APHAJMANII: No, I just want you to realize the nature of the problem and
how it should be handled. My image of a "salesman" is not very
suitable, and if you want me to, I'll apologize and ask you to
excuse my error.

FATHER [*vengefully*]: Don't hit me on the head and then try to placate
me. You're just as bad as your younger brother. I've given up any
hope that you two will ever tend to my dying body or my
corpse.[15] It's better to lose both my sons this very day than to have
to suffer and be disappointed the rest of my life. There is no need
for any more discussion. I'm fed up with all this argument.[16]

APHAJMANII [*standing up*]: If that's the way you want it, it's fine with me.
At least it makes me feel better to know that I didn't make the first
move. You turned against me, not I against you.

[*At this point,* MOTHER *can no longer hold back her tears.*]

MOTHER [*sobbing*]: What kind of *karma* has made me survive to this
day? Why didn't I die the last time I was sick, so that it would
have been over and done with?

APHAJMANII [*feels moved but tries to hold back expressing his feelings.
Walks toward* MOTHER *and kneels down beside her*]: Nobody
wants to hurt you, Mother. But don't you think you should give us
a chance to do the things we believe in? What would be left to a
man if he could not do what he believed. There will be a day when
Mother will come to understand and will realize that we are not
such bad sons, after all.

[APHAJMANII *stands, walks toward the wings on the right, and returns in
a moment with his luggage.* FATHER *continues to sit downcast, and*
MOTHER *continues sobbing. Expressing his uneasiness,* MORA *sits
down.* APHAJMANII *walks over to* MORA, *and taps him with his finger to
get his attention.* MORA *stands up.*]

---

15. In the original Thai, literally, "entrusting my ghost or my illness to you
two." The nursing of the parent during his or her terminal illness and later the
washing and removal of the corpse to the temple, as preludes to eventual cremation, represent the most irrevocable filial obligations in Thailand.

16. Literally, "bargaining, teasing, and playing with words in a hostile way."

APHAJMANII: I'm leaving for now, Mother. I'm going, Father.

[*Nobody looks up.* MORA *is about to lift the palms of his hands to pay a respectful goodbye, but when he perceives the parents' state, he stops his movement.* APHAJMANII *and* MORA *walk out the wings on the left.* FATHER *and* MOTHER *are still sitting in the same position. Curtain falls.*]

I Am a University Student

Introduction

For those who are accustomed to thinking of university students as one of the major forces of Thai political life—as perpetrators of the 1973 Student Revolution and as protagonists-cum-victims of the 1976 coup—it is easy to forget that things were not always that way. In fact, for the decade and a half prior to October 1973, students were among the most politically quiescent elements of Thai society. Their inactivity was made all the more striking by the fact that it was during this period that so many other students around the world—in Japan, Indonesia, Mexico, France, and the United States—were in constant, overt opposition to their governments. Before 1973, students had not played an organized role in national political life since 1957, when General Sarit Thanarat used them, briefly but successfully, to demonstrate against the Phibun-Phao "dirty election," marking the onset of Sarit's own coup against the Phibun government.[1]

After Sarit's ascent to power, the students quickly reverted to their traditional role as junior members of the Thai establishment. In a nation in which only .60 of 1 percent of the population had been to college, they saw themselves, quite realistically, as "future leaders of the country." Too, in an expanding economy of "national development," they had a vested interest in maintaining the social and political status quo. However, as the years went on, the corrupt, inefficient, and morally whimsical nature of the Sarit-Thanom-Prapart regimes became increasingly obvious and onerous to them, and after Thanom abrogated the constitution in 1971 they became an active force in Thai politics. Thus, although they were one of the last student populations to become politically active during this period in world history, theirs was also the only student movement that actually caused the downfall of not one but two of their nation's governments.[2]

The following poem by Suchit Wongthed, written in 1968, recalls the

218

more traditional apprenticeship of Thailand's "future leaders" with intense satire, but also with extraordinary accuracy. Suchit has said that he cast his judgment in this form because a more direct criticism of his classmates' attitudes and lifestyle would have fallen on deaf ears. The poem hits home not only because it correctly describes the actual behavior of some Chulalongkorn and Thammasat undergraduates but more importantly because it reveals the fantasies and self-image of the vast majority. This was a time when the most prestigious student position on campus was that of "cheerleader"—the person who was responsible for mobilizing fellow students to show the "spirit" of their faculty (or college) at university assemblies and to support their faculty teams and who also had the right to discipline recalcitrants. These "cheerleaders" were often elected to office after an immense expenditure of funds for feasts at Chinese restaurants and visitations to popular brothels. The Chulalongkorn University Ball was one of the major social events of the year, and the annual Chulalongkorn–Thammasat Soccer Game at the National Stadium was almost equivalent to a national holiday. It was a time when Thailand's most popular and respected female professor was so acclaimed because of the personal interest she took in the way her students dressed, wore their hair, and carried on with men.

That young people should have such interests is, of course, not at all unusual. What is unusual is that while these things played such a critical role in the total experience of university students, they were virtually unrecognized and unreported in the numerous accounts of student life of this period. The English-language literature on Thai students during this time reflected, and perhaps even reinforced, this same kind of intellectual denial. (See Schuler and Thamavit 1958; Guskin 1964; Hollinger 1965; Prizzia and Sinsawasdi 1974.) When Suchit's poem was published, it opened the eyes of thousands of educated Thai to what was so obvious, but previously unperceived, and it also contributed to the changing nature of student life itself. In this sense, it fulfilled one of the highest functions of the poetic and literary enterprise.

NOTES

1. There are some Thai who argue that the 1973 Student Revolution was identical in political orchestration to the 1957 situation, with General Kris Sivara using the students, as Sarit had used them in 1957, as a frontal force to assault his military seniors, Thanom and Prapart. While this argument has a certain aesthetic and logical appeal, it ignores all the other, more critical factors in the two situations that were fundamentally different from one another, although it does say something about a Thai willingness to perceive historical events as a result of conspiracy.

2. And although it was not their intention, they were the precipitant to the downfall of a third government in October 1976.

I Am a University Student

Suchit Wongthed

I am a university student[1]
With the fortune of high-class association
This evening I will wend my way to the ball
And enjoy the charms of beautiful flowers.[2]

I am a university student
Elegant and handsome as a lion
The brain of the Thai realm
Tonight I will indulge my passion to my fill.

I am a university student
You lowly people, don't you know me?
My belt buckle, buttons, and tie pin?[3]
Get out—don't stand in my way.

First published in 1968; Reprinted in *Thasana* 1 (February 1973). Prasarnmitr Teachers University, Bangkok.

1. The title of the poem refers to students enrolled at Chulalongkorn and Thammasat universities in Bangkok. In Thai, personal pronouns are both optional and highly variable in meaning. The "I" appearing in the title and in the first line of almost every stanza is *kuu,* which explicitly conveys pride, assertion, and a demand for attention. The line might more accurately, but more awkwardly, read: "Listen here, I am a university student."

2. The traditional symbol of the young Thai woman.

3. These are usually worn as part of the uniform of university students and display the shield of the wearer's university; the buttons are typically worn on the blouses of female students. During the 1973–1976 period a large number of students, particularly those at Thammasat, intentionally changed their uniforms and to assert their proletarian commitments wore instead "the five *jauau*": long hair, rumpled shirt, jeans, flip-flop rubber sandals, and shoulderbags made by Thailand's tribal peoples. In Thai, the names of each of these items begins with the consonant *jauau.*

I am a university student
My campus is spacious and broad
I taste many subjects without interruption
In this great, comfortable city.

I am a university student
My stride has dignity and panache
Come the darkness and I will go the whole night
Following my marathon in our Sri Ayuthia.[4]

Hey, I am a university student
With awareness and intellect as great as a mountain
Let the angel, Phra In, with his sword do battle with me
I studied under the Americans and am expert.

I am a university student
Luxurious, able, and established
Tomorrow I must go to a party
To mingle with others like me with degrees.

Just listen
I am a university student
Silence—listen—to my philosophy
I am from the university.

. . . I am from the university
Do you know? Do you see? How about that?
It won't be long before we all die
So better seize all we can now.

---

4. Sri Ayuthia is another, more gracious, name for the city of Bangkok.

Social Work

Introduction

"Social Work" is drawn from a book entitled *Dongyen* [The cool jungle], the name of a fictionalized village that is supposed to be located somewhere in Thailand's Northeast. Dongyen is a place that has become heavily involved in the communist insurgency, and the purpose of the book is to describe some of the human consequences of that involvement. The "authors" do this by using a favorite Thai literary form: they select a number of heroes and heroines, assign each to a chapter that describes very different kinds of situations and reactions, and simply allow the presence of the single theme—in this case, the impact of the insurgency on the community—to unify the work aesthetically. Nine of the twelve portraits in the book are supposedly written by 'Go Bangkok and three by Vasit Dejkunjorn, but the two authors are probably one and the same person.[1]

Since the attitudes of the "authors" toward the insurgency are very clear, the book contains no hidden ideological messages. What it does contain are superbly realistic descriptions of some of the most important character types to be found in Thailand. In this story, *Khunying* Bawalaam is much more than a caricature or stereotype. Anybody who has spent time in Thailand is immediately familiar with the kind of situation portrayed in "Social Work," not only in terms of the gross attributes of "the rural-urban gap" but, more importantly, in terms of such things as the clothes in which the heroine is dressed, the baroque language of the public speeches, and the various motivations that are assigned to the *Khunying* and her colleagues. The only motivation that goes unspecified, if only because it is so obvious to ordinary Thai readers, is that in Thailand this kind of "social work" occurs principally because it is so much fun, that is, it provides the ladies with a justification to get away together on an outing, one that is even spiced with a tinge of danger. While some readers might consider this particular motivation to be ultimate proof of all that is wrong with the Thai social order, most Thai readers consider it so patently reasonable as not even to be questioned. The ironic ending to the story might suggest that the author himself questions it. But in his own observations about writing *Dongyen,* Vasit is explicit in saying that his sole purpose is to describe things the way they are and not to pass glib judgments on larger political or moral issues.

It is Vasit's attention to detail, particularly the detail of context and meaning, that makes his account of the *Khunying* so unerring. For example, in his reference to the *Khunying*'s musings about her husband's affair, the "other woman" is no mundane beauty—a movie actress, model, or courtesan. Rather, she is a nightclub singer, the siren of modern Siamese fantasy whose voice and lyrics can seduce even the most powerful of men. And in that very same line, the affair is phrased not as a certainty but only as a possibility, an expression of the wife's perennial hope that her worries are unnecessary. It is also an expression of the fact that husbands and wives in this class really lead separate lives and much of the time do not know what the other is doing. This same sense of veracity emerges a few lines later in Vasit's description of the excitement that Thai feel when someone mentions a delicacy that one has waited a lifetime—and in this case, ventured hundreds of kilometers—to eat. The comments of the deputy district officer second grade are an integral part of the scene: the young gallant flirting with the older woman about the size of the local fauna and, in an inimitable Thai way, reinforcing the discussion of food with a faint suggestion of sex. Several times in the text Vasit refers to the ill-managed public address system. While there is a touch of the burlesque in his description, the fact remains that one simply does not hear a public address in rural Thailand without the p.a. system going wrong at least once. It is as intrinsic to the public meeting as is the speaker's use of kinship terms when addressing the audience.

There is an important historical dimension to this story. Although *Dongyen* does not carry a date of publication, contextual considerations suggest that it was published in the late 1960s—when the kinds of visits described in the story were just beginning to catch on. By 1973–1974, Bangkok women's groups were actually competing with one another on the number of times they could visit villages in dangerous areas[2]; the wife of a former prime minister was particularly famous for riding the pillion of a motorcycle to make her visits. By 1976, the fashion (and perhaps the ideology or political reality) had changed, and instead of visiting villages these ladies began to call at provincial hospitals to bring gifts to police and soldiers who had been wounded in battles against the insurgents.

Born in 1929, the author, Vasit Dejkunjorn, is one of the most unlikely members of his society. The son of a provincial education officer, he spent his early years in Thailand's Northeast before going to Bangkok to continue his studies. He did his undergraduate work at Chulalongkorn University where he was famous as a humorist and essayist, and for a period of time also wrote for M. R. Khukrit Pramoj's various publications. He considers Khukrit a major influence in the early years of his career.

Since childhood, Vasit had the notion of becoming a policeman. He fulfilled his dream by becoming an officer in the Thai National Police Department; he also received an M.A. in police administration from a university in the United States. His career as a policeman has been *sui generis:* he was editor of the *Police Journal* for a period of time; was teacher and lecturer to hundreds of junior grade noncommissioned officers in police training programs; and in the 1960s held various policy-making posts in the government's anti-insurgency programs. More recently, he was attached to the palace where, as permanent Chief Police Officer of the Royal Court, he was promoted to the rank of lieutenant-general. During the Student Revolution of October 1973, Vasit was the major liaison between the king, the students, and various military groups and played the critical role in defusing the situation, perhaps saving hundreds of lives. Until his recent departure from the palace, he was viewed as one of the royal family's most influential advisors.

Vasit derives intense pleasure from his writing, and during the many years he has worked as a policeman he has always managed to find time to pursue this interest. In fact, to most educated Thai he is more recognizable as an author than as a policeman. Almost all of his work has been in social satire. His single most famous book is his 1975 *Khwaamphid-phlaad Khong Naaj Maak* or "The flaws of Mr. Betel Nut"—"betel nut" being the translation of a Thai transliteration for "Marx." In what is perhaps the only lampoon of Karl Marx to be written in *any* language, Vasit criticizes Marx for being, among other things, a headstrong son, an irresponsible husband, and a "hippie type" in his personal habits and social dreams. The disrobing of the emperor is done in a twitting, ironic way, as if in the mind of the author Karl Marx were really not that different from *Khunying* Bawalaam.

NOTES

1. On the back cover of the book is a photo of the senior author, but it is clearly a photo of Vasit; all the accompanying biographical facts, also attributed to the senior author, apply equally well to Vasit; and the writing style in all twelve stories is strikingly similar.

2. During this same period, student, farmer, and political groups of all kinds also competed with each other in visiting activities. For a village view of the value of all such visits, see Khamsing Srinawk's "I Lost My Teeth."

Social Work

VASIT DEJKUNJORN

Late in the morning of that day, Baan Dongyen's temple was bubbling with much more activity than usual. Cars of various makes—cars that were made by Westerners and Japanese but that were used by Thai[1]— entered the temple grounds and parked in tight, neat rows. Men and women dressed in the khaki-colored uniform of the civil service stepped from the cars and dispersed throughout the area.

For the most part, these people were senior civil servants. They included the province governor, the deputy governor, the superintendent of the provincial police, the provincial education officer, the provincial tax collector, the provincial customs officer, and others of that type. They stood around chatting in groups, as though they had not seen each other in months.[2] The lesser among them were clerks and other employees who, together with the commune headman and other headmen, their deputies, and the commune health worker, were each lending a hand at setting up tables and chairs in the temple pavilion. The district education officer and the teachers of the Baan Dongyen School were inspecting and counting the boys and girls who had assembled. The headman of Baan Dongyen went through a roll call of the adults and, using a Central Plain pronunciation that he thought appropriate to the situation, produced names that sounded so weird that people were not at all sure whether they had heard their own name or somebody else's. It was not until some-

---

From 'Go Bangkok and Vasit Dejkunjorn, *Dongyen* (Bangkok: Supha Wong-chanachaj Press, n.d.).

1. This fillip is double-edged: while it states how clever the Thai are in using the expertise of others it is also a reminder that they pay for the privilege.

2. Even though they all work in the same building they may not have seen each other in months. Studied avoidance is not unusual in many provincial administrative situations, and it is precisely the kind of event described in this story that provides an occasion for chitchat.

one speaking in northeastern dialect reassured them that their names had indeed been called that the owners of these names, the majority of whom were old women and men, began timidly to line themselves up with the others, in accordance with the headman's instructions.

Standing alert and facing outward, a long line of armed police and green-uniformed members of the Village Volunteer Security Force surrounded the temple. Officials of the PsyOp Unit (the acronym for "Psychological Operations") were setting up the loudspeakers in the temple pavilion. They tried the microphone, blowing into it like hoarse water buffaloes. Then in a voice that could be heard throughout Baan Dongyen village they announced:

> Beloved brothers and sisters of Dongyen. Today, around 10:00 A.M., the Executive Committee and the members of the National Women's Voluntary Social Workers Association will be here to distribute clothes, pads and pencils, and other necessary things to the pupils of Baan Dongyen School and to our senior citizens. The Executive Committee and the members of the Voluntary Women's Association . . . oops, Women's Voluntary[3] . . . (the sound of paper crackling through the loudspeakers) . . . I mean the National Women's Voluntary Social Workers Association . . . (a heavy sigh) . . . will arrive by bus. So, on this occasion, the Provincial Governor and his lady together with the senior officials of our province and their wives have come to greet them at Temple Baan Dongyen. And as the Executive Committee and the members of the . . . Workers . . . (the sound of paper crackling once again) . . . National Women's Voluntary Social Workers Association . . . (another sigh, although not as heavy as the first time) . . . Association have gone out of their way . . . travelling such a long distance, overnight from the city of Bangkok . . . to show their kindness of heart and friendship by bringing clothes and other things to distribute to their children and grandchildren, nieces and nephews, and aunts and uncles. Therefore, we would like to invite all the brothers and sisters of Baan Dongyen to join together in welcoming them in a spirit of unity. . . .

And at that point the sound of *"Siamanusti"*[4] blasted forth to drown out the speaker's final words.

---

3. The confusion is not only a result of the wordy nature of the organization's title (in the original, eight words and fifteen syllables) but also a result of the high frequency of "s" sounds. Thus, in Thai the title reads *Sa-maa-khom Sa-tri Aa-saa Sa-mak Sang-khom Song-khrau Haeaeng Chaad,* which makes it all sound like "Peter Piper Picked a Peck of Pickled Peppers."

4. A drums and flourishes patriotic song.

Not until about eleven o'clock did the big blue "BUS"[5] enter Baan Dongyen and make its way to the temple, led by a maroon-colored police Jeep and followed by a pale green Land Rover, a bright green Jeep (both belonging to some provincial government agency), and another maroon police Jeep that represented the tail of the procession. Hanging from both sides of that "BUS" were large pieces of white cloth on which were written in dark letters "National Women's Voluntary Social Workers Association."

That "BUS" was so wide and high that it was unable to get through the gate of the temple, so it had to be parked outside in front. When the door opened, out stepped a woman who was no longer young and who was beginning to get fat. She was wearing a sheer, long-sleeved blouse, loud-colored bell-bottomed pants, a wide-brimmed hat, and toting a large handbag. Her fingernails and toenails were painted bright red. It was impossible to say whether her eyes were large or small, normal or cross-eyed, since she wore a giant-sized pair of sunglasses which covered most of her face.

The provincial governor stepped forward before anyone else, saluting respectfully. His wife performed a respectful *waj*[6] and then using her husband as a shield, took cover.

"*Khunying,* are you well?"[7] said the provincial governor.

"Oh, sir, and you're the *Thaan Phuu Waa?*"[8] She did not reply to his question. She used to protest when people, following the tendency, addressed her with the title *"Khunying,"* but after a while she grew weary from having to object to their good will.

"*Thaan Phuu Waa,* would you please get someone to unload the things from the bus?" she ordered with her question. Meanwhile, the "Executive Committee and the members" of that organization with the name that was beyond the ability of any of the inhabitants either to pronounce correctly or to remember came straggling out of the "BUS." They gathered aimlessly by the side of the vehicle, each dressed in the style of the *Khunying,* and each wearing glasses of various makes and styles.

---

5. In the original, this is written in quotation marks, upper case, and is a transliteration, not a translation, of the English word "bus"—all of which is intended as a barb against the self-importance of the vehicle's occupants.

6. The Thai gesture of greeting and respect.

7. Although in most contexts this phrasing *("Khunying, sabaaj dii ryy khrab?")* represents the most ordinary salutation, in this context it clearly suggests a double entendre, the second meaning being, *"Khunying,* are you normal?" The term *"Khunying"* is an official title conferred by the king on women who have made contributions to society. If speakers use the title inappropriately, it is usually to be on the safe side of politeness.

8. The short and familiar form of the title for "provincial governor."

"I must also apologize to you, *Thaan Phuu Waa,* for having arrived later than scheduled," she said after remembering that it was the right thing to say. "That's just the way we women are. Before getting started, one of us has to wait for her friend. And then that one has to wait for this one. And this one has to wait for that one."

She laughed as if this were hilarious. And the provincial governor, who probably felt the same, joined in the laughter. In the meantime, those "someones" whose duty it was to unload things from the bus began to perform their tasks. They of course were the same people who had earlier set up the pavilion being used to welcome the visitors. The governor then invited the *Khunying* and her entourage to enter and to rest under the canopy of the pavilion. The *Khunying,* walking past the rows of civil servants, students, and other residents, scattered smiles to the right and to the left—all the way through.

When they reached the canopy, the people who were arranging the things that were to be given away had only just begun, so there was plenty of time for the prologue. The governor nodded in signal to three or four female secretaries to bring some cold towels, coconut juice, and bottled drinks to the committee and members of the visiting association. The *Khunying* introduced the committee and those members so swiftly that it was beyond the governor's capacity to remember, aside from a few surnames that he recognized as identical to those of some of the senior officials in the inner circle of the civil, police, and military departments.

When the arranging of the gifts on the platform had been completed, the governor stepped forward to the microphone. The officer in command of the province's PsyOp Unit adjusted the amplifier, and a sound like the howling of a dog filled the area. The governor turned his reprimanding eyes toward the official and the sound of the howling dog ceased. Without faltering, the governor turned to the microphone, and in a smooth and polite voice said:

Dear fathers and mothers and brothers and sisters of Baan Dongyen. Today, we are honored and we are also fortunate to have visiting us the Executive Committee and some of the members of the Association of Volunteer Women Working Socially for the Nation.[9] But before the gifts are handed out, I would like to invite *Khunying* Bawalaam,[10] the association's vice president, to address us and to explain to all our fathers and mothers and brothers and sisters the purpose of this visit to

---

9. The governor's "mistake" here is as suggestive in Thai as it is in English, i.e., that with only a slight reinterpretation his words could be read as a euphemism for "working girls." In Thai, the words are *Sa-maa-khom Aa-saa Sa-mak Sa-tri Song-khrau Sang-khom Haeaeng Chaad.*
10. In Thai, *Bawalaam* means "dangling beads."

Baan Dongyen on the part of the Executive Committee and members of the Women's Association Volunteering Socially.

Mrs. Bawalaam, who had been illegally appointed *"Khunying,"* adroitly stepped forward to take the place of the governor. It was obvious that she was familiar with a microphone and versed in public speaking.

My dear Provincial Governor, honorable civil servants, and all brothers and sisters of Baan Dongyen. In the name of the National Women's Voluntary Social Workers Association (after the comments by the governor, she was not sure she got the name of the association right, but she was absolutely sure that it was too long) I thank you for giving us the opportunity to visit Baan Dongyen today. Before saying anything else, I would like to tell you that even though we live so many hundreds of kilometers away in Bangkok we are very familiar with the current situation and what is going on in this province, this district, and especially in Baan Dongyen.

She stopped speaking, not to swallow her saliva or to lick her lips, which were beginning to get dry in the hot weather, but only to look for someone. And when she could not locate that person, she frowned, her eyebrows revealing her disappointment and frustration.

. . . We all know very well . . . (she gazed out over the rims of what were probably the largest sunglasses in the world) . . . the great ill fortune that has befallen the brothers and sisters of Baan Dongyen . . . the fate that you must deal with. We are well aware of the menacing threats and intimidations that our dear brothers and sisters are receiving from the communid![11]

Her eyes glanced around once more. Her spirits were lifted when she saw the person she wanted to see making his way through the crowd with his camera and flash equipment. She straightened herself up to look as tall and elegant as possible and smiled toward the camera, while continuing to speak.

. . . Because we care about the well-being and welfare of our brothers and sisters . . . (she really did not know the difference in the meaning

---

11. To the educated Thai reader this rural lower-class pronunciation of "Communist" reads almost like an absurd anticlimax to everything that precedes it. Its absurdity derives either from the ludicrous nature of Mrs. Bawalaam trying to imitate a village pronunciation and/or her inability to conceal fully her own nonelite speech patterns.

of the two ideas) . . . we the members of the National Women's Voluntary Social Association, numbering approximately five hundred,[12]
each of us a housewife who is married to a government official, a mer-
chant, or a Thai head of household,[13] with love and concern for our
brothers and sisters of the same nation, especially our brothers and sisters of Baan Dongyen, have together sacrificed our personal income,
each according to her ability and her faith and belief in this cause. And
with the sum of money thus obtained, we bought things, namely
clothes and school items, which our brothers and sisters can now see
set before you. . . .

She turned to her right, believing this to be her most photogenic side,
to accept the flash of the camera.

The things we have brought today may not be of very much value,
and there might not be enough for everybody, since our funds were
limited. So we have to give them specifically to our children and
nephews and nieces who are still of school age and to our older uncles
and aunts who need special care and attention. But it is our hope that
our brothers and sisters of Baan Dongyen will consider them symbols
of the love, regard, and concern which the Thai people of the central
region in the capital city of Bangkok have for our brothers and sisters
in the northeastern community of Baan Dongyen, as tokens of our
closeness and unity—those qualities which are the most necessary
things in our fight against the aggression of the communid. . . .

On the occasion of our visit to Baan Dongyen today, I, in the name
of the National Women's Voluntary Social Workers Association . . .
(she paused, slightly out of breath) . . . I would like to take this
opportunity to invoke the grace of The Three Gems and all the Sacred
Things in this Universe. . . .

When the *Khunying* ended her speech, the governor, uncertain about
whether it was appropriate, slowly began to clap his hands, followed in
chorus by the civil servants and citizens. The theme of the song "Auspicious Occasion and Spirit of Victory" burst forth from the loudspeakers.
Out of habit, everyone stood and held himself at attention. The deputy
provincial governor raised his right hand in salute, but when he realized
he was not wearing a hat and there was no specific reason to salute, he
quickly drew his hand down and turned an embarrassed smile at one

---

12. In Thai, the number five hundred suggests the eccentric or pejorative.
Thus, Thai speak of "five hundred kinds of madness" and "five hundred bandits."
13. These are three aphoristic categories that indicate respectability.

dried-out, skinny member of the association who stood nearby, defenseless against the wind.

The sound of the song stopped abruptly, well before it was supposed to, because the officer in command of the PsyOp Unit had switched off the amplifier. While that officer was discussing with other officials whether it was even suitable to play such a song, the deputy provincial governor, acting to correct the situation, nodded to the principal of the Baan Dongyen School to bring the children forward to receive the gifts from the *Khunying*.

In less than an hour, all the gifts that had been brought by the association had reached the hands of their recipients. When the last item had been given, the governor stepped to the microphone once again.

> In the name of the citizens of Baan Dongyen, I would like to say that I am overwhelmed with gratitude to the National Association Aiding Society Women to Volunteer, and particularly to *Khunying* Bawalaam, the vice president, and to the Executive Committee and the honorable members of the association who with diligence have travelled overnight risking many dangers and difficulties and who have come here today to bring these gifts to our children, nephews, nieces, uncles, and aunts. The villagers of Baan Dongyen will inscribe this act of virtue upon their hearts and will cherish it until their dying day. . . .
>
> I believe that this kind of visit by the association on this occasion will make every citizen of Dongyen realize that we do not exist isolated and alone, but that our brothers and sisters who live in another part of Thailand still care and have concern for us and think about us. This feeling will naturally bring about our unity and a spirit of joining forces that will give us strength which will enable us to fight with courage and achieve victory against the enemies' aggression, especially the aggression of the communist[14] bandits!
>
> Finally, in the name of the civil servants and the citizens of the Province, I. . . .

Mrs. Bawalaam, the vice president of the National Women's Voluntary Social Workers Association, stood there listening to the eloquent speech of the provincial governor, her eyes spying the news reporter. She was pleased that the young man was busily recording in his small notebook the governor's words. She knew from experience that in a few days news that the National Women's Voluntary Social Workers Association, "under the leadership of Mrs. Bawalaam, the vice president (she so much hated the title "Mrs.," but there was no choice) had brought clothes and other

---

14. The governor's pronunciation is perfect.

necessities to the children and poor people of Baan Dongyen, a subverted area," would appear on some page of a leading newspaper in Bangkok. And later, praise of her would resound throughout the capital's high society. Her name would be mentioned often, and probably in some cases with envy.

She sighed in pleasure and smiled to herself unself-consciously. The news of each one of her "social work" projects not only raised her own social status and made it more secure, but in the same proportion also raised the official status of her husband, the general. And that wasn't all. It also eased her loss of pride, that loss of pride that resulted from her husband's affections being diverted to that slutty nightclub singer, the one he might be secretly keeping.

The trace of the smile on her face became an angry scowl as she thought of this. But the cheers from the people around her brought her out of her mental trap.

"Shall we return to Provincial Headquarters for lunch, *Khunying?*" the governor asked smoothly and with an air of respect.

Khunying looked at her wristwatch and tried to display a look of wide-eyed surprise, but as to how successful she was, no one will ever know because of that pair of sunglasses.

"It may be rather late in the afternoon when we get there," the governor said apologetically, "but it will probably be worth our hunger. That shop is the most famous restaurant in the Northeast. And I have already ordered them to prepare some *plaa byyk*."[15]

"*Plaa byyk!*" The piercing voice of one of the committee members had exploded. "I'll die! I've been waiting so many years to taste some! Governor, isn't this the fish they say is supposed to be deep-fried whole in simmering oil and when it's done it is so crunchy and delicious . . . ?"

"Probably not, Madame . . . ," the young second-grade deputy district officer who was standing next to her hastened to explain, chuckling, ". . . the *plaa byyk* around here are as big as water buffalo. Frying one would require a special pan about five meters in diameter. And after frying it probably would not be crunchy either. . . ."

He did not finish what he had wanted to say because his eyes had met those of the governor.

"You do know about this evening, don't you, *Khunying?*" the provincial governor glared at the young deputy district officer. "The Provincial Red Cross has invited the Executive Committee and the members of the National Association of Voluntary Society Women to have dinner on the beach by the Mekhong River. And there will be a performance of the

---

15. *Plaa byyk* is a species of giant catfish found only in the Mekhong River. Eating of the fish supposedly brings good luck and well-being.

Serng Saak Mong, the modernized version of the traditional northeastern rice-pestle dance.

About fifteen minutes later, the only people remaining in the Baan Dongyen Temple area were the commune headman, the hamlet headman, the commune police inspector, some deputy hamlet headmen, the commune health worker, and six or seven men and women together with teachers and students who were helping to put away the tables and chairs. Some were picking up empty bottles, coconut shells, cold towels covered with red dust,[16] glasses, and trays and were placing them in a small truck whose driver had started the engine and was waiting to get going. Some people were walking around picking up empty plastic bags that had been scattered throughout the area.

Almost at the same time, two men in the prime of life, each carrying a pole across his shoulder from which a large basket was suspended at each end, walked across the field that was on the eastern side of Baan Dongyen. They headed straight toward the line of trees ahead of them. The things in the baskets were probably heavy because the pole each carried across his shoulder had bent into a deep bow. One man followed the other, and neither said a word. They frequently glanced behind them and sideways to be sure that they were not being followed.

About an hour after they had passed into the dense forest called "Dongyen," the two men came to a big tree where they stopped, put down their baskets, and used the cloth from around their waist to wipe off their sweat. At that moment, the last rays of the setting sun touched the tree tops of Dongyen, spreading a golden hue over the entire forest.

With incredible silence, two other men, also in their prime, appeared behind the first two. They were both dressed in black, were bareheaded, wore flip-flops on their feet, and carried small automatic guns.

Neither side displayed any acknowledgment or uttered any words of greeting. The pair that had just arrived went to the four baskets and threw aside the large leaves that covered them so as to examine what was inside, wrapped under plastic. When satisfied, they lifted the heavy baskets across their shoulders and disappeared silently, leaving the same way that had come.

Each plastic package in the baskets was printed in beautiful Thai letters. The letters read: "Gift from the National Women's Voluntary Social Workers Association."

---

16. Red dust is the most ubiquitous feature of Thailand's Northeast.

Headman Thuj

Introduction

In terms of money spent, men mobilized, agencies created, and expectations stimulated, the most significant activity in Thailand during the past twenty-five years has been "national development." From its inception, the basic logic of "development" was to accelerate the process of changing Thailand from a society of semi-isolated, economically undeveloped peasant communities into a modern, integrated, agricultural/industrial nation.

The statistics of development—the number of roads built, villages electrified, latrines and public address systems installed—demonstrate that technologically development has been a booming success. However, to most Thai the human consequences of all this activity have been considerably more ambiguous. While several of the writings in this book testify to the inherent merit of development and its associated ideology of "public service" (see particularly Puey Ungphakorn's "The Quality of Life of a Southeast Asian"), they are more poignantly statements of how this process and ideology have been violated ("Madame Lamhab"), frustrated ("Relations with Colleagues"), or subverted by human vanity ("Social Work"); in one ("Fulfilling One's Duty"), the author uses the contrast between the long-term gain and short-term pain of development as the background for his drama.

At the popular level, the quintessential Thai view of development is embodied in the popular song, "*Phuujaj* Lii" ("Headman Lii"). To call this tune merely "popular" is to understate an extraordinary cultural phenomenon. From 1965 to 1968 one could literally go nowhere in Thailand without hearing this song at least ten times a day: it blasted from radios, was on the lips of toddlers, stimulated an unknown number of additional stanzas and competing versions, and even made its way to American TV, where it was sung on "The Johnny Carson Show."

234

The song's lyrics describe *Phuujaj* Lii assembling his villagers to inform them of the latest government directive to raise ducks and pigs in order to improve their income and diet. However, instead of using the commonplace word for "pigs" *(muu)*, the headman uses the elegant Pali word that is written on the directive—*sukauaun*. When a villager asks what *sukauaun* means, the headman, ignorant himself, replies, "ordinary little dogs." In another stanza, the headman looks at the clear sky through his sunglasses—which, in imitation of his bureaucratic superiors, he wears as a symbol of his own modernity—and declares that it is going to rain. The song continues in this vein for several stanzas.

While most Thai view "*Phuujaj* Lii" as a satire on the naiveté of villagers, others consider it a caricature on the pretensions and stupidities of bureaucrats. In either case, by pointing to the confusion that can ensue from even the simplest elements of "development," the song encapsulated the spirit of the most important public issue of the era.

The following short story, "Headman Thuj," although known to a considerably smaller audience, partakes of this same spirit. More important, unlike "*Phuujaj* Lii," it represents a village, rather than a Bangkok, perspective on development and thus is a considerably more realistic, gentle, and homely portrait of the meaning of development to those for whom the whole enterprise was intended. In fact, of all the selections in this volume, this story comes closest to describing the aura and idiom of village life as it is actually experienced. The spirit of relaxation that animates the telling of the story; the anthropomorphizing of the dove; the frank, but easy, preoccupation with bowel movements and other things anal; the tainting of shrimp paste by toothpaste; and the simple imagery ("the aroma of the new rice," the feet of infants being "as big as shells")—are all precisely the kinds of things that villagers would attend to in telling the story, although perhaps not with the narrative subtlety that the author controls.

Little is known about Phutthapon Angkinan other than he was an instructor at Prasarnmitr College of Education in Bangkok. The journal in which the story originally appeared is no longer published.

Headman Thuj

PHUTTHAPON ANGKINAN

Dawn had not yet broken, but the cocks were busily crowing away like the alarm on little Tick's (Tiraphong's) clock during the exam season.[1] Feeling restless, *Kamnan* Thuj tossed and turned.[2] "It's morning." He was conscious of that even if his eyes were still closed. Life in the forest in the morning hinges on nature; there are no rules, only a system based on habits.

This morning as well, habit caused *Kamnan* Thuj of Ban Hua Dong to feel like popping out of his mosquito net, particularly at this time, since his bowels rumbled in turmoil, urging excretion. In the breadfruit grove at the end of the field, Song Kuk, the big dove that he had so often tried to decoy, was cooing a greeting to the dawn. The bird was so intelligent in averting the *kamnan*'s ruses that the headman had all but given up trying to catch him. Song Kuk's song was very inviting. If it had been any other morning, he would have been off some time ago shuffling in his sarong to duck behind the bush to listen to the dove's song.

It was not because of the influence of several bottles of Maeae Khoong[3] that he had fetched for the development officers—those he

---

From Nithat Khurukaakowit, ed., *Eegalak* (Bangkok: The Academic Club of Prasarnmitr Teachers College, 1972): 25–28.

1. While "little Tick" is a thoroughly acceptable nickname, it is in this context also a play on words, i.e., exactly like most English speakers, Thai hear the sound of a clock as "tick tock, tick tock."

2. In rural Thailand there are two types of headmen: *phuujajbaan* and *kamnan*. The former is an elected head of a hamlet; the latter (himself a *phuujajbaan*) is the elected head of a commune, or group of individual hamlets. The title (and protagonist) of this story is a *kamnan*, elected to his position by his fellow hamlet headmen.

3. One of the more expensive brands of domestic whiskey.

teasingly called "The Four-Armed Gods."[4] They had come for a plenary meeting to develop Ban Hua Dong into a model subdistrict. And now, one example of development had just yesterday been completed in *Kamnan* Thuj's house compound.

Development work caused great excitement in *Kamnan* Thuj, a man of fifty years of age. The new dirt road led the way for vehicles from the provincial town to come into the village. The well was dug with the objective of starting a system of running water for the commune. The Community Center was constructed to replace his own front lawn as the meeting place of the Commune Council. Along with these were the district officials' comforting words that in three years at most, Hua Dong commune would be a model subdistrict and he, as its head, would receive a prize for being a model *kamnan*. He might even be granted an honorary degree for what had been accomplished.

However, development also caused quite a disturbance in *Kamnan* Thuj's life. Even worse than that, Lamjaj, his faithful wife, along with the district officials, had impressed upon him the responsibilities he had for being a model villager, a pioneer in a changing world, or to use a modern term, the "fashion leader of the village."[5] Anyhow, there were many new things that he could not help being rather proud of, like the portable transistor radio. Lamjaj had it on loud from morning till late at night. Country songs, *likee*,[6] and city soap operas alternated with advertisements for all kinds of luxurious goods ranging from houses as grand as royal palaces, different makes of cars, household equipment and wares, down to and including quality toilet paper so soft that it tickles your ass.

Many of these things were accepted only half-heartedly by *Kamnan* Thuj. They would be thrown away in a moment of carelessness, for they were a waste of money and against his habits. A toothbrush, for example. For fifty-odd years, his teeth had been perfectly white and shiny, as strong as a bull's teeth. But Lamjaj got bossy one day and bought him that thing. Its bristles pricked his gums until they hurt. The toothpaste tasted strange. Worse, it made his shrimp-paste sauce taste insipid. He used it for two days, then out it went. He turned back to his usual *khauauj* bush twig. You chew one end of the twig until it is soft, and then

---

4. This is a particularly apt play on words. The Thai term for "development" is *phatthanakauaun* and the term for "Four-Armed Gods" is the phonetically similar *phra sii kauaun*. In addition, the "Four-Armed God" in the Thai pantheon is *Phra* Narai, the Maintainer of the Universe—the god who is constantly developing things.

5. The term here for "fashion" is a Thai transliteration, not a translation, of the English word, and the use of a foreign word underscores how important the matter really is.

6. *Likee* is folk drama.

use it to scrub your teeth. It tastes slightly bitter. He composed his own advertisement: "Whiter, cheaper, and better tasting than any other brand." This was employed on his dog, Aaj Daang, who, whenever he heard it, wagged his tail excitedly.

The *kamnan*'s calloused feet were as thick as water buffaloes' hooves for they had been trodding the fields since they were only as big as shells. No thorns and pricks he stepped on would ever drink his blood; they would be picked out with a needle without any bother. But now that he is a *kamnan* in a development project, he has had to acquire a pair of shoes to wear for meetings at the district office. An hour after putting the shoes on, he was shedding tears, "Holy Father and Mother, save me this time!" They squeezed so tightly his toes almost broke, and they also pinched the skin off the back of his feet. He staggered away from the meeting like a one-legged cripple. It was both painful and embarrassing, but he did not dare take them off. Back home, he had to lie on his back for a few days because his lymph glands were so swollen and painful. Finally, he found comfort in a pair of oversized sneakers and thick socks, which helped save his face as the leader of development. Of course, he would only wear them at meetings in the district office.

Some symbols of development worried *Kamnan* Thuj much more than the toothbrush or shoes. These things seemed to mean so much to the development officers and the project. *Kamnan* Thuj remembered the words of the leader of the Four-Armed Gods: "Let me say first that the project that is most important for development is the upgrading of the people's health and welfare, because the country can only prosper if its citizens are strong and healthy, and if they know how to protect themselves from disease. This is done by using appropriate behavior. We should begin with an essential place in our daily life. That is a toilet. . . ." The leader paused for a moment staring into *Kamnan* Thuj's eyes and continued with emphasis. "There isn't even one in your house. As leader of this project, I have ordered the workers to build one at your home, which will serve as an example for others."

The subject of the toilet had stunned *Kamnan* Thuj. It is not that he was too ignorant to know what it was. He had even used one himself— out of necessity, while at a meeting in the district office. It was a square box that radiated unpleasant odors and on which you had to sit carefully so as not to fall off. What was worse was the feeling of being confined in a narrow little room and being suffocated by the disgusting odor. To his mind, it was the same as being put in a filthy prison cell.

The sun was appearing above the mountain range which served as the backdrop to the Hua Dong commune. The bold cock had stopped crowing and instead was making a courting sound with a young hen. Song Kuk, however, was cooing at a faster rhythm, and *Kamnan* Thuj's stomach began to churn even more. *Kamnan* Thuj decided to get out of the mosquito net under which he had been lying awake and restless. He tightened his sarong knot, felt around for his tobacco and tinder box, and walked out behind the house, turning his head so as not to acknowledge the toilet which still smelled of the damp, new cement. At the edge of the field behind the house, he picked a twig from the *khauauj* bush, ripped off its leaves, and chewed on the broken end. Its bitter and minty taste suddenly lifted his spirits. He looked farther away at the fields where rice plants were swelling with grain. "This year's harvest looks promising. . . . Please, let's not have any mice or a price drop." He placed his palms together in a gesture of homage toward the sky. He happily breathed in the aroma of the new rice.

His foot slipped forward and he almost fell. His mind had switched back to its original track. He took a look around as if afraid to be seen, feeling a bit embarrassed. "If anyone ever finds out that *Kamnan* Thuj of Hua Dong commune, the model of development, still comes out to the middle of the field to perform his bodily function even though he has a toilet, how could I ever show my face? . . . And what will I do if Lamjaj finds out? She will be telling the whole village for days on end." Song Kuk's cooing was touched with pathos as the mellow drawn-out voice dropped at the end with a "kuk." He sounded like a bird of great authority, very comforting, and rather strangely, made one feel relaxed. On second thought, "He is much better off being his own boss. If I were to put him into a cage, he would not be half as arrogant and dignified. . . ."

The *khauauj* twig in his mouth was drained of its taste as he approached his destination, the tree grove. *Kamnan* Thuj—a traitor to toilets, the symbols of development—gazed around, looking for a suitable spot. All of a sudden, he jerked, startled by the sight of Lamjaj who seemed to come out of nowhere. "What are you doing here?" Her voice was shaking with alarm.

But the one who was asking was too frightened to notice anything. He answered automatically, "Oh! I've come to listen to the dove," and unwittingly asked in return, "What about you, why are you here?" He looked closely at the place where his good wife had abruptly appeared. His eyes widened, for a lump of human waste sat there as evidence. He laughed out loud. His harassed feeling ceased at that moment. "Ha ha! So Lamjaj, you too have sneaked out here to listen to the cooing of the dove."

3

The Deterioration of Thai Life

Lord Buddha, Help Me?

Introduction

Whatever its aesthetic merit, the following account of the odyssey of Mahaa Bunman by Suchit Wongthed approaches the central problems of contemporary Thailand more closely and comprehensively than perhaps any other piece in this collection. At its most obvious level, the story is a description of the hero's lost of faith in Buddhism and its encompassing moral power. The loss here relates to Bunman's commitment to the authenticity of the Thai Buddhist world view, a loss that is so inherently threatening to most Thai that the author has to provide himself (and his readers) a way out—mainly by suggesting the possibility that Bunman's amulets may not be genuine and that if he can deceive himself about the potency of his own amulets, he can also deceive himself about the potency of Buddhism and its definitions of reality. It is important to note that in terms of the exposition and continuity of the narrative, this possibility is only intimated, never declared, although in context it is not easy for a sensitive reader to miss it.

At another level, the story documents one of the most profound changes that has occurred in Thailand during the past quarter of a century—the redefining of the universe so that it is no longer primarily a moral universe but rather a pragmatic and secular one. Two or three decades ago (or during the author's childhood), an ex-monk like Mahaa Bunman would have had little difficulty in finding a good position. Potential employers would have been lined up to recruit a person of such virtue and knowledge. Possession of the *Parien* III would have been proof of the applicant's capacity for learning; his long service of "ten lents" would have been demonstration of his constancy and dedication; and, above all, the mere fact that he had worn the yellow robes would have been evidence of his essential goodness. However, the world has changed, and where moral experience and training were once necessary

241

conditions for insuring that a job would be well done, they are no longer sufficient conditions for operating a complex, technological society. As the text itself indicates, Bunman did not really believe the message of "all those who shook their heads when he said he had graduated *Parien* III."

At still another level, the story is a brilliant presentation of the relationship between poverty and self-esteem. Thailand is not a place where people are likely to starve: as those without work can always return to their villages, ex-monks can always return to their temples. However, for those who are forced to return to their earlier status, the retreat can be as personally devastating as starvation itself. The pain is particularly acute in this account because the hero's re-entry into the world of human beings seems to be motivated mainly by psychological considerations, that is, "to demonstrate that he is a man, to show how a man becomes full in fighting the world." This is a powerful drive for many Thai, who perceive the monkly state, quite realistically, as solipsistic and socially passive, without external stimulation or challenge. A monk can simply "be"; he does not necessarily have "to do" anything. And of course his biological existence is dependent upon what laypersons choose to give him. His state is in sharp contrast to the world of human beings who must compete and fight for their own survival and who, whether they succeed or fail, are vibrant "full men." Thus, to leave the monkly state for the "devilish state" demands a major marshalling of one's resources, and is not a decision that is lightly reached. To try to be a "man" and then be forced to acknowledge failure can be, as the story demonstrates, a psychologically brutalizing experience. Bunman's burden is not made any easier by the fact that he was apparently always a man without social resources. Even before being ordained as a monk he went about "naively, with nobody to depend on, nobody to know or to know him, nobody to serve or to serve him." This may also be the author's way of emphasizing the isolating, lonely nature of the Thai urban experience.

The hero's isolation amid the din and chaos of Bangkok is perhaps the most insistent theme of the story. Bunman's remark that since leaving the monkhood, "nobody even cared to ask when he left or even whether he was married" is almost excruciating in its plaintiveness, since these particular questions represent the simplest expressions of traditional Thai civility. In times past, any stranger would have asked. Similarly, his comment on "the loss of the country's trade balance" is an expression not of his understanding of the human consequences of abstract economic forces but simply an attempt to use one of those catch phrases of modern life that, by the sheer mystery of its meaning, can somehow assuage the pain that one is feeling.

Suchit Wongthed is one of the most prolific members of Thailand's literary community. The son of a farmer, he was born in 1945 in Prachinburi in the Central Plain, and spent twelve years as a temple boy—both in the village in which he was reared and in Bangkok. Living at the temple in Bangkok under the sponsorship of a monk, he attended secondary school and later entered Silapakorn University where he studied archaeology and history. Because of work obligations, he spent six years at Silapakorn before obtaining his degree and going to work as a writer for M. R. Khukrit Pramoj's *Siam Rath* newspaper and *Chaawkrung* magazine. Although he spoke little English, he was able to read it, and in 1971 he went to the United States, ostensibly "to study the American publishing industry," but mainly to be close to his wife-to-be, who was studying for a master's degree in anthropology. It was during his year in America that he wrote "Getting Drunk Abroad" and "Madame Lamhab," the latter being stimulated by an account in a Thai newspaper he regularly read at the Cornell University library.

After returning to Bangkok in 1972, he disagreed with Khukrit over what he says was a minor political matter (e.g., "Khukrit said my politics were too progressive, and I said I didn't know anything about politics"), and when he was fired he started his own publishing house. He has since edited and written for some of the nation's finest journals and also started a Thai-language magazine concerned with archaeology and tourism. Although the latter is partially supported by the indigenous Thai tourist industry, its extraordinary success is testimony to the rapid maturation of Thai cultural tastes and the diffusion of these tastes to an increasingly larger audience.

Many of Suchit's writings contain references to aspects of Thai art, archaeology, and literature. He does this not for rhetorical purposes nor to parade his expertise but simply out of deep commitment to what he believes are the most valuable elements of the Thai cultural heritage and the idea that such knowledge should be both preserved and disseminated. These kinds of interests serve to label him as one of the more conservative voices of Thailand's intellectual community.

Lord Buddha, Help Me?

SUCHIT WONGTHED

Mahaa Bunman has paid respect to Thaan Phra Khruu Waj with a fluid *beencaangkhapradit*.[1]

After putting on his polished black shoes, he dutifully tucks his shirt into his pants and wipes the dust from his trousers. The pants are shiny, made of material imported from Japan.

He takes a comb from his back pocket and draws it over his hair, hair that now almost covers the back of his neck. The pomade he uses—one of the best-selling brands—makes his black hair gleam.

Finished combing, he puts the comb back into his pocket and then smooths the hair at the sides of his head with the clean palms of his hands. As he steps away from the terraced area in front of Thaan Phra Khruu Waj's dormitory, Maha Bunman pats the top of his head a few times with his right hand. He realizes that his hair has grown quite long. He is all smiles because he intends to grow his hair in a proper style, like Charin Nanthanakhorn.[2]

Mahaa Bunman walks toward the front of the monastery through one of the ritual halls. This ritual hall is in a Chinese style, a style that was very influential during the reign of King Rama III. This form lacks the *Chauau Faa, Bai Rakaa,* and *Naak Sadung* that are characteristic elements of most Thai temples. There is only the *Naa Ban* eve and lintel

---

First published *Chayapryk* Magazine (December 1969); Reprinted in Suchart Sawadsii, ed., *Thanon Sajj Thii Nam Paj Suu Khwaamtaaj* [The road that leads to death, vol. 2, Urban scene, collected contemporary Thai short stories] (Bangkok: Duang Kamol Publishers, 1975).

1. *Mahaa* is an honorific for a learned monk or ex-monk; Than Phra Khruu Waj is a senior monk who officiated at Mahaa Bunman's own ordination many years earlier; a *beencaangkhapradit* is a series of extremely elaborate body movements for showing respect to senior monks and Buddha images.

2. A popular male vocalist of the period.

decorated with Chinese porcelain and colorful chinaware. The wall of the ritual hall, coated with white stucco, is brilliant.

Mahaa Bunman looks at the wall with a smile because during his priesthood he had painted it with his own hands. He had been a monk at this temple for ten lents, until he reached the level of *Parien* III and could proudly enjoy the title of "Buddhist Scholar of the First Rank."[3]

He had resigned from the monkhood into this devilish state almost three months ago and had been out of work for three months as well. Today is the most brutal day. He has never known such a day in his life. He is so glad he has the chance to face this day. It is the day to demonstrate that he is a man, to show how a man becomes full in fighting the world.

At the *wat* entrance facing Mahachaj Road, Mahaa Bunman stands with a parched smile on his face. At the moment, what he craves is a glass of iced Chinese coffee. Turning left toward the Pauaum Mahaakaan Wall near the Chalerm Thai Theatre on Rajadamnern Avenue, he sees the Golden Mountain beyond the roofs of the low buildings. He sees the sharp, pointed top of the Looha Praasaat on Raachanaddaa Temple. Mahaa Bunman thinks of the time of his own monkhood when he used to go up to the top of the Golden Mountain and the top of the Mondop of Looha Praasaat. This was even before the municipality reconstructed it.

He walks on aimlessly—but deep in his thoughts.

His stomach rumbles like thunder during the rainy season. Intermittently, the Air[4] in his stomach swells up, and his throat becomes constricted. His body trembles. The trembling is greater than that of *Phra* Wesandorn expressing his anger toward Chuuchok, who had beaten the two royal children from Bana Sala.[5] *Phra* Wesandorn could control his emotions, but Mahaa Bunman cannot. He is trembling even more than the Watsakaan Brahman who had been beaten with a bamboo rod. His flesh, his veins are all trembling.

Mahaa Bunman is trembling from hunger. His last few coins had been spent that morning on a cup of coffee and half a package of Khled Thong cigarettes.

Mahaa Bunman is furious at himself for having first gone to Thaan Phra Khruu Waj's dormitory. He thought there would be something left to eat there, so he went directly, without considering whether there was anyone else who might help him.

---

3. The Thai monastic order recognizes nine levels of "*parien*hood," or expertise in knowledge of Buddhism. *Parien* IX is the highest rank. Thus, the attainment of *Parien* III, while an achievement, is not extraordinary. Also, in this context, the phrase "ten lents" means ten consecutive years.

4. As one of the Four Elements in the human body.

5. Both this and the following allusion are taken from the Jataka tales, or stories of the various lives of the Lord Buddha.

His thoughts went back to when he arrived at the dormitory. It was already one in the afternoon.[6]

"How are you sir?" He had greeted and paid obeisance to the monk at the same time.

"It's you. . . . I'm well. What about you?"

"I'm well, sir."

"Where are you working?" Thaan Phra Khruu Waj's question had pierced into Mahaa Bunman's heart.

"My friend asked me to wait for a job that was coming up at the Religious Affairs Department. I am not doing anything now. Do you have any work for me?"

"What about working at the morgue?"[7] Thaan Phra Khruu Waj laughs from deep in his throat while offering his guest a kettle of tea, betel nut and leaves, and cigarettes.

Mahaa Bunman puts his two hands up to pay respect, then pours out the tea to drink, thinking that he would much prefer it be rice.

He drinks the whole cup. He can no longer bear it, so he asks indirectly, "Some cake would be nice." He gets up and walks toward the kitchen. "I miss the cake they have at the monastery. The kind you buy outside is not as tasty."

"We don't have any," answered Thaan Phra Khruu Waj. "Nobody went out to receive food today. Mr. Klieng made merit by offering us breakfast, and the air force captain living behind the monastery invited us for the noonday meal. So we didn't go out on our begging rounds today. . . ."

Mahaa Bunman stops walking to wipe off his perspiration. He is crossing the bridge over the canal between Wat Thepthidaran and Wat Rajanaddharam. Thinking back to what happened earlier, his heart sinks. He had pretended he would like some cake so he could look into the kitchen to find something to eat. What a pity.

He feels that this is a brutal day. But his second thoughts make him feel proud that he has left the monkhood to fight the world. Yet the world is so cruel to him.

He's sorry that he guessed so wrong. At first, he thought he would be

---

6. A monk's major meal of the day must begin by 11:00 A.M. and, when completed, the monk can eat no solids again until the following morning. By 1:00 P.M., any leftovers from this meal would presumably be available to visitors and hangers-on.

7. In the original Thai, this is intended as a wry comment rather than as a realistic suggestion. Working at a morgue is for those at the bottom of the occupational ladder, for whom there are no longer any alternatives. At the same time, such persons are considered strange and perhaps supernaturally endowed: they are thought to have special talents that permit them to come to terms with the malevolent spirits that inhabit such places. The monk's comment is primarily a recognition of the likelihood that things must be difficult for his guest.

out of work for, at the most, a month. His religion degree should have helped him get a job without any difficulty. But it was all wrong. All those people shook their heads when he said he had graduated *Parien* III. Nowadays they want people with university degrees, not with *Parien* certificates.

Bunman's hand touches his heart, and then moves down into his shirt, caressing the stainless steel necklace he bought right after he had left the monkhood. He moves his hand down a bit and pulls out the bunch of Buddha amulets on the necklace. But then he drops them back onto his chest: *Somdej, Somkauau, Kring, Kampaeaeng Kayeeng.*[8] All had come from Wat Mahathat at Sanam Luang.

Mahaa Bunman feels the grievance in his heart. Why do his *Luang Phauau* do nothing to help their son? Their son has always been virtuous, both in front and behind, both privately and publicly.

He starts wondering about the nature of Virtue. What can Virtue do for him, other than bring him starvation like this?

Feeling weak and dry, he walks past the Chalerm Thai Theatre. He looks angrily at the poster in front of the movie house. His jealousy is awakened by a young couple sitting in an air-conditioned restaurant. A girl strolls toward him displaying her knees and thighs, and he feels embarrassed, but he can't keep himself from glancing at them.

He thinks of the village of his birth, of his home district, over a hundred kilometers from the provincial capital. Then he tries not to think anymore of his home. He had left home and had become a novice many years ago and then moved to a temple in Bangkok—naively, with nobody to depend on, nobody to know or to know him, nobody to serve or to serve him. He was alone when Thaan Phra Khruu Waj offered him his yellow robes on the day he was ordained at age twenty.

Mahaa Bunman had made up his mind to resign from the monkhood when this year's lent was over. He wanted to come out into the inviting human world. But it turned into disappointment.

The friend who promised to get him a job in the Religious Affairs Department has given him money several times. But he is too embarrassed to ask for help again. He has to wait for several days to pass before again asking for a favor.

This world is so cruel. People in the city are so selfish. It's impossible

---

8. These are the names of amulets which, when genuine, are considered among the most potent of all Buddha amulets. However, the fact that the amulets had come from Wat Mahathat at Sanam Luang—an open marketplace—raises doubts in a Thai reader's mind about their authenticity. The lines that follow, however, indicate clearly that Mahaa Bunman is unaware of this possibility. The *Luang Phauau* are various personifications of the Lord Buddha which the amulets symbolize. (In other contexts, *Luang Phauau* may mean a monk who is highly knowledgeable about the supernatural.)

to depend on anyone, even for a short time. Everyone works like mad to earn his living. Nobody cares about anyone else, or asks if anyone else is happy.

Damn it! Since he left the monkhood nobody even cared to ask when he left or even whether he was married.

He is a little disappointed with society. But he feels proud to have a chance to fight against hunger. From his years in the monkhood, he had become used to going without dinner. But once he started eating again, he couldn't do without it. Now, when he has had nothing to eat he truly suffers.

Mahaa Bunman pauses to sit down on a stone bench next to the theatre. He thinks of the shabby room he rents. He hasn't paid this month's rent yet. Angry at himself, he strikes his head with his knuckles: "I should not have rented the room. In fact, I should have stayed on at the temple. That would have been all right."[9]

But he was too embarrassed to do that, and also, he wanted to show off his ability.

He has no property he can sell for money. Taking his clothes to the pawnshop is out of the question because he has only one good outfit, which he is wearing. There's another one he keeps in reserve, but not even the Chinaman would want that. And even if he wanted to, he wouldn't dare enter a pawnshop.

He never thought that the life of a layman would be so difficult and miserable. The world is so confusing. It is all turmoil, indecency, and without justice.[10]

"How can I, who studied for my *Parien* III until my head almost fell apart, still be without a job?

"While in the monkhood, I never transgressed even a minor precept. Why have not good deeds led to good results? Or are the words of the Lord Buddha already out of date?

"If so, why do good deeds? What for? I might as well have become a thief, a terrorist, a bank robber, or a purse snatcher . . . or return to the monkhood and become a twice-ordained man.[11]

"Its embarrassing to be called 'Bunman—One Secure in His Merit.'

---

9. This is not meant to imply that he should have continued to be a monk. Rather, he would have lived at the temple as a temporary guest or temple boy. Some Bangkok temples house more guests than monks.

10. Although these words may seem unpersuasively abstract in English, most Thai readers would know that they come from actual observations of the Lord Buddha and a famous mantra used in Buddhist meditation.

11. The meaning here is clearly pejorative. Although it is permissible for a Thai male to be ordained an unlimited number of times during the course of his adult life, it is expected that all ordinations after the first will be limited in tenure and will have a specific merit-making purpose (e.g., making merit for a recently deceased parent). Here, the notion of a "twice-ordained man" (literally, "a man of

I ought to change my name to 'Bunmauaung—One Whose Merit is Murky.'

"Why the hell did I leave the monkhood?

"Should I commit suicide?"

The more he thinks, the more uncomfortable he becomes. He starts feeling sick to his stomach. He smells the stinking car exhaust. He can't stand the dust rising from the street. Maybe it would be good to pass out so that he would be taken to a hospital, where he would be fed.

There's nothing attractive about Rajadamnern Avenue today.[12]

Mahaa Bunman becomes extremely angry. He clenches his fists tightly. His body stiffens. He looks around and, forgetting himself, spits on the street.

"This Thai society is decadent and morally shabby. You can't ask anyone for help.

"The rich are so rich. They have so much to eat that they cannot even finish their food. The poor are so poor that they cannot even buy a glass of coffee to lubricate the engine of the body.

"Society is diseased. People compete with each other so much that the poor almost choke to death over their own jealousy.

"If all the money that is poured into sexual obsessions were used to help people like me the prosperity of the country would increase.

"But who would sacrifice?

"Our morality has deteriorated.

"They cut the heads from Buddha images to sell to the market. They undermine our Buddhist religion, even though it has been our respected faith for many thousands of years. Every day morality is disappearing from men's hearts. Sooner or later, without doubt, there will not be any. See, nobody is going to give me any help. Generosity is fading from people's hearts."

Mahaa Bunman covers his face with his two hands, hopeless about his misdirected fate.

"Why do people today have such wicked hearts? This is so much an age of confusion and madness. One group of people has tried to spend several hundred thousand million to build an electronic machine just to send two people to walk on the moon, while several hundred thousand others are waiting for help to survive with a little less pain and poverty."

Mahaa Bunman thinks of the extravagance of people in his country, a country in which the majority do not live well or eat well. He looks at

---

two ritual halls") refers to someone who has been in the monkhood for many years, disrobes, and later returns because he could not survive in the world of ordinary men. Such individuals are considered acceptable monks but not acceptable men—tempered, of course, by a Thai sense of tolerance.

12. A broad boulevard, Rajadamnern Avenue (literally, "The King's Way") is universally recognized as Bangkok's most handsome thoroughfare.

himself as an example: he is starving and is living in difficulty even though he had studied so hard to become a *Parien* III, a first-rank Buddhist scholar. But there are others, a small part of the population who lead luxurious lives in the capital city.

This city is full of products that have caused the loss of the country's trade balance. It is full of places of entertainment that are excessive and unnecessary, places of sex that are the cause of vice and crime. All these are poisons which destroy the leaders who are responsible for the country and which, with every breath we take, draw our youth into the lower depths.

Mahaa Bunman is so angry. He spits onto the street. He looks up at the sky and stands up energetically. He stuffs his hands into his pockets. For an instant he tells himself, "I won't give in."

Mahaa Bunman makes a resolute decision to do something to survive, and he sees the way.

Although he has never thought of doing something like this, this time he will have to do it for. . . .

Mahaa Bunman spits in front of the pawnshop, the government pawnshop near Samraan Raad Police Station. His left hand holds something so tightly that it could never be seen, even by somebody trained in clairvoyance.

There is no use having the strongest and most consistent faith. Mahaa Bunman will return to the temple again. Perhaps luck will later take his side—if not much, a little. He has always thought it is impossible for a person to be unlucky all the time.

Mahaa Bunman looks around. He slowly bends down over the slightly open cover of the sewer system near the side of the road. He quickly drops what he holds in his left hand into the sewer and recovers quickly to leave the spot where he had been standing.

Mahaa Bunman murmurs to himself: "I had to do this *Luang Phauau*. Even four of you together couldn't help me get what I wanted . . . even the little things. Go your own way. I'll go mine. You are not even any good for the pawnshop."

Mahaa Bunman walks across the street. He feels relieved around his neck. No more obligation.

Glossary for an Underdeveloped Country

Introduction

Over the years observers of Thai language behavior (Bilmes 1976; Brown 1974 and 1976; Haas 1951 and 1957; Phillips 1965; Mosel 1961) have noted the great pleasure that most Thai derive from their verbal forms— by fulfilling them, playing with them, and occasionally even violating them. The most intellectually challenging of these are the prosodic forms of poetry (see Mosel 1961), but the most spontaneous and perhaps creative are the verbal inversions in certain kinds of word games. Among these, the best known is probably *kham phuan*.[1] In this volume the clearest example of the Thai talent at verbal play is "Concerning *Farang*."

The following selection by Serin Punnahitanon partakes of this tradition, but its effectiveness depends much more upon the subtlety of the author's logic than it does upon the concatenation of sounds and meanings. By the same token, its message is much less frivolous and more cynical than that which is usually associated with verbal play. Indeed, among the many Thai readers with whom the editor has discussed it, there is a genuine division about the aesthetic merit of this work over precisely these points. Some (a literal-minded minority) say the glossary fails at its purpose simply because the issues it addresses are too serious to be treated flippantly, and the author has trivialized and demeaned them without really being amusing. On the other hand, the majority say that Thai culture itself has become so misshapen (at least with respect to the matters addressed here) that it can no longer be convincingly conceptualized except in terms of such forms as parody, caricature, and satire. Clearly the aim of such forms is not only to amuse but to clarify and edify, as well as to help those who have to live in such a milieu to maintain their emotional perspective.

Thai conversation and writing are often punctuated with the kind of aphoristic imagery that is presented here. What is extraordinary about Serin's effort is the concentrated nature of his offering (and this English-language version is an abridgment of a much longer statement). Too, with the few exceptions indicated in the notes, almost all of his imagery is a product of his own critical imagination, although it obviously uses the rhythms and juxtapositions of traditional Thai homiletic thinking.

As the title suggests, the focus here is on the corrupting features of modern Thai bureaucratic practice. The author has explicitly said that he prepared the glossary because of his increasing concern about the readiness of many young Thai university people to be co-opted by the Thai bureaucratic establishment of the period and also because of his hatred of the "three tyrants" (Thanom, Prapart, and the former's son, Narong) who controlled that establishment.

The author is a professor of sociology at Chulalongkorn University and is more widely known among the educated public for his contributions to public opinion research than for his contributions to social criticism. Born in 1931, he graduated in political science from Chulalongkorn University in 1952. He went on to receive an M.A. in political science from the University of New Hampshire in 1958 and a Ph.D. in sociology from the University of Indiana in 1971.

NOTE

1. *Kham phuan* might be called "silent stinky pinky." In American stinky pinky, person *A* would say, "I am thinking of a cadaverous Marxist," to which person *B* might reply, "a dead red." However, *kham phuan* differs from stinky pinky in at least three critical respects: (1) the play involves switching the consonants (usually, although not always, the initial and final consonants) of *A*'s statement; (2) the switching is always implied or imagined, but never actually said; (3) the game is not a parlor game but a diversion from ordinary conversation, where *B* picks up on *A*'s implied switch (and by so doing sometimes makes *A* aware for the very first time of the potentialities of his utterance), responds with his own, to which *A* then responds with another, and the dialogue of implied switches continues until one of the participants can no longer produce and the game ends in laughter. Because the game emerges out of workaday communication, it means that the participants are forever attentive, at some level of consciousness, to the latent sounds and meanings of utterances. The most famous *kham phuan* frame is *hen mii* ("see the bear") which everyone hears as *men hii* ("your vulva smells"). The *kham phuan* principle also operates in contexts other than two-person games. Thus, in his poem "What Kind of Boat?" Sulak Sivaraksa clearly intended the line *"nang kau kra dum"* ("They sit picking at their buttons, smirking their insipid smiles") to be perceived by attentive readers as *"nang kum ka dauau"* ("They sit holding their cocks, smiling their insipid smirks").

Glossary for an Underdeveloped Country: A Sample

Serin Punnahitanon

Politics: An institution that teaches one instantaneously how to be deceitful and devious. It is the human stage upon which the lives of people are bought and sold cheaply. Some politicians are capable of selling everything, including their wives and children, relatives or friends, and even their own motherland.

Honest Man: One of the following types

a. one who acts contrary to social custom when the majority of people regard venality as a way of life;

b. one who is condemned and derided as a fool for not snatching at opportunities;

c. one who is often deceived and cheated for having "trusted in the way and the people";[1]

d. one who has accumulated GOOD WILL for himself which is used by wife and children and brothers and sisters to ease the pursuit of their own pernicious activities.

Good Man: There are many such types

a. one who is not afraid of sin, for he already fears poverty;[2]

b. one who is minimally bad, or the least bad, since there is no way to choose a really good man;

c. one who has already gone to hell but upon whom virtue is forced by those who are left behind;

From *Wicharanayan* (September 14, 1972): 19–24. Abridged.

1. Although set in quotes in the original, this is a normal Thai way of expressing faith and optimism.
2. A very familiar Thai aphorism.

d. one who believes that making merit will cleanse him of sins previously committed.

Praises and Promotions: The product of mixing a twisted tongue with saliva. If nowadays honors and titles were still to be given, a person who receives praises and promotions would initially be appointed "*Khun* Yes Man." Later on, if he performs well, he would be appointed to "*Luang* Perpetual Sycophant," and his next title would be "*Phra* Shin Licker," while awaiting the higher post of "*Phrayaa* Foot Rest." And should he perform other meritorious services, he would be granted the title of "*Chao Phrayaa* Virtue Murderer."[3]

Pseudo-Intellectual: One who has sold himself into the hands of vice, expert at alchemy, utilizing his knowledge to deceive and to persuade people to see the discus as the lotus.[4] One who is a victim of those who eat[5] the city in their pursuit of power and authority. There is nothing as crooked as these so-called intellectuals.

Policy: Principles or procedures that may not be based on knowledge or reasons. When put into practice, some policies naturally cancel all reasons completely. And of course, only policies without reasons can protect personal interests or those of one's group.

Reasons: These are always subservient to policies. Reasons do not necessarily have intrinsic worth, particularly when they come from foolish, devious, or power-crazed people. The reason why some people in power are not necessarily reasonable is because they want to test just how powerful they are.

Economizing: A form of economic behavior and also a popular proper name,[6] although the owners of such proper names may belie their names. *Economizing* is not something the ruling classes have to do, althought it is a rule for people who live from hand to mouth. The nation's economy will prosper only when the majority of people economize in order to allow the minority to spend luxuriously.

---

3. The terms *Khun, Luang, Phra, Phrayaa* and *Chao Phrayaa* are noble titles awarded to commoners in ascending degrees of importance; the descent down the body expresses increasing degrees of contempt.

4. The discus is the weapon of the devil; the lotus is a symbol of Buddhism, and thus goodness.

5. The traditional way of describing the prerogatives of royal officials who ruled an area.

6. The word is *Prayad,* a common name for a Thai male. Unlike Occidentals, all Thai know and appreciate the meanings of their names.

Leader: One who often orders or asks others to make sacrifices or even to die in his place. The position of leader is such that it is legitimately monopolized, for its holder often believes that he is the Incarnate of Heaven who was born only to carry out His mission. A good and easy-to-find leader blames others for his faults (for he alone cannot shoulder all the blame, something which should be distributed all around to everyone) but he appropriates all praise to himself (because there is ample room in his swollen head to store it).

Chair: An ordinary piece of furniture, by no means expensive, but with a special significance that makes people vie for its ownership (in some cases to the point of killing each other). Some chairs are said to possess magical powers of such magnitude that they grant jewels, rings, and money. Therefore, sitters do not stand up to allow others to occupy their places. Some have sat there for so long that their friends have to throw them out by force. Some have sat so long that spiders spin their webs all around them, without their knowing it. Some just sit and die there.

Discussion: An activity which utilizes more saliva than knowledge. Also, a mechanism that helps the speaker appear incredibly more knowledgeable. For certain types of individuals—those unwilling to act on their beliefs—it is a means for reducing shame. It is mainly an activity which offers opportunities for those who "aspire to greatness" to advertise themselves freely with their foolish listeners serving as their ladders. For some, *Discussion* results in the fulfilling of hopes to become famous.

Buck-Passing:[7] An action that occurs without the use of a buck and can possibly turn those involved into goats. Its most important characteristic is that it involves two or more people (or two or more groups). These parties carry on in the following ways:

    a. One avoids any damage to his own position by disclaiming responsibility and by shifting the blame to another in a lower position. The latter, having received the stinking substance passed onto him, looks for another person in a still lower position. But if by chance he does not know to whom to pass it, he becomes, according to tradition, "the scapegoat."

    b. Not complying with the role of scapegoat who receives the stinking substance, and not passing it on, he discloses the origin and nature of the matter to an *Audience,* in which case, he becomes "a goat in search of his own doom."

    Buck-Passing needs no rules. The thicker skinned are better at it, and the more powerful pass more accurately and with greater frequency.

---

7. The original Thai speaks of "drum throwing," but the meaning is identical.

Buck-Passing, wherever it occurs, always results in damage to the public.

The Scapegoat: This type is quite different from the *Farang* breed of "scapegoat." Unlike the innocent or naive *Farang* type, this kind can see through the complexity of an issue. *The Scapegoat* fears the powerful person above him more than he does his own doom or that of his family. He consents to die for an evil person, thinking that he will be praised and flattered for his efforts.

What Kind of Boat?

Introduction

The following poem is a result of a stroke of serendipity. It was discovered by the editor completely by accident and is one of the least-known writings of one of Thailand's most important intellectual figures; in fact, in recent correspondence, the author, Sulak Sivaraksa, indicated that he had forgotten that he had even written the poem.

It is, nevertheless, a very unusual document. Most of Sulak's more famous writings tend to be flamboyant in language, preachy in style, and, while focusing on important issues, ephemeral in their impact. Too, they rarely convey much of the complex and integrated intellectual position that underlies them and which, explicit or not, animates almost everything that Sulak writes.

This work has a strikingly different quality. Whether a result of the event that stimulated it or of his frame of mind at the time, Sulak lays out in this poem some of the principal elements of his "position" on Thai society, because, though written in verse form, the statement has some of the attributes of a position paper.

The poem was written on the occasion of the completion of the then new National Institute of Development Administration (popularly known as NIDA), an institution that was funded in part by the Thai government and in part by the Ford Foundation. The establishment of the institute was marked by considerable controversy within the Thai and American academic communities, the foundation itself, and even within the highest levels of the Thai and U.S. governments. Whatever the nature or merit of the controversy, Sulak saw the situation as a crystallization of much of what he considered to be wrong with Thai society during this period.

To Sulak, the central issue of Thai life (or life in any society) is the identification and perpetuation of human excellence: how to find and train people who will make wise decisions and who will give the best of themselves (and in so doing, will also fulfill themselves) in furthering the highest purposes of their culture. Sulak sees this as an extremely complex process involving long-term commitments, the benevolent nurturing of the young and the honest monitoring of their performance, the constant guarding and reevaluation of standards, and, perhaps most important, the inculcation of a sense of integrity. From his point of view, bureaucratic practices and values (and NIDA as a symbol of the popularity of such values) are inimical to all of this, in part because they substitute mechanical and universalistic criteria for considerations of excellence and in part because they pretend to solve the problems of society while in fact exacerbating them. For the comparative historian, it is interesting to note that while at the time Americans were protesting this "do not fold, spindle, or mutilate" mentality on the grounds that it dehumanized people (e.g., the Free Speech Movement, the Greening of America, and the like), Sulak was protesting it on the grounds that it produced an inferior product. The point of view is an inimitable synthesis of Thai elitism and Thai practicality.

Perhaps an even more basic criticism—"basic" in the sense that it strikes at an even more unquestioned premise of Thai life—is Sulak's attack against his fellow Thai for accepting foreign largesse as an alternative to expending their own energy and effort. He writes as a person who at the time was himself a recipient of foreign aid, the journal he edited, *Sangkhomsaat Parithat* [Social science review], being supported largely by a grant from the Asia Foundation, a San Francisco–based organization. Sulak's criticism of foreign largesse is precise. He protests the pretense and interpersonal fraudulence that accompanies it ("Just talk big— they will fall for it"), the misuse that is made of it ("Degrees? We will give them away with generosity"), and, although it is never made explicit in the poem, the sentiment of self-abasement that ultimately lies behind soliciting and accepting it. Again, the thrust of Sulak's position is the necessity to maintain one's own sense of honesty, integrity, and value.

Sulak's attack against the pretense and posturing that occurs in Thai life is the most fully ramified theme of the poem. But Sulak's position here is more focused than it would seem. Puffery and preening are characteristic features of Thai culture, and Sulak does not oppose them as a source of personal pleasure or as a legitimate symbol either of one's accomplishments or of one's deeply professed values. Sulak himself was famous throughout Bangkok for his wearing of the *phaanung* on formal occasions. The *phaanung,* a wide loincloth-like garment, was the traditional formal dress of Thai men, particularly royalty, and to Sulak it was an explicit symbol of his commitment to civility, the aesthetically attractive, and the uniquely Thai; in a famous essay, he created a fictional club called "The Phaanung Society" that was dedicated to the perpetuation of such values. What Sulak opposes about pretense is its use as an end in itself or its use as a cover for incompetence, irrelevance, or fraud. In the poem, Sulak is particularly exercised by the fact that Thai should want to pose as *farang* and, because they are such practiced poseurs, perhaps succeed at their pretense ("Even better than *farang* at what they know"). What is so distressing to him is that in their mad pursuit of high status and rank—which to Sulak are useful but ultimately third-rate human values—Thai are so ready to relinquish their own identity.

These views of the world, emerging out of a personal background that was in no sense extraordinary, reveal a person who from early childhood was enraptured by the values and great men of his culture. Sulak was born in 1933, the son of a chief clerk of a Western import-export firm, and was educated at Assumption College in Bangkok before leaving for England at the age of nineteen. Even before reaching adolescence, he had gone through most of the available writings of Prince Damrong Rajanubhab, the architect of Thailand's system of modern education and public administration. Another of his childhood heroes was Prince Narisara Nuwatiwongse, designer of Bangkok's Marble Temple and Thailand's greatest composer-musician of the early twentieth-century period. Prince Damrong's impact on him was sufficiently great that more than thirty years later Sulak undertook a study (actually funded by the Ford Foundation) of Prince Damrong's contributions to Thai intellectual history.

Sulak spent nine years in England studying history, philosophy, and law. On his return to Thailand, he became the principal disciple of *Phya* Anuman Rajadhon—philologist, ethnographer, and literary critic and at the time the doyen of the Thai scholarly world. He also came under the informal protection of Prince Dhaninivat, regent of Thailand and president of the Privy Council, and Prince Wan, who had just retired from the presidency of the General Assembly of the United Nations. The halo of patronage provided by these two most senior and prestigious princes was later to prove critical in ensuring Sulak's safety while he was out on his numerous sallies against the inadequacies of a changing Thai society. Very few people or institutions escaped Sulak's evaluation—including the king (in a metaphor comparing him with King Chulalongkorn) and M. R. Khukrit Pramoj. Sulak's criticisms of Khukrit have continued intermittently for two decades and have yet to elicit a direct reply. While he occasionally praises his self-selected adversary, the thrust of his view is that Khukrit is a fallen idol—a pretentious, and thus false, version of the "great man" of Thailand. While all of this might seem somewhat juvenile, it in fact relates to precisely the same issues raised in the poem: how are excellence, success, pretense, and fraud to be identified and judged?

During the middle and late 1960s the principal forum for Sulak's views was the journal *Sangkhomsaat Parithat,* which he established, operated, and developed into Thailand's major intellectual magazine. It is not fortuitous that most of the materials appearing in this book was first published in *Sangkhomsaat Parithat*. Reflecting the times and its charter—but also Sulak's character—the journal was successfully apolitical during his tenure as editor. It was not until Suchart Sawadsii assumed editorship in the late 1960s that its thrust began to change and it very quickly became the major source of Thai protest against the Vietnam War. While serving as editor, Sulak also established the first university bookstores in Thailand and did considerable travelling in provincial and rural Thailand stirring up apolitical intellectual controversy.

In recent years, Sulak has established his own publishing house, translated several books into Thai, and written several of his own, the latter tending to be increasingly "political" in nature; for example, addressing the reality of Marxism, he lauds it for its commitment to social justice but condemns it for its indifference to the spiritual needs of man. With the passage of time, his intellectual style has also become increasingly mellow.[1] This is in part a function of the fact that he has lately become the major liaison linking the intellectual life of Thailand with the intellectual life of the international world. He is the "favorite" lecturer or discussant on the humanities and Buddhism in Thailand at international conferences, and during 1977–1978 he taught Thai studies at Berkeley, Cornell, and the University of Toronto. He has also travelled extensively in China, Japan, and throughout Southeast Asia.

Sulak's influence, however, will always be greatest within Thailand. Although he is not the spokesman for any "school" and has had perhaps fewer disciples than his fame would warrant, he has had a profound personal impact on a number of people whose work appears in this book—particularly Suchit Wongthed, Suchart Sawadsii, and Angkarn Kalayaanaphong. Suchit—whose own writing reflects strikingly different interests and values—cites Sulak's integrity, his knowledge and appreciation of premodern Thailand, and his communication of both the propriety and joy of being daring as his most valuable legacy.

NOTE

1. However, his style did not become sufficiently mellow to prevent him from being indicted on a charge of lèse majesté in August 1984. The charges were eventually dropped, in part because of strong pressures from the international legal and intellectual community.

What Kind of Boat?

SULAK SIVARAKSA

There are so many good boats.
Why are they not used for crossing the river?
Instead they choose the boats that leak.
And when a good job is really needed,
They find only imposters to do the work.

An old Siamese saying

Among the Thai people in this era
  The degree alone is the symbol of success.
Masks are worn to deceive others
  And to gain congratulations and approval.
The more one struts, the more credible one is,
  The larger the boasts, the greater the expertise.
Bosses busy themselves in this and that[1]
  While uncontrolled subordinates create havoc.
When not at their meetings
  They sit picking at their buttons, smirking their insipid smiles.[2]
They call their plagiarism "creative writing"
  And present it to the boss as proof of their merit.
The boss reads it, and cannot possibly understand
  But he does not dare to say anything.

From *Sangkhomsaat Parithat* 3, no. 2 (1965).

1. The busyness of bosses is in part prompted by their need to demonstrate that they have the expertise to deal with all problems and in part by the need to prove that they are always seeking opportunities to expand their responsibilities, power, and little empires.

2. The symbolism of "meetings" in Thailand is akin to the symbolism of being "in conference" in the United States: it is meant to suggest something secretive, inviolable, and terribly important, although it also has a latent meaning of fraudulence, e.g., that the purpose of the meeting is really quite unimportant or that a participant is simply using it as a cover for doing something or being somewhere else. Button-picking is the perfect posture of the person who is doing nothing, and the insipid smile is the act of someone who is simply too lazy to do anything more. However, both these expressions have another meaning; if the consonant order of the original Thai is mentally inverted (and *nang kau kra dum* becomes *nang kum ka dauau*), the line would read: "They sit holding their cocks, smiling their insipid smirks."

For to open his mouth would betray him as a *Phuujaj* Lii,[3]
  Proclaiming his stupidity for all the world to hear.
The subordinates speak their "foot fit,"[4]
  With English and American swagger.
The more they speak, the more credible they seem,
  Even better than *farang* at what they know.
Oh, *farang*—they are really quite stupid,
  Always believing the bravado of their older Thai brothers.[5]
Whatever we want, they give.
  Just talk big—they will fall for it.
If you ask only for a little bit, they think you are flattering them
    and do not need it.
  But if you ask for something grand, it suits their disposition.
Whether the project is feasible
  Or whether it is absurd—that is not what matters.
What matters is the way you act.
  Act big and you will get what you want.
Creating academies with a snap of the fingers,
  It is an easy thing, in fact the simplest thing, to do.
Once you have the money . . .
  Are there really any other problems? Just let me know.
Teachers? Oh, that is no issue.
  What is important are the curricula and the children.
Have loads of them and make them all jazzy.
  Degrees? We will give them away with generosity.[6]
Everybody is happy.
  There will be no suffering, no difficulty.[7] How could there be?
Teachers with degrees from abroad.
  Give them money. They will come running.
To teach those courses with the Indian names,[8]

---

3. The hero of the most popular song of this period. For an explanation of the symbolism of *Phuujaj* Lii, see the Introduction to "Headman Thuj," p. 234.

4. This is a contraction of "foot, fit, four, five" which is a phrase of Thai gibberish used to mock the sounds of spoken English.

5. By referring to the Thai as "older brothers," the author is making their bravado more persuasive or credible to native Thai readers.

6. The terms here are the same terms that are used to describe the giving of alms when making Buddhist merit.

7. Again, the author uses the Buddhist canonical terms for "suffering" and "difficulty."

8. The term here for "Indian" is *Khaeaeg*, a word that is always charged with a bit of ridicule. While the author is referring to names taken from Pali and Sanskrit, names that ought to be respected for their sacred qualities, he is also deriding the way they are adulterated and misused. Thus, to speak of Pali and Sanskrit as "*Khaeaeg* languages" is like referring to Latin as "that Wop language."

Those weird words that required research expeditions to be
discovered.
While the translations from *farang* are done verbatim,
    And are passed off as new books.
The graduates that result from all of this,
    Whether bright-eyed or dull-witted,
Are in the end all leveled off.
    They all are given the same degrees.
The big shots of this world
    Act as if they are skilled in everything—from the beginning to the end,
Each a universal expert
    With hundreds of responsibilities—and that is hardly a little.
Where do they get the eyes?
    To see who is who?
To see whether it is a good boat or a leaky boat.
    To them, they are all the same—just boats.

I Lost My Teeth

Introduction

When the following story by Khamsing Srinawk was first published it was clearly intended as a wry commentary on the quality of contemporary Thai life, not as a statement of statistical or sociological reality. However, times have changed in Thailand, and what would have once been mainly testimony to an author's sense of irony would now be considered a description of a common occurrence of the workaday world.

The rise in the frequency of crime is a near-universal phenomenon of the latter part of the twentieth century. In Thailand, as in most places, it seems to be associated with the breakdown in family and community controls, the increasing anonymity of the individual, and the randomness and uncertainty of the sanctions that are applied against it. The high incidence of unpunished official crime, particularly among members of the bureaucratic elite, further contributes to the absence of effective sanctions as well as to a general atmosphere of criminal permissiveness on the one hand and social resignation on the other.

Whatever its ultimate causes, the actual frequency of crime in Thailand is extraordinary. The United States is widely acknowledged as having the highest homicide rate in the industrialized world. The homicide rate for Thailand for 1975–1976, the most recent year for which the editor has adequate data, was more than three times that of the United States (13,479 murders in a population of 42.9 million versus 20,427 in a population of 213.5 million). Particularly striking was the fact that homicide in rural areas (where the figures would be expected to be greatly underreported) exceeded that of urban areas by more than two to one. In fact, during this same period, murder became such a banal issue (or perhaps a macabre one) that otherwise respectable Thai would cite the prevailing cost of hiring an assassin in Chiengmai ($25) as compared with Bangkok ($75).

264

Whatever the nature of the statistics, the actual experiencing of a crime will probably remain a relatively isolated event in the lives of most people. What is most distressing about crime, apart from the enervation of constantly having to be wary, is that it serves as a recurring reminder of the inadequacy of one's expectations and of one's ability to read the world correctly. As the victim of this story poignantly tells us, "Nowadays things around here are so confusing. You can't tell who's a bad guy and who's a good one." And he lays out some of the evidence of this reality: that in the modern world everybody smiles the same way, irrespective of motives. Even the potential victims are forced to smile constantly. The markers for distinguishing between people no longer work. Nowadays everybody is intrusive: they come from everywhere, "right into our kitchens to find out how we are doing . . . from places nobody has ever even heard of." It is as if there is no longer any social distance by which to maintain a sense of civility or privacy. Not even the jungle affords protection anymore.

I Lost My Teeth

KHAMSING SRINAWK

He first greeted me with a sullen question: "Why don't you ask what happened to my teeth?" I was struck dumb for a moment not knowing what to say. In fact I had noticed the deformity on his pale face when I first glanced at him. Even so, my brain was not fast enough to come up with an answer to the sudden question. I did not know how to incorporate a greeting into a reply so as to keep the atmosphere easy and to avoid hurting his feelings any further.

Actually, I had heard a bit about his misfortune, but the information was superficial and confusing. It had been passed on by word of mouth and you could not be sure how accurate it was. The first wave of rumor indicated he had been shot dead; then it changed to his having been shot almost dead but having survived. It was not until I met him personally and heard the story from his own mouth that I knew that all he actually received was a blow to his face. The whole thing might be called a trivial matter compared to other robberies—considering he lost only two hundred and some *baht,* an old pistol, and four teeth. A sporting person would say that people give away more than that to their friends. But then it is only a small matter to me because it was not I who lost two hundred *baht,* an old pistol, and four teeth. For the person who did, the tired and gloomy face and the odd sounds pouring through his deformed oral cavity seemed to express a different viewpoint. After listening to him grumble away for a while, I started to voice my own unsympathetic opinion. "You had the gun with you. Why did you let them strike you so easily?"

I had not yet finished my sentence when his face, that a moment ago

Published originally in *Sangkhomsaat Parithat* (August 1973); reprinted in Khamsing Srinawk, *Khamphaeng* (Bangkok: Puthuchorn Publishers, 1975).

had calmed down to normal, turned back to scowling. His eyes, still buried in his cheekbones, flashed out a piercing glance.

"I bought the thing with just that thought in mind: to protect myself against robbers and thieves. But you know, nowadays things around here are so confusing. You can't tell who's a bad guy and who's a good one. Come out and live here for a while—you'll see what I mean. Especially a village like ours that's in the jungle. People outside seem so worried about us. Week after week and month after month we have to mold a smile on our faces with never any time to close our mouths. Like idiots, we smile back at anybody who turns up to visit us. They come right into our kitchens to find out how we are doing, to make our acquaintance, to ask about our livelihood. Questions after questions. Some come from the subdistrict office; some come from the offices of the district, province or the capital, and some come from the outside world, from places nobody has ever even heard of. Every one of them seems to have his own forced smile. They must have practiced fixing their facial expressions from the same teacher. When the good guys can smile, the bad guys can, too. Then what use can a gun be . . . ?

"That afternoon, the day I lost my teeth, these people filed through the gate, all with broad grins on their faces. One of them came straight to where I was shoveling husks from under the storehouse. Another went toward the pigsty where my wife and my little son were pouring bran into the trough. Three gathered in front of the stairs to the house. I looked up and smiled. Before the smile had spread fully over my lips, a gun was nudged into my waist and I was ordered to put the hoe down. . . .

"At that instant, the three who were waiting at the foot of the stairs all ran up into the house and started searching for things they might fancy. I was stupified by this for a while. When I recovered, I felt rage building up inside me. The sight of three people moving around upstairs gradually became blurred because tears were welling up in my eyes. I said, 'If you are so brave and bold, why are you picking on people like me who live from hand to mouth? Why don't you go and rob those people who are overwhelmed by wealth?'

" 'Who?'

" 'Those moneymen and millionaires who ride around in big cars and walk with their bellies sticking out in . . .' Before I could finish my sentence, the bastard swung the gunstock at my mouth and snapped: 'What a loud mouth.' I was laid out at his feet with four of my teeth stuck down my throat."

"Did you report this to the authorities?"

"Yes."

"What did they say?"

"Nothing. They just acknowledged my report."

"Did you tell them the details?"

"Yes, every detail. Oh, but I didn't tell them what I had said before they hit me."

"Why not?"

"Like I said, everything is mixed up these days and you can't tell who's a good guy and who's a bad guy. Who knows what would have happened? I might have lost all the rest of my teeth."

The Chao Phrayaa River
Is on the Verge of Dying

Introduction

In one of those phrasings that catches the fancy of journalists, Bangkok was in the mid-1970s repeatedly described in the Thai press as "the sixth filthiest major city in the world." Other than some unidentified "UN commission," no source for this statistic was ever cited, there was never any specification of the five "filthier" cities, nor was there any clarification of the meaning of "filth."

Whatever the truth of such a statistic, there is no doubt that since the end of World War II, Bangkok has been transformed from a tree lined, safe, and graciously livable city of approximately 750,000 people into a gray, discordant, and at times physically oppressive megalopolis of 5 million. Where once only a few blocks of Chinatown were flooded during rainy season, now almost one-third of the city is occasionally under water between May and August. While Bangkok traffic is both a local joke and a superb manifestation of the Thai capacity to be patient, it is also the source of a semipermanent cloud that hovers over the city like a giant mantle. From an airplane, this cloud can be seen from hundreds of miles away as an enormous gray glob in an azure sky. Unlike Los Angeles or Mexico City there are no mountains to hem it in. It just hangs. Bangkok's cars (which if laid end-to-end would be twice as long as the city's roadways) have also caused major changes in the lifestyle of the city's inhabitants. Where fifteen years ago people awakened at 7:00 A.M. to get to work or school by 8:00 A.M., they now rise at 5:00 and sometimes at 4:00 in order "to beat the traffic." Similarly, every prospective social visit, shopping excursion, or outing to a movie that requires travel beyond one's immediate neighborhood is first evaluated in terms of whether it is worth the discomfort that the trip entails.

While exhaust fumes are the most dramatic expression of the fouling of the city's environment, there are others equally insidious: noise pollution, both from street traffic and from the long-tailed motor boats whose wails reverberate over Bangkok's few remaining canals; the wholesale destruction of the trees that once shaded the city's major roads and that contributed so providentially to the simple comforts of tropical living; the uninformed use of hazardous industrial materials, such as using lead waste from a battery factory to surface a suburban road on which children played and later died.

It is not easy to characterize the Thai response to these ecological realities. There are some citizens who view pollution simply as an inevitable concomitant of modernization and who take comfort in the belief that most of the world's cities share the same problems to a greater or lesser extent, even if Bangkok's share is somewhat greater. There are others who literally do not see or experience the pollution, seemingly having "adapted" to the new environment, perhaps even in a psychobiological sense. However, since both the environment and the adaptation are historically both so recent, the effectiveness of such adaptation is of course problematic. Among these people are those Thai who have a fundamentally benign vision of their natural world and who, following King Ramkhamhaeng's thirteenth-century view, genuinely believe that their Thai realm will always have "rice in the fields and fish in the streams." And there are others who, like M. R. Khukrit Pramoj in the following essay, are increasingly worried about the natural state of their Asian Arcady.

This essay is included for a number of reasons. First, it was one of the earliest expressions of concern about environmental degradation to be voiced by a major, respected public figure. Although the concepts of "ecology" and "environmental protection" were already in the Thai air when the article appeared, they had little meaning or impact, being viewed as just another example of the kind of faddish jargon brought home by Thai students returning from their overseas study. Whether or not these fashionable categories actually played a role in his own thinking, Khukrit was one of the first senior members of the Thai establishment to express them in an idiom that made sense to a Thai audience.

Second, despite its brevity, the essay is a superb example of Khukrit's special kind of eloquence when addressing a complex social problem. Lesser writers would have simply lamented the pollution or condemned the polluters and let the matter go at that. But Khukrit uses images that call forth much more subtle and powerful kinds of sentiments: the continuity of Thai history; the responsibility of each generation—but particularly the living one—to keep the sacred trust of its ancestors; the utility of nature and how all human existence is contingent upon its continued health; and the aesthetic sensibilities and accomplishments of the Thai people. While all of this may seem to be a somewhat rococo approach to a public issue, it is precisely this kind of perception and elaboration that lies at the basis of Khukrit's intellectual persuasiveness and ultimately his political power.

There may also be a deeper, religious factor operating here. Eleven years earlier, in an essay entitled *Huang Mahanop* [The vast expanse], 1959, Khukrit brought together Buddhist and biological notions that emphasized, among other things, man's sharing of the universe with all living creatures and his special responsibilities not to disrupt natural processes. Although these notions do not appear explicitly in this essay, they obviously form part of the background of his thinking.

Khukrit's commitment to the aesthetic in Thai life also merits special mention. Himself a man of impeccable taste (in the design of his home, clothes, gardens, and the like), Khukrit believes that his nation's traditional art—particularly its architecture, religious imagery, and graphic designs—represent some of the finest creations of mankind, rivalling their equivalents from any of the other great civilizations of the world. To him, Thai art represents an authentic source of national achievement and pride and must be preserved at all costs. Thus, his reference to these matters in this essay (and in most of his other writings) must be understood not as a mere turn of phrase or elite affectation but rather as an underscoring of what he considers to be the most valuable expressions of his national identity.

Khukrit's imagery also builds upon one of those little coincidences, never fortuitous in the Thai way of thinking, that play such a crucial role in linking human beings to natural and social events. It is never even hinted at in the text, but Khukrit knows that many of his readers are aware that he was actually born on the Chao Phrayaa River. At the time, his father was commander of the king's Northern Army and was travelling throughout the northern provinces establishing new military garrisons. His mother was on her way to Phitsanulok to join her husband, and since it was dry season preferred the comfort of going by boat. Travelling by day, the boat would tie up for the night at a convenient dock, usually at one of the numerous temples that bordered on the river. It was next to one of these riverine temples in In Buri District of Singburi Province that Khukrit was born on the morning of April 20, 1911. It is the auspiciousness of this site in Khukrit's own experience—the selectivity of fate and how it affected his own ties to eternity—that adds special power to his message.

Finally, note must be taken of that inimitable Khukrit touch at the end of the essay when he transforms the whole tone of the piece by taking a jab at Bangkok's municipal government. While to the Western reader this ending is jarring, and in its mockery seems to subvert the import of everything that precedes it, this is hardly its effect in Thai. There is no doubt that it is a form of comic relief, but it is a humor that makes light of the reader's psychological burden, not the importance of the message. If anything, in its contrast it reinforces the message and makes it more memorable. Furthermore, it is a way of bringing the reader back to reality, even if it is a harsh reality. For both Khukrit and his readers know that, when all is said and done, the only way the pollution of Bangkok is going to be reduced is if the government puts its hand to it—with commitment, money, personnel, laws, and powerful sanctions against offenders—and that on the basis of its record, the likelihood of the Bangkok Municipality succeeding at this task is extremely low. That reality is the ultimate irony.

The Chao Phrayaa River Is on the Verge of Dying

M. R. Khukrit Pramoj

The Chao Phrayaa River is on the verge of dying from an incurable disease.[1] His descendants can now only sit, keeping a bedside vigil, waiting for him to die.

It will not be long before he will surely breathe his last, and then begin to rot, stink, and become offensive.

When you think about it, it is such a pity and so disheartening.

If the Chao Phrayaa were a human being, he would be the longest serving *Chao Phrayaa* in the history of the royal service, and he would be the oldest witness to the chronicle of events that comprise the history of the Thai nation.

The Chao Phrayaa River witnessed a group of Thai of high culture, civilization, and artistic excellence erect the Buddha image of Wat Phrachao Phanancherng on his bank and helped carry the boats of brick, mortar, and sand necessary for its construction until it was completed and became an object of veneration for the Thai people that has continued to the present day.

The Chao Phrayaa River has been in royal service since the reign of

Originally published in *Siam Rath,* January 20, 1970; reprinted in *Caag Naa Haa Nangsyyphim Siam Rath* [From page five of the *Siam Rath*] (Bangkok: 'Rong Wongsawaan and His Young Friends Publishing Co., July 1970).

1. The Thai lexicon is particularly rich in terms describing death. Here, the term for "dying," *anicakam,* is typically used to refer to the death of a nobleman. Since the name of the river, "Chao Phrayaa," is identical to the highest rank of conferred nobility, this particular verb for describing its death is perfect. The title, "Chao Phrayaa" also creates a special paradox. While the word for river in Thai is *maeaenaam,* meaning "mother of waters," the noble title of this particular river is used almost exclusively for men. In the translation that follows, the river is personified as a male.

King Utong.[2] He participated in the royal service by transporting the materials for the construction of the capital. During one period, he was the moat on one side of the city that protected the capital against the enemies of the king. If during the dry season the enemy laid siege to the city, during the rainy season the Chao Phrayaa would rise up and flood his bank, compelling the enemy to withdraw its forces and depart.

The streams of the Chao Phrayaa River have been nourishing rice, vegetables, and all the other crops of the Thai people for uncountable ages, enabling us to feed our bodies and thus exist, maintaining the continuity of the nation to the present day.

If one tried to count the number of royal princes and princesses who bathed in the Chao Phrayaa, he would find the task endless.

The Chao Phrayaa River was the oldest and most trusted aide of King Naresuan the Great and the most intimate courtier of his royal brother, *Somdet Phra* Ekatotsarot,[3] witnessing his private affairs one night when the royal barge capsized at Bang Nang In.

Later he was in the royal service of the king of Thonburi.

And since then he has been in the service of the dynasty of the Radtanakosin[4] capital for one hundred and eighty-eight consecutive years.

Whenever "His Majesty travels through water,"[5] the Chao Phrayaa River is always in his gracious service.

But the life of the Chao Phrayaa River is now coming to a close.

This is because his children and grandchildren and their descendants have betrayed him. Not only do they refuse to take decent care of him. They even pour into him all kinds of deadly organisms and filth that make it impossible for him to maintain his life any longer.

And when the Chao Phrayaa River has finished his life it is doubtful whether his children and grandchildren will be able to continue their own lives much longer.

---

2. The founder of the Ayuthian dynasty in 1350.

3. Known respectively as "The Black Prince" and "The White Prince" (because of their complexions), these two brothers ruled Thailand successively between 1590 and 1610 (or perhaps as late as 1620). King Naresuan was Ayuthia's great warrior-king who, mounted on an elephant, slew the Burmese crown prince and expelled the Burmese forces in 1593. The reference to "private affairs" concerns Prince Ekatotsarot being struck by a sudden storm while on the river and being shipwrecked in a neighboring village where he dallied with a pretty village lass, which resulted in the birth of a son. Although the historical record is most ambiguous, this son may have been the man who thirty years later, but with no direct aid or influence from his genitor, ascended to the throne as King Prasart Thong and ruled Thailand between 1630 and 1655.

This is not the only instance where Khukrit refers to a boat capsizing on the Chao Phrayaa. One of his most famous novels is *Laaj Chiiwid* [Several lives], which describes in flashback the lives of several passengers who have drowned when their boat capsizes on the river during a storm.

4. The official name of Bangkok.

5. The first verse of a royal barge song, well known to most Thai.

Because running through the heart of our great capital city of Krungthep will be a stream of poison.

The death of the Chao Phrayaa River is only one of several deaths that are impending around us.

If we do nothing about this matter, before long not a single heirloom from our paternal or maternal ancestors will be left for us to see.

The Reclining Buddha of Wat Phoo is approaching its demise.

Its face is already fractured.

It will not be long before it will crack apart and separate. The head will split off from the neck. The whole body will fall shattering into shards of broken brick.

The honored architects who built the Reclining Buddha and Wat Phrachetuphon had calculated that their work would surely last to the end of the world.

But they did not take into account the weight and the vibration of the vehicles moving on the streets of today.

They had no way of knowing that anyone would be bringing in ten-wheeled trucks that would drive around their temple compound day and night.

And they never imagined that next to the ritual hall enclosing the Reclining Buddha there would be a bus terminal.

It is not only the Reclining Buddha or Wat Phrachetuphon.

The days are also numbered for all the other sacred places in Krungthep that our ancestors built so felicitously, and with such faith and expertise.

The ritual hall of Wat Phrasri Saakayamuni, the chapel of Wat Suthat, Wat Srakeed, Wat Raadchabophit, Wat Boworniweed,

The Giant Swing,

The Brahman Temple,

or even the Grand Palace itself.

If we are unable to control the vibration of the traffic, which every day becomes more congested,

If we are unable to divert our everyday movement from these places,

The complete royal title of the Radtanakosin City—"The Royal Capital City of Abounding Charm, Pleasure, and Beauty, Replete with Great Palaces and Possessions that Fulfill All Wants, the Abode of the Gods—will become meaningless.[6]

Nobody will know to what it refers.

Sometimes we do things without reflecting on their consequences or without realizing that their long-term effects can be deleterious.

Some high-ranking official—who this big shot was, I do not know—

---

6. Different Thai recognize different versions of the "complete" royal title of Bangkok. The version used in the original text here is *Raadchathanii buriirom udomraadchaniweed mahaasathaan saryngkhaan awataansathid.*

went abroad for a good time, probably to Venice, saw pigeons being fed in the square in front of the San Marco Church, thought it all so charming, and remembering it, did the same thing here.

He fed the pigeons at the Square of the Giant Swing in front of the ritual hall of Wat Suthat.

San Marco Church is built of stone. Its front gable is flat and smooth, made of gold-colored tiles that were laid out into mosaics.

Even under such conditions, they constantly have to control the pigeons to prevent them from getting up there and causing destruction.

But the front gables of the ritual hall and chapel of Wat Suthat are panelled of wood that has been carved into elaborate, protruding bas-reliefs and has also been decorated with gold leaf and mirrored glass.

The huge flock of pigeons that is forever multiplying makes its home under the eaves of the temple where they have their nests and happily lay their eggs.

No matter how much they keep repairing the damage, they cannot contend with the birds.

The birds' droppings just keep coming, fouling everything.

And in their scratching and scraping to build their nests, they deface the intricately carved wood, which will eventually be destroyed.

The future growth of Krungthep will have to be harmful to its inhabitants.

Such growth necessarily poisons the earth and the air and is hazardous to human life as well as animal life.

No one has yet considered how this problem can be solved—whether it concerns the lesser domain of our sacred places, mansions, or palaces or the larger domain of the safety of all the inhabitants of Krungthep.

Do not blame this whole thing only on the municipality.

Because although we have municipal governments in this Thailand, having them is the same as not having them.

Relations with Colleagues

Introduction

Like racial or ethnic prejudice in the United States, "official corruption" in Thailand is one of the most persistent and inescapable attributes of national life. Individually, many Thai feel a deep sense of shame about the role that corruption plays in their society, but whether this sentiment is significant in reducing its incidence is problematic. Most argue that although corruption occurs at all levels of the social order, its magnitude is greatest among members of the bureaucratic elite—which of course is the very factor that makes remedial action against it so difficult. (See Scott 1972; Neher 1977; Somvichian 1978.)

As something that is behaviorally real, shameful, and illegal, corruption is not easily measured, and most discussions of it are based upon a kind of conventional wisdom. Thus, villagers with whom the editor worked several years ago simply assumed that 10 to 20 percent (they resisted all entreaties to be more precise) of the budget of *any* government project was illegally siphoned off by the officials responsible for the project. More recently, the secretary-general of the 1977 Thanin government's Anti-Corruption Committee claimed that over a third of Thailand's national budget found its way into the private pockets of government officials. Whether ultimately true or false, the sheer magnitude of these figures suggests that, whatever else corruption in Thailand may be, it is unsubtle, forbearable, and commonplace.

The following selection is a chapter from a novel, *Naaj Amphur Patiwad* [The revolutionary district officer], that has corruption as its major theme. The revolutionary nature of the hero refers to his revolt against the corruption, privilege, and indifference that the author perceives as pervading every part of the administrative system of rural Thailand. At the end of the novel, the revolution fails when the district officer goes mad and the narrator, the provincial clerk called "Cha," is promoted to his position. "Cha" is like the hero in his decency and kindness, but he is totally unlike him in his realism and in his readiness to accommodate the status quo.

Although District Officer Ruamphol is portrayed in simple, transparent terms, it is not easy to characterize his cultural status. On the one hand, he is something of a cultural "dope," a Candide-like character who drives men of affairs crazy with his simple-minded mouthing of the rules. In fact, to some Thai readers his lectures on the value of rules are almost cloying in their triteness. On the other hand, he also has the quality of a Billy Budd—the innocent who is absolutely right in his personal ethics, cultural goals, and even in his willingness to sacrifice himself to the larger social good. From this perspective, Ruamphol's concern with rules has a ritualistic quality that almost echoes the rhythm and tenor of Buddhist preaching. On balance, the majority of Thai readers are probably more likely to consider Ruamphol a figure of respect than of ridicule.

The villain of the story is drawn much more clearly than is the hero. Like most Thai villains, he is a person who knows no limits and simply commits one self-aggrandizing or antisocial act after another. He is also a man devoid of almost all personality. In fact, the only thing that we are told about his character is that, in contrast to the hero, he uses stealth and imagination, constantly trying to cover his tracks and to seem other than what he is. In general, it is what he does, not what he is—and certainly not what he thinks or feels—that defines him.

To most Westerners, the deputy governor insinuates himself as the drama's true heavy, endorsing the villain in his evil ways and cajoling the hero to violate regulations. Although later in the book he is shown to have his own interests in the matter (the chief accountant turns out to be his wife's brother), at this point he is very much a man trying to resolve the bickering of his subordinates, if only by siding with the majority. Too, from a Thai point of view, a man who counsels evil is never as wicked as the man who does it. Since each person is morally free, there is always the possibility that the former may be testing the latter; more important, on the scales of justice, committing an evil act is always more significant than its motivation.

Although the personalities of some of the principals may not be fully developed, there are other aspects of the story—contextual references, turns of phrase, details of meaning—that make the account poignantly realistic for most Thai readers. Thus, the allusions to a context of constant bickering, the signing of grievance petitions by "citizens" (not "villagers" or "peasants"), the affronts felt by colleagues, point to one of the central themes of bureaucratic life in the provinces.

More subtle is the way the author directs the reader's attention to some of the larger structural problems of the Thai administrative system, problems that permit and perhaps even create the discord that is shown in the story. As early as the fourth paragraph, he has the deputy governor say that the hero is "destroying all the unity." A few paragraphs later the meaning of this phrase if amplified with the comment "you do not coordinate your own work with his." To the ordinary Thai reader, these are two of the most pointed euphemisms for describing (or trying to conceal) some of the irremedial problems of the Thai bureaucratic system: functionaries being more responsive to their own departmental and ministerial superiors in Bangkok than to their colleagues on the scene with whom they are supposed to be doing a job; the breakdown in the system of bureaucratic authority; the chaos this all creates for citizens, the supposed clients of bureaucratic activity; the fact that the system has not yet devised any sanctions or rewards for insuring "unity" and "coordination." Thus, very early the author has suggested to the reader that the problem of corruption and honesty is not merely a question of individual evil but is very much a systemic problem, deeply rooted in the flaws and inconsistencies of Thai bureaucratic organization.

The author of *Naaj Amphur Patiwad,* who publishes under the name "Bunchookh Chiamwiriya," is a man who has devoted much of his adult life to the subject matter of his novel. Born in the late 1930s, he worked as a schoolteacher, policeman, and district officer—the last in one of the more politically "sensitive" districts of Nakornphanom Province, on the Laotian border, in Thailand's Northeast. He is a graduate of the Faculty of Political Science at Chulalongkorn University and of the Ministry of Interior's District Officers Academy. He also received an M.A. degree at an American university where he wrote a thesis entitled "The Administrative Responsibility of the District Officer in Thailand." In 1972, he resigned from the Ministry of Interior and has since supported himself with his writing—in part by working as a newspaper columnist and in part from his fiction. Among his numerous efforts are such titles as (in Thai) *The Interior Ministry—By Birth and Rearing, The Interior Ministry's Mafia, The Interior Ministry's Guardian Angel,* and *The Mobilized District Officer.*

Naaj Amphur Patiwad is Bunchookh's most famous work, having won a prize for being the Finest Thai Novel of 1975 and for reputedly having sold more than a hundred thousand copies within a year of its publication. Since most Thai fiction rarely has lifetime sales of more than twenty thousand copies, the author's accomplishment, if accurate, is extraordinary. Bunchookh is one of the few authors in Thailand whose pen name has successfully concealed his real name.

Relations with Colleagues

"Bunchookh Chiamwiriya"

Two months later, a special incident occurred in that district up there on the mountain. According to the official police investigation there was sufficient evidence from the scene to indicate that the district's Second-Class Public Health Center had been set on fire. It was not simply an accident.

There was that afternoon after the deputy governor had finished his long meeting with the chief of the district police, the chief accountant, and the district public health officer. He came out of the room to spit[1] it all at me: "I'm going to explode! That damn district officer is going to drive me crazy. That's what he is going to do."

"What's the problem now, sir?"

"And what else is new? He's causing all kinds of problems again—he's destroying all the unity—between the Health Department, the Accounting Division, and the police." He answered with a tone of voice and a look that indicated he was totally fed up with the thing.

"They had lined up with their complaints."

"It looks as if he's made a mountain out of a mole hill and that there's going to be a big fuss, sir."

"Exactly. That's what he's done. Would you radio him and tell him to come in and see me again."

"Yes sir. Would it be better for him to come today or tomorrow?"

"Have him come to see me tomorrow."

Thus, District Officer Ruamphol came in to spend the night in town.

From *Naaj Amphur Patiwad* [The revolutionary district officer] (Bangkok: Banakid Publishers, 1975).

1. This imagery is quite intentional. The traditional name for a provincial governor is "the royal spittoon," and each person further down the bureaucratic ladder is the symbolic recipient of his superior's spittle.

He arrived very late. The next morning, he met me at the coffee shop in the market, and we sat for a while chatting, sipping our coffee, as was the practice.

"I guess you know why the deputy governor wanted to see me again."

He called me "Cha," which was the short way of referring to my position as provincial clerk.

"I don't know, sir." I lied, as a matter of etiquette. "He told me to radio you. So following his orders, I radioed, that's all."

We chatted on in an amusing way about unimportant things. And then we began to walk toward Provincial Headquarters to meet the deputy governor. We saw him just as we reached the foot of the staircase. He was unusually early for work this day.

"Let's talk in Cha's office. It's a little more spacious. My inner office is too narrow and stuffy—like a rat hole." The deputy governor swung the cafe doors open and walked straight into my room. "It's still early morning. The air here is a lot fresher than it is in my air-conditioned office."

When both of them sat down I quietly prepared to take my leave. The deputy governor waved me back, beckoning me to join them. "It's all right, Cha. It's all right for you to sit down and be here."

"Is there anything of an official nature for which you require my services, sir?" the district officer asked. This was one of the most familiar questions of a person of his rank.

"No," was the deputy governor's curt answer. "But it seems as if you're on the way to starting a big fire all over again."

"About what, sir?"

"What do you have going on against the district public health officer? Nothing, huh?"

"I still don't understand your question, sir."

"He came with a lot of complaints. For example, he said that you're interfering in his work too much and that you do not coordinate your own work with his. How about explaining all of this to me."

"In fact, I don't like saying anything behind my colleagues' backs. I would hope that we could have a special understanding among ourselves. But if you want me to explain myself, I guess I'll have to say something about this. Personally, I regard the district public health officer and his wife as people to whom I am grateful, even obligated. During my very first night in the district . . . well, they welcomed me and gave me a place to sleep so that I would have a roof over my head."

"That's right. He told me about that, and that you don't know what gratitude is."

The district officer stopped short and sat there, blinking his eyes in his confusion.

"What happened was unexpected," the district officer explained. "It all started with the governor's directive that decisive action be taken against the people who were trespassing on the public land, the land that is supposed to be used only for cattle grazing. The problem had been hanging on since the last district officer was here. I didn't want it to turn into a violent confrontation against the squatters, so I called a meeting of all the division chiefs, who elected a committee to arrange a meeting with the citizens who were squatting to discuss the matter with them. The committee was made up of the deputy district officer (he's a second-class official), the district land officer, the district officer of cooperatives, and the chief of the district police. This should have settled the matter, because we already had set aside some land, for both living and cultivating, at a place only a half kilometer away from the cattle-grazing area. When the committee explained this to the villagers, they promised that they would move down to the site that had been arranged. But the next day, they broke their promise and insisted on staying where they were.

"It was during this period that the district public health officer became very hostile and came around to pour out his complaints against me for not appointing him to be a member of the committee. I explained that the selection of the committee was made by all the people attending the meeting and not by me alone and that this was clear to everyone who was there. He said that in not selecting him as a committee member I did not do the right thing, and neither did the others who were at the meeting.

"Later, I found out what was behind the whole thing. The truth was that the trespassers on this public land were actually the district public health officer and two or three of his relatives. They had staked out several hundred *rai*,[2] really good land that was adjacent to a mountain stream and a pond. There were forty other villagers who had migrated from elsewhere who were also trespassing, but they occupied very small plots of land, not more than ten *rai* each. Therefore, there was hardly anybody in their group who objected to the committee's decision. But the district public health officer and his relatives persuaded and encouraged these people to protest, buying them off by offering to loan them a lot of money—all as a way of building up their own power and influence. More than that, he even drafted a petition for the villagers to sign that laid claim to the whole area outside the reserved land, and this was sent to the headquarters of the Revolutionary Group and the Communist Suppression Operations Command at Suan Ryyn Rydii.[3] He also tried to tell

---

2. One *rai* equals .40 of an acre.

3. "The Revolutionary Group" is the title of the Sarit-Thanom-Prapart group that came to power in 1957 and ruled Thailand continuously until October 1973. The Communist Suppression Operations Command (also known as "CSOC," and later changed to "ISOC," or Internal Security Operations Command) was a special agency concerned with rural security, which supposedly had the power to resolve problems of interagency cooperation, particularly between the army, police, and Department of Local Affairs.

them that they had nothing to worry about, because if the matter went to court, the fine would be only 500 *baht*,[4] and after the fine was paid, they would be allowed to stay on and would not be forced to move.

"So this problem has remained unsettled to this day. We've not been able either to swallow it or to spit it out. The governor reprimanded me for not enforcing the law and the regulations of the Revolutionary Group by warning the trespassers that they faced imprisonment, fines, and the confiscation of their property and all the tools they may have used in their trespass. The district public health officer was not happy with me over this matter, and this was just the first thing."

District Officer Ruamphol stopped talking and then sighed uncomfortably.

"Well then, you could have solved the problem by drafting a proposal to go up through channels that would have turned that particular piece of land into a site for living and cultivating," the deputy governor advised.

"I understood that to have tried that would have been very difficult. It would not have been approved, because that particular piece of land is located within the national forest reserve. Even now the district public health officer and his gang are all having a good time up there cutting down koa and rosewood trees to make charcoal[5]—which they then sell. Another thing: the citizens from the four nearby villages who for a long time have benefitted from grazing their cattle in the area clearly would not permit it. The conflict between the two groups has already started."

The deputy governor sat in quiet silence and then asked: "And what about those two midwives?"

"The first one was stationed at the district's Second-Class Public Health Center. Her husband was a police sergeant-major. She had a friendly disposition, was attentive to her work, and got on with and was loved by all the villagers. However, she and the district public health officer's wife are like turmeric and lime. They were always exchanging words. At the time of her annual review, when an evaluation had to be made of her performance, the public health officer decided that she did not deserve a promotion or salary increase. When the matter was sent up to me, I discussed it with several people and concluded that we should give her a one-step promotion as an encouragement for those who do good work. Therefore, in the space provided for the district officer's opinion, I signed my name proposing the increase. However, two or three days later, after I had sent the list of people meriting promotion and salary increases up to the province, the district public health officer blew his top. He came into see me and carried on in the most heated way."

"What you did was not right," the deputy governor protested. "In

---

4. Approximately US$25.00.
5. These hardwood trees are typically used for furniture, not charcoal.

matters of work performance, you always have to support the person's immediate supervisor. You have to approve the public health officer's recommendation—whatever it was. This is one of the most important principles of bureaucratic action. The provincial public health officer has already discussed this matter with me, and I and the governor will endorse the proposals of our district and provincial public health officers."

"Yes, sir—as you wish. It must depend upon your judgment.

"Now, as for the problem with the second midwife, she was the niece of the district public health officer. She had been assigned to one of the district's Commune Nurse's Stations as an obstetrical nurse. She had received a scholarship for her nursing education and according to the contract was under obligation to work in that Nurse's Station. But the district public health officer moved her out of the village station and into the District Public Health Center in town. Then one day, one of the village women went into labor and her relatives carried her to that Commune Nurse's Station, and both the mother and the unborn child died. The principal of the local school and the commune headman were furious. They drew up a grievance petition and sent it to the Department of Public Health and to the Revolutionary Group. The petition accused her of neglecting her duties and of leaving her post at the Nurse's Station, thus causing the death of a human being. When this incident occurred, the district public health officer asked me to help by issuing an order that directed her to serve and to expedite the work at the District Public Health Center—thus providing some evidence that would free him of blame. I was happy to do this for him. But he wanted me to issue a false order, one that was dated five months earlier than the day the incident happened. The clerks could not do this for him because in the log books kept at the District Office all orders issued at the district are numbered chronologically, by day, month, and year. The public health officer again blew his top and accused me of not cooperating with him, of not joining together with him in our work, and he would not accept any of my explanations—not a single one."

"How dense can you be? Why didn't you open the log, see if there were any orders that were unimportant or no longer valid, and then use the number of that order for this new one, entering it on the same page? You would just have to make sure that the new order was affixed properly, so that the original was not visible. That would have settled the matter. Everything would have been fine, legal, and proper.

"And what about the Public Health Center being set on fire? How come you didn't give them any cooperation?"

"The district public health officer asked me to report that the communist terrorists forced their way into the district and set fire to the Health Center. But I couldn't do that—because it wasn't true. I'd just be stirring

up the pot and creating a situation. The Health Center is located in
between the Police Station and District Headquarters; it's hidden next to
the barracks used by the Voluntary Security Forces and the police. No
communist terrorist wants to look down the throat of a cobra. That's
what it would be like if they tried to force their way into a place like that,
located downtown next to everything else. And even if it were true, I
would still have to wait on the results of the investigation by the police.
After the fire, several petitions and unsigned letters were sent to the
Department of Public Health in Bangkok, in the province, and also in the
district. Some of the nurses insisted that the district public health officer
set the fire himself in order to destroy evidence of his own malfeasance.
There were other rumors that villagers were taking revenge against him
for treating them in a rude and obnoxious manner, for extorting money
from them, and for refusing to provide them with medicine when they
were in need. They were so full of revenge that they sneaked in and
burned up the whole place.

"The public health officer and two of his followers then came to ask
for temporary use of some space in the District Headquarters that they
could use until the new Public Health Center was built. One of my deputy district officers arranged some room for him. Then still another
problem arose. Officials in other offices, in other sections of the district
administration, began to wonder about what kind of privileges he had
over other civil servants in not having to sign his time sheets in Book
Number Ten of the Civil Service Registry. He then announced that he was
subject only to the regulations of the Department of Public Health and
that he was not under the jurisdiction of the district, as were all other
officials. So people became disgusted with him.

"Someone gave him a copy of the Act Governing the Administration of
the Nation to read, which is the basic code governing the organization of
the bureaucracy and which is known to every government official. Then
he came running in to see me damning and slandering the whole bureaucratic system in the most unsavory way. He was just like those people
who are ignorant of the laws and of bureaucratic rules and traditions,
who never take an interest in studying government handbooks, and who
use their spare time only to read dime novels."

An amused smile flashed across the dark and serious face of the narrator of this tale. When he realized that everyone was listening attentively,
he took control of the situation and proceeded.

"I had to answer his many questions about the way the bureaucracy
operated, and I had to explain to him that in living our lives we do not all
go our own separate ways, that we live together in and as a society, and
that under such conditions rules and regulations on how we live together
are required. We must have a social structure and an administrative system that is well organized so that it will create efficiency and good

results. In a family, there are a father and mother. In a school, there are a principal and several other teachers. In the governmental sphere, there is a prime minister. In the same way, the Act Governing the Administration of the Nation provides that at every level there is a supervisor who will take responsibility for the work done at that level—the district level, the province level, and then the department and ministry levels. There is nothing wrong with that arrangement. Every bureaucratic system in the world is the same, no matter the country, no matter the language. There is an administrator responsible for work at every level. For example, in America there is a governor who is the center of the administration at the state level and there is a city manager who is the axis of administration at the city level, just as there are governors and district officers who control things at the province and district levels in our country. There are some small differences between countries, but these differences are limited to minor matters of governmental practice and to the basic, overarching conditions of each society—that's all.

"I really tried my best, and I thought I had explained to him that there was nothing hateful about signing one's name in the time book and that by no means would he lose face in doing that. I also told him that I wasn't one of those people who was excited by things like status, prestige, rank, and honor. I too signed my name every day—following the general procedure. Whenever I had to go on a field trip, I would record it in the column 'Field Duty.' Some nights I had to work all night, until dawn. Right now, each of us is working hard, together, without a day off and without knowing whether it is day or night. If we get fed up with things, we don't sign our names immediately. We can do it later when we feel better, at some other time. Our officials are not so persnickety as to draw a red line as soon as office hours begin. Furthermore, signing the time sheet can sometimes prove to be useful. If, unfortunately, someone accused you of deserting your official duties—which, if more than fifteen days, could be punished by permanent dismissal from government service, never to be reinstated, for the rest of your life—this book could be used as significant evidence and could have a very positive effect upon you. Of course, if the evidence is not in the book, it could have a negative effect, too.

"Instead of trying to understand what I was saying to him, the district public health officer raised hell, screaming that he could work anywhere he wanted, and that the District Headquarters and its offices were not important. And then he ordered his subordinates to move his office into his own house."

"The provincial public health officer has already come to see me and the governor about this. He said he was the one who ordered the move."

"Yes, sir. And soon there was some more trouble. The midwife and her husband, who is a police sergeant-major, sent a petition to the Public Health Department, to the Revolutionary Group, to the governor, and also to me claiming that she was a woman and that she was forced to work all alone with the district public health officer under conditions that were no better than working in an isolated hay barn or lumber shed. She was afraid of possible scandal. I suppose you already know this story."

The deputy governor nodded his head in acknowledgment.

"When this story came out for all to hear, the district health officer made a report, predating it several days, asking for his office to be moved to his own home and requesting me to sign my name, acknowledging it and approving it. Moreover, he threatened me, saying that he was well acquainted with the wife of an influential person in our ministry and that he would go see her and ask her to get me transferred—any time he chooses to. It gave me a damn headache!

"It sounds like a hilarious story, but it's really not the kind of thing that makes you smile. On top of that, after the incident of the fire, the district public health officer refused to do any work. Whenever sick people came to see him, he used the excuse of having no medicine to treat them. He told them that if they wanted to complain, they should go and complain to those who were responsible for the fire!"

Fishiness in the Night

Introduction

Chitr Phoumisak, the author of the following poem, may or may not prove to be the most important Thai writer of this century. Whatever history's ultimate judgment, it will probably be based upon larger political events that are still to unfold rather than upon the inherent merit of the man, his ideas, or his writings. This particular poem is a very small— and, Chitr's more ardent defenders might claim, irrelevant—part of his total intellectual and aesthetic output. However, its subject matter is of considerable historical and cultural significance, and the view that Chitr is affirming here is, in the opinion of many who knew him, one of the more salient expressions of his character.

Chitr was a man of many parts, and all but a few of them were characterized by controversy. He was born in Prachinburi in the Central Plain in 1930 and was killed by the Thai police in either 1965 or 1966. Not only the date but the circumstances surrounding his death are shrouded in disagreement. Bangkok press reports of May 1965 describe him as having been in police custody for several months and killed when "attempting to escape" while being transferred from one prison to another. Other reports, principally those upon which a poem and popular song entitled "Chitr Phoumisak" are based, had him in May 1966 fighting with the communist insurgents in the Northeast when, in search of supplies, he was ambushed by the police. The legend that has since developed around Chitr has the officer responsible for the ambush being rewarded with a fourfold promotion in rank.

Exactly how or why Chitr discovered his Marxism is uncertain. Chitr was an insatiable reader, and some who have studied his intellectual development believe that the interest may have been stimulated by the books he borrowed from the United States Information Agency library and perhaps also the Russian Embassy. What is certain is that prior to his discovery of Marxism, Chitr was already known for his stunning use of Thai prosodic forms and for his work in historical and literary analysis. Even before his enrollment at Chulalongkorn University in 1952, he was an informal disciple of Prince Dhaninivat, regent of Thailand and president of the Privy Council (the same prince who a decade later was also the patron of Sulak Sivaraksa) and during his first two years at the university he studied under *Phya* Anuman Rajadhon, at the time the acknowledged conservator of Thailand's philological and ethnographic traditions. These two stalwarts of the *sakdinaa* system (a concept later reinvented by Chitr to mean "feudalism," mainly in a pejorative sense) guided his early interests in traditional Thai literature and music and helped him get started in historical studies. There were other, less famous faculty members against whom he also later reacted.

It was in 1953 as editor of a Chulalongkorn literary journal that he entered public awareness, principally because his budding Marxism became cause for the journal's suppression. This notoriety was reinforced when, in an associated incident, he was thrown off the stage of the auditorium at Chulalongkorn by a group of Faculty of Engineering students; he was subsequently suspended from the university by school authorities. He later worked as a tourist guide (his spoken English was excellent) and as an instructor in a Bangkok teacher's college. Although he spent several years in jail as a political prisoner—where he did much of his writing—he eventually managed to earn his degree from Chulalongkorn.

Chitr wrote voluminously, both under his real name and various pseudonyms such as "Thipakorn" and " Somsamai Sriisuuthornphaan." Although for several years his manuscripts were circulated, discussed, and hailed, they were not readily available, principally because of publishers' fears of confiscation or more severe forms of official retribution. His best known work to date is *Chomnaa Sakdinaa Thai* [The face of Thai feudalism], which is the first Marxist analysis of Thai history; although first printed in 1956–1957, it was not published and openly sold until after the events of October 1973. Some of his best essays on Thai poetry, art, and literature have been collected into a volume entitled *Silapa Phya Chiiwid, Silapa Phya Prachaachorn* [Art for life, art for the people], which was published under his real name in 1972.

Whatever position Chitr ultimately assumes in the pantheon of communist heroes, there is no doubt that he was one of the most powerful and imaginative writers of his time. In his use of and control over the aesthetics of the Thai language (rhythms, word choice, modes of suggestion) he is most often compared with *Luang* Vichitr Vadakan who, from the 1930s through the 1950s, was Thailand's great philosopher-historian of right-wing nationalism. (That such a comparison should even be made—e.g., that regard for the Thai language should supersede irreconcilable political differences—is in itself inimitably Thai.) In his intellectual style, Chitr is most frequently compared with Seksan Prasertkul. While the latter is judged to be considerably more analytic, cosmopolitan, and flexible in his grasp of social and political realities, Chitr is judged to have much greater sensitivity to the unstated assumptions of his culture and to how ordinary Thai think.

In personal manner, Chitr was a soft-spoken, thoughtful, and gentle man. However, when the subject turned to questions of politics or the social order, his soft-spokenness often turned into rage and his thoughtfulness seemed to succumb to the tyranny of his own abstractions. Chitr is the only Thai the editor has ever met who, for all his sophistication in other ways, actually argued that "religion is the opium of the Thai people."

Chitr's readiness to express his rage is clear in the following poem. It must be emphasized, however, that for all his anger he is not being unrealistic or excessive in his portrait of the role of sex in the life of Bangkok during the early 1960s. If there is any flaw in this account it is only in the suggestion, as in the final stanza, that the sale of sex somehow arrived with the American airmen who descended on Thailand during this period. Sex has always been sold in Thailand and has been a major element of Thai economic and cultural life, affecting family relations, politics, the structure of social obligations, recreational patterns, folklore, and the like. What was unique about the situation in the early 1960s was, on the one hand, its brassy exhibitionism and, on the other, the acknowledgment of its public, institutionalized nature in the writings of Thai literary figures and critics. It was during this period that the "Patpong" and "New Petchburi Road" areas emerged as major tourist attractions, rivalling in their cultural impact the role of Place Pigalle in Paris, the Wanchai area in Hong Kong, and a few years later the changed nature of the Times Square area of New York. This was also the period when 'Rong Wongsawaan was writing novels of Thai brothel life in vivid detail, including descriptions of the incantations and other ritual practices used by prostitutes to attract customers. And above all, as suggested by the poem, this was the period when the public was becoming increasingly aware of and titillated by (if only because of the sheer numbers of women involved) the dalliances of Field Marshal Sarit Thanarat, the leader of the nation.

What the Thai attitude toward all of this actually was has never been clear. While some Thai view all sexual behavior as essentially the private business of individuals and others actively approved the contribution that it was and is making to the nation's economy, there are others who saw it as a form of nonsense and still others who were deeply shamed by it. People who knew Chitr say that he was very much a prude and that he would have written this kind of poem even if he had never been a Marxist. Others say that he was a true believer and that he saw these practices as another form of class exploitation and as an expression of the debauchery of the ruling classes.

Like many of Chitr's poems, this one in the original Thai is known only by the prosodic form of which it is meant to be an example—in this case, a *khloong siisuphaab;* the English title here is a creation of the editor. However, Chitr wrote several *khloong siisuphaab* that reflect the same sentiments and issues that appear in this verse, suggesting that the subject matter was very important to him.

All native Thai with whom the editor has discussed this poem share a universal admiration of Chitr's ability to adhere to the rhyming rules of the poetic form and at the same time to be so evocative and precise in the use of his language. A few pointed particularly to the final stanza and to its extraordinary juxtaposition of elements: on the one hand, the throbbing, vital sounds of the northeastern mouth organ echoing off rain clouds—in themselves the harbingers of rice, health, wealth, and fecundity—and how this inevitably leads to the northeastern maiden's delicate and modest evasions; and, on the other hand, how all of this idealized past has been suddenly and totally violated by the foreign legionnaires and their undreamed of and corrupting riches.

Fishiness in the Night

CHITR PHOUMISAK

The capital of Siam is suffocating from fishiness.[1] It is an odor stronger
    than fish itself.
The greatest of the wicked are swallowing and wallowing in a slimy sea
    of sex.
"Hiding in the Shadows,"[2] slaves to their pimps, promiscuously strewn
    upon the streets.
Outlawed,[3] forbidden—they cover themselves with darkness.

There are the call girls—their creamy white, sweet complexions.
The widows of absent-minded husbands—spreading their legs wide open
    for trade.
The sex boats meandering on the river, places for careless orgies.
Saen Saeb Canal[4] wincing from the madness of lust, suffocating from its
    fishy smells.

First published in *Prachathipatj* Newspaper (1964); reprinted in Chonitraa Kla-
dyuu, ed., *Songthaj* (Bangkok: Suksit Siam Press, 1975).

1. There is an immediate double meaning here: the odor of fish and the odor of
sexuality, particularly the female genitals. The allusions to fishiness throughout
the poem are expressions of moral revulsion, not of physical repulsion; in the
abstract, the odor would be considered physically attractive and even seductive,
or would otherwise be ignored.
2. This is simply an attempt to give a name to the unknown prostitutes.
3. After 700 years of totally open commerce, brothels and streetwalking were
made officially illegal in the late 1950s.
4. Saen Saeb Canal is a major canal leading eastward out of Bangkok. The
name literally means "100,000 stings," referring to the mosquitoes that once
infested the area. While the allusion to the canal is in part a play on words
("sting" and "wince") the canal is also cited because it was another locale for mar-
itime brothels and because Bangkok's most elite red-light district ("the Soi Klang
area") was located on some of the lanes leading down to it.

Services for bathing and massaging—around the clock and without end.
Young men and women massage each other, their desire rising, until the
pleasure stings.
The new style of cutting hair. It's super![5] All fatigue is forgotten, right?
"After your haircut, do you want a massage? Do you want a massage?
She is a young masseuse—an expert."[6]

Beauticians to improve the charm and the skin of women.
Beautician schools overflowing, bountiful.
Young women teachers whose nubile aroma, like love potion, stimulates
the passions.
Young men who come to enroll, supporting education, and overflowing
the classrooms.

There are bowling alleys—gaudy, gay, and noisy.[7]
Young punks, their eyes darting everywhere, taking in the asses of young
women.
"Who is that? She's pretty (but used)." "I'm a big man's mistress! Who
else? Stupid! Who are you to ask?"
In their group, laughing loudly, demanding attention, feigning excitement, they throw their bowling balls screaming, "Wow . . .
whee . . . whoo . . . I did it. . . . Hey. . . . "

There are the kept women—burgeoning, vigorous—who when first
popped[8] are like tender, young mangoes.
Teenagers whose nubile young swellings, the size of eggs, are displayed
so proudly.

---

5. The original Thai here is *man,* one of those words found in every language
that resists easy translation. The dictionary translations of *man* are "nuttiness"
and "crunchiness," and indeed *man* has these qualities. But *man* is the absolute
perfect state of anything: a *mamuang man* is a mango that is perfect for eating; a
thauaud man plaa is a fried fish patty that is fried fish perfection. That which is
man is so superb that no name can be given to it—other than *man.*

6. The question that is asked—in an almost undeviating linguistic frame—of
every customer at the hundreds of combination barber shops–massage parlors
that abound in Bangkok.

7. When the bowling alley first came to Thailand from the United States in the
early 1960s it became instantaneously popular among the upper and upper middle classes as a place to spend a relaxing evening socializing, placing bets on each
others' skills, and the like. However, within a very few years some became
famous as gathering places for ne'er-do-wells, expensive prostitutes, and the idle
sons of the *nouveaux riches.* See Suchit Wongthed's "Getting Drunk Abroad,"
elsewhere in this volume, for another view of the symbolism of the bowling alley.

8. While this metaphor obviously concerns the deflowering of a virgin, its
imagery relates to the sound of biting into firm fruit. As should now be apparent,
much of the language of sex in Thailand uses imagery of eating, swallowing, and
tasting.

The dirty old hens and madames flatter them, cajole them—and tempt
    them ("100,000 *baht,* diamond rings, Taunus cars")[9]
And after the decrepit old bull has eaten his green grass ("It was great!"),
    he is exhausted, unable to breathe, gurgling in his own spittle.

(In the past) the Northeast was alive with the sound of the *khaen*[10] echo-
    ing off the rain clouds.
Maidens were modest, and in their manner turned away from the gaze of
    men.
(But now) they are delirious over their foreign soldiers, boasting of lovers
    who throw money at them.
They promenade, proposing their beautiful flesh for sale along the side of
    the road.

---

9. This and the following line have reference to the sexual excesses of the then
premier of Thailand, Field Marshal Sarit Thanarat. After Sarit's death in 1963,
more than a hundred women declared themselves publicly as having been among
his favorites. The Taunus, a German-made car of the period, was one of Sarit's
best-known gifts to his paramours, supposedly symbolizing that the recipient was
indeed a "favorite."

10. The northeastern mouth organ, and the most distinctive symbol of this
region of the country.

4

The Politicization of Experience

My Beloved Brother, Thamnu . . .

Introduction

The most salient feature of Thai public life during the past half century has been the continuing dialectic between military-oligarchical and democratic forms of government and the coups and elections that brought them into existence. Since 1932, there have been, depending upon one's method of counting, at least sixteen such coups—nine "successful" and seven "unsuccessful." The number of "genuine" elections has been more difficult to count, because many have served mainly to sanction or legitimize a preceding coup, although elections occurring in the period immediately following World War II and during 1973–1976 were authentic expressions of the democratic process.

On November 17, 1971, one of Thailand's numerous coups occurred. As such things go, it was not a particularly momentous event in Thai history. Known as the "Silent Coup," it was conducted by edict rather than guns and involved the suspension of the constitution, parliament, political parties, as well as the rights of free speech, assembly, and free press by the regime of Field Marshal Thanom Kittikachorn, the incumbent prime minister. In its political motivation, this coup was essentially an act of domination on the part of the Thanom government vis-à-vis expressions of independence from a parliament, half of whose members the Thanom group had itself appointed.

In the flow of Thai history, the coup is in part remembered for having created some of the conditions that led to the Student Revolution two years later (and the ultimate downfall of the Thanom regime) and for the fact that some of the leading members of the inner group of the Thanom government declared themselves against it. Included were the director of the prime minister's own Executive Office and the prime minister's own brother—both generals. However, to the majority of the educated public, the single most memorable aspect of the coup was not its long-term con-

296

sequences nor its politics, but rather the extraordinary letter that it stimulated from Dr. Puey Ungphakorn—a letter widely recognized as the most eloquent exposition of the nature and importance of democracy to be written in the Thai language.

The letter is presented here not only because of its historical and literary interest but because it helps define the special position that its author has come to hold in Thai society.

At the time of the coup, Puey was out of the country serving as a visiting professor at Cambridge University, so it was impossible for him to respond to the immediate implications of the event. The letter was written three months later, after he made some brief visits to Thailand, and was initially intended to be a private communication from a respected and trusted lieutenant to a friend and senior colleague of several years. The latter is important because the letter never would have been written —or have taken the form that it does—without such prior personal involvements. In fact, although the phrasing of the letter suggests in English a certain amount of grandstanding, it is really a ritual language used by a person who finds himself in a delicate situation; he is in fundamental disagreement on matters of principle with a man who is not only his bureaucratic senior but an esteemed friend. This kind of conflict between social structural values (the dictates of one's role) and moral values (the dictates of one's conscience) is something with which most Thai are familiar, and here Puey deals with the conflict by couching his protest in the language of endearment and analogy. From this point of view, the allegory of "Thai Chareon Village" should be seen not merely as a literary device but rather as a subtle and gracious way of dealing with a personal (as well as cultural) dilemma.

To what extent Puey actually expected his letter to have any influence on Thanom or to elicit a response has never been clear. However, having never received an acknowledgment and having mentioned the letter to several friends, Puey eventually permitted it to be copied and distributed privately. It was soon referred to frequently in the Thai press and finally was published in its entirety in April 1972, immediately becoming a cynosure of both admiration and controversy ("Did Puey really write it?" or "Where is this 'Thai Chareon Village'?"). The publication of the letter was prompted by the hope that public pressure would contribute to the restoration of the constitution, parliament, and democratic freedoms.[1]

The elements of the analogy are straightforward. "Thai Chareon Village" ("Progressive Thai village") refers to the nation; the "Village Chief" or *"Phuujajbaan"* refers to the prime minister; "Village Rules" to the constitution; "Village Assembly" to parliament; and "villagers" to the nation's citizens. The one element of the letter that is a bit double-edged is the signature "Khem Yenying." This was Puey's code name during World War II when, as a member of the Free Thai Movement (which as a student in England he helped organize), he parachuted into Thailand, was captured almost immediately, and remained a prisoner until the war ended a short time later. While the use of the name is meant to convey the author's patriotic commitments, it also suggests the sense of once again being made a prisoner in his own country.

The significance of the letter derives not only from its content or circumstance, but from the fact that its author, Puey Ungphakorn, is one of the very few, if perhaps the only, Thai of his generation who over the years has taken on some of the attributes of a cultural hero. However, Puey's "heroism" is comprised of several elements, most of which have as much to do with what he symbolizes as with what he has actually done, and a few of which have made him a figure of enmity as well as one of respect and admiration. As with any cultural hero, his "position" is as much a function of the aspirations and flaws of his society as they are of his own talent and character.

Puey was an extremely successful bureaucrat who through the combination of his own competence, good luck, and sense of diplomacy played a central role in Thailand's economic development and in the strengthening of its system of higher education. This success began in the late 1950s when, as one of the nation's first Ph.D.'s in economics (from the London School of Economics), he became director of the Budget Bureau of the newly installed government of Field Marshal Sarit Thanarat. The Sarit government had come into power by coup d'etat, and while Puey certainly had no sympathy for either Sarit's despotic ways or extraordinary corruption (see Chaloemtiarana 1979), he did have the dictator's support, as well as extraordinary professional freedom, to help initiate Thailand's long-term development programs.

When he became governor of the Bank of Thailand (a position he held for the next twelve years), he quickly attracted the attention of international agencies, foreign governments, and the international financial community for the integrity of his financial planning and management. His international stature was recognized ceremoniously in 1964 when he became the first Thai recipient of the Magsaysay Award for public service. Equally important, this international recognition gave him an influence with Sarit, Thanom, and their cohort far exceeding his bureaucratic position, as they sought his aid and advice as a troubleshooter for Thailand's monetary interests, particularly in matters that they had botched or in which they were suspected to have their own private interests (e.g., remedying Sarit's mishandling of Thailand's participation in an International Tin Council; preventing a kickback scandal over the foreign printing of Thailand's currency).

In 1966 Puey became the dean of the Faculty of Economics at his alma mater, Thammasat University, where his work with the Rockefeller Foundation and with foreign scholars dramatically up-graded the training of Thailand's future technocrats. He also instituted a long-term research project on raising the productivity and economic level of Thai villagers. It was during this period that he was invited to serve as a visiting professor at both Cambridge and Princeton universities and was appointed to the governing boards of such organizations as the International Council for Educational Development, the East-West Center, the Asian Institute of Management, and the International Food Policy Research Institute.

This kind of international esteem was unprecedented for a Thai bureaucrat-educator who had been born the fourth son of an immigrant Chinese fishmonger and Thai mother and whose entire career was completely a function of his own talent rather than of family, class, or ethnic advantage. Puey's double Thai-Chinese identity was something that he was never permitted to forget, particularly in his early days during the regime of Field Marshal Phibun Songkhram, although he confounded his critics further by marrying his English sweetheart from his student days in London. In a society where love and sex have always had political overtones, this was seen by some as additional evidence of Puey's cosmopolitan outlook but by others as a denial of his Thai heritage. Those who know him best say simply that it was one more expression of his characteristic independence in matters that were truly important to him, and to that extent, they add, he was being a "genuine Thai."

After the Student Revolution of October 1973, Puey was catapulted into political prominence and, along with M. R. Khukrit Pramoj, was broadly promoted as one of the two major candidates for the post of prime minister in the elected government that would follow the interim regime of Sanya Thammasak. However, after a great deal of self-examination, Puey disavowed all interest in such a candidacy and returned to Thammasat where he was appointed rector. Puey's explanation (one he had used several times in the past when offered political appointment) was that when he had joined the Free Thai Movement, thirty years earlier, he had taken an oath never to seek or to accept political appointment until after reaching the age of retirement and that to become a candidate, even in a free election, would be a violation of that oath. Some have argued, however, that Puey's withdrawal was based upon more tough-minded reasons: that with his more mature understanding of the nature of Thai society, he accurately foresaw that the upcoming democratic period would be inherently unstable, dangerous, and short-lived and that in his realism he was also aware of his own limitations as a politician, particularly in his dealings with the palace and with the military.

On the evening of the coup of October 6, 1976, Puey was nearly lynched by a right-wing mob while he was fleeing Thailand for his own safety. He has since settled in England. For a period of time he played the leading role in gaining the support of interested Westerners to help

Thai who, like himself, had been forced to leave their homeland, and he also publicly cautioned that if the polarization of Thai society were to continue it would eventually lead to civil war. He soon after became dangerously ill—many Thai say as a result of the trauma he experienced during and after the coup—and although his health has improved somewhat, he has essentially retired from Thai public life.

Puey's status as a cultural hero derives from several obvious, but special, features of his career and character. His most significant, if paradoxical, attribute was his willingness to work for the Thai bureaucratic establishment and yet maintain his moral independence, intellectual creativity, and sense of social responsibility. In the *realpolitik* world in which most Thai live, his capacity to strike a compromise between what was objectively possible and morally desirable was an extraordinary achievement. It had particular impact on younger people, almost all of whose models have traditionally been either successful rogues who manipulate their social environment for their own advantage or martyrs, fools, and failures who succumb to it. That Puey's success should come in the area of economic development had a quality of practicality that was especially meaningful to most Thai. Too, his style had a certain aesthetic appeal; he always acted with modesty, good humor, civility, and with an awareness that his actions might help improve the Thai world rather than revolutionize it. This last point represented his greatest strength, because unlike those who merely dreamed or talked about changing Thailand, he was actually doing it. And to do it under the aegis of scoundrels like Sarit made his effort even more commendable.

Connected to this was his deep sense of incorruptibility. Over the years, he held a variety of jobs and served on a number of commissions that, in terms of standard Thai corruption practices, could have made him a wealthy man. But unlike many of his bureaucratic peers, he lived modestly in a wooden house, had few or no servants (his wife was known for doing her own cooking and laundry), no retinue, and did not use a driver—all of which to most Thai was *prima facie* evidence of his honesty. Further, Puey's incorruptibility was more than merely passive. As an economist, he was keenly aware that official corruption was depriving the Thai treasury of inordinately large sums, and in public addresses and statements he would often include selections of his "anticorruption poetry"—thinly veiled, but cutting, poetic attacks against the specific acts of the very highest government officials.

Puey's career is also powerful evidence of how education—as contrasted to wealth, political power, and connections—could be used to climb the Thai status system. There were, of course, many others who followed a similar route. But he is perhaps the clearest public example of how technocracy, professionalism, expertise, and the long-term education that these presumed are beginning to work the kind of quiet transformation that will ultimately alter the very nature and structure of Thai society.

Yet, for all these propitious attributes, Puey is also viewed by many sensitive Thai as one of his nation's tragic heroes—partly as a result of his own fate and decision but, more importantly, as a result of the tragic nature of Thai society. Some of his acts of heroism resulted in failure: his World War II parachuting exploit as a Free Thai agent ended almost immediately after it started with his imprisonment; for all its truth and eloquence, his letter to "My Beloved Brother, Thamnu" had absolutely no influence on Thanom's decisions; and although the Student Revolution, conducted by many of his own disciples, involved the kind of integrity that he so often taught and symbolized, he could not see it through to its logical consequence by assuming political power and leadership. Some Thai say that these "failings" were ultimately the result of his *karma* or *phromlikhid* (see n. 2, p. 144) and, as precipitates of fate, were literally beyond his capacity to control. In fact, some who have taken this position say that from a karmic point of view, Puey actually did see the Student Revolution through to its "logical" consequence—that consequence being its destruction in the coup of October 1976 and Puey's own flight from Thailand.

The majority opinion, however, is that although his tragic heroism might be personal and karmic, it is much more obviously social and political and that like many of the *wirachon* (political heroes) of this period of Thai history, Puey was simply playing out his role in the larger tragedy of his society. There is obviously a strong undercurrent of fatalism to this approach as well. Many say that for all his service to his nation, his honesty, and his international reputation, there was no way that Puey could have avoided being made into a symbol of villainy ("Communist," "destroyer of unity," "the biggest of all the Ung's")[2] by the political right of Thailand. Thus, although he spoke out against the unending student demonstrations of 1975–1976 as being both ineffective and self-destructive,[3] and even denied his students any use of the Thammasat campus as a base for mounting public demonstrations, he was nevertheless assigned blame for their occurrence. Similarly, there was no way that he could deal with the guilt-by-association thinking that linked him to Pridi Phanomyong. The kingdom's regent and later prime minister during the early 1940s and immediately after World War II, Pridi was the founder of Thammasat, the person who had sponsored Puey's government fellowship to study in England, and Puey's senior collaborator in the Free Thai Movement. But Pridi had also been implicated in the 1946 regicide of King Ananda, had fled Thailand, and during his thirty-year banishment from his country was never forgiven nor forgotten, particularly by certain elements at the palace. Although Puey's success during this same thirty-year period had nothing to do with Pridi and occurred despite Puey's earlier ties to him, the fact of those ties was also never forgiven nor forgotten.

Since October 1976, Puey's stature in Thailand has grown into something of a legend. Given the savage way he was treated upon his departure, his subsequent illness, and the quiet dignity with which he and his family responded to the events which followed in Thailand, this was perhaps inevitable. Unlike Pridi decades earlier or even his own students at the time, he was not even alleged to have violated any law. His only sin was to be an innocent by-stander to a horrible event in Thai history, although many Thai also feel deep sympathy toward him for being unable to protect his students against the horrors of the event. Juxtaposed against his earlier contributions, his life appears to many of his countrymen as the fulfillment of their sense of both tragedy and heroism.

There are others who point out that because real life is always both more complex and prosaic than dramaturgic views of it, Puey came out of this situation much better than the "tragic hero" metaphor suggests, that is, while the events of October 1976 turned him into a martyr or failure in Thailand, it also resulted in his return to the milieu which had provided him with his higher education, his wife, the pleasures of rationality and civility, as well as the continued esteem of his colleagues in the international technocratic and educational community. It had inadvertently also given him a much larger position in the history of twentieth-century Thailand. These were not insignificant satisfactions for a man sixty years of age—although the onset of his illness soon altered the total meaning of the situation. Moreover, it may be that he would have gladly relinquished most of them for the satisfaction of knowing that the kind of situation he had hoped for in "My Beloved Brother, Thamnu . . ." had been finally and permanently established in Thailand. But as he reminds us in his letter, and as every Thai knows with absolute certainty, "how clearly we see the impermanence of all things!"

NOTES

1. In discussions with the editor six years earlier and in reference to totally different matters, Puey pointed out that he would never publicly criticize the actions of the Thai government or its leaders without first expressing his criticism to these persons in private: "They have to know where you stand. Otherwise it would be calamitous." His handling of this letter was clearly in accord with this long-standing practice.

2. This has reference to Puey's half-Chinese origins. The other "Ung's" are presumably both Puey's own children and those Thammasat students who were presumed to have some Chinese background.

3. It is significant that some student leaders also saw their demonstrations as "ineffective and self-destructive" (e.g., as turning public opinion further against them) but, like characters in a drama that they themselves had written, felt that they "had no choice" but to continue their marches. They said that "not to march was to 'give the stage' over to the organizations of the far right." This dramaturgic conception of the nature of human events is similar to the way most Thai conceive of Puey's behavior and fate.

My Beloved Brother, Thamnu . . .

Puey Ungphakorn

February 1972

My Beloved Brother, Thamnu,

Two years ago, when I left our beloved Thai Chareon Village, now so many miles away, you, Brother Thamnu, as the Village Chief, had undertaken to do two things which meant much to our village, in my eyes and everyone else's. Moreover, they meant much to the future of our village. You set up the new "Village Rules" as the supreme authority.

This meant that the Thai Chareon villagers would be able to hold on to and respect those rules as the fundamental principles of their everyday life. Their lives would be better and our village would become more developed than in the days when we had only a few authoritarian rulers. Along with implementing the new Rules, you made possible peaceful change in the structure of village authority. And you, Brother Thamnu, arranged to have the villagers select among themselves those persons who would speak for them.

Those men who were selected got together and called themselves the Village Assembly. They had the power and the responsibility to make rules for our village, based on the principle of popular sovereignty. The principle which you followed was "right makes might, not might makes right—and right derives from the people." This really meant that the supreme power came from the collective moral spirit of all the citizens of Thai Chareon Village.

I was not sure then that I liked all the Rules, and was not sure that all the assemblymen were good men. But I admired you, the Honourable

First published in *Chaawbaan* 1, no. 4 (April 1972). This English-language version is from Puey Ungphakorn, *Best Wishes to Asia* (Bangkok: Klett Thai Publications, 1975).

Village Chief—*Phuujajbaan* Thamnu Kiatkong—for having the patience to create the new Rules and give them a chance. It was better to have the Rules than to have no rules at all. And it was better to have an Assembly than to have no assembly.

Now, how clearly we see the impermanence of all things! Not long after I left our village I heard that suddenly you had changed your mind; that together with some of your friends, you had announced the annulment of the Village Rules and dissolved the Village Assembly. The village has now gone back to the system whereby it is ruled according to the will of the Village Chief and his friends, alone. In this case, it is still Brother Thamnu and his Deputy Village Chief, his Assistant Village Chief, and so on—the same group, minus a few.

I have carefully considered the causes which you, Brother Thamnu, and your men have cited as reasons for this change. I have spent a considerable length of time waiting to see whether, after the Village Rules were given up, the existing bad conditions in our village would be corrected miraculously and something wonderful occur. But alas, there has not been the slightest sign of the magical changes that were promised. In some instances, the situation has even become worse—for example, concerning the troubles along our village borders. Not feeling quite sure of myself (because I was looking from afar), I took two trips back to our village, with my eyes and my ears wide open. The result was a definite confirmation of my original beliefs that, with sincere intention, our problems of crime, external subversion, economic growth, and youth development could have been solved without having to give up the Village Rules. If necessary, the Village Assembly could have been reselected, with the Rules retained.

This most important issue is the new limitation on the villagers' rights. Now the villagers are not allowed to think, speak, or write freely. Public meetings concerning governmental affairs of our beloved village have been banned. This has prevented the village from receiving the benefits of the intelligent thinking of all the villagers, collectively and as individuals.

You, Brother Thamnu, may argue that the change already has been blessed by the village officials and the villagers alike, except for a few who are "unsound." . . . I would beg to inform you that, as far as the officials are concerned, they personally benefit from living without the Assembly. They do not have to be bothered by men from the Assembly. In short, now there is no one to stand in their way.

As for the villagers, you know very well that they cling to the motto "Survival of the Fittest."[1] I can confirm this point, as I too was once a

---

1. This line from *Phra Aphajmanii* has been translated elsewhere in this volume as "To know how to survive is the greatest good." The phrasing used here is Dr. Puey's own translation.

kind of chief, contributing to the work of our village. At that time, I never found anyone who would argue with me, whether I happened to be right or wrong. They all knew the secret way to "survive." As for the claim that there has been very little opposition—this is quite valid, and is due to the omnipresence of your armed guards, Brother Thamnu. Your friends have been there since the beginning, ready to challenge all those who oppose you. Fear works as magic to weaken the cries of the opposition. If you would know how the villagers really feel, abandon intimidation.

Nevertheless, my letter is not intended to oppose you personally, Brother Thamnu. Rather, I would like to expound on the very point which you and I once agreed on. That is, "We shall work to develop our Thai Chareon Village." Development, after all, can be truly beneficial only when it is carried out in all aspects—social, economic, moral, cultural, educational, and political, with an eye towards security.

As for the political aspects of development, during the twenty years of my personal association with you I have always heard that my Brother Thamnu (and his friends) believe in democracy. (The Reds are trying to wipe out democracy—so we claim—and it is true.) You exhausted the time, care, brains, and money of the village for almost ten years to devise a new set of Village Rules. I sincerely admire democracy, just as you (and your friends) do.

Nowadays, civilised villages usually are interested in the environment which, if polluted further, will greatly endanger the human species. They fear the wrong application of science and technology, the black smoke from automobile exhaust pipes, or factories, or the poisonous chemical effects of industrialisation. In our Thai Chareon Village, there are indeed such terrible environmental conditions. But they are by no means as bad as the poison of fear caused by intimidation, and the uncontrolled use of selfish power (whether used towards "justifiable" ends or not). Fear damages the intellect. The intellect, being damaged, sometimes becomes paralysed. Or worse things happen—the intellect, deprived and depressed, bursts out in reaction. This has been happening in many other villages, as is frequently reported in the press.

I agree with you, Brother Thamnu, that the external threat to our village must be done away with completely. But when our villagers are constantly exposed to coercion and frightening threats from within, and their intellects cannot be used in honourable channels as our ancestors often used theirs to save our country—and when more power breeds more fear—this is a time of danger! In biology it is said that the nerves can force the eyes to close. The time during which our eyes are closed is a time of potential disaster, for who knows but that our enemies may take advantage of their opportunity in the blinking of an eye?

Another factor which I consider very important is this. You are over

sixty; I am close to sixty. We are both close to taking leave of this world.
I have as much ambition as you do, for I too hope to leave behind to our
younger generation a world and a village which are worthy places to live
in; to leave behind a village as "free" as its name; and one which is developed, capable of effecting change through peaceful means, according to
the Rules. To accomplish as much as this, if nothing more, would be considered a great heritage for future generations.

Some people ask: "Should we permit the youth of today to enjoy rights
and freedom according to the Village Rules?" Many of today's youth
show disgustingly bad behaviour. I get rather disgusted myself at times.
But you, Brother Thamnu, gave me a job which required close association with our youth for a number of years.[2] I have carefully and objectively observed them and have found that, rather than being full of contempt, I am full of pride for our Thai Chareon Village youngsters.

They are humble, unlike the youth of other villages. I sympathize with
them. They have been taught by us to love democracy (which was a correct thing for us to teach them), and to enjoy expressing themselves freely
in thinking, writing, speaking, and associating with others (which was
also the right thing to do, according to all the past Village Rules).

These teachings which we have imparted to them are impressed upon
their hearts. They were overjoyed when the new Village Rules were
created for the use of the entire village. This act fulfilled their hope and
anticipation, as it corresponded to what we had taught them to feel. But
those Rules had such a short life, a life that was taken away so suddenly.
No one knows when the Rules will come to life again. Who would not
feel the loss? Who would not be disappointed? They were hoping to have
a part to play in developing our village according to the Rules. Nevertheless, our youth have remained calm. They suppress their fear when making requests to us. They still believe in the good and sincere intentions of
their elders. How can one help being kind to them and proud of them?

For these numerous reasons, and with my sincere respect for you, I beg
you, please, to hurry to bring the Village Rules back into use again. As
soon as possible, maybe in the middle of 1972, or at the latest, by the end
of the year. Please allow the Thai Chareon villagers to live according to
the principle of human rights, and elect a new Assembly quickly. This
would be a priceless gift to the villagers, for the present and for the
future.

Respectfully yours,
Khem Yenying

---

2. At the time, Puey was still dean of Faculty of Economics at Thammasat University.

The Big Shot as Toad

Introduction

One of the most pervasive themes of Thai culture is the *phuujaj-phuunauauj* ("big man–little man") relationship—a complex of attitudes, ethics, sanctions, and linguistic features that define the importance of superordination and subordination in the total social life of the Thai. The theme and its variations are found in virtually every social domain: the family, government, business, the monkhood, voluntary associations, dyadic contracts, and, if it is not a contradiction in terms, even in peer groups.[1] The dynamics of the theme have been analyzed in a variety of ways in the historical and social science literature (Chaloemtiarana 1979; Hanks 1962, 1966, and 1975; Kemp 1980; Keyes 1970; Moerman 1969; Phillips 1965; Rabibhadana 1969 and 1975; Riggs 1966; Rubin 1973) and aspects of the theme emerge repeatedly in other stories in this volume. It represents the central issue in "Paradise Preserved"; the views of villagers held by the different narrators in "Fulfilling One's Duty," "Social Work," and "Headman Thuj"; the hero's view of his boss in "A Day in the Life of Pat"; the reciprocal views of father and sons in *Naaj Aphajmanii;* and is immanent to the perceptions of everyone in "The Wholesome Intention of *Khunnaaj* Saajbua."

However, for all of its ubiquity and historical depth, the credibility of the superordinate-subordinate relationship is not without challenge. In "What Kind of Boat?" Sulak Sivaraksa attacks superordinates for their pretensions and subordinates for their laziness and, in general, is critical of a system that places so much emphasis upon the superficialities of forms and so little on the substance of performance. A related criticism is implicit to "Big Shots and *Likee,*" where superordinates are described as interested mainly in the perquisites and theatrics of power rather than in actually doing anything. And in Anand Seenakhan's "Chewing Out a Special Class," intense criticism is directed against the corruption practiced by many social superiors, although Anand is more interested in exposing corruption than he is in challenging the *phuujaj-phuunauauj* paradigm as such.

The following essay by Anud Aaphaaphirom is different from these in that it represents a rejection of the paradigm that is total and absolute. In fact, the author's rage is so overwhelming that in certain places his message becomes incoherent (although in aesthetic contrast, in other places quite elegant). Also, because of its particular imagery, the essay is perhaps even emotionally upsetting to some Thai readers. This is probably not unintentional because the statement is meant to be read as much for what it says about the author's rhetorical talent as for what it says about the nature of the Thai social order. It is presented here not because it is intellectually persuasive but to illustrate how far the rejection of this aspect of traditional Thai culture has actually come, at least at the level of exhortatory performance.

The term that has been translated here as "big shot" is *phuujaj,* which denotes superior status in a generic, nonspecific, and emotionally neutral way. The English glosses "big man," "the head man," and "Mr. Big" would all be equally possible. In fact, *phuujaj* is in itself so emotionally neutral that it serves to enhance the virulence of the feelings that the author is trying to convey. Under most circumstances one would simply not admit to wanting to kill or destroy *phuujaj* merely because they were *phuujaj,* and one would certainly not admit this in direct juxtaposition to building a society where "There will only be people who love one another as fellow human beings."

The image of the toad should not be taken lightly. There is nothing in the Occident that has quite the symbolic power to stimulate the kind of revulsion that the toad *(khaangkhok)* stimulates in the Thai imagination. The response of some Westerners to cockroaches or bats perhaps suggests something of the nature of the revulsion, but little of its intensity. The bug in Kafka's *Metamorphosis* alludes to the type of anxiety that such creatures can stimulate, but it too misses the point that is being made here. Thai explain it as a result of the toad's inherent noxiousness (mere contact can result in skin infection), its ugliness (its capacity to inflate its head, which some *phuujaj* do as well), and its uselessness (unlike frogs or tadpoles, toads cannot be eaten).[2]

Anud Aaphaaphirom is an interesting and, during the early 1970s, influential member of Thailand's intellectual community. A member of a conservative Thai family (an older brother has been a high-ranking minister in several recent governments), he studied literature and history at Chulalongkorn University, from where he graduated in 1965. He later worked for Thailand's largest publishing house editing a children's magazine and an educational journal and slowly began to develop an interest in Marxism and leftist political action. It was during this period that he wrote "The Big Shot as Toad" and also published an influential "progressive" children's comic book series. After October 1973, his political interests bloomed and he essentially became a Maoist-oriented propogandist, seminar leader, and organizer working among university students. He was known to be extremely effective at this work, and his public personality is reputed to have even undergone a change—from a silent, stubborn person of recondite ideas he had become a confident and spellbinding public speaker. He is also reported to have been deeply affected by the concept of the Cultural Revolution as it was implemented in China and had hopes of replicating the same kind of thing in Thailand. After October 1976, he went into the jungle almost immediately, but very soon went on to China where he wrote for "The Voice of the Free Thai People" radio station. He, his writer wife, and child are reported to have returned to Bangkok in 1981, where they have since been living quietly and where he is also reported to have undertaken a major personal reevaluation of his social and political views.

NOTES

1. The *phuujaj-phuunauauj* relationship is simply one of a whole series of stylistically similar relationships, each one of which takes its specific meaning from the context of its usage. Its most obvious variants are: *phii-nauaung* (older sibling–younger sibling, often in a fictional sense); *phuujaj-dek* (adults-children, frequently irrespective of actual ages); *phauaukhun-luug* (paternalistic king and/or leader–his subjects or followers as his children); *phauaubaan-luugbaan* (village leader–village member or follower); *aacaan-luugsid* (teacher-disciple); *phuunam-phuutaam* (leader-follower); *phuuthaw–luug laan* (those of father's and mother's status–those of the status of children, nephews, nieces, and grandchildren).

2. These perceptions of toads are not at variance with the biological facts. Apparently, the toads of mainland Southeast Asia are extraordinary creatures. Some species secrete poisons from their pores, others from a gland near the corner of their eyes, and others by spraying poisonous urine. They have been observed copulating with toad corpses, even rotting corpses. Some secrete a noxious froth from their skins. Because of their toxicity they are the prey of very few other animals or birds. At the same time, they are obdurate about their own deaths, being able to live without food or even without parts of their own bodies for excessively long periods.

The Big Shot as Toad

ANUD AAPHAAPHIROM

Amidst all the vulgarity there is to see there is nothing as ugly as a toad's head.

Dedicating its life to aimless hopping, with no one to give it any attention, a toad considers itself so great. Hardly. A toad is really rather useless.

It sits so arrogantly and proudly. Nothing less than a beating to its head would cause it to become aware.

Perhaps it is good to know that there is something even more obnoxious than a toad's head. It is something more disgusting and obstinate. It is what we call the "big shot."

For beating, oh toad, a big shot is much to be preferred.

Toad, you may wonder what is the so-called "big shot." It is something that is supposed to be made of a number of years, of knowledge, of higher degrees, and of position.

But no matter what the big shot is supposedly made of, he is in truth all arrogance and intransigence.

Find me a big shot who is not like a toad.

When the pride of thinking oneself better than others prompts one to call oneself a big shot, arrogance follows suit.

He is arrogant of always being in the right, and insists on doing what he knows is wrong.

He is arrogant in taking upon himself the power to grant others pardon, and in denying his own guilt to himself.

He is arrogant in not showing mercy, and in shamelessly allowing others to die in the name of his greatness.

From *Chaturat* 1, no. 1 (August 1970). The publication of this journal was terminated by the Thai government after only a few issues. A second, very different *Chaturat* began publication in the spring of 1975.

He is arrogant in telling children to pay him respect, and indecent in his refusal to be courteous to others. That is enough. I cannot describe it any more. The big shot makes me nauseous.

I think of the day that he will bleed from his head, so that he will realize:

That by nature a man is one unit of his species, and no one man can boast of any greater right to live than others.

That socially, people own their society equally, and no one person has the right to monopolize that ownership.

And that humanistically, everyone has the right to enjoy life and to grow in his own way without compulsion.

But will these big shots know? Or would they rather die in ignorance and arrogance?

I will kill the big shots. I will no longer listen to them because they all mean to lie and deceive.

The state is like a father who rules the children under his care. But its brazen desire is to make people submit and to surrender their lives to it. And the big shots who maintain and govern the state have the power to lie. This is their deceitfulness, their filth—the filth of big shots who have built their filthy society.

Death is their tomorrow. The big shots live by the Dharma of death and envy life and the living. They destroy the newborn of everything as they appropriate all in the movement to their own death.

And that is why in the eyes which gleam with arrogance and superiority, I see shadows of envy mingled with anxiety.

"Be patient," the big shot counsels the likes of me. "Do not try to advance in haste, but let us continue to sit on your head."

Toads, now you can all understand the repulsiveness that lies within the sanctimonious and degree-filled head of the big shot.

You understand how I loathe big shots more than toads. As long as they exist I will not strike you.

Enough of the stubborn big shots. I will destroy them clean and build a new society without them. There will only be people who love one another as fellow human beings.

Isn't it funny? To think that just by building a society without toads, all people will be clean and safe from ugliness and dirt.

This we can easily do by not growing up to become toads, and by not allowing toad-headed people to dominate us.

I will make a society for people—not for toads—to live in. I will make a society that is owned by people, not toads. For to do otherwise would be to live forever in a nation of half humans and half beasts.

Stages of Democracy

Introduction

Of all the changes that resulted from the Student Revolution of October 1973, perhaps the most significant was the "proletariatization" of Thai politics: the broadening of political participation (although by no means the control of political power) by the creation and proliferation of political organizations at all levels of Thai society and simultaneously the entry of politics into previously untouched areas of Thai life. This politicization process led to as many as fifty-four officially registered political parties in the country, each one sufficiently viable to run candidates for public office.

On the left of the political spectrum, newly created farmers' organizations, student organizations, cooperatives, labor unions, and anticorruption organizations were all intensely active, both in their search for public support and in their attempts to represent the interests and expand the memberships of their previously unorganized constituencies. During this period, there literally was not a day when a demonstration, strike, rally, or some other large-scale public activity was not occurring somewhere in Thailand. It was in fact the very openness of the left's activities[1] that ultimately contributed to its demise—very early by threats to or assassinations of its more highly visible members and finally in the bloody events of October 6, 1976.

On the right of the political spectrum, there was also intense organization, but initially of a more concealed, less public nature—if only because the Student Revolution was itself a direct negation of what the political right had symbolized. However, by the middle of 1975, at least three rightist organizations, all with overlapping memberships, had made their way into the public's consciousness.

The largest, most broadly based, and viable of these organizations was Luugsya Chaawbaan (Tiger Cubs and Village Scouts). With the support

312

of the palace and using organizational forms based on Communist models and the American 4-H Club movement, this organization's membership is reputed to have grown by mid-1976 to more than one million people, most of whom were villagers. Although these extraordinary numbers were probably a result of its recreational activities—dance, music, and sewing contests; in-country tours; fairs and dinners—the organization's principal functions were political mobilization and education. It was the members of a branch of this organization that on the evening of October 6, 1976, at Don Muang Airport attempted to lynch the then rector of Thammasat University, Dr. Puey Ungphakorn.

A second organization was Krathing Daeaeng (Red Gaurs)[2]. Organized by a high-ranking officer of the Border Patrol Police, the active membership of this group probably did not exceed fifteen hundred men, most of whom were unemployed or unattached urban youth (many recent arrivals from villages) whom the organization also housed, fed, and otherwise cared for. Functioning mainly as un-uniformed storm troopers, they did most of the killing and burning that occurred at Thammasat University immediately prior to the October 1976 military coup.

The third organization, Naawaphon (Nine Circles)[3], was the best known of the rightist groups, if only because its principal function was the dissemination of rightist propaganda in its numerous publications, lectures, radio broadcasts, and public happenings, such as the staging of "thank you" rallies in front of the U.S. Embassy, often to the extreme embarrassment of the latter. Naawaphon was also well known because of its flamboyant leader, Wattana Kiawimol. When he returned from the United States, where he ostensibly studied international relations, he utilized not the Ph.D. he claimed to have received from Seton Hall University but rather the mobilization and propaganda techniques of American preacher Billy Graham to create Naawaphon. He was also familiar with communism from having served as a personal advisor to one of Thailand's most respected military officers, the general in charge of the Internal Security Operations Command.

The following essay was excerpted from a column appearing in the weekly newspaper published by Naawaphon. The column, "Stages of Democracy," was a regular offering of Chart Premridii, whose reputation, whatever it may be, is based solely on this effort. The thrust of the article is a discussion of how the battle against "the Communists" can be compared to a soccer game in which the Communists are attempting to achieve the fifty-one goals enumerated in the article. Nowhere is there a specification of who "the Communists" are, although the author's allusions suggest that he is referring to acknowledged Communists rather than to the leftist movement in general.

For all of its expository disorganization, the enumeration has certain fascinating features. First, irrespective of the author's attributing the source of all problems to "the Communists," the list is, with a few exceptions, an extraordinarily accurate and comprehensive summation of most of the fundamental problems of Thai society as they are conceived and verbalized by the majority of Thai—whatever their political views. As a set of propositions, rather than explanations, the list is essentially a description of the confusions of the contemporary Thai world and an unabashed recognition of the inadequacy of traditional Thai institutions to provide emotional support to the nation's citizenry or even to function properly. Perhaps the only major problem area that the author omits is pollution. But since the antipollution concern has tended to be identified with left-leaning groups, this omission may have been intentional.

Second, despite its mish-mash, grab-bag quality, the list was prepared with considerable thought: part of it was published during the week of September 11–17, 1975, and the balance was published the following week. It is clear that the author felt nothing could be omitted. In fact, some native Thai readers who have examined the list suspect that it may have actually been written by a committee, each of whose members insisted that certain items be included.

Finally, one Thai reader suggested that the list is such an excellent account of the flaws of Thai society that it might have been written as a left-wing satire on rightist views and somehow planted in the Naawaphon newspaper. Although voiced with tongue in cheek, this observation does reflect the spirit of intrigue that characterized the period or, as another Thai noted, perhaps more of the confusion.

NOTES

1. This excludes the Communist Party of Thailand which during this entire period continued to be illegal and also continued its jungle-based insurgency.

2. The gaur is the wild Southeast Asian buffalo.

3. The precise meaning and symbolism of Naawaphon is unclear, even to its own members. It sometimes refers to the nine-tiered umbrella that symbolizes the office of the king; at other times it refers to the nine specific kings of the Chakri dynasty; in other contexts it may refer to the nine heavens of the Thai universe; and some claim it refers to nine generals who allegedly created the organization.

Stages of Democracy

Chart Premridii

. . . In this soccer game, the Communists are trying to accomplish the following:

1. They make the people disorderly, undisciplined, and irresponsible.
2. They make the people feel the economic gap that exists between the rich and the poor.
3. They try to make the people feel inferior in their living conditions.
4. They try to make people who are ignorant and incapable have an attitude of opposition to everything.
5. They try to deny people the opportunities to study.
6. They try to support the existence of large numbers of thugs and thieves.
7. They cut the protection that the people have been provided by their leaders and chiefs.
8. They make the people as poor as possible.
9. They create panic among government officials for the purpose of making the government officials incapable of looking after the people.
10. They make the people lead a way of life that is so unsuitable to their real conditions that it causes corruption.
11. They try to make leaders lose their sense of firmness and resoluteness.
12. They try to fill the bureaucratic system with red tape and this gives birth to corruption.
13. They try to make use of flaws in the law in order to make their propaganda campaigns easier.

Excerpted from *Kaenprachaachon* Newspaper, September 11–17, 1975, and September 18–24, 1975.

14. They make difficulties for enforcement officers so that they cannot carry out their suppressive functions and also so that they cannot be proper patrons to their followers. [This means that the superiors in the law enforcement and crime suppression system are so busy that they cannot attend to the needs of their subordinates. Any high official in the Thai bureaucracy has two functions: one is to do his bureaucratic job and the other is to attend to his subordinates. But if he is busy trying to clear up the mess that enemies have caused, the officer will have neither the time nor the energy to attend to the needs of his inferiors.]

15. They try to make people who have low incomes seek higher and higher incomes without knowing the meaning of the word "enough."

16. They try to make the people lose their sense of obligation to their families.

17. They try to make everything have a high price so that in the end people will not be able to cope economically. [This attributes to the Communists the ability to manipulate prices and thus cause inflation, so that ultimately people will not be able to cope and the system will fail.]

18. They try to make the people hostile toward education that is helpful in everyday life.

19. They make the people feel alone and morose.

20. They make the people hate the old style of education and the kind of civilization that currently exists.

21. They try to influence the people of the nation to cooperate with the new system.

22. They try to make the people alienated from being educated in their own morality, ethics, and religion.

23. They try to make the people have no leisure time to ponder ideas and to follow their own professions.

24. They make the capitalists hate the workers and the workers hate the capitalists.

25. They make the people not have their own land for making their living.

26. They cause people to misunderstand and to lose awareness of the freedom they already have.

27. They try to make the people alienated from the truthful information provided by the government.

28. They try to make the people feel that they are not Thai and that their institutions are not important.

29. They try to make the people lack a sense of community and public responsibility.

30. They make the people feel that every Thai leader is not good enough to lead the nation to democracy.

31. They try to make people feel that in every case there is no justice.
32. They try to make Thai officials turn their backs on fulfilling regulations.
33. They try to make the people love the new system.
34. They try to prevent every commodity from reaching the hands of the people.
35. They try to make corruption in every sphere.
36. They try to make the system of work loose and inefficient.
37. They try to make the people feel that they, the people, are big and powerful without limitation.
38. They try to create confusion and disorder.
39. They try to make people sensitive to the class system.
40. They try to build up politicians who will support Communist ideology in Thailand.
41. They try to make people take addictive drugs as much as possible.
42. They try to make people love evil as much as possible [evil being to love gambling, whoring, drinking, taking drugs, etc.].
43. They try to make people have a sense of confidence in Mao, Ho Chi Minh, and Lenin.
44. They try to make the Thai people lose their sense of value of what it is to be a Thai.
45. They try to make the Thai people have faith in new values.
46. They try to make Thai students give less attention to their studies [and, by implication, spend more of their time organizing demonstrations and making speeches, etc.]
47. They try to make intellectuals—for example, teachers—have a sense of enthusiasm about democracy.
48. They try to make teachers bring the Communist system into education.
49. They try to alter and thus distort educational fundamentals—philosophy, psychology, history, social studies and technology—by changing them in new educational directions which represent pure communism.
50. They try to support movies, books, and newspapers which will be persuasive in every way and to the greatest possible extent give sympathy to the Communists.
51. They try to arouse people to hate everything that is Thai.

A Day in the Life of Pat

Introduction

If anti-Americanism was one of the major themes of Thai intellectual life during the early 1970s, its easiest target was the CIA. The CIA had two images in Thailand: to the majority of an indifferent public it was the harmless one of handsome James Bond characters making love to beautiful women and striking evil men dead. The other, held by the educated public, was the considerably more realistic one of large numbers of nameless men who, among other things, helped finance and train the Thai police since the early 1950s; supported and trained the Meo Army in Laos during the 1960s; financed and organized early anti-communist insurgent activities throughout Thailand's Northeast, North, and South; supported (unbeknownst to its editor and any of its contributors) Thailand's first general intellectual journal; and authored a bogus letter from supposed insurgents to the Thai government. The people who knew of these things were also aware of the CIA's activities in other countries of the world, and "CIA" became synonymous with *any* American activity of which the writer or speaker diapproved.

The following selection represents a somewhat novel, light, and obviously more sophisticated view of the nature of CIA activities in Thailand. The magazine in which it appeared, *Chaturat,* was until October 1976 the most professional and politically mature news weekly in the country.

The story refers to negotiations between the Thai and U.S. governments over the continued retention of U.S. military forces—particularly electronic specialists at the large Ramasuun spy facility in northern Thailand—after the March 20, 1976, deadline for the withdrawal of all American soldiers. The story was written before that deadline. On March 20, the U.S. government was presented with a gentle, but clear, ultimatum to leave, and four months later all but 270 U.S. soldiers

318

departed Thailand—more than a quarter of a century after they had first arrived.

The author is clearly a person who knows his facts. Although "Pat" is a fictional creation, "Hugh" is the real first name of the CIA Station Chief in Thailand at the time, and Hugh's car was a Mercedes, then the preferred car of men of wealth or power. The black license plate on Pat's less expensive Toyota is meant to suggest either that Pat is not sufficiently important to merit a white diplomatic license plate or that he is concealing his CIA affiliation. The phrase "Hugh can do it!" is an allusion to "We Can Do It!," the slogan of the Social Action Party, the party of the then prime minister of Thailand, M. R. Khukrit Pramoj. As with most continually repeated political slogans, the phrase became an object of approval for some but an object of laughter and derision for others. The phrase may have also been meant to suggest a mysterious relationship between the CIA and the Social Action Party, although it was actually the party's leader who expelled the U.S. military forces. The "third floor of the white building" on Wireless Road is known to house the offices of the CIA at the U.S. Embassy, and the "Thermae" is a well-known Bangkok massage parlor, believed to be patronized mainly by foreigners.

The piece also contains some distinctively Thai touches: the meteorological reference to the changing state of Thai-Chinese relations; the whirring computer at the embassy suggesting the computers at Ramasuun (which are never mentioned in the story); and, at the end, the Thai view of a lackey's absolute faith in the power and wisdom of his own boss.

For comments on the author, see the Introduction to "A Telephone Conversation the Night the Dogs Howled."

A Day in the Life of Pat

The weather this morning, along Wireless Road, is exceptionally cool, although the Thai Meteorological Bureau has already announced that the air currents from the cold zone in Mainland China had stopped their thrust of cold temperature into Thailand.

On the third floor of the white building, the humming sound of the code machine is still audible, and the small radar device on the roof under the white dome is revolving at the same angle as the communications satellite.

Yesterday, Pat spent a late night at the Thermae because Ustinov, a press correspondent from *Pravda,* had treated him to three bottles of brandy, which he had brought with him when he had moved to Thailand from the Soviet Embassy in India. Pat's personality, however, befits a CIA official in every respect. He had been phoned at four o'clock in the morning to prepare his transmission of special news to Washington. Since serving in Vietnam, he had become weary of the content of these cables. Here, in Thailand, it was no different. Nothing exciting. Thailand had become particularly boring since the arrival of the new ambassador from Laos. It was particularly aggravating to try to spell the names of those Thai politicians. At least when he was in Vietnam the names of those hundreds of Vietnamese politicians who had been bought off were spelled in an understandable alphabet. But the Thai names are almost impossible to change into English.

He could remember almost all the names of those Thai politicians who had already been bought off by the Agency. At least, he had worked out his own system for rendering these names into English. But a problem arose when another group of politicians whom the Agency knew threw that first group of people out of power. That was just over two years ago.

From *Chaturat* 2, no. 33 (February 24, 1976).

For him, the inability of Asian politicians to remain in power very long was one great pain. When he had been transferred to Wireless Road he had been told by Tom, the Agency's old communications officer, that it would be better than in Saigon. Tom said that the names of the politicians here are a bit more constant than those in Vietnam.

However, the news that he was to transmit today again made him feel rather peevish. What's this? He had spent so much time memorizing the names of the politicians the Agency had been buying these past two years and his report today suggested that, sooner or later, he would have to go through the process all over again. The Thai government had set up so many conditions for our continued stay in this country. Pat wasn't sure what the people on the third floor were doing, but he remembered that it was just last month that he had reported to Washington that "the person with whom we talked told us that there would not be any problems in our being able to continue to stay here." He wanted to shout out loud, "Why the hell don't you increase the payoff so I won't have to go through this whole damn thing again?" Although he wanted to shout, he knew no one would hear him because the room was not only sound-proof but had been constructed with walls that not even the microwaves from the Russian Embassy could penetrate. Pat got down to work seriously, reporting the long news in front of him. The humming noise of the code computer this morning resembled the mocking tone of an electronic machine which laughed at a person like him, saying: "You are different from me. You have to memorize and waste time. My potential is far greater than yours."

Pat drove out in his Toyota with the black licence plate, thinking that tonight he would see Ustinov at the Thermae and would tell him, for his own good, that he should know how difficult it is to get any power in Southeast Asia. The politicians here are just too capricious. No one can afford the high price of buying off these people. They never kept their promises. Ustinov, however, wants to build his own reputation and he probably would not listen.

Before Pat's car turned onto Ploenchit Road, he saw a black Mercedes turning into Wireless Road. He smiled for the first time since he had awakened. Seeing that Mercedes, he thought to himself: "Hugh can do it!" Alone in his car, he shouted out loud, "Hugh can do it!"

The Paradise of the President's Wife

Introduction

While the impact of the West on Thailand's economy and political and administrative institutions is now well documented (for varying views, see Caldwell 1971; Darling 1965 and 1978; Hanks 1952 and 1968; Ingram 1955; Lobe 1977; Riggs 1966; Siffin 1966; Vella 1955; Wilson 1970; Wyatt 1969), almost nothing is known about Western influence in such areas as philosophical speculation, aesthetic forms, or intellectual styles. The little that is known strongly suggests that although there has been some influence it has been of an unlikely, serendipitous nature, reflecting the idiosyncratic decisions of those introducing the foreign material.

Thus, the very first novel to be published in the Thai language was Thai neither in subject matter nor authorship but was a 1902 translation of a Victorian melodrama entitled *Vendetta* (in Thai *Khwaam Phayaabaat*) by a then important, but now forgotten and no longer published, English writer named Marie Corelli.[1] Sixty years later, Sulak Sivaraksa translated some of the writings of Plato, including those on Socrates, into Thai. Sulak has said that although he was fully aware that the Thai audience for such writings was very small, he made the translations available because he thought that "these great Western thinkers would stimulate us to think about and to value some of the great Siamese ideas that are found in Buddhism and in the Thai tradition." In recent years, Chitr Phoumisak's posthumously published *Chomnaa Sakdinaa Thai* [The face of Thai feudalism] has been widely hailed as the first, great Marxist analysis of Thai history. While the "greatness" of Chitr's effort was clearly a function of the timeliness of its 1974 publication and the fact that it was the first such analysis, Chitr's own understanding of Marxism was opaque in the extreme. Thus, in discussing the rise of capitalism in Thailand and in the West, Chitr speaks of Western capitalism following directly after the "medieval dark ages," simply by-passing five hundred years of Western history. (For another view on Chitr's Marxist scholarship, see Reynolds and Lysa 1983.)

The following poem by Suchart Sawadsii is a modern expression of this kind of intercultural confusion. The poem is presented here not in denigration of its aesthetic value but simply to document the occurrence of such confusion as an inevitable part of the process of cross-cultural communication. In fact, if one were to set aside the poem's implausible elements, it remains a poignant and extremely powerful statement of revulsion against the Vietnam War.

The work was published in 1973 when Richard Nixon was president of the United States, and the "President's Wife" of the title ostensibly refers to Pat Nixon. For Americans accustomed to perceiving Pat Nixon as a symbol of either the sexless or sexually deprived American woman, the inappropriateness of Suchart's imagery is obvious.[2] However, the problem here is really bicultural. Even if Suchart had been "correct" from an American point of view, his symbolism would have missed the mark from a Thai point of view.

We showed this poem to fifteen university-educated Thai of both sexes, and the universal response was perplexity. The perplexity derived not from the symbolism of Mrs. Nixon, about whom nothing was known or fantasized, but rather from the symbolism of sexual sadism. Some informants volunteered that they "had heard about such things" and that it is something that "appears sometimes in *farang* culture," but that it otherwise made no sense to them. In defense of the author, the majority observed that Suchart "must have been experimenting in the poem" or "he wanted to show how strange some *farang* were," but they had difficulty identifying the emotional basis of the author's point. The only part of the poem that was genuinely meaningful to all of them was the assumption that, once under the sheets, a wife had extraordinary power over all her husband's decisions.

For the vast majority of Thai, sex is perceived as simple, primitive fun. It is certainly true that it also has a multiplicity of secondary functions: the assertion of social rank, political power, interpersonal dominance, and male solidarity.[3] But nowhere in Thai culture can one find a recognizable association between the pleasures of sex and the perversions of violence. Even rape in Thailand tends to be a group matter (again, male solidarity) rather than the character disorder of an individual acting alone.

Thai culture is changing with extraordinary rapidity, and it is quite possible that what was previously unknown is now mused over, gossiped about, and even experimented with. The problem with the imagery of a poem like this is that it is impossible to judge whether the author is awakening a critical part of the Thai unconscious (as was the case of the "women's lib" issue in "Madame Lamhab") or whether he is simplying playing with an alien idea that is as ephemeral as all the other fads that pass through Bangkok.

There may be a deeper meaning to all of this. If poetry is viewed as, and in this instance actually is, a vehicle for the expression of the creative imagination—rather than merely as a conveyor of conventional meanings (intracultural or intercultural)—then Suchart's effort must be considered completely legitimate. Indeed, the distinguished literary scholar Harold Bloom has argued that advances in poetry, and presumably in thought, cannot take place without the willful and perverse distortion of historically prior meanings. He explicitly asserts that "Poetic Influence [in our case, the influence of one cultural tradition upon another] . . . always proceeds by a misreading of the prior poet, an act of creative correction that is actually and necessarily a misinterpretation" (Bloom 1973: 30). Thus, conventional American perceptions notwithstanding, who is to say that Suchart is *actually* wrong about Mrs. Nixon's sexual fantasies and their influence upon her husband and world history? In fact, to deny her the possibility of such fantasies is to deny her ultimate humanity. And who is also to say that in bringing all of this to the attention of a "naive" Thai audience Suchart is not simply trying to expose one of the critical repressions of the Thai experience?

Born shortly after World War II, Suchart was brought up in modest circumstances in Ayuthia Province in Thailand's Central Plain. He started to write seriously while attending Thammasat University and worked for several years on *Sangkhomsaat Parithat*. A poet, journalist, short-story writer, and editor, he has bloomed into one of the major figures of Thailand's literary world, in part through his own creative work and in part through his editorship of publications such as *The World of Books*. Although he reads English easily, he does not speak it comfortably, and thus, unlike some of his colleagues, he has not worked at developing liaisons with the international literary community. However, within Thailand he has achieved considerable influence as an intellectual pacesetter, continually experimenting with new literary styles, topics, and publications. He is married to the writer known by the pen name "Sri Daawruang," and they have one child.

NOTES

1. Corelli's importance derives from the fact that she was the favorite author of both Queen Victoria and Prime Minister Gladstone.

2. That Mrs. Nixon was indeed such a symbol in the American public's imagination is attested to by the genre of jokes concerning the Nixons' presumed sex life, one of the most famous of which is, "He gets into bed with his necktie on."

3. For examples of the first three, see "I Am a University Student," "Fishiness

in the Night," "The Wholesome Intention of *Khunnaaj* Saajbua," and "Madame Lamhab." The role of male solidarity is best demonstrated by the fact that Thai men almost always visit brothels in the company of other men, rather than by themselves. All these attributes also appear in the novels of 'Rong Wongsawaan, who is Thailand's most accomplished and sensitive author on the role of sex in human affairs. While violence appears repeatedly in 'Rong's writings—between pimps and prostitutes, seducer and seduced—it is always a violence of interpersonal dominance, never a violence that intrudes upon or confuses the physical pleasures of lovemaking.

The Paradise of the President's Wife

SUCHART SAWADSII

Do you remember?
You dreamed of seeing young Asian men when in your lust you were
    reaching climax
You dreamed of seeing the torn bodies of children lying in the middle of
    fields of rice
You heard the screaming, moaning sounds of the exploding bombs
    hurtling through the skies of the monsoon season
You listened to the sound of the bass *ranad*[1] playing in the funeral
    procession carrying the dead whose final breath had been fouled
    by chemicals.

Do you remember?
You reached your peak when you saw the tender rice seedlings being
    consumed by napalm
You closed your eyes in bliss when the bullets pierced into the bodies
    spurting blood in all directions
You kissed the lips of the tan warriors when they were writhing in their
    deaths
You embraced what was left of the corpses of the insignificant farmers.

Do you remember?
The woe you planted that was watered with the tears of mothers who
    lost their children
The gall and misery you so generously gave to the women who lost their
    husbands

From *Sanyaan: Siang Phya Sangkhom Maj* 1, no. 1 (October 1973).

1. The *ranad* is the Thai xylophone.

The water and ploughs that turned the Plain of Jars into a fishing pond
The rice seeds that you flung at the farmers so that they would fight
       among each other.

Do you remember?
You dreamed of seeing young Asian men
You lovingly embraced the phallus carrying you to paradise
From Washington D.C. to Hanoi.

"Scum of the Earth" and "Man and Buffalo"

Introduction

The following selections are the lyrics of two of the most popular Thai songs of the mid-1970s. They are presented here because of their social and historical interest, rather than their intellectual or aesthetic value. It is our sense that the cultural significance of both songs is much more a function of their accompanying music, their genres, and the manner in which they were presented to the public than it is of their lyrics per se. Nevertheless, because lyrics are frequently crystallizations of the cant and conventional wisdom of the period in which they are written, they can be telling social documents. In this instance, they convey a highly polarized vision of the nature of Thai society—which is of course precisely what their authors intended.

Of the two, "Scum of the Earth" *("Nak Phaeaendin")* had by far the greater impact upon the public.[1] It was written by a Thai Army major, Boonsong Hakritsuk, and was sung to a military march that was as compelling in Thai as perhaps Meredith Wilson's "Seventy-Six Trombones" is in English. It was originally played on the radio station operated by the army's armored forces but soon was heard constantly on virtually every radio station in the nation. As a cultural phenomenon it was probably second only to *"Phuujaj* Lii" (see the Introduction to "Headman Thuj") in its popularity among the general public, making it one of the two most frequently sung and hummed Thai songs of the past twenty years. While it is impossible to judge its significance as a rallying cry for rightist political mobilization, it clearly had some role in demonstrating to the general public how thoroughly grim even popular culture had become. Whereas a decade earlier *"Phuujaj* Lii" had merely poked fun at the naiveté of villagers or the pretensions of bureaucrats, *"Nak Phaeaendin"* was actually calling other Thai the equivalent of "scum of the earth."

On the other side of the political spectrum, "Man and Buffalo" is even more grim; it calls for the death of the bourgeois oppressors, although some might claim that its greater anger is perhaps justified. However, the total context of the song is very different from that of its right-wing counterpart. The words are reputed to be based on a poem by Chitr Phoumisak, but they were arranged as lyrics by Surachai Chanthimathorn for this song by the "Caravan Singers," the most popular of the numerous groups playing *dontrii phya chiiwid* ("music for life") or *phleeng phya chiiwid* ("songs for life") that emerged during the 1970s.

The *nakdontrii phya chiiwid* ("musicians for life") essentially created a new genre of Thai music. Integrating traditional Thai string instruments (the northern *syng* and the Central Plain *saw*) with the modern guitar and harmonica, and reworking some of the song patterns of traditional Thai folk music into a modern idiom, they sang of the social problems of farmers, the urban poor, and young people.[2] These themes of social protest were a dramatic departure from what for years had been the standard themes of Thai popular music—unrequited love, personal aspiration, and interpersonal misunderstanding—all of which they downgraded as the characteristic fare of bourgeois self-interest.

Dontrii phya chiiwid also differed from most popular music in the stirring and infectious qualities of its rhythms. Thus, however morose the lyrics of "Man and Buffalo" may seem in printed form, they are made to sound, in the company of their music, like a paean to the optimism and commitment of the peasantry. The exciting quality of the *phleeng phya chiiwid* "sound" made the music of the "Caravan Singers" among the bestselling of all tapes and records in the music markets of the nation's larger cities.

Yet, for all their popularity and their concern with social issues and even social mobilization, the *nakdontrii phya chiiwid* never produced a song that gained the kind of mass attention that was awarded to *"Nak Phaeaendin"*. This was a result of a number of factors: their inability to gain the support of any of the mass media; their unwillingness to address themes that appealed to Thai society as a whole (as contrasted to "oppressed" subsocietal groups); the simple fact that they were all young people and thus were seen as representing the limited interests of the young; and the parochial, often weird, nature of their rhetoric. This last trait is particularly apparent in "Man and Buffalo," where after some moving sentiments on the nobility of work and the trust that exists between the farmer and his buffalo, the verse is virtually violated by the howler, "the excess value of our labor." Thai colleagues say that this Marxist lyric has no musical purpose and aesthetically is as out of joint in the original Thai as it is in this translation.

NOTES

1. The title of the song (and of the refrain) in Thai, *"Nak Phaeaendin"*, means literally "burden on the realm" or "weight on the land." The title "Scum of the Earth" was assigned to the song by Thailand's English-language press. Language-sensitive bilingual Thai have said that in emotional overtones the translation "Scum of the Earth" is very much on target.

2. Some Thai have said that the *nakdontrii phya chiiwid* borrowed directly from the style and themes of Americans such as Bob Dylan and Crosby, Stills, Nash, and Young and that their greatest talent lay in their ability to synthesize these foreign elements with traditional Thai folk music. However, they were probably not aware that many of their American borrowings were themselves modern versions of traditional American folk music and thus that both they and the Americans were practicing parallel forms of a kind of "musical nativism."

"Scum of the Earth"

Scum of the Earth, Scum of the Earth
Scum of the Earth, Scum of the Earth
These are those who are the scum of the earth:

Whoever calls himself "Thai," whose body looks like that of a Thai, who
  lives in the shade of the Golden Bo tree of our royal land,
But who in his heart thinks always of destroying our realm.
Whoever sees Thai as slaves, who has contempt for the Thai race, Thai
  land,
But who earns his living by exploiting our resources, while reviling
  us as slaves.

(Refrain)

Whoever agitates the Thai people into disunity
Whoever mobilizes them into confusion and disorder
Whoever divides us into camps fighting each other
Whoever praises other nations but abuses our own
Whoever can be bought off to kill even a Thai,[1] and who curries the
  favor of other nations as if they were relatives.

(Refrain)

Although music and lyrics were freely distributed, this translation is based upon
the lyrics reprinted in *Khwaanryan* Magazine (June 14, 1976).

1. The logic of this grammar is meant to suggest that he who can be bought off
to kill a Thai is more despicable than he who can be bought off to kill someone of
another nationality.

Whoever sells himself and his nation
Whoever helps the enemy to destroy our Thai forces and prevents us
      from retaliating
Whoever lulls us as our enemies attack
Whoever thinks of doing evil to us and pushes us around
Whoever wants to do away with Thai traditions
Whoever supports the prejudice of dangerous doctrines and spreads them
      through our homeland.

(Refrain)

"Man and Buffalo"

Man tills the land with other men
Man tills the land with the buffalo
Man and buffalo have the depth of meaning that comes from their having
      worked together forever.
Happiness and fulfillment have come from this.

Let us go, all of us together
To carry guns and plants to the fields
Because of the poverty and sorrow we have borne for so long
That have reversed the flow of our tears
As we suffered in our hearts all hardship.
However anxious you are, do not be afraid.

These are the lyrics and music of death
For having had our manhood broken
By the bourgeoisie who, elevating themselves into a superior class, have
      devoured the excess value of our labor
Contemptuous of the peasant class
Reviling us as savages.
Truly and surely the oppressors will die.

From *Phleeng Phya Chiiwid* [Songs for life], by Caravan Singers (Bangkok: Bopit Press, 1975).

Oh! Temple, Temple of Bot!

Introduction

Of all the accounts and analyses of the October 1973 Student Revolution,[1] none has had as great a historical and cultural impact, or elicited as strong an emotional response, as the following poem by Suchit Wongthed. It was written on the morning of October 11, 1973, the second day of the five-day crisis, and was stimulated both by the author's sense of the momentous nature of the event and his anxiety over its impending violence.

Although the power of the poem derives from the timeliness of its publication on October 13, Suchit's incorporation of the title and two stanzas of one of the most beloved lullabys of the Ayuthian period gives the verse an aura of historical and sentimental reinforcement that is arresting in the extreme. Equally important, Suchit used the prosodic form of that eighteenth-century lullaby (the *bod hee klauaum* style), which further suggests its classical roots. In a very real sense, these historical allusions are meant to memorialize the Student Revolution as one of the great series of events of Thai history, equal in symbolic significance to the Bangrachan defense against the Burmese invasion of 1767 in which Ayuthia was destroyed. It is too early to tell whether the events of that week could ever take on such mythological significance, but at the time this was clearly the author's intent and the way the poem was received by many of those who read or heard it.

Suchit's resurrection of the *Khun* Thauaung theme has had continuous impact on the Thai imagination since 1973. After the coup d'etat of October 6, 1976, leftist students who had gone into the jungle (many of whom had earlier participated in the October 1973 events) began referring to each other and to potential recruits as "*Nok Khun* Thauaung." More recently, *Chaw Khun* Thauaung has become less politicized and aesthetically more generalized as the archetypical symbol of the young martyr in search of justice, goodness, and integrity. In fact, the haunting quality of the original line, *"Chaw Khun* Thauaung *paj plon"* ("my son *Khun* Thauaung, who has gone to strike the enemy") has made the phrase virtually synonymous with the condition of futile, unrequited human goodness—a condition where virtue is never only its own reward but rather where it always has karmic consequences for its perpetrator. The mere fact that these consequences may emerge in future lives and worlds makes it less an act of futility or martyrdom in the Western sense and more an act with its own ultimate cosmic justice.

Other elements of the poem are crafted with similar care. The narrator of the verse is the loving, succouring mother. The father is "also here and waits," but like almost all Thai fathers, his role is considerably more distant and passive than that of his wife. As the source of all sad lullabies (and *all* Thai lullabies are sad, mainly because sleep is the closest parallel to death and human helplessness), she also pleads with her son to hear her cries. Her cries are not intended to do anything, other than to express maternal care, commitment, and pride. *Khun* Thauaung himself is "a frail, slight figure," made that way "from many years of hard study"—a very different kind of hero from the bumptious, arrogant show-off that just five years earlier represented Suchit's version of the Thai undergraduate. (See "I Am a University Student.") However, it is this frail figure who feels such "loyalty" and "gratitude" toward his land that he will risk his life to defend its constitution.

This final reference is particularly telling because it demonstrates that for Suchit, if not the vast majority of students, the purpose of the events of that week, at least as of October 13, was the same as that of all earlier student political protests in Thailand: to defend the integrity of the constitution and not to create the circumstances for revolutionary social or political change. This is a very conservative conception and differs fundamentally from the more socially imaginative views of someone like Seksan Prasertkul, whose essay, "On the Thai Left," follows this selection.

NOTE

1. In English, the most frequently cited analyses are Heinze 1974, Prizzia and Sinsawasdi 1974 and Zimmerman 1974. In Thai, the essays are simply too numerous to cite, although probably the most intellectually elegant is the analysis by Saneh Chammarik, *Lakkaan, Sithi, Seriphaab Lang Patiwat Tula 2516* [Principles, rights, and freedoms after the Revolution of October 1973].

Oh! Temple, Temple of Bot!

SUCHIT WONGTHED

Oh! Temple, Temple of Bot![1]
With its seven palm trees.
Where is my son *Khun* Thauaung, who has gone to strike the enemy?
He is gone so long and is not yet returned home.

Packed some rice in palm leaf,
Punted my boat in search of him.
Rumors have spread
That my dear son *Khun* Thauaung has passed away.

Making my way by rickety bus
Travelling by train
The clickety-clack like cries of parrots calling[2]
"My son *Khun* Thauaung . . . My son *Khun* Thauaung."

You left our home
When day was dawning.
You paused, telling younger brothers and sisters
You would be gone for many days.

First published in *Thai Rath* Newspaper (Bangkok), October 13, 1973, and frequently reprinted.

1. In the original Thai, the title is "*Wat* Erj, *Wat* Bot!" which is meant to have emotive, rather than denotative, meaning.

2. In the original, this passage reads "*nok kaeaew, nok khun thauaung,*" meaning "green parrots and gold-beaked mynah birds." In Thai, the names of these two talking birds are more closely associated semantically than "sheep and goats" or "lions and tigers" are in English. Here, however, the name of the mynah bird is precisely the same as that of the hero. Thus, the parrot, while not in itself a critical symbol, is calling for his semantically inseparable mate.

Going to fight for freedom and for that which is ours
For the integrity of Bangrachan.[3]
Oh! My dear son! My singing bird!
You walked down and left our home.

You carried a shoulderbag slung across you
With the books you have read by moonlight[4]
And also your notebooks
That since last night were stained with tears.

My *Khun* Thauaung, you wept
In the house till late at night
Over the flowering *champee*s[5] that were struck by bullets
And strewn onto the River Chao Phrayaa.

Son! My lovely son!
Do not resist
Mother's cries.
Father is also here and waits, looking only for you.

You are not a warrior
Who carries the scars of his calling
You are only a frail, slight figure
From many years of hard study.

Mother knows that her dearest child
Has loyalty
And your father too knows
Of your gratitude to this land.

But what others know these things about you?
They who hear of you are not the Lord Indra
They are only ordinary people,
Human beings blinded by the influence of power.

You said you knew
So you turned to nonviolence in your struggle.
Mother and Father have since been waiting
So many days, so many days.

---

3. Name of a village whose inhabitants fought to the death against the Burmese during the destruction of Ayuthia in 1767.

4. After lanterns were extinguished and all others had gone to sleep.

5. Magnolias, symbols of flowering youth. However, because of the shape of the bud, also a clear symbol of bullets and thus of assertiveness and martial activity.

The *sannoo* flower blooms at dawn
Oh! The *katkaw* flower blooms at sunset[6]
At the end of Buddhist lent, we walk in search
At the glorious Monument of Democracy.

There is no trace of my dear *Khun* Thauaung
There, only the Constitution looms.
Mother and Father mourn our loss
But so proud of our dear son.

---

6. Both this and the preceding line are taken directly from a well-known folk song of love and fun.

On the Thai Left

Introduction

One of the more dramatic consequences of the 1973 Student Revolution was the explosion in the availability and popularity of Marxist writings, most of which had been banned during the preceding sixteen years. Almost overnight the major bookstores of Bangkok and the bookstalls in and around the Pramane Grounds near Thammasat University began to sell large numbers of Thai translations of the writings of Marx, Mao, Ho Chi Minh, Ché Guevara, and to a lesser extent Lenin and Trotsky. Posters, decals, and slogans of these Communist heroes were also widely exhibited.

For all of its visibility, the intellectual and cultural meaning of this Marxist florescence was never clear. Although some of the literature was undoubtedly read, some of it was also meant for sheer display. Thus, for many people simple possession of these books and pamphlets was almost a kind of radical chic, serving very much the same function as the "five *jauau*"—long hair, rumpled shirt, jeans, flip-flop rubber sandals, and shoulderbags made by Thailand's tribal peoples. All were symbolic markers either for asserting the wearer's freedom from the constraints of traditional Thai bourgeois values or his identification with his newly discovered proletarian commitments.

Because none of the authors of the Marxist literature was Thai, however, none of it addressed Thai issues in any kind of direct or focused way. Indeed, from the point of view of intellectual history, one of the most ironic aspects of the thirty-six month period between October 1973 and October 1976 was that, despite the outpouring of Marxist literature, there was virtually no writing on the nature, purposes, or premises of Thai Marxism. This is not to deny that Thai Marxists were also writing about Thailand, but their writings were more nihilistic than they were Marxist, focusing almost exclusively on the flaws of traditional Thai society and not on any vision of a Thai Marxist state or even how Thai-

339

land and Marxism might fit together. The writings by and comments on Chitr Phoumisak and Anud Aaphaaphirom, elsewhere in this volume, reveal these kinds of attitudes quite clearly.

In retrospect, there are several obvious, if partial, reasons for this apparent indifference: the recency and suddenness of the 1973 revolution caught them unprepared; whether planned or fortuitous, they decided to devote their energies to recruitment, mobilization, and social action (strikes, organizing farmers) rather than to thinking through ideological goals; the "hard-core" Marxists, the insurgents of the Communist Party of Thailand (CPT), had been so long dominated by Maoist doctrine and a Chinese world view that they could not see that their situation required something more distinctively Thai; and, with the possible exception of Chitr Phoumisak, whose vision of Thailand always focused on the past not on the future, none of the Marxist groups had ever developed any socially recognized intellectual leaders. It may well be that some of the Marxists decided on tactical grounds to defer the formulation of their ideological positions until they were more secure politically or militarily, although stylistically such a decision would not be in accord with usual Marxist practice. Events after October 1976 strongly suggest that, of all these reasons, the domination of alien Marxist views—Chinese, Vietnamese, even Khmer—was perhaps the critical factor in inhibiting the development of a Thai Marxist conception.

The following essay by Seksan Prasertkul is the only statement we could locate that is even vaguely suggestive of what a Thai approach to Marxism might have been during the 1973 to 1976 period. Whatever chord it might strike in a contemporary Western reader, it was for the period in which it was written a remarkable document. For one thing, it contains none of the rage and little of the cant that is usually associated with Marxist writings of those years. Cant is not totally absent: the identification of "Marxism" as "science" is one of those ritual phrasings for asserting the explanatory superiority of Marxist principles. But Seksan's use of such code words has none of the spirit of intellectual infallibility that accompanies most Marxist interpretation. On the contrary, the thrust of the essay is its plea for reflection, self-examination, and self-understanding.

Second, from the point of view of intellectual style, it is perhaps the most subtly and tightly argued essay in this volume. The author obviously enjoys analysis in its own right as a kind of mental exercise, and the style of his reasoning—his catholicity, his use of juxtaposition and contrast, his enumeration of the complexity of the issues—adds significantly to the impact of his message. Although his mode of exposition is by no means typically Thai, its suppleness is pleasurable to the Thai reader, if only because it is such an obvious exception to the formulaic format of most Marxist thinking.

Third, and more substantively, the essay is extraordinary in its concern with "spiritual values" and "mental considerations." Although this is perhaps the least lucid aspect of the piece, the mere fact that Seksan feels compelled to address the concepts of *winjaan* and *khunkhaathangcidcaj*, to assert their reality and to insist that they are not any less significant to Marxists than are "material things," makes the essay almost a subversion of traditional Marxist dogma. Almost equally subversive is his insistence that the "beauty" and "morality" of things be considered as important as their "scientific benefit."

Seksan does not attempt to justify his positions in this regard. However, one has the sense throughout the essay that he is primarily a Thai and secondarily a Marxist and that in any struggle between his dual identities the former will always be dominant. Thus, not even Marxist dogma can force him to relinquish his prior and more fundamental Thai Buddhist premises about the nature of human happiness and inner, "spiritual" experience. In a few places, these priorities are made quite explicit. The underlying theme here suggests a very different kind of Marxism than was espoused, for example, by someone like Chitr, who was revolted by religious concepts and "spiritual values."

Following from this, and perhaps most important, the essay is an attack against the tyranny of dogma and its symbols, including some of the then current symbols of "leftism" (hair, dress, speech styles). Very early in the argument he points out that the legitimacy of Marxism depends upon its "applicability . . . to the actual conditions of society," not to its "reasonableness" or "elegance of . . . logic" or its ability to "provide a ready-made formula. . . . " Later he attacks his peers for their ideological rigidity, moral arrogance, and intellectual superficiality. He is particularly exercised by those who have no historical perspective, who are incapable of comprehending that earlier generations had their own responsibilities and their own heroes, and who cannot see that all people must act in terms of their own historical contexts and not in terms of Platonic absolutes. There is one line in which he suggests that contemporary Marxists might become sufficiently "reactionary" as to try to obstruct the next generation from realizing the need for even further change when that time comes. Again, the whole time perspective here seems to be based not upon the Marxist conception of an alternating dialectic but rather upon the most basic notion of Thai Buddhism—that change is inherent, inexorable, and unending.

Seksan Prasertkul is one of the most well-known and controversial members of Thai society. However, as the preceding commentary suggests, he also resists facile identification. At various times he has been called "Thailand's Lenin," "the future Ho Chi Minh of Thailand," and more recently, "Siam's Trotsky." He is reported to be amused by such labels, if only because they are simultaneously so overinflated and so simple-minded. From his point of view, they also have little "applicability . . . to the actual conditions of society."

Born in 1949 in Chachoengsao Province in the Central Plain, he is the third of six children. His father was a fisherman and his mother a market vendor. His early education was at a village temple school, and later he attended secondary school in the town of Cholburi. In 1966 he became an American Field Service exchange student and spent a year in the United States living in Wisconsin. It was in the American Midwest where, in his own view, "my political education began." The Anti-Vietnam War Movement had just started, and he observed directly how moral outrage could be mobilized politically.

After his return to Thailand, he entered Thammasat University, where his intellectual talents were immediately recognized and where, along with a few other extraordinary students, he was enrolled in an experimental seminar in which the members were required to read political theory from primary sources, almost all in Western languages. He also became the public relations officer of the National Students Center of Thailand. It was in that capacity that in October 1973 he emerged as the principal leader and hero of the Student Revolution.

During the following year, he devoted most of his energies to public speaking and to mobilizing various student groups and was widely perceived as one of the most left-leaning members of the student leadership group. Although his public image was that of political activist rather than political thinker, he did manage to do some writing during this period, of which "On the Thai Left" is a good example.

After the right-wing reaction began to set in, he and his wife-to-be, Chiranaan, fled to Europe where they travelled and where he did some writing, mainly in English. Two of his efforts were translated and published in *Le Monde*.

Sometime after October 1976, the couple was known to have joined up with communist insurgent groups in Thailand's north, but almost immediately there were rumors of major differences between Seksan and the Maoist leadership of the insurgents, most of these differences focusing on the issue of what Thai Marxism ought to be. One of the major symbols of these differences was the fact, constantly noted, that Seksan never became a member of the CPT. While this status may have permitted him to maintain his intellectual independence, it also denied him any significant influence.

By fall 1980, he and Chiranaan had become so disenchanted with the CPT—with both their political vision and their failure to influence Thai villagers—that they returned with their young child to Bangkok where they asked to be left alone and permitted to resume their private lives. Thai governmental authorities accommodated these requests. Both Seksan and Chiranaan are presently enrolled in graduate programs at an American university.

On the Thai Left

SEKSAN PRASERTKUL

Whoever witnessed closely the bloody events of October must have realized that the vast majority of demonstrators were not secondary school
and university students but rather the general public. The reason why so
many people joined in the demonstration was not only because they
believed that Thailand should have a constitution or democracy, which
would thus make it the peer of most of the civilized nations of the world,
but also because they felt the repression, frustration, and misery of the
people that was produced by the exploiting and tyrannical politico-eco-
nomic system.

Under such circumstances, it is only natural that the ideas that developed after the October crisis were those that emphasized political
change. The publication of books on socialism, the scheduling of seminars and debates, the holding of exhibitions on the different problems
of the people were all significant indications that more and more of the
Thai people had begun to seek a new direction for their society and that
this new direction of change had to arise from the deepest roots of
society.

In this current of new thoughts, one school of thought inevitably
forced itself into awareness. This was Marxist Materialism, a school
whose teachings had long been forbidden in Thailand and which in the
future might be forbidden again, although nobody knows when. This
school of thought encompasses all leftist teachings, and those that spread
into Thailand took many forms, including the classical Marxism of
Marx and Engels, the thoughts of Lenin and Trotsky who were the
heroes of the Russian Revolution, the ideas of Mao Tse-tung, the present
leader of the People's Republic of China, down through the ideas of Ché
Guevara, the Latin American guerilla war fighter who died just a few
years ago.

From Seksan Prasertkul, *Iangkhaang Phrachaachon* [Taking the people's side]
(Bangkok: Saengchan Book Club, 1974).

Whatever their differences, all the forms of Marxism that entered the country had one thing in common, that is, they all looked at problems from the scientific point of view, considering the nature and scope of the situation and the dialectic law as the major principles in laying down the purpose and method of social change. Those who were interested in studying these ideas were generally the young intellectual writers and, inevitably, the progressive students who considered themselves the spearhead in the fight to protect the rights and liberties as well as the vested interests of the people.

The admission of foreign thoughts and ideas into Thai society should not be judged as something improper, particularly when it is obvious that contemporary Thailand needs change and change needs direction. If Thai society cannot provide the structure of thought necessary for dealing with contemporary problems, the acceptance of new thoughts from elsewhere should be considered legitimate. Those ideas that are in accord with conditions in society will flourish, while those that do not relate to reality will not prevail and will eventually wither away.

However, this does not mean that Marxist thought will provide a ready-made formula for dealing with the problems of our country, Thailand. The acceptance of these thoughts concerning the nature of social change depends not only upon their reasonableness and strength, or the elegance of their logic, but depends also upon their capacity to be understood by the public, to be genuinely accepted as social goals, and upon their applicability, both as principles and methods, to the actual conditions of society. It is certain that a large majority of the young leftists still lack both the experience and maturity that would enable them to proceed and to fulfill effectively the complex task that has been pointed to above. However, it is not too late—and the time is ripe—to start analyzing ourselves now.

Analysis

We shall start at the beginning, which is concerned with the scientific nature of Marxist thought. While Marxism does provide some basic philosophical guides, the important feature of Marxism is that it is a means of analyzing social problems that will help us gain a better insight into human beings and the evolution of human society. In times past, a large number of young leftists accepted Marxist thought as a metaphysical philosophy or as a new system of value judgments rather than using its scientific characteristics to diagnose problems or to plan action. Those people would use some of the phrases or some of the other elements of Marxist thought to create their own rigid standards or their own set of personal values and, using such criteria, would be quick to evaluate others on the basis of their thought, everyday speech, jobs, or even on the basis of their dress style. Those who deviated from the prescribed definition would immediately be branded "Idealists," "Rightist Reactionaries," or "Revisionists," depending upon the vocabulary that one could dig up to use for lashing out at others. Actually, such behavior is not very different from the behavior of the conservative rightist groups: it represents a way of thinking that views the world in advance as something fixed; it is insensitive to the fact that people exist in different circumstances; and it judges people merely on the basis of superficial appearances. It is something that is done without analysis and without research. For such persons, whoever acts differently is readily labelled as "an enemy to be treated unmercifully."

It is true that in the fight against the exploiting social system we have a definite enemy whom we must confront and defeat. But if we persist in labelling people in advance, we may not be able to distinguish between friends and foes. We might end up fighting even against those whose moral consciousness is on the people's side.[1] Some young leftists make a major error when they insult progressive thinkers and writers, slandering them as unrealistic reactionaries simply because they work under the capitalist system and do not express themselves in as violent a manner as their critics desire. How can we call this way of thinking "scientific thought"? It is a way of looking at people without considering their social development, without thoroughly analyzing beforehand the fact that during the dark age of dictatorship the very first thing that emerged was thought, and when this thought developed quantitatively and reached a certain level, it became action and defiant movement—all of these things having occurred in recent times. Those who fight today cannot claim that they are more important or fearless than their predecessors who ten years earlier fought only with their ideas. In each period of history the duties and responsibilities of people differ. Fighters of each generation might be considered metaphorically as levels of soil being laid into an abyss of vice that is eventually filled and disappears. Therefore, those who would trample upon earlier generations of thinkers cannot claim that they understand society from a scientific point of view. People like this who perceive the world solely from the point of view of their own limited personal experience are those who have reactionary characteristics and who would be ready to obstruct the next generation, which might realize the need for still further stages of change.

The scientific method of Marxist thought does not exist for the purpose of producing a set of personal values, but rather as a guide for

---

1. In the original Thai, the phrasing here is a clear allusion to the title of the collection in which this essay appears, *Iangkhaang Phrachaachon* [Taking the people's side], and is intended to reinforce Seksan's position that the critical issue is "people," not ideological categories.

analyzing and researching the relationship between man and society, so that we may gain understanding into the nature of the dynamics of behavior and various other phenomena in our country and thus be able to bring about a change that will promote social progress most efficiently. As is the case with other branches of scientific thought, one must utilize three steps in order to be a Marxist: learning, practice, and mastery. These things will permit self-examination and will insure that our thoughts will not drift from the roots of reality. On the other hand, if the majority of the Thai people still do not think in a way that is scientific and this nonscientific view influences their behavior, we who do think scientifically should deal with this as a condition that we must study and try to understand, not as a condition that we condemn.

At this point in the discussion, many people may argue that if we are to accept or assign importance to a nonscientific way of thinking, are we any better than those Idealists or Liberals who will accept just anything? What is the value of stressing the superiority of scientific thought? This kind of doubt involves a rather profound issue. All leftists should right from the beginning question themselves in such matters in order to make sure that they know what they are fighting for. The ultimate goal of Marxism touches upon human beings, human beings with lives and with souls.[2] Human beings are the only creatures that derive their happiness from society and who feel their happiness in that context. "Materialistic thought" does not mean that we attribute greater significance to material things than to mental or spiritual ones. Rather, it is a way of explaining the relationship between matters of the mind and the conditions of society. In fact, from the point of view of its physical character, the mind is really no different from any other part of a human being. When the mind has been stimulated and embellished by various influences, it creates its own system of thinking and feeling, including the way such feelings are expressed. The mind develops and later has the capacity to control the behavior patterns and actions of human beings in society, which means being able to determine material conditions and social conditions as well. Mental and other material factors have their own relationships and influence each other reciprocally. From this point of view, the mind is of great importance in establishing the value of the actions that man undertakes or the things that he touches. It is the mind that defines sorrow or happiness, the content or discontent that man experiences. Therefore, if our

---

2. The term that has been translated here as "souls" is *winjaan,* which refers to the psychobiological energy or motivational power with which human beings are born and which they carry through their cycles of reincarnation. It should be noted that the balance of this paragraph is as ambiguous in the original Thai as it is in this translation and, whatever its essential meaning, is intended as a reply to critics who argue that Marxist materialism ignores the spiritual and emotional dimensions of human beings.

ultimate goal is the happiness of mankind we must always take account of the mind operating in this manner. The fact that man touches the world and material things with his mind does not mean that the mind can alter or transform things as they actually are scientifically. The mind only performs the function of acknowledging the existence of things and of judging their value, and this of course is one of the things that most clearly identifies the nature of man. The point is that man admires things not only because he perceives the scientific benefit that may be derived from them but also because of their other qualities, such as their beauty, morality, or code of behavior.

A large number of young leftists are still confused about what are called "spiritual values" and "idealism."[3] They assume that they are the same things and that Marxists consider them to be repulsive and things to be eliminated. Unlike "spiritual values," "idealism" is not a common possession of human beings. "Idealism" represents merely another stream of thought which argues that the mind or cognition is something pure, independent of social conditions. Marxism is opposed to this school of thought because history has proven that it has come to serve as the instrument of the ruling class in imprisoning people in a morass of misery and bitterness out of which they dare not arise and fight. For example, Roman Catholic priests in ancient times used religious ideas as instruments to obtain for themselves wealth and veneration and to indoctrinate the people into accepting their existing state. It is certain, therefore, that the idealism involved in tyrannizing and exploiting people in society is something that we must fight to overcome. There are many examples of tyrannizing idealism in Thai society. An obvious illustration is the idealism of the class system of our feudal period.

There is another reason for Marxism's opposition to idealism. Marx saw the weaknesses in the views of the metaphysical philosophers of earlier generations who would tend to derive hypotheses from abstract values and who by constructing lengthy chains of cause and effect would create their own social systems, which in reality could never be put into practice. Furthermore, this form of idealism can create a dictatorial consciousness in certain instances. For example, the upholding of law and order or ethical codes without considering the sources of that law and other aspects of the social situation can result in the unjust use of the power of the state. The fact that street vendors are arrested or that farmers are accused and brought to trial by capitalists without the government taking steps to prevent such actions demonstrates very well how

---

3. The translation "spiritual values" comes close, but not quite, to the original Thai term *khunkhaathangcidcaj.* The latter pertains to the emotional nature of human beings and to a presumed inner goodness of the human heart. The term for "idealism," on the other hand, *khwaamkhidcidniyom,* is identical to the Occidental notion of a "Platonic absolute."

metaphysical idealism coincides with the basic class interests of the ruling groups of Thailand.

Therefore, it is now obvious that idealism and spiritual values are not the same things. The fact that we appreciate the importance of spiritual or mental considerations and that we accept the significance of man as a person does not mean that we favor a form of individualism that diminishes the importance of society. This entire explanation serves merely to clarify the humanitarian goals of the leftists. Certainly no leftist would dare to deny the importance of society. Thai society, as it is presently constituted, has the power to deprive us of those things that are of value to mankind, material or spiritual. Therefore, we have to change the system of social relationships and the structure of the society into something new, something that will result in the social order being a positive rather than a negative force and which will create conditions that will permit people to achieve their greatest happiness. When leftists oppose the search for personal happiness they first ought to distinguish between the kind of happiness that is not dangerous to society as a whole and the kind of happiness that is based upon the exploitation of others. We should not hypothesize in advance that personal happiness is always evil, because that would be equivalent to destroying the goals we have set for ourselves regarding human beings. The reason that we refrain from searching for our own personal happiness in many ways is because we have the duty of being the spearhead in changing our country. In addition to refraining from indulging in the kind of happiness that is based on immoral social activities (for example, consorting with prostitutes, organizing extravagant social affairs) we have also to refrain from certain types of happiness because of the nature of our struggle or because the movement's tactics and strategies require it (for example, avoiding wearing long hair in order to be able to get along with the population and being disciplined in our everyday life).

Finally, since we are now able to distinguish between idealism and spiritual values and know how to analyze problems scientifically, we should also make friends with those people who have a constructive approach to things, and we should regard it as an investment for further social change and improvement. For example, in Thai society we will find a large number of people who out of a sense of pity and empathy are ready to stand by those who are poor. These persons would be ready to be a supporting force in any struggle for the people. We have already seen evidence of this kind in the October struggle. Many military officials opposed the idea of attacking the students and the citizenry because it went against their own moral consciousness. At the same time, many people helped the university students, by providing moral and financial support, simply because they did not like the behavior of the corrupt and arrogant ruling group.

It is of extreme importance to gain understanding into the feelings and thoughts of human beings when we are establishing the strategy and tactics of the struggle. Such understanding not only helps to distinguish between friends and foes in order to establish a united front. Even more important from a leftist point of view, a view which assigns major significance to the people's efforts in bringing about change, is the fact that the state of their minds represents one of the fundamental conditions of society. We cannot expect the poor to understand and to agree automatically with our ideas. Rather, we must first adapt ourselves to them. No matter how personal or individualistic their thoughts may be, we must accept such ideas and find a way to communicate meaningfully in their language. Certainly, in climbing a mountain you have to begin at the foot of the mountain. In the same manner, change must begin with existing conditions. Since the events of October, many of the young leftists have tried to express their leftism in an open and ostentatious way, particularly in the way they have dressed and used language. Some have even gone so far as to advocate the taking over of state power and using violence in various forms, without considering time, place, and audience. Some have been adamant in being repulsive to those who do not have leftist ideas, regarding the latter as people not worthy to be talked with. At the same time they have limited their own communication to those who already agree with them in their own group. Such behavior can have highly negative effects upon the movement. It creates alarm among the people, driving them into a state of rejection. Furthermore, it may stir up the enemies of the movement to the point that they may decide to eliminate the left altogether, immediately and quickly, while the left is still weak. We should note that such attitudes are really not very different from those held by Idealists and Liberals who stress individualism and the value of people doing their own thing as major principles. They reject the necessity to adapt to existing social conditions, and thus preclude progress and movement. Furthermore, if we dwell only on the most superficial characteristics of leftism, we will be creating a weakness which will give the dictatorial group or the enemies of the people an easy opportunity to infiltrate and sabotage our movement. They would subvert the movement by making it seem acceptable and trustworthy solely on the basis of ornamental considerations.

In conclusion, it is obvious that the scientific thought of Marxism can be beneficial only if it is implemented. Since each human society has its own characteristics, it is important for us to study and to gain a good understanding of the nature of Thai society so that we are able to carry out our work effectively and make it coincide most fully with the desires of the people. Social change is, more or less, like a problem in mathematics. We may use the same formula to analyze problems and to find solutions to them. However, the solutions do not have to be the same in every case. Each solution depends upon the nature of each problem. Most certainly for Thailand, every change must grow out of the roots of Thai society and not those of China, Russia, Cuba, or Vietnam.

Marxist ideology arises out of a love of humanity and a faith and trust in people. However, in the current of prejudice that exists in contemporary Thai society, leftists must work extremely hard to prove their truthfulness and integrity to the people.

Chewing Out a Special Class

Introduction

The following essay by Anand Seenaakhan is included in this volume because of the quality of its language rather than the importance of its subject matter or the persuasiveness of its point of view. It represents a mode of discourse that one encounters frequently in Thailand but which is all but absent from our other selections. The others almost all aim at being aesthetically disciplined and polished, subtle, and often intellectually complex; too, the message is almost always more important than the author or his emotional state. Here, however, the point is very different. Instead of trying to be disciplined, the aim is to be unabashed, transparent, emotionally direct, even a bit uncontrolled. In fact, the intensity with which Anand asserts his point of view is considered to be just as important as the merit of that view. Further, the style recognizes and permits a high degree of cognitive discontinuity and scatter—ideas are flung all over the place.

One typically finds this mode of exposition in political speeches and public interviews, although it is by no means limited to those contexts. It is mainly a masculine, essentially macho, idiom, shared by military personalities, *nagleeng* (hoodlum-protectors), politicians, and others who wish to demonstrate that they are absolutely certain about their own beliefs and positions. There is no doubt that part of the demonstration of their certainty (which often is also theatrical) is the ease with which they toss off thoughts that are so obviously unclear, confusing, or illogical—as if to emphasize that they are above such matters. In recent times, the most celebrated exemplars of this idiom were General Prapart Charusathien and former interior minister Samak Sundaravej. However, the Western reader should not miss the point about the cultural meaning of this kind of communicative style: its effectiveness has little to do with the clarity or logic of its message but rather with the candor, self-confidence, and conviction of the author. In Thailand, and probably many other places on earth, a person's verbal forcefulness often has its own inherent validity.

The essay also contains numerous passages of genuine intellectual merit. Particularly telling is the author's application of traditional metaphors of Thai rhetoric: tall trees on level ground versus grass on the peaks of mountains; ghosts that try simultaneously to align the feet and heads of sleeping human beings; weaver birds caught in the hunter's net; corrupt officials as harrassing flies. That these flies should be harrassing livestock, as symbols of human beings, is a metaphor associated explicitly with Anand.

In other places Anand makes pointed use of some of the most valued aphorisms of the Thai world view, for example, the necessity to "take into consideration other factors and analyze all these things deeply and profoundly, examining their pros and cons, in order to construct a new approach. . . ." For many Thai, this is the only legitimate way to discover useful or truthful knowledge. In the very same sentence (and several other places in the text) an appeal is also made to the Thai appreciation of Thai uniqueness—"the only country that is unlike any other country in the world." This "chosen people" concept, while in no sense institutionalized and rarely made even obvious, is nevertheless a widely shared Thai notion about Thailand. It is an attribute of Siamese identity that is constantly stimulated as a source of pride, self-satisfaction, and patriotism.

Other portions of the text are more problematic. Thus, the extent to which Anand's view of the world reflects a more generalized Thai world view is dubious. For all the emphasis that Thai place on the continuities of nature and on man's links to other animals the central theme of Thai thought is man's special nature as a morally accountable creature. From this perspective, notions of competing species and survival of the fittest (or destruction of the least fit) are irrelevant. For most Thai, all creatures should and do live, and as a morally accountable creature, man has the additional responsibility of insuring their existence. Many reflective Thai would suggest that if, as a result of social and psychological changes, man's exploitation of the universe may now be characterized by methods that are "more cunning, tactful, secretive, and subtle," such qualities apply just as readily to acts of responsibility and benevolence as they do irresponsibility and malevolence. They are the qualities of being "civilized."

Anand Seenaakhan is both historically and symbolically one of the most provocative members of Thai society. A police officer for much of his adult life, he holds an M.A. in public administration from the University of Indiana and a certificate in "criminal investigation" from the University of Kentucky. During the early 1970s, he achieved considerable fame for the publication of two books, *A.T.R.: Antaraaj* and *Khon Nauauk Khauauk,* both of whose titles are plays on words. The first can be translated as "Police director-general: danger," and is an account of the corruption, malfeasance, and venality that Anand encountered in the Thai National Police Department. (*A.T.R.* can also be read as an abbreviation for *"aj tua raaj"* or "damn dangerous beast.") The title of the second might be translated as "The stabled nonconformist," and refers to a human being who is so alienated from his society, and who is also so enraged by the contradictions between its ideals and realities, that he feels like a corralled animal. This image is cited so frequently in Anand's writings that it has taken on some of the qualities of a logo.

As might be expected, Anand's attacks on his bureaucratic superiors eventually led to his discharge from the police department, allegedly for refusing to obey orders but for other professional flaws as well. Thus, as an officer with the rank of major, he was arrested for leading a police mob that ransacked the home of then prime minister M. R. Khukrit Pramoj during a political demonstration, although Anand claimed he was merely trying to calm the situation.

A.T.R. was published soon after the Student Revolution, and if his attacks against his own bureaucratic institution stimulated the ire of his superiors, they simultaneously made him an instant hero to thousands of people, particularly university students. For a brief period, leftist undergraduates thought of him as an ally and even called him "Thailand's Left-Wing Cop." However, as demonstrated in the accompanying essay, this was sheer wish-fulfillment on their part. Anand's political vision is, if anything, highly conservative. He condemns those who do not live their lives according to the traditional values of Thai society and is totally accepting of those values themselves.

Anand's most significant attribute, at least theatrically, is his heroism. This is expressed in his readiness to place himself in genuine danger (vis-à-vis his police supervisors, among others), to articulate thoughts that others are too fearful to express, and to voice these thoughts in an outrageous rhetoric. Soon after his termination from the police force, Anand helped found the Chanuan Anti-Corruption Movement. As the principal spokesman for this movement, he travelled from area to area giving speeches in which he condemned—by name and in great detail—the alleged corrupt activities of leading local businessmen, politicians, and government officials. This often led to violent confrontations between local henchmen and Anand's own bodyguards, including a few occasions when he was literally stoned out of town by local mobs.

In July 1976, Anand temporarily relinquished his efforts to reform the Thai polity and, leaving his wife and two children, entered the Buddhist monkhood where he suggested he would remain the rest of his life. While in the monkhood, he began a campaign of intense criticism against the kingdom's most learned monk. After leaving the monkhood he was arrested and has since been serving a prison term for *lèse majesté*.

Notwithstanding his eccentricities, Anand's position in Thai society is neither insignificant nor unique. He emerged at a time when actual historical circumstances—the Student Revolution and its massive expression of revulsion against official excess—reinforced his own vision of the flawed nature of Thai life. For all its outrageous qualities, his message had an impact on elements of even the educated public. He may have been confused, but he was also fearless and critical—qualities that many proper Thai might hesitate to exhibit themselves but which they quietly, perhaps even secretly, admire in others. His message also had a certain substantive appeal. Thus, however dubious it might be as a scientific statement or as an abstract moral principle, there is a peculiar persuasiveness to the notion (at least to some members of the Thai elite) that there may be a biological-evolutionary basis to the inequities of the traditional Thai social order.

At the same time, what Anand (and others playing similar symbolic roles) never realized is that even charisma is eventually routinized, that public appreciation is never self-sustaining, and that there comes a time when people must turn away from his kind of emotional intensity and toward things that are more familiar and stable—even with their customary warts. Like Seksan Prasertkul on the political left and Wattana Kiawimol on the far political right, Anand attracted a large following and eventually fell from public grace.

Chewing Out a Special Class

ANAND SEENAAKHAN

There are few words in Thai which the social reformists of the new generation use in their speech and writings as much as the word "class." It is a new word which reflects the political advancement of the user and which has an impressive meaning to the young radicals of the new generation.

The word "class" also has a variety of other applications, such as "class society," "class struggle," "class differences," "proletariat class," "middle class," "capitalist class," and "the exploiting class." Some people appreciate these terms, while others find them repulsive; and there are many who consider them incomprehensible. Even those who apply these words may themselves not understand them very clearly.

The "class theory" is a product of thought of the philosophers of various nationalities who contrived it out of the conditions of the places they were born, their own intelligence, and the psychological suffering they experienced as a result of unfair treatment and material deprivation.

In general, we all accept the fact that since the beginning of the historical record of mankind, our world has never known a period which has been free of human beings struggling with and exploiting each other. This struggle has undergone a process of development through time. Before the historical period, it was a personal, human struggle, without ideology, in which individuals fought selfishly for their own survival, and although those who were strong, large, and sturdily built had an advantage over their opponents, their victories were ultimately thwarted by younger generations as a result of the infirmities and facts of old age. This kind of personal struggle then changed to the type of struggle which

From Anand Seenaakhan, *Sawa Kaansygsaa* [Educational junk] (Bangkok: Privately published by Thai Mitr Thai Business Ltd., ca. 1975).

involved conflicts of benefits regarding nationality, religious doctrines, beliefs, and the search for ways and means to gain economic advantage over others.

According to the theories of Western social revolutionaries, the current period is the period of "class struggle," a hypothetical transitional stage between the end of feudalism and the beginning of capitalism [*sic*], and this struggle is moving forward toward socialism and finally communism.

The struggle between lords and slaves, landlords and tenants, the poor and the rich are all labelled by the revolutionaries of the new generation as the struggle between "feudalists, capitalists, and the proletariat," which is further specified as the struggle between "the exploiting class and the exploited class."

The revolutionaries who imported such theories have raised their own expectations and now indulge in the fantasy that one day in the near future, these struggles will come to an end with the victory of the proletariat. This will involve the annihilation of both the feudalists and the capitalists, leaving only one class in existence, the proletariat class.

Those idealists may have forgotten the fact that the proletariat who have had their victory must bear the responsibility for building their nation and for creating a new set of rules for governing—in order that balance and order in society are maintained.

To express it another way, liquid needs a container. Similarly, a society needs a group of planners to lay out the policies which will provide that society with a framework.

Therefore, change in a political system is not very different from a transfer of liquid into a vacuum. If the latter were the case, it would imply that society would disappear in the same manner as liquid.[1]

It is impossible for any society—in the past, present, or future—to be free of human beings persecuting each other or of differences in social and economic status. Analyses from various points of view will persuade us of this truth.

From the point of view of nature, no matter how high large trees stand above level ground, they are always lower than grasses that grow on the tops of mountains. According to the principles governing the nature of animals, larger fish nourish themselves by feeding on smaller fish, birds nourish themselves by feeding on insects, and stronger animals prey upon weaker ones. Human beings represent one type of animal, and, as animals in nature, they exploit and persecute others in the same ways as do other creatures. Their only difference lies in the fact that once humans became more civilized and more sensitive to feelings of shame, they

---

1. In the original Thai text, this analogy also turns back upon itself, that is, the analogy becomes the premise of the very argument it is meant to illustrate.

changed from brutal and violent ways of exploitation to methods that were more cunning, tactful, secretive, and subtle.[2]

From the point of view of religious doctrine, we all accept the fact that our good deeds in this lifetime will have positive and beneficial effects upon us, and that our evil actions will have negative effects. Religion places particular emphasis on the idea that man's past performances will determine his future; that those who have performed good deeds will be well rewarded with intellectual enlightenment and that those who have been industrious, perservering, and have earned their livings honestly and intelligently will be rewarded with high economic status. It is impossible to provide for the equal distribution of these things to everybody. Each person must accumulate his own good deeds during his lifetime. They are things which cannot be seized by struggle or by use of force.

From the point of view of economics or our interest in material things, it is evident that the natural resources that man has discovered and has used for his survival are decreasing in the same proportion that the world's population is increasing. Since supply cannot equal demand, people struggle against each other naturally, trying to take advantage of each other and to grasp as much as they can, not only for their own survival but for the survival of their families and friends as well.

In other words, from the religious and economic perspectives, and using one's own experiences as criteria, the point is clear that man's nature is to feel that "nothing is ever enough." Human beings have the passion of anger as well as the capacity for illusion, and pressured by limited amounts of natural resources they, therefore, try to take advantage of others, to seize what they desire, to annihilate those in possession of the materials they want, and finally to claim possession of such things as against the claims of others. The same applies to the case of the proletariat. With the annihilation of all other classes, they will finally turn to annihilating themselves.

From a social point of view, we find those who are virtuous and those who are evil-minded in every society. The behavior of those people have different consequences. Unintelligent people use their labor while the intelligent ones use their brains. Marx argued that the products resulting from the use of physical power and brain power must be equal. Those who are idle must be rewarded as equally as those who are industrious. The state must be able to arrange an efficient system of control. However, Marx may have forgotten the fact that the state machinery is, in fact, comprised of the people themselves, those who are diligent and idle

---

2. In Thailand this view of man is Brahmanic in origin, and precedes any influence that Hobbes or Darwin may have had. Its imagery suggests its derivation from concepts of statecraft expounded in the *Arthashastra,* the Sanskrit text on polity.

as well as ignorant and intelligent. Therefore, the problems of society are based upon the problem of having people of different qualities.

The "class trash" I have been referring to are not in the least aware of the fact that events in Russia, Cuba, Bolivia, or Chile all occurred in different manners, times, places, and environments. They all occurred entirely as a result of situations which were ripe in those places, every one of which is completely different from that of Thailand.

If we wish to make a comparison, we should think of some of the "class trash" who are particularly ambitious and unknowledgeable as actually being not too different from those ghosts who believe that they are able to keep the heads and toes of people who fall asleep on a temple pavilion always equal and aligned. Once these ghosts manage to get the heads of the people lined up, the feet go out of line; so then they pull the feet to get them in line; and when they look back, they see the heads are out of line again. These stupid, idiotic ghosts are never able to keep the heads and feet of those who are sleeping lined up all the time. Similarly, it is not possible to provide for the absolute equality of everybody in a society. However, it is possible to provide for order and discipline in a society by means of arranging people in groups in the same way as we would arrange people in a line, from low to high, or vice versa, in hierarchical order. Once the status gap of the people or groups of people is narrowed so that they are closer to each other, there would be very little difference. Consequently, persecution of each other would be more difficult, since each would have almost equal bargaining power.

If we would, on the contrary, bring those at the head and end of the line together or bring those with high and low potential together, the differences would be obvious and under such circumstances a great deal of persecution would obtain.

Therefore, in every society there must be a ruling class which will be responsible for maintaining order in that society, which will prevent the widening of the gap or the differences between people, and which will protect underdogs from being persecuted.

In some developing countries, especially Thailand, the government or its officials who should, in fact, be carrying out such duties, abuse their power by opening the channels for the capitalists to gain an upper hand over other groups in the society and they also use their positions to persecute and exploit others for their own personal benefit; instead of being the balancer which maintains justice in the society, they themselves make society more unbalanced.

There is only one ideal method for narrowing the gap between the classes—between government officials and the public and between capitalists and workers—and that is to eliminate all bad officials by every means available. These people, without any sense of humanitarianism, not only seek to grasp as much as they can for their own personal benefit and for the benefit of their followers, but they also allow themselves to become the instrument of the capitalists in their bloodsucking suppression of working people.

No matter which point of view one uses, one will not find equality resulting from the behavior patterns that are used by men in their societies. This lack of equality has created class differences in all stages of human history. The more differences there are in any society, the more oppression, persecution, and exploitation there will be.

In the same manner, the more exploitation there is in any society, the more imbalance is created and the less justice prevails. And under such circumstances, there is less tranquility.

Many people accept the idea that efforts to narrow the gap between classes will have only beneficial effects on society. However, such efforts must be implemented carefully, systematically, gradually, using the right knowledge, and must be done with courage, tolerance, and devotion. After the great changes of October 14–15, 1973, the orators and writers who took it upon themselves to become the social reformers of the new generation sprouted like mushrooms after a rain. They began the most outrageous verbal attacks against the ruling groups, ruthlessly, brutally, and unreasonably slandering the capitalists while, at the same time, instigating the workers to join forces and to oppose the existing conditions of society forcefully and violently. They did this on the basis of their belief that neither the tyrants nor the exploiting capitalists will be persuaded to relinquish the advantages that they have over others and will succumb only to the use of power and force.

These social reformers of the new generation are under the illusion that they are the scholarly authorities on class theory or, taking themselves seriously, that they are the heroes of the nation and thus are able to apply the entire original thoughts of Marx and Lenin, Ché Guevara, Ho Chi Minh, or Mao Tse-tung to Thai society, with the purpose of reforming Thai society. But they do this without studying our disciplines, traditions, culture, values, and beliefs, and the relevance of these alien thoughts to our situation. Also, they do not take into consideration other significant factors and analyze all these things deeply and profoundly, examining their pros and cons, in order to construct a new approach which would be appropriate to the conditions of the country, the only country that is unlike any other country in the world. Therefore, what these people have done has not only been unhelpful in narrowing the class gap in Thai society but has been responsible for widening the existing gap further. Thus, these social reformers, misguided by their own illusions, should be called "class trash."

Even though the group of corrupt officials that I have been discussing are decadent and a social waste, they are a tight, firmly established, and highly influential group. They are made up of people who share the benefits of wealth, status, position, and prestige, which are themselves the ultimate desires of human beings imbued with various passions and prejudices. Thus, this group of rotten government officials is no different from a swarm of flies that harass livestock. Should anyone try to eliminate them, they would react like mad dogs, biting everything in their way, no matter whom and no matter where.

Therefore, fearing that getting close to them will get one into trouble, no one pays any attention to them. Why should one pollute his hands with dirt and smell if it is not necessary? This, however, is an extremely selfish attitude.

Since no one dares to touch them, these evil flies, these mad dogs, have developed the illusion that they are a group of privileged people or saints, and they incessantly inflict greater evil on society. The more venal they become, the more followers they seek to help them cover up their venality. These people are another type of "class trash."

Everyone should know how to eliminate class trash. We should know it as well as we know how to get rid of ordinary garbage. In order to do it productively and effectively, we must cooperate continually, courageously, and devotedly and consider it to be part of our duties and responsibilities. We must not develop the attitude that we will each go our own way or show no concern on the grounds that it is none of our business.

However, since most of us have allowed ourselves to be so narrow-minded for such a long time—to the extent that some of us believe that our narrow personal worlds represent the entire world—most of us think that there is no need to struggle.

Some groups of people have been so overcome by their own narrow-mindedness that their minds have been virtually paralyzed. Pitifully, they have lost all strength to struggle even for their own survival in their own worlds.

Our struggle against the class trash is comparable to the plight of weaverbirds caught in a hunter's net. If we keep haggling with each other, refusing to cooperate or to take action, simply awaiting our death, all of us will be dominated by this class trash for generations and generations. However, if we cooperate, not even the hunter's trap nor this class trash can withstand our force.

If we accept the fact that the struggle of the working class cannot be won by their getting on their knees and folding their hands in supplication, we must accept the same fact in the struggle against the class trash.

Owing to the prestige and influence of our religion and His Majesty the King since ancient times and to the sacred spirits of the national heroes of October 14, 1973, may this "class trash" be in righteousness, gain moral consciousness, change their character, and make efforts to contribute to society instead of resorting to violent measures to solve crises, which would have negative results on all sides.

Are you ready to begin now? For us, our struggle has been going on since. . . .

October 14, 1973

5

The Search for the Good Life

The Quality of Life of a Southeast Asian
A Chain Letter

The Quality of Life of a Southeast Asian
and A Chain Letter

Introduction

These last two statements are the result of the editor's search for a particular kind of material—how Thai thinkers conceptualize the nature of the
"good life" and what they reasonably expect of themselves and of their
society. Although there is clearly some concern for these matters (mainly
as specific goals, unstated premises, and asides), that concern has not yet
been institutionalized into a literature of aspiration and self-assessment.
As most of the preceding selections demonstrate, the thrust of the Thai
literary effort is toward criticizing (and to a lesser extent, approving)
what is rather than toward formulating a conception of what might be
reasonably sought for or attained. Certain modes or genres of "hope"
that are obvious in the West simply play no role in the Siamese intellectual context. Thus, there is no established commencement rhetoric or
visionary oratory (Martin Luther King, Jr.'s, "I Have a Dream"), utopian
literature (Samuel Butler's *Erewhon,* Edward Bellamy's *Looking Backward 2000–1887,* B. F. Skinner's *Walden Two,* Charles Reich's *Greening
of America*), or futurology (the writings of such people as Herman Kahn
or Buckminster Fuller).[1]

There are good cultural reasons for this. Thai colleagues with whom
the matter has been discussed say that any cataloguing of the "good life"
would be viewed as intellectually pretentious, as something to be undertaken only by the genuinely learned or the outrageously bold.[2] Related to
this is the more specific notion that any concern with the future suggests
an interest in what is inherently unknown, and thus inherently supernatural, and to that extent requires that the author have some special ritual
talent or be willing to take some risks. (The curse that appears at the end
of the second selection partakes of this kind of reasoning.) In contrast to
this type of explanation is the suggestion that any specification of the
"good life" would have to be virtually axiomatic to be persuasive, focus-

ing on things that everybody already agrees are desirable, such as health, wealth, security, and so on. And still different from these reasons is the idea that concern with a future "good life" is out of phase with fatalistic Buddhist premises about the inherent nature of the human condition.

Despite the cogency of these arguments, the search turned up a few items that do convey a conception of what the good Thai life might be. However, given the contexts from which they arise, they should not be considered either consensual or representative statements of "a Thai point of view." Also, the fact that they reflect socioeconomic and political interests—rather than philosophical, aesthetic, or psychological ones—is completely a function of Thai intellectual reality rather than of the mode of selection.

"The Quality of Life of a Southeast Asian," by Puey Ungphakorn, was originally written in the mid-1960s as an appendix to a document entitled "Thoughts on Southeast Asia's Development for 1980." Written in English for an international audience, it was meant to serve as a ratio-nale for some of Thailand's newly implemented development activities. (That the intended audience was non-Thai is suggested by the fact that the original subtitle speaks of "A Chronicle of Hope from Womb to Tomb," not from "Womb to Crematorium," and the essay contains no statement about preferring cremation to burial.) In 1976, several years after the "development era" had actually been in place—but also after most of his earlier hopes had still not been fulfilled—the author rewrote the statement in Thai as part of a professional biography he had prepared in celebration of his sixtieth birthday.[3] That it should be reissued on this occasion, and for the first time in Thai, is clear indication that at least for the author it represented unfinished business of the highest order. The rendition here is a synthesis of the two versions.

The essay is vintage Puey Ungphakorn, combining an infinity of aspi-ration ("so that I can have access to the intellectual and technical knowl-edge of all mankind") with the most down-to-earth practicalities ("let them cremate, not bury, me, so that others will have land to live on"). Although much of its content emerges out of the author's experience as governor of the Bank of Thailand (1959–1971) and director of the Bud-get Bureau during the early years of the Sarit regime (1958–1960), it is in fact a highly personal statement which in many details is at variance with the priorities of the governments he served. None of those regimes ever concerned itself with worker participation in the organization or deci-sions of the factories that employed them or with the question of equal opportunity between the sexes. While the essay focuses on some things that have been long known but recently lost (clean air and water, urban greenery)[4], there are also other things that would be totally novel in the Thai experience (social security and survivor benefits, estate taxes). Puey's concern with the latter is particularly poignant because it was his advocacy of just these kinds of social policies—policies that have been central features of Western capitalism for almost half a century—that ultimately lead to the extreme right accusing him of being a Communist and to his departure from Thailand and public life.

It should also be pointed out that not all of Puey's aspirations have gone unfulfilled. In 1970, the Thai government finally made family planning official government policy and semi-free medical services have also become a firmly established feature of Thai rural life.

The second piece is of an entirely different nature. It came through the mail in December 1975 as an unsigned, mimeographed letter. Because the phenomenon of the chain letter is both recent and rare in Thailand, it is difficult to pinpoint the psychological impact of a statement like this. Thai who know about chain letters say that they are used mainly to propagate religious messages, sometimes also asking for donations, and this sacred association would not be lost upon a reader. The purposes such letters serve in the West—get-rich-quick schemes, political propaganda, accumulating valuables like reprints and premium stamps (see Dundes 1966 and Dundes and Pagter 1975)—are apparently unknown to most Thai, although this letter is certainly an attempt to experiment with the form as a political message.

In its secrecy, however, this chain letter is reminiscent of a traditional Thai form, the *bad sonthee,* or unsigned "surprise card," which for centuries Thai have left with one another to express their secret displeasure with the addressee's behavior and to urge him or her to shape up. Although to include a curse at the end, as the letter does, is extremely rare (if only because most authors of a curse are aware they are simultaneously inviting retaliation), it is the single element of the letter that most impresses and worries Thai readers. It is the *possibility* that one might be a traitor or that one might be interested only in one's own survival—and thus always the object of the author's potential wrath—that gives the letter a certain indeterminate power; that it is written in a clear and civil manner also contributes to its legitimacy. On the other hand, since the author of the curse is unknown, and his credibility uncertain, it is unclear whether one should take the threat too seriously. Ultimately, the matter must remain unsettled, but also unsettling—which is precisely what was intended.

From our point of view, the most interesting feature of the letter is that it conceives of the good Thai life as a straight and narrow version of the way Thai society already is. The notion is that through a blood, sweat, and tears kind of conservatism, plus a dedicated attentiveness to any conceivable expression of communist subversion, the realities of Thai society can be transformed into an ideal Thai society—although admittedly the only feature defining the latter is that it is a place where people do what they are supposed to do. Perhaps the letter's most intriguing element is the spirit of self-denial that runs through it. It repeatedly asks that Thai relinquish their traditional hedonism ("Avoid preoccupation with temptations or with places of entertainment") and opportunism (by rejecting the Sunthorn Phuu ethic that survival is the greatest good) and replace them with an ethic of national unity and mutual cooperation and assistance ("Be willing, at all times, to sacrifice personal happiness to the common good"). It even utilizes the Puey Ungphakornian notion of "ful-filling your duty of paying taxes so that it may . . . be used to promote further development for the benefit of all your countrymen," indicating that the principal audience for the letter is the upper-middle-class and upper-class members of Thai society who are supposed to pay the bulk of such taxes.

What is intriguing about these sentiments is that while on their face they seem obvious and even banal, they are seen by the author as requiring a secret document, reinforced by a ritual curse, as their vehicle of expression. While this may be simply another expression of Thai polit-ical theatrics, it is much more likely a manifestation of the deep anxiety that many Thai feel, or believe that their compatriots must be made to feel, about the state of their nation in the modern world.

NOTES

1. Several related issues should be noted. First, if there is no significant "uto-pian literature," neither is there a literature of anxiety about the future (e.g., equivalents of Orwell, Aldous Huxley, Alvin Toffler, and the like), although the Thai world does abound with magico-religious predictions, both positive and negative, large and small. Perhaps the most famous of these is the prophecy attributed to Rama I (c. 1800) predicting only ten monarchs of the Chakri dynasty and several specific events whose symbolism could easily be interpreted as having actually occurred, e.g., the prediction of the appearance of "white birds" during the current era being the American airmen who flew from Thailand during the Vietnam War (see Morell and Samudavanija 1981:309). Second, if there are few codifications of the "good life" there is certainly a rich magico-reli-gious literature on the tactics to be used to obtain those things in life whose "goodness" is completely self-evident, such as money, status, wealth, love, viril-ity, beauty, respect, and the like. In this respect, it is probably not fortuitous that the best-selling trade book in the history of Thailand is Dale Carnegie's *How to Win Friends and Influence People,* available in at least nine different translations. All such literature, of course, assumes the validity of the prevailing value system and focuses mainly on getting more of the same. By the same token it is inherently unreflective and nonanalytic about its own premises. This literature also relates to the rich *mauau duu* complex (seer or shaman, including *luang phauau,* or monks with supernatural powers; see "A Telephone Conversation the Night the Dogs Howled") that plays such a central role in Thai life. Third, a sufficient num-ber of Thai readers are interested in the future to be able to maintain a small, but vigorous, genre of science fiction writing, some of which is borrowed directly from the West and Japan. This interest is also fed by TV movies and cartoons, some of the most popular of which concern interplanetary travel.

2. The line between these two qualities is by no means fixed, its location being a function of the public personality projected by an individual. For certain persons there are no problems. Whatever the real truth, Thai consensus would define Puey Ungphakorn as more learned than bold, M. R. Khukrit Pramoj as learned and bold in equal amounts (although probably more "clever" than either learned or bold), and Sulak Sivaraksa as perhaps more bold than learned, mainly because of his comparative youth. But for other individuals, the public definition is more ambiguous. Among the contributors to this volume, a person like Anand Seenakhan is seen by many as a figure of genuine admiration (because of his courage, dedication, and even his capacity to earn a foreign degree) and by others as a figure of derision (for being so bombastic and unrealistic).

3. Although the annual celebration of birthdays is a borrowing from the West, those marking the end of a twelve-year lunar cycle have always been considered important. Among these, the celebration of the beginning of the fifth cycle is perhaps the most significant and personally satisfying in the life of an adult male. At the age of sixty a man is still sufficiently close to his prime for his accomplishments to be remembered and honored realistically, and yet he is sufficiently old for all to begin to think about his legacy to future generations. The celebration of the sixth cycle is also significant, but by the time a man reaches seventy-two, his accomplishments have become more mythical and his legacy has become the primary basis for judging him.

4. The disappearance of Bangkok's trees, malls, and public lawns since the end of World War II is one of the great Thai tragedies of the twentieth century. It has been made even more painful by the fact that because there had always been so much greenery in the capital it was never considered necessary to preserve large areas for public parks. The result is that at the present time Bangkok has fewer public park areas than any other major city of the tropical world.

The Quality of Life of a Southeast Asian

PUEY UNGPHAKORN

A Chronicle of Hope from Womb to Crematorium

While in my mother's womb, I want to have good nutrition and access to maternal and child welfare care.

I do not want to have as many brothers and sisters as my parents had, and I do not want my mother to have another child too soon after me.

I do not care whether my parents are formally married, but I want them to live together in reasonable harmony and to be caring toward their children.

I want good nutrition for my mother and myself during the first few years of my life when my brain is developing and when my future mental and physical capacity is determined.

I—and my sisters, too—want to go to school to obtain the knowledge to earn a living and to learn about some of the good things of life. If I have the aptitude for higher education, I should have the opportunity to pursue that course, irrespective of whether my parents are rich or poor or from the city or village.

When I leave school I want a meaningful job, one in which I can feel the satisfaction of making a contribution to society.

I want to live in a society in which there is law and order, and where I will not be molested or threatened.

I want my country to relate effectively and equitably to the outside world, so that I can have access to the intellectual and technical knowledge of all mankind, as well as to foreign capital, which can be used for the common good.

Adapted from Puey Ungphakorn, *Best Wishes for Asia* (1975), and *Liaw Lang Lae Naa* [Looking backward, looking forward] (Bangkok: Klett Thai Publications, 1976).

368

I would like my country to get a fair price abroad for the products that I and my fellow citizens create.

As a farmer, I would like to have my own plot of land and a system which would give me access to credit, to new agricultural technologies, to markets, and to fair prices for my products.

As a worker, I would like to have some share, some sense of participation in the factory or company in which I work.

As a human being, I would like to be able to read inexpensive newspapers and paperback books and also be able to listen to radio and television (without too much interruption from the advertisements).

I want to enjoy good health and sanitation, and I expect the government to provide free immunizations and other preventative medical services, as well as good, inexpensive, and readily available curative services.

I must have some leisure time to spend with my family, and access to green parks, and to be able to participate in or enjoy the arts, and to attend traditional social and religious festivals.

I want clean air to breathe and pure water to drink.

I want to be able to join with others in cooperatives, clubs, or unions so that I will be able to help others, and they help me, in things that each of us cannot do by ourselves or cannot do well.

All the things I have asked for above, I do not want free. I shall be pleased to pay the taxes that I owe according to my means.

I want the opportunity to participate in the society around me and to be able to shape the decisions of the economic and social as well as the political institutions that affect my life and the fate of my country.

My wife wants the same opportunities as I do, and both of us want access to the knowledge and means of family planning.

In our old age, my wife and I expect some form of social security to which we have contributed all along.

When I die, I hope it is not a futile death, such as in a war that was started by someone else, a civil war, a car accident, by air or water pollution, or as a result of political poisoning.

When I die, and if I happen to have some wealth remaining, I would like an adequate amount to be kept for my wife and any of my children who are still young, but the rest should be spent by the government to make it possible for others to enjoy life, too.

When I am dead, let them cremate, not bury, me, so that others will have land to live on and to make a living. Let there be no elaborate funeral ceremonies.

This is what life is all about, and what development should seek to achieve for all.

A Chain Letter

Dear Thai patriot,

This letter is sent to all Thai patriots who are determined to take a stand against our enemies and to fight in defense of our beloved nation, so that it will not come under foreign domination. When you receive this letter, please send at least ten copies of it to your friends and relatives within seven days. As a Thai citizen, you will be proud that you have performed this duty, as small as it is, to help preserve the independence and maintain the survival of the nation.

As we are now aware, the Communists are pushing forward their infiltration of the Thai nation by manipulating the people and using them as their political instrument. This is the same procedure they successfully used in our neighboring countries, until finally, after inflicting much grief and sorrow, beyond which words cannot express, the reins of power were taken over by foreign forces. Unfortunately, it is now already too late to remedy this situation. Our nation has maintained our independence for over seven hundred years. If we, Thai people, do not unite in the defense of our nation, we will undoubtedly lose it in the same way as our neighboring countries. Thailand belongs to the people of the whole nation. It is, therefore, our duty to fight by legitimate means for our survival and the existence of our nation. If you regard this as the duty and responsibility of only the government, and none of your own concern, it would be disastrous for yourself as well as for the nation. Thai patriots! Let us now wake up! Unite and cooperate with each other appropriately in order to defend our nation, religion, monarchy, and freedom in the following ways:

1. Pursue a simple and nonextravagant life. Avoid preoccupation with temptations or with places of entertainment. Be hard-working, industri-

---

Author, source, and distribution unknown.

ous, and earn an honest living. Be just, noncorrupt, and avoid exploitation of others in undertaking any kind of business.

2. For those who are government officials, respect and conform to the regulations of the Civil Service. Perform your duties effectively. Do not take advantage of your official position, either in material things or in time. Be willing, at all times, to sacrifice personal happiness to the common good. Do not harass citizens and do not be arrogant.

3. Treat people of all classes with equality. Give assistance and support to the poor and encourage them to help themselves. Help to reduce the gap between the rich and the poor by fulfilling your duty of paying taxes so that it may, in turn, be used to promote further development for the benefit of all your countrymen.

4. In every way possible, condemn publicly those who are evil and support those who are virtuous. Express your opinion condemning any obvious corruption so that the government may impose punishment upon those who are responsible for it.

5. Make observations of the actions and behavior of organizations and people who seek to undermine and subvert the security of the nation. Reveal their actions and make it known to the public through the mass media, letter writing, propaganda leaflets, and by word of mouth, so that the Thai people will not be lured into their enemy's trap. If you keep what you know to yourself or show apathy to the situation or follow the proverb, "To know how to survive is the greatest good,"[1] you would only be giving way to the minority of the people who have the malicious purpose of sabotaging the nation. Let us, the majority who love our country, who want to see Thailand free from the danger of communism, wake up and have a say in the maintenance of our nation's independence.

6. Do not fear the rumor that says that Thailand has no chance of surviving. Let us unify our efforts and our force in order to fight the Communists who seek to destroy our nation. If the Thai people will only cooperate with and assist one another, even to a small extent, Thailand will be able to maintain her independence. We must not forget that Thailand has never been under any foreign power's domination and we will not allow that to happen, not in the near or even the far future.

7. Do not give support to the Communist forces and do not vote for the Communist Party and the left-wing parties. Do not fall into the trap of believing that the Communist system is an ideal system. In reality, that

---

1. This is one of the most famous lines of Thai literature. From Sunthorn Phuu's early nineteenth-century classic, *Phra Aphajmanii,* it was part of the advice that a teacher-hermit gave *Phra* Aphajmanii's son after the latter was deceived and had almost died. Over the years, the phrase has almost always been used in an approving way, although in recent years, as suggested here, some Thai have come to consider the advice to be subversive. See also nn. 9 and 10 in *Naaj Aphajmanii.*

system is only a fraud. (From my own experience) I discovered that the people in the Communist countries (the common people) are forced to work like machines and are left with no element of their humanity. They are deprived of all rights and liberties while those in leadership positions gain the upper hand and simply give orders. Do not let yourself be lured by Communist or leftist propaganda, which receives support from foreign nations that seek the power to rule our country (and to install Communist or leftist leaders).

Let this patriotic message help unite the Thai people in our efforts to maintain the independence of our nation. As it was expressed in the words of His Majesty the King, New Year's Day 1976:

"WE FIGHT"

The ancestors of Thailand
Sacrificed their blood and flesh.
So that descendants of the future
Thailand must exist in the future,
Despite threats of massacre,
Fight here! Fight here! Fight till
  our last drop of blood
We must defend our nation
We will uphold our honor and national
  integrity.

Defended the nation, and
We therefore must pursue our duty
Will have a land upon which to live.
Allow no one to destroy it.
We will fight and refuse escape.
Fight till the last survivor.

Traitors! Come! Fight with us!
We will fight and will not withdraw,
  not one step back.[2]

Best wishes to those who forward copies of this letter to their friends. May you and your family have a long, prosperous, and progressive life, free of all ailments. However, if among those who receive this letter there are traitors who betray the nation, religion, king, and people, and who flee in search of only their own survival, let them be cursed, and let them and their families never find a prosperous and progressive life. Let them deserve all the evil that will befall them for the rest of their lives for having inflicted disaster upon their fellow countrymen, their religion, and king.

From
"The Thai Patriots"

---

2. As in the original Thai, this poem should be read across, not down.

Bibliography

Anderson, Benedict R. O'G.
  1977 "Withdrawal Symptoms: Social and Cultural Aspects of the October 6 Coup." *Bulletin for Concerned Asian Scholars* 9 (3): 13–30.

Attagara, Kingkeo
  1961 "The Ramayana Epic in Thailand and Southeast Asia." *Journal of the Assam Research Society* 15:3–21.

Attagara, Kingkeo, ed.
  1976 *Khati Chon Withayaa* [Folk wisdom]. Documents in Didactic Parables, No. 184. Bangkok: Kromakaanfoeoekhatkhruu.

Bantock, G. H.
  1966 *The Implications of Literacy.* Leicester: Leicester University Press.

Barry, Jean
  1967 *Thai Students in the United States: A Study in Attitude Change.* Cornell Thailand Project Interim Report Series No. 11, Data Paper No. 66. Ithaca: Southeast Asia Program, Cornell University.

Becker, Alton L.
  1979 "Text Building, Epistemology, and Aesthetics in Javanese Shadow Theatre." In *The Imagination of Reality: Essays in Southeast Asian Coherence Systems,* ed. A. L. Becker and Aram A. Yengoyan, pp. 211–243. Norwood, NJ: Ablex Publishing Corp.

Bellamy, Edward
  1888 *Looking Backward 2000–1887.* New York: Modern Library.

Berreman, Gerald D.
  1966 "Anemic and Emetic Analyses in Social Anthropology." *American Anthropologist* 68 (2): 346–354.

Bilmes, Jack
  1975 "Misinformation and Ambiguity in Verbal Interaction: A Northern Thai Example." *International Journal of the Sociology of Language* 5:63–75.
  1976 "Rules and Rhetoric: Negotiating the Social Order in a Thai Village." *Journal of Anthropological Research* 32 (1): 44–57.

Bloom, Harold
1973 *The Anxiety of Influence: A Theory of Poetry.* New York: Oxford University Press.

Boon, James A.
1977 *The Anthropological Romance of Bali, 1597–1972: Dynamic Perspectives in Marriage and Caste, Politics and Religion.* Cambridge: Cambridge University Press.

Boonlue, M. L.
1972 *Surat Naari.* Bangkok: Phrae Phitthaya.

Brown, J. Marvin, ed.
1974 *Small Talk. A.U.A. Language Center Thai Course, Book A.* Prepared by Adrian S. Palmer with the assistance of Sasi Jungsatitkul. Bangkok: American Universities Association Language Center.

Brown, J. Marvin
1976 "Dead Consonants or Dead Tones?" In *Tai Linguistics in Honor of Fang Kuei Li,* ed. Thomas W. Gething, Jimmy G. Harris, and Pranee Kullavanijaya. Bangkok: Chulalongkorn University Press.

Butler, Samuel
[1872]
1976 *Erewhon.* London: Penguin Books.

Cadet, J. M.
1971 *The Ramakien: The Thai Epic.* Tokyo and Palo Alto: Kodansha International.

Caldwell, J. Alexander
1974 *American Economic Aid to Thailand.* Lexington, MA: Lexington Books.

Caulfield, Genevieve
1961 *Three Thai Tales: The Loyal Boatman and the King, Love Conquers All, A Reconciliation.* Bangkok: Progress Bookstore.

Chaloemtiarana, Thak
1979 *Thailand: The Politics of Despotic Paternalism.* Bangkok: Social Science Association of Thailand.

Chammarik, Saneh
1976 "Thai Politics and the October Revolution." *Journal of Social Science Review* (Bangkok) 1 (1): 1–41.

Chantornvong, Sombat
1981 "Religious Literature in Thai Political Perspective: The Case of the Maha Chat Kamluang." In *Essays on Literature and Society in Southeast Asia,* ed. Tham Seong Chee, pp. 187–205. Singapore: Singapore University Press.

Chappell, Wallace
1972 "Monohra." In *Traditional Asian Plays,* ed. James R. Brandon. New York: Hill and Wang.

Chaudhuri, P. C. Roy
1976 *Folk Tales of Thailand.* New Delhi: Sterling Publishers.

Chenvidyakarn, Montri
1978 *The Political Economy of Siam, 1910–1931.* Bangkok: Social Science Association of Thailand.

Chitakasem, Manas
 1982 "The Development of Political and Social Consciousness in Thai Short Stories." In *The Short Story in Southeast Asia,* ed. J. H. C. S. Davidson and H. Cordell. London: School of Oriental and African Studies, University of London.

Cipolla, Carlo
 1969 *Literacy and Development in the West.* Harmondsworth: Penguin Books.

Colby, Benjamin N.
 1975 "Culture Grammars." *Science* 187:913–919.

Colby, Benjamin N., James W. Fernandez, and David B. Kronenfeld
 1981 "Toward a Convergence of Cognitive and Symbolic Anthropology." *American Ethnologist* 8 (3): 422–450.

Cressy, David
 1980 *Literacy and the Social Order: Reading and Writing in Tudor and Stuart England.* Cambridge: Cambridge University Press.

Darling, Frank
 1965 *Thailand and the United States.* Washington D.C.: Public Affairs Press.
 1978 "Thailand in 1977: The Search for Stability and Progress." *Asian Survey* 18 (2): 153–163.

Davis, Richard
 1974 "Tolerance and Intolerance of Ambiguity in Northern Thai Myth and Ritual." *Ethnology* 13 (1): 1–24.

de Fels, Jacqueline
 1975 "Popular Literature in Thailand." *Journal of the Siam Soceity* 63 (2): 219–238.

Dhaninivat, H. H. Prince
 1947 "Siamese Versions of the Panji Romance." In *India Antiqua,* pp. 95–101. Leyden: E. J. Brill.
 1954 "The Royal Kathin." *Standard* (Bangkok) (410): 11–12, 29.
 1961 "The Ramakien: A Siamese Version of the Story of Rama." In *Burma Research Society, Fiftieth Anniversary Publications No. 1: Some of the Papers Read at the Fiftieth Anniversary Conference,* pp. 33–45. Rangoon: Burma Research Society.

Dhiravegin, Likhit
 1984 *Social Change and Contemporary Thai Politics: An Analysis of the Interrelationship between the Society and the Polity.* Faculty of Political Science Monograph Series No. 5. Bangkok: Research Center, Faculty of Political Science, Thammasat University.

Disch, Robert, ed.
 1973 *The Future of Literacy.* Englewood Cliffs, NJ: Prentice-Hall, Inc.

Drans, Jean
 1947 *Histoire de Nang Manira et Histoire de Song Thong, Deux Recits du Recueil des Cinquante Jataka, traduits du Siamois.* Tokyo: Presses Salesiennes.

Dundes, Alan, ed.
   1965 *The Study of Folklore.* Englewood Cliffs, NJ: Prentice-Hall, Inc.
   1966 "Chain Letter: A Folk Geometric Progression." *Northwest Folklore* 1:14–19.
   1980 *Interpreting Folklore.* Bloomington: Indiana University Press.

Dundes, Alan, and Carl R. Pagter
   1975 *Work Hard and You Shall Be Rewarded: Urban Folklore from the Paperwork Empire.* American Folklore Society Memoir Series, Vol. 62. Austin, TX.

Eisenstein, Elizabeth
   1979 *The Printing Press as an Agent of Change: Communication and Cultural Transformation in Early Modern Europe.* New York: Cambridge University Press.

Feinstein, Alan S.
   1969 *Folk Tales from Siam.* South Brunswick, NJ: A. S. Barnes.

Fischer, John L.
   1963 "The Sociopsychological Analysis of Folktales." *Current Anthropology* 4:235–295.

Frake, Charles O.
   1962 "Cultural Ecology and Ethnography." *American Anthropologist* 64 (1): 53–59.

Fuller, R. Buckminster
   1969 *Utopia or Oblivion: The Prospects for Mankind.* New York: Overlook Press.
   1976 *And It Came to Pass—Not to Stay.* New York: Macmillan Co.
   1981 *Critical Path.* New York: St. Martin's Press.

Gedney, William J.
   1982 "Patrons and Practitioners: The Chakri Monarchs and Literature." Paper presented at the Rattanakosin Conference, Northern Illinois University, November 11–13, 1982.

Geertz, Clifford
   1972 "Deep Play: Notes on the Balinese Cockfight." *Daedalus* 101 (1): 1–37.
   1973 *The Interpretation of Cultures.* New York: Basic Books, Inc.
   1976 "Art As a Cultural System." *Modern Language Notes* 91:1473–1499.
   1980a "Blurred Genres." *American Scholar* 49:165–179.
   1980b *Negara: The Theatre-State in Nineteenth Century Bali.* Princeton: Princeton University Press.

Ginsburg, Henry D.
   1972 "The Manora Dance-Drama: An Introduction." *Journal of the Siam Society* 60 (2): 169–181.

Girling, John L. S.
   1968 "Northeast Thailand: Tomorrow's Viet-Nam?" *Foreign Affairs* 46: 388–397.
   1977 "Thailand, the Coup and Its Implications." *Pacific Affairs* 50 (3): 387–405.
   1981 *Thailand: Society and Politics.* Ithaca: Cornell University Press.

Goodenough, Ward
   1956 "Componential Analysis and the Study of Meaning." *Language* 32:195–216.

1957 "Cultural Anthropology and Linguistics." In *Report of the Seventh Annual Round Table Meeting of Linguistics and Language Study,* ed. Paul L. Garvin, pp. 167–173. Washington, D.C.: Georgetown University.

Goody, Jack
1977 *The Domestication of the Savage Mind.* Cambridge: Cambridge University Press.

Goody, Jack, and Ian Watt
1963 "The Consequences of Literacy." *Comparative Studies in Society and History* 4:304–345.

Gough, Kathleen
1968 "Literacy in Kerala." In *Literacy in Traditional Societies,* ed. Jack Goody, pp. 132–160. Cambridge: Cambridge University Press.

Graburn, Nelson H. H.
1978 " 'I Like Things To Look More Different Than That Stuff Did': An Experiment in Cross-Cultural Art Appreciation." In *Art in Society: Studies in Style, Culture, and Aesthetics,* ed. Michael Greenhalgh and Vincent Megaw, pp. 51–70. London: Duckworth Publishers.

Graff, Harvey J.
1976 *Literacy In History: An Interdisciplinary Research Bibliography.* Chicago: The Newberry Library.
1979 *The Literacy Myth: Literacy and Social Structure in the Nineteenth Century City.* New York: Academic Press.

Guskin, Alan E.
1964 *Changing Values of Thai College Students.* Bangkok: Faculty of Education, Chulalongkorn University.

Haas, Mary R.
1951 "Interlingual Word Taboos." *American Anthropologist* 53 (3): 338–344.
1957 "Thai Word-Games." *Journal of American Folklore* 70:173–175.

Hanks, Lucien M., Jr.
1952/ "A Note on Psycho-Social Tensions in a Thai Village after the Advent of
1953 Occidental Technology." *Economic Development and Cultural Change* 1:394–396.
1962 "Merit and Power in the Thai Social Order." *American Anthropologist* 64 (1): 247–261.
1966 "The Corporation and the Entourage: A Comparison of Thai and American Social Organization." *Catalyst* 2:55–63.
1968 "American Aid is Damaging Thai Society." *Transaction* (October): 29–34.
1975 "The Thai Social Order as Entourage and Circle." In *Change and Persistence in Thai Society,* ed. G. William Skinner and A. Thomas Kirsch, pp. 197–218. Ithaca: Cornell University Press.

Hanks, Lucien M., Jr., and Herbert P. Phillips
1961 "A Young Thai from the Countryside: A Psychosocial Analysis." In *Studying Personality Cross-Culturally,* ed. Bert Kaplan, pp. 637–656. Evanston, IL: Row, Peterson and Co.

Harman, David
1970 "Illiteracy: An Overview." *Harvard Educational Review* 40 (2): 226–243.

Havelock, Eric
    1963 *Preface to Plato.* Cambridge: Harvard University Press.
    1976 *Origins of Western Literacy.* Toronto: Ontario Institute for Studies in Education.

Heinze, Ruth-Inge
    1974 "Ten Days in October—Students vs. the Military: An Account of the Student Uprising in Thailand." *Asian Survey* 14 (6): 491–508.

Hollinger, Carol
    1965 "Mai Pen Rai *Means Never Mind.*" Boston: Houghton Mifflin Co.

Huxley, Aldous
    1923 *Brave New World.* New York: Harper and Row.

Ingersoll, Fern S.
    1973 *Sang Thong: A Dance-Drama from Thailand. Written by King Rama II and the Poets of His Court.* Rutland, VT: Charles E. Tuttle Co.

Ingram, James C.
    1955 *Economic Changes in Thailand since 1850.* Stanford: Stanford University Press.

Jumbala, Prudhisan
    1974 "Towards a Theory of Group Formation in Thai Society and Pressure Groups in Thailand after the October 1973 Uprising." *Asian Survey* 14 (6): 530–545.
    1977 "The Democratic Experiment in Thailand, 1973–1976." *Dyason House Papers* (Melbourne) 3 (3): 1–6.

Kahn, Herman
    1976 *The Next Two Hundred Years.* New York: William Morrow and Co.

Kasetsiri, Charnvit
    1976 *The Rise of Ayudhya: A History of Siam in the Fourteenth and Fifteenth Centuries.* New York: Oxford University Press.

Kemp, Jeremy
    1980 "From Kinship to Patron-Clientage: The Manipulation of Personal Relations." Paper presented at the Thai-European Seminar on Contemporary Thailand, 28–30 May, 1980. University of Amsterdam Anthropological-Sociological Centre, Department of South and Southeast Asian Studies.

Kershaw, Roger
    1979 " 'Unlimited Sovereignty' in Cambodia: The View from Bangkok." *The World Today,* March.
    1980 "Modernizing the Thai Monarchy? Theory and Practice of Two Intellectuals Turned Prime Minister." Paper presented at the Thai-European Seminar on Contemporary Thailand, 28–30 May, 1980. University of Amsterdam Anthropological-Sociological Centre, Department of South and Southeast Asian Studies.

Keyes, Charles F.
    1970 "Local Leadership in Rural Thailand." In *Local Authority and Administration in Thailand,* ed. Fred R. Von der Mehden and David A. Wilson. Los Angeles: University of California Academic Advisory Council on Thailand.
    1977 "Millennialism, Theravada Buddhism, and Thai Society." *Journal of Asian Studies* 36:283–302.

Khoman, Thanat
1973 "Thailand in the Midst of Changes." In *Trends in Thailand,* ed. Rajaret-
      nam and Lim So Jean, pp. 110–114. Singapore: Institute of Southeast
      Asian Studies.

Khruakaew, Paitoon
1970 *Laksanaa Sangkhom Thai* [The characteristics of Thai society]. Bang-
      kok: Liang Sieng Chungcharoen Press.

Kroeber, Alfred L.
1948 *Anthropology.* New York: Harcourt, Brace and Co.
1951 "The Novel in Asia and Europe." *University of California Publications
      in Semitic Philology* 9:233–241.

Krueger, Kermit
1969 *The Serpent Prince: Folk Tales from Northeastern Thailand.* New York:
      World Publishing Co.

Krull, G., and D. Melchers
1966 *Tales from Siam.* London: Hale.

Lafont, Pierre-Bernard
1983 "La Roman Thai Contemporain Miroir d'une Société." *Ethnos* 48:195–
      204.

LeMay, Reginald S.
1930 *Siamese Tales Old and New: The Four Riddles and Other Stories. With
      Some Reflections on the Tales.* London: Noel Douglas.

Lévi-Strauss, Claude
1963 *Structural Anthropology.* Translated Claire Jacobson and Brooke
      Grundfest Schoepf. New York: Basic Books, Inc.

LeVine, Kenneth
1982 "Functional Literacy: Fond Illusion and False Economies." *Harvard
      Educational Review* 52 (3): 249–266.

Lobe, Thomas
1977 *United States National Security Policy and Aid to the Thailand Police.*
      University of Denver Monograph Series in World Affairs. Colorado:
      University of Denver.

Malinowski, Bronislaw
1922 *Argonauts of the Western Pacific.* New York: E. P. Dutton and Co.

Moerman, Michael
1969 "A Thai Village Headman as Synaptic Leader." *Journal of Asian Studies*
      28:535–549.

Morell, David, and Chai-anan Samudavanija
1979 "Leadership Capabilities and Insurgency in Thailand." *Asian Survey* 19
      (4): 315–332.
1981 *Political Conflict in Thailand: Reform, Reaction, Revolution.* Cam-
      bridge, MA: Oelgeschlager, Gunn and Hain.

Mosel, James N.
1961 *Trends and Structure in Contemporary Thai Poetry, with Translations
      and Bibliography.* Department of Far Eastern Studies, Data Paper No.
      43. Ithaca: Southeast Asia Program, Cornell University.

Muecke, Marjorie A.
1980 "The Village Scouts of Thailand." *Asian Survey* 20 (4): 407–427.

National Statistical Office, Thailand
    1965 *Statistical Yearbook, No. 26.*
    1981 *Statistical Yearbook, No. 42.*

Neher, Clark D.
    1977 "Political Corruption in a Thai Province." *Journal of Developing Areas*
          11 (4): 479–492.
    1979 *Modern Thai Politics.* Rev. ed. Cambridge, MA: Schenkman Publishing
          Co.

Nida, Eugene A.
    1975 *Componential Analysis of Meaning.* The Hague: Mouton.

Numnonda, Thamsook
    1977 "When Thailand Followed the Leader" (in English). *Social Science
          Review* 3:197–223.
    1978 "Pibulsongkram's Thai Nation-Building Programme during the Japa-
          nese Military Presence, 1941–1945." *Journal of Southeast Asian Studies*
          9 (2): 234–247.

Orwell, George
    1949 *Nineteen Eighty-Four.* New York: Harcourt, Brace and Co.

Palmer, Bernard
    1972 "The Thai Student: A Study in Educational Acculturation." Ph.D. dis-
          sertation, University of California, Berkeley.

Phillips, Herbert P.
    1958 "The Election Ritual in a Thai Village." *Journal of Social Issues* 14 (4):
          36–50.
    1963 "Relationships between Personality and Social Structure in a Siamese
          Peasant Community." *Human Organization* 22 (2): 105–108.
    1965 *Thai Peasant Personality.* Berkeley: University of California Press.
    1975 "The Culture of Siamese Intellectuals." In *Change and Persistence in
          Thai Society,* ed. G. William Skinner and A. Thomas Kirsch, pp. 324–
          357. Ithaca: Cornell University Press.

Poolthupya, Srisurang
    1981 "Social Change as Seen in Modern Thai Literature." In *Essays on Litera-
          ture and Society in Southeast Asia,* ed. Tham Seong Chee, pp. 206–
          215. Singapore: Singapore University Press.

Postel-Coster, E.
    1970 "The Use of Written Sources in Cultural Anthropology." In *Anniversary
          Contributions to Anthropology: Twelve Essays.* Leiden Ethnological
          Society. Leiden: E. J. Brill.

Pramoj, M. R. Seni
    1958 "Poetic Translations from the Siamese: Selected Verses of Sri Praj and
          Sunthon Bhu." *Journal of the Siam Society* 46 (2): 215–216.
    1965 *Interpretive Translations of Thai Poetry by M. R. Seni Pramoj.* Bang-
          kok: SEATO.

Prizzia, Ross, and Narong Sinsawasdi
    1974 *Thailand: Student Activism and Political Change.* Bangkok: Allied
          Printers.

Purachatra (Prince Prem Chaya)
 1949 *Magic Lotus, A Romantic Fantasy: An Adaptation for the English Stage of the Fifteenth-Century Siamese Classic* Pra Law. 2nd ed. Bangkok: Chatra Books.
 1955 *The Story of Khun Chang Khun Phan.* Bangkok: Chatra Books.
 1959 "The Birth of Khun Chang and Khun Phan." *Orient Review and Literary Digest* 5 (3): 17–25; 5 (5): 38–56; 5 (6): 18–37.

Rabibhadana, Akin
 1975 "Bangkok Slum: Aspects of Social Organization." Ph.D. dissertation, Cornell University.

Rajadhon, Phya Anuman
 1956 *Thai Literature and* Swasdi raksa. Thailand Culture Series No. 3, 4th ed. Bangkok: The National Culture Institute.
 1961 *Thai Literature in Relation to the Diffusion of Her Cultures.* Thai Culture, New Series, No. 9. Bangkok: The Fine Arts Department.
 1968 *Essays on Thai Folklore.* Bangkok: The Social Science Association Press of Thailand.

Rakwijit, Somchai
 1974 *The Jungle Leads the Village.* Translated Chaumsri Race. Bangkok: USOM.
 1976 *Security Situation in Thailand: Trends in Thailand II.* Singapore: Institute of Southeast Asian Studies.

Redfield, Robert
 1955 "The Social Organization of Tradition." *Far Eastern Quarterly* 15 (1): 13–21.

Reich, Charles A.
 1970 *Greening of America.* New York: Random House.

Reynolds, Craig J., and Hong Lysa
 1983 "Marxism in Thai Historical Studies." *Journal of Asian Studies* 43 (1): 77–104.

Riggs, Fred W.
 1966 *Thailand: Modernization of a Bureaucratic Polity.* Honolulu: East West Center Press.

Rubin, Herbert J.
 1973 "Will and Awe: Illustration of Thai Villager Dependency upon Officials." *Journal of Asian Studies* 32:425–444.

Rutnin, Mattani
 1975 *The Siamese Theatre: A Collection of Reprints from the Journal of the Siam Society.* Bangkok: The Siam Society.
 1978 "Modern Thai Literature: The Process of Modernization and the Transformation of Values." *East Asian Cultural Studies* 17 (1–4): 1–132.

Sangchai, Somporn
 1976 *Coalition Behavior in Modern Thai Politics: A Thai Perspective.* Institute of Southeast Asian Studies Occasional Paper No. 41. Singapore: Institute of Southeast Asian Studies.

Saveng, Phinith
 1975 "Contemporary Lao Literature." *Journal of the Siam Society* 63 (2): 240–250.

Schuler, Edgar A., and Vibul Thamavit
  1958 *Public Opinion among Thai Students: A Study of Opinions, Attitudes, and Values Held by a Random Sample of Students in Colleges and Universities, Thailand, 1958.* Bangkok: Faculty of Social Administration, Thammasat University.

Schweisguth, P.
  1951 *Étude sur la Littérature Siamoise.* Paris: Adrien Maisonneuve.

Scott, James C.
  1972 *Comparative Political Corruption.* Englewood Cliffs, NJ: Prentice-Hall.

Senanan, Wibha
  1975 *The Genesis of the Novel in Thailand.* Bangkok: Thai Watana Panich Co., Ltd.

Sibunruang, Jit Kawem
  1954 *Siamese Folktales: Narrated in English with Illustrations by Saeng Aroon Rataksikorn.* Bangkok: Don Bosco Technical School and Orphanage.

Siffin, William J.
  1966 *The Thai Bureaucracy: Institutional Change and Development.* Honolulu: East-West Center Press.

Simmonds, E. H. S.
  1963 "Thai Narrative Poetry: Palace and Provincial Texts of an Episode from *Khun Chang Khun Phaen.*" *Asia Major* 10(December): 279–299.
  1965 "Siamese (Thai)." In *Eros: An Inquiry into the Theme of Lovers' Meetings and Partings at Dawn in Poetry,* ed. Arthur T. Hatto, pp. 186–195. London: Mouton.
  1971 "Mahoorasap II. The Thai National Library Manuscript." *Bulletin of the School of Oriental and African Studies* 34 (1): 119–131.

Sivaraksa, Sulak
  1973 *Siam Through a Looking Glass: A Critique.* Bangkok: Suksit Siam.
  1980 *Siam in Crisis.* Bangkok: Komol Keemthong Foundation.

Skinner, B. F.
  1948 *Walden Two.* New York: Macmillan Co.

Somvichian, Kamol
  1978 "The Oyster and the Shell: Thai Bureaucrats in Politics." *Asian Survey* 18 (8): 829–837.

Spearman, Diana
  1966 *The Novel and Society.* New York: Barnes and Noble.

Srinawk, Khamsing
  1973 *The Politician and Other Stories.* London and Kuala Lumpur: Oxford University Press.

Sturtevant, William C.
  1964 "Studies in Ethnoscience." *American Anthropologist* 66 (3): 99–131.

Suksamran, Sombuun
  1977 *Political Buddhism in Southeast Asia: The Role of the Sangha in the Modernization of Thailand.* London: C. Hurst and Co.

1980 "Buddhism and Socio-Political Change: An Interaction of Buddhism with Politics in Contemporary Thailand," Paper presented at the Thai-European Seminar on Social Change in Contemporary Thailand, 28–30 May, 1980. University of Amsterdam Anthropological-Sociological Centre, Department of South and Southeast Asian Studies.

Tambiah, S. J.
1970 *Buddhism and the Spirit Cults in North-East Thailand.* Cambridge: Cambridge University Press.
1976 *World Conquerer and World Renouncer: A Study of Buddhism and Polity in Thailand against a Historical Background.* Cambridge: Cambridge University Press.

Tanham, George K.
1974 *Trial in Thailand.* New York: Crane, Russak.

Terwiel, B. J.
1975 *Monks and Magic.* Bangkok: Scandinavian Institute of Asian Studies.

Textor, Robert Bayard
1973 *Roster of the Gods: An Ethnography of the Supernatural in a Thai Village.* 6 vols. New Haven: Human Relations Area Files.

Thomas, M. Ladd
1975 Political Violence in the Muslim Provinces of Southern Thailand. Institute of Southeast Asian Studies Occasional Paper, No. 28. Singapore: Institute of Southeast Asian Studies.

Thongthew-Ratarasarn, Somchintana
1979 *The Socio-Cultural Setting of Love Magic in Central Thailand.* Wisconsin Papers on Southeast Asia, No. 2. Madison, WI: Center for Southeast Asian Studies, University of Wisconsin-Madison.

Toelken, Barre
1979 *The Dynamics of Folklore.* Boston: Houghton Mifflin Co.

Toffler, Alvin
1970 *Future Shock.* New York: Random House.
1972 *The Futurists.* New York: Random House.

Toth, Marian Davies
1971 *Tales from Thailand.* Rutland, VT: Charles E. Tuttle Co.

Turton, Andrew, Jonathan Fast, and Malcolm Caldwell, eds.
1978 *Thailand: Roots of Conflict.* Nottingham: Spokesman.

UNESCO
1982 *Statistical Yearbook.*

Vella, Walter F.
1955 *The Impact of the West on Government in Thailand.* Berkeley: University of California Press.

Wedel, Yuangrat
1982 "Current Thai Radical Ideology: The Returnees from the Jungle." *Contemporary Southeast Asia* 4:1–18.

Wells, Margaretta B.
1964 *Thai Fairy Tales.* Bangkok: Church of Christ.

Wilson, David A.
1962 *Politics in Thailand.* Ithaca: Cornell University Press.
1970 *The United States and the Future of Thailand.* New York: Praeger.

Wyatt, David K.
  1969 *The Politics of Reform in Thailand: Education in the Reign of King Chulalongkorn.* New Haven: Yale University Press.
  1982 "The 'Subtle Revolution' of King Rama I of Siam." In *Moral Order and the Question of Change: Essays on Southeast Asian Thought,* ed. David K. Wyatt and Alexander Woodside, pp. 9–52. Yale University Southeast Asia Monograph Series No. 24. New Haven: Yale University Press.

Yupho, Dhanit
  1963 *The Khon and Lakon: Dance Dramas Presented by the Department of Fine Arts.* Bangkok: Department of Fine Arts.

Zimmerman, Robert F.
  1974 "Student 'Revolution' in Thailand: The End of the Thai Bureaucratic Polity?" *Asian Survey* 14 (6): 509–529.
  1978 *Reflections on the Collapse of Democracy in Thailand.* Institute of Southeast Asian Studies Occasional Paper, No. 50. Singapore: Institute of Southeast Asian Studies.

Index

Herbert P. Phillips is professor of anthropology and chairman of the Group in Asian Studies at the University of California, Berkeley. A graduate of Harvard College (A.B.) and Cornell University (Ph.D.), he has also taught at Michigan State University and Thammasat University in Bangkok. He has conducted research in Thailand periodically for more than two decades and is the author of *Thai Peasant Personality* and numerous articles and essays on Thailand.

 Production Notes

This book was designed by Roger Eggers.
Composition and paging were done on the
Quadex Composing System and typesetting on
the Compugraphic 8400 by the design and
production staff of University of Hawaii Press.

The text and display typeface is Sabon.

Offset presswork and binding were done by
Vail-Ballou Press, Inc. Text paper is Glatfelter
Offset Vellum, basis 45.